TEXAS REAL ESTATE AGENCY

JOHN REILLY
THOMAS TERRELL

Real Estate Education Company
a division of Dearborn Financial Publishing, Inc.

Publisher: Carol L. Luitjens
Acquisitions Editor: Margaret M. Maloney
Project Editor: Michal E. Eichenbaum
Art and Design Manager: Lucy Jenkins

Published by Real Estate Education Company,
a division of Dearborn Financial Publishing, Inc.

94 95 96 10 9 8 7 6 5 4 3 2 1

Library of Congress Cataloging-in-Publication Data

Reilly, John W.
Texas real estate agency / John Reilly, Thomas Terrell.
p. cm.
Includes index.
ISBN 0-7931-0985-X (paper)
1. Real estate business—Law and legislation—Texas. I. Terrell, Thomas. II. Title.
KFT1482.R4R45 1994
346.76404'37—dc20
[347.6406437] 94-27751
CIP

TABLE OF CONTENTS

ACKNOWLEDGEMENTS

The authors wish to thank those who reviewed the drafts of this manuscript, including James E. George, Ed.D., Professional Development Institute, University of North Texas, North Denton, and John Wesley Tomblin, J. Wesley Tomblin & Associates, Austin.

INTRODUCTION

The 1980s and early '90s have witnessed front-page headlines and cover stories about the issues surrounding who represents who in a real estate transaction and why it makes a difference. Federal and state regulatory agencies, lawyers, industry trade associations and real estate educators entered into spirited debate and fact-finding, some trying to reach a consensus, others advocating a particular position. Major studies on the issue of agency were prepared by the Federal Trade Commission (FTC), the Association of License Law Officials (ARELLO), the National Association of REALTORS® (NAR®), the Hawaii Real Estate Commission and the California Department of Real Estate.

On September 1, 1988, for the first time in Texas, a written disclosure notice as to who an agent represents was made mandatory. From that point on, a new agency task force, committee, Senate or House sub-committee or industry seminar was set up almost continually by someone with a new question, a new problem or a new solution. These forums were sponsored by many different organizations, most relevant the Texas state legislature, the Texas Real Estate Commission, the Texas Association of REALTORS®, the Texas Real Estate Buyer's Agents Association, the Independent Brokers of America and the Texas Realty Council. Almost every real estate school in the state, whether a private, proprietary school or a university-level program, became engaged in the issue. Slowly, at first, and then faster, the opinions and positions hardened and widened, and the financial impact of the implementation of Texas common law concepts of agency began to be realized at all levels of the industry. To date, at least 44 states have passed some form of agency disclosure requirement.

The various studies and committee findings point to a need to clarify the concept of representing buyers and tenants in real estate transactions versus exclusively representing sellers and landlords. All the studies stress a pressing need to clearly articulate agency relationships. While many solutions to the dilemma of agency have been offered, the common thread is a heavy emphasis on education designed to create an awareness of the importance of making informed choices about appropriate representation and working relationships. The NAR®'s *Report of the Presidential Advisory Group on Agency,* issued in March, 1992, set forth a number of significant recommendations founded on the principles of informed consent and freedom of choice. Buyers, sellers, tenants, landlords and brokers should be free to select from a range of business relationships that best meet their needs.

Consumers, as well as real estate licensees, may be confused about representation and about what level of service the real estate licensee provides when acting as an agent for a buyer instead of a seller. And, the nature of these services is continually expanding. Today, a broker has to be current in such diverse areas as state disclosure laws affecting property condition, agency, closing, lending and fair housing; zoning and building restrictions; financing alternatives; appraisal, survey and insulation standards; and contract provisions and meanings.

Much is expected of today's real estate licensee (*See* Appendices B and C). Real estate professionals, acting as agents, face increasing legal and ethical accountability to their clients, who have placed their financial futures, in the form of home equity, in the licensee's care. And the same responsibility applies to commercial broker as it does to the residential broker: According to the Texas Real Estate Commission, "Agency law and disclosure requirements exist equally for all brokers . . . The commercial broker is subject to the same statutory requirements and rules as are residential brokers."

Real estate licensees should be as comfortable and competent in discussing their role in a real estate transaction and who they represent as they are, for example, in discussing the routine use of exclusive listings over open listings. A significant part of a real estate licensee's job is to provide helpful services to the general public as potential customers, keeping in mind the potential benefit to his or her clients. It is of paramount importance for a licensee to distinguish a client from a customer, for it is only by virtue of his or her relationship to a client that a licensee is legally and appropriately characterized as a real estate *agent.* In Texas, if a real estate licensee is acting as an agent in a real estate transaction, he or she must make that relationship clear to everyone else involved in the transaction. He or she must understand what kinds of services result from what kinds of duties and in which direction—and for whose benefit—the streams of duties, services and responsibilities flow in any given circumstance.

So how does *Texas Real Estate Agency* help the real estate professional or student become more aware of his or her role and who he or she represents? The first two chapters introduce the subject of agency, its meaning and creation, and then discuss the different choices of agency representation: subagency, dual agency, single agency, seller agency and buyer agency. There is also some discussion of "non-agency" roles, such as "transaction broker," "middleman," "finder," "facilitator" and "independent contractor."

Following chapters present a practical approach to handling agency in everyday practice. There is sample dialogue to illustrate how to approach certain agency situations and a forecast of what to expect as more and more states attempt to redefine, refine and expand upon statutory definitions of agency and revamp agency disclosure laws.

In addition to an extensive bibliography and a special section on ethical responsibilities, appendices provide relevant forms, notices and sample clauses to consider in listing and sales contracts as well as Texas statutes and Real Estate Commission rules relevant to agency. Appendix D contains annotations of more than 600 legal decisions on agency issues from all 50 states.

Throughout this book, we use real life examples and practical discussion cases. Even though the examples are generally based on residential sales transaction, **the principles illustrated apply equally to leases and commercial real estate.**

ABOUT THE AUTHORS

John Reilly is a real estate educator and attorney currently practicing in Honolulu. He is a member of the New York, California, Hawaii and federal bars, as well as a REALTOR® licensed in Hawaii. He is past president of the Real Estate Educators Association and holds their prestigious DREI designation. Reilly is a law school professor, lecturer and licensed real estate instructor. He is widely regarded as one of the top national experts on agency disclosure, having served as a consultant to the Association of Real Estate License Law Officials (ARELLO). Reilly is the author of *The Language of Real Estate,* 3rd Edition, *Questions & Answers To Help You Pass the Real Estate Exam,* 4th Edition (with Paige Vitousek), *Agency Relationships in Real Estate,* 2nd Edition and *Agency Relationships in California Real Estate* (with Martha R. Williams).

Thomas Terrell is a licensed real estate broker and a TREC-approved real estate educator. He has served as an expert witness in litigation involving real estate agency and licensing issues and has taught real estate courses at the University of Texas at Arlington, Texas Wesleyan College, Texas Christian University, The American College of Real Estate, Cedar Valley College, North Lake College, Real Estate Training Institute and the University of North Texas Greater Development Institute. Additionally, Terrell has taught programs for the Greater Dallas Association of REALTORS® as well as the Boards of REALTORS® in Denton, Arlington, Fort Worth, Garland, Irving, Weatherford and Mineral Wells.

CHAPTER

1 THE REAL ESTATE LICENSEE

The real estate licensee plays a key role in the purchase and sale of property, and most real estate transactions involve at least one real estate licensee. Still there is often disagreement as to what a licensee's role should be and who it is he or she, as an agent, represents. To begin our understanding of real estate representation in a marketing system, we'll define *agency* and discuss why there continues to be so much interest in the topic.

This chapter will cover:

- What is Agency?
  - Definition
  - Client or customer?
- Who Does the Real Estate Licensee Represent?
- Why Is There Increased Interest in Agency?
  - Complexity
  - Greater Consumer Representation
  - Use of More Than One Broker
  - Greater Broker Professionalism
  - Increased Litigation Against Real Estate Brokers
  - State agency disclosure laws

WHAT IS AGENCY?

To the average person, talk of agency and agents conjures visions of high-priced athletes or movie stars and their representatives negotiating million-dollar contacts. The next most common picture of agency is of an attorney drawing a will or handling some other legal matter. Few people think of agents or agency when they buy or sell real estate, yet that is how the average person will most likely encounter agency and agents—when making the largest financial investment of his or her life.

Too few people—including real estate licensees when they are acting as agents—appreciate the intricacies of the traditional legal concept of agency as applied by courts to real estate agents and the general public. The law on agency is clear and straightforward, but its application in the real estate brokerage business has become quite complex, especially with the emergence of buyer representation as an acceptable form of practice.

Definition

In the most general terms, an *agent is anyone who represents the interests of another person (the* principal *or* client*) in dealings with others.* In an agency relationship a person consents to use the services of others to accomplish what they cannot or do not want to do themselves.

Two ideas are essential to agency relationships. First, the agent is regarded as an expert upon whom the principal relies for specialized professional advice. Second, an agency relationship involves money or property, and the agent has a fiduciary responsibility to his or her principal. This means that the agent must work in behalf of the client's best financial interests at all times. In many professions, including real estate, an agent is called a *fiduciary.* In some instances, an agent many use the services of another agent to act on behalf of his or her client. This second agent is usually called a *subagent,* a relationship discussed in greater detail in Chapter 5.

Client or Customer?

In this book we will use the terms *client* and *customer.* These are not precisely defined legal terms, but they are helpful in focusing on the role of the real estate agent. A *client* is commonly understood to mean a person, called a *principal,* who engages the professional advice and/or services of another, called an *agent,* and whose interests are protected by the specific duties and loyalties of a fiduciary relationship. A *customer* is a person who purchases property or services without the protection of a fiduciary relationship; one who receives services primarily given on behalf of and for the benefit of another person (the client). Clients are represented by agents. Customers represent themselves. An agent works **for a client,** providing services and advice, and works **with a customer,** giving information.

WHO DOES THE AGENT REPRESENT?

The question of whether an agency relationship in a real estate transaction has been created is a question of fact, one a jury or hearing officer might be called upon to determine. The particular circumstance of each case must be examined to determine if the agent represents the buyer, seller or both. Because of the ease with which agency relationships may be created and the absence of any formalities or written agreements, a real estate licensee unwittingly may be held to be an agent in a so-called unintended or accidental agency. William D. North, past executive vice president of the National Association of REALTORS® (NAR®), stated, "It's often hard to tell which party the broker represents, and both the buyer and seller are apt to visualize the broker as 'their' broker."

A jury might find that the conduct of both the licensee and the consumer demonstrated that the consumer authorized the licensee to act on his or her behalf and that the licensee did so act, thus creating a principal-agent relationship. Such a finding has serious legal, economic and ethical consequences to a broker, salesperson, seller and buyer.

WHY IS THERE INCREASED INTEREST IN AGENCY?

The issue of agency relationships in real estate is not new. There are several reasons why there is an increased interest in the question of who the agent represents.

Complexity

Buying a home is an investment decision as well as a practical consideration. With today's rapid property turnover rate, many consumers are buying, selling and buying again, each time better understanding the importance of receiving sound, objective advice and counsel in addition to accurate factual information about the property under evaluation. These repeat buyers recognize the distinction between advice and information, especially with so much money at stake. They recognize that as customers they are entitled to any accurate, relevant information the broker might possess, but as clients they are additionally entitled to advice and opinions, such as suggested negotiating strategies in light of the other party's marketing position.

Greater Consumer Representation

Both the buyer and seller increasingly have come to expect professionalism and competence from licensed real estate agents. After all, state licensing requirements demand a higher knowledge and competency level for brokers and salespersons than for the average person. A judicial trend is emerging, away from the tradition of *caveat emptor* ("Let the buyer beware") and toward greater consumer protection and professional accountability on the part of the real estate agent. Frequently, real estate agents are the most visible experts in the transaction, and both the buyer and seller tend to defer to their agents' judgment and skill.

Use of More Than One Broker

A 1983 Federal Trade Commission study on national residential brokerage practices noted that 66% of the home sales studied involved two brokers or salespersons and more than half involved the services of two brokerage firms. With two brokers participating in one transaction, it is not surprising that buyers and sellers sometimes question who the participating brokers really represent. To some, it seems a natural division of labor that the listing broker represents the seller and another broker represents the buyer. Many buyers are surprised when told later that "their" agent actually represented the seller.

Greater Broker Professionalism

In the past, the listing broker was hired primarily to find a buyer. Today, it is likely that another broker will find the buyer. The seller looks to the listing broker to protect his or her best financial interests in the form of professional advice and counsel as to the soundness of the buyer's offer.

Many agents are emphasizing the variety and quality of services they offer, rather than emphasizing their salesmanship and matchmaking skills. Real estate agents are promoting themselves as advisors, problem-solvers and data interpreters rather than solely as information-providers. Brokers are expected to be generally knowledgeable in such areas as, among others, taxation, law, mortgage planning, contract preparation, investment analysis, finance, appraisal and property management. The law and the industry itself are demanding higher standards of skill, care and due diligence from the broker, in promoting the client's best interests, in treating everyone honestly, in spotting potential problems and in recommending the use of experts when necessary.

Increased Litigation Against Real Estate Brokers

All the previous reasons are important, but a key reason for increased interest in agency is litigation. Usually, a real estate lawsuit results from something other than agency, such as breach of contract, misrepresentation or a decision by one of the contracting parties to rescind. However, after a lawsuit is filed, the issue of who represented who becomes the focal point in the majority of cases. Traditionally, brokers do not discuss or disclose who they represent. Therefore, lawyers seeking to set aside a transaction search for an undisclosed, often unintended dual agency. For example, a lawyer interviewing a buyer-client prior to filing a misrepresentation action might ask the buyer, "How were you treated by the broker you worked with? Did you think that the broker was your agent? Did you know that your broker was really the legal agent of the seller? How do you feel about that now?"

An undisclosed—or inadequately disclosed—dual agency can be grounds for not paying a brokerage commission or used as a basis to rescind a purchase contract between a buyer and seller. Because there probably would be a factual dispute as to whether a dual agency existed, it is likely that any legal action would proceed to a full trial and not be dismissed at a preliminary stage, unless the threat of a long, costly trial causes the parties to settle out of court. An innocent broker may be upset to learn that his or her errors and omissions insurance carrier wants to settle to keep down expenses, whereas the broker wants to fight the case to protect his or her reputation. Although the risk of a lawsuit cannot be completely eliminated, many potential suits can be avoided with some early, basic agency disclosure.

State Agency Disclosure Laws

Nearly every state has passed legislation requiring real estate licensees to disclose who it is they represent in each transaction. Some laws permit simple oral disclosure, other laws mandate the use of specific disclosure forms. [Texas has a very stringent agency disclosure law requiring the use of specific forms.] In all cases, the salesperson faces the likelihood that the buyer or seller will want to know what the role of the salesperson will be. A salesperson who is not comfortable discussing his or her role may find the prospective client switching to a more competent real estate licensee.

SUMMARY

From the most basic residential real estate transaction to the most complex commercial deal, it is important to understand who the licensee represents as agent and what services will—or cannot by law—be provided. There is an increased interest in clarifying agency issues, as highlighted by expanded professional liability suits against real estate agents.

By developing a positive awareness of agency relationships, the real estate professional, when acting as an agent, will be able to adapt to consumer demands for greater representation in today's real estate marketplace.

KEY POINTS

- Real estate licensees may work for clients in a principal-agent relationship or they may work for customers in a non-agency relationship.

- A client has a legal right to expect accurate information, advice, counsel and informed opinions. A customer has a legal right to expect only accurate information.
- An undisclosed, underdisclosed or accidental dual agency may result in a lawsuit for rescission, forfeiture of commission, money damages or disciplinary action.

SUGGESTIONS FOR BROKERS

Develop a company agency disclosure policy that emphasizes awareness of the various agency situations your salespeople will encounter in daily practice. The goal is to assist your sales staff in becoming comfortable in disclosing who they represent, consistent with your established company policy.

DISCUSSION QUESTIONS

1. What are some of the reasons for filing a lawsuit as a result of a real estate transaction?
2. What is the difference between a broker providing advice and a broker providing information?
3. What are some of the reasons for the increased interest in agency?
4. What is the essential difference between a client and a customer?
5. What are some of the courses of action a lawyer may choose to take against a real estate licensee who fails to properly disclose his or her agency on behalf of his or her client?

CHAPTER

2 AGENCY RELATIONSHIPS

In any real estate transaction, a variety of agency relationships may be created. For this reason, agency relationships, when not clearly defined and recognized, may be a source of confusion and misunderstanding to buyers, sellers, real estate salespeople, brokers, lawyers and judges. Preconceived notions about the right to representation and misapplied terminology often create roadblocks to greater understanding.

This chapter discusses the following subjects:

- Sources of Confusion
- Conflicting Interests
    - Identification Problems
- Some Basic Agency Relationships
- The Licensee's Role
- Fiduciary Duties and Responsibilities
    - Loyalty
    - Confidentiality
    - Full Disclosure
        - Relationships
        - Other Offers
        - Status of Earnest Money
        - Buyer's Financial Condition
        - Property Value
        - Commission Split
        - Contract Provisions
    - Obedience
    - Reasonable Skill and Care
    - Accounting
- Scope of Authority
- Duties to Others
    - Watch What Is Said
- Avoid Misrepresentation

Figure 2.1 Special Agency Relationships

ONLY ONE BROKER IN THE TRANSACTION

If Broker Acts as Agent for Seller Only

- Buyer unrepresented
- Full written disclosure
- Acts as agent to seller, non-agent to buyer

If Broker Acts as Agent for Buyer Only

- Seller unrepresented
- Full written disclosure
- Acts as agent to buyer, non-agent to seller

If Broker Acts as Dual Agent for Both Buyer and Seller

- To buyer and seller, licensee is a dual agent
- Full written disclosure and written consent of both buyer and seller required by law, otherwise deemed undisclosed, underdisclosed or unintended and violates TRELA 15(a)(6)(D) and 15C as well as DTPA

MORE THAN ONE BROKER IN THE TRANSACTION

If One Broker Acts as Seller's Agent and Another Acts as Subagent of Seller

- Buyer unrepresented
- Full, timely written disclosure to the buyer
- To buyer all licensees are non-agents, to seller all are agents, even if classed as subagents

If One Broker Acts as Buyer's Agent and Another Acts as Subagent of the Buyer

- Seller unrepresented
- Full, timely written disclosure to the seller
- To seller all licensees are not agents; to the buyer all are agents

If One Broker Acts as Seller's Agent and Another Acts as Buyer's Agent

- Full, timely written disclosure by each broker to the party he or she does not represent
- Broker acting as agent to seller not as agent to the buyer. Broker acting as agent to buyer is not an agent of the seller

If One Broker Acts as Seller's Agent and Another Acts as Seller's Subagent and Buyer's Agent

- Full disclosure and consent of both parties; otherwise the dual agency is undisclosed or underdisclosed and illegal
- Broker acting as seller's agent is a non-agent to the buyer. Other broker is dual agent to buyer and seller

One Broker Acts as Agent for Seller or Buyer and Another Acts in a Nonrepresentative Capacity (Non-Agent)

- The non-agent is generally referred to as a *finder, consultant, transaction coordinator, transaction broker, independent contractor, middleman* or *facilitator* (all are non-agents)
- Full disclosure by each broker to any party the broker does not represent in an agent capacity (i.e., where broker is a non-agent as to that party)

Note: All disclosures of agency must made in writing to the party the licensee does not represent. The exception to this rule is dual agency. In dual agency situations the broker must not only make written disclosure to each party of his or her representation but must obtain, in writing, the informed consent of all parties after due diligence to make full disclosure of the prospective dual representation, the limitations of dual agency and its potential effect on the position of each principal. The written agreements must set forth the source of any expected compensation to the real estate broker. Under Texas statutes, failure to do any of the above makes the dual representation illegal as a matter of law. (TRELA Section 15C)

SOURCES OF CONFUSION

Some of the possible agency relationships that may occur in the course of a transaction are illustrated in Figure 2.1. With all these possible relationships and necessary disclosures and consents, it is not surprising that there may be some confusion over who the agent represents. Confusion can result in consumer dissatisfaction and, in some cases, litigation.

The following are common misconceptions concerning agency relationships in real estate:

- "The broker always represents the seller because that's who pays the commission."
- "Brokers always represents whoever pays them."
- "The listing broker can share commissions only with a subagent, not a buyer's broker."
- "A broker can never represent both the buyer and the seller, even if they both approve the dual agency."
- "A listing broker cannot sell the broker's own listings to an unrepresented buyer without creating a dual agency."
- "Both buyer and seller must have separate real estate agents from different companies."
- "In an in-house sale the firm can represent both the buyer and the seller without creating a dual agency, provided each is working with a salesperson from a different branch office."
- "A member of a MLS is automatically a subagent of the seller and cannot represent the buyer."
- "The role of the broker is that of a mediator or facilitator, not that of an advocate in an adversarial relationship between buyers and sellers."

Most brokers have heard similar misstatements and misconceptions and could probably add a few more. What is clear from these statements is that there is a great deal of interest in the topic of agency representation, myth concerning whom the broker represents and confusion and misunderstanding over the proper role of the broker in the real estate transaction.

The confusion may arise from the disparity between the apparent relationships among seller, broker and buyer and the legal relationships among them that are created by agency law, statute, administrative law and custom. Other causes for the confusion are the ease of creating agency relationships and the variety of working relationships that may exist.

CONFLICTING INTEREST

Each participant in a typical real estate transaction has a distinct interest:

- The seller hopes to sell the property quickly at the highest price with the most favorable terms.
- The buyer expects to select the best property for the lowest price with the most favorable terms.

- The listing broker wants to sell the property quickly at the best terms the market will bring.
- The selling broker, if he is a seller's subagent, wants to sell the property for the best price and terms for the seller.
- The buyer's broker wants to find the best property at the best price and terms possible for the buyer.

All brokers like to avoid disputes, dissension and lawsuits. They would like to create a "win-win" situation so they can receive referral from buyer and seller alike. In addition, brokers are likely to have licensed associates working for them who also are interested in smooth closings and receipt of their commission checks. The potential for conflict is increased by an individual licensee's personal financial stake in an early closing (in order to receive the commission money) and as big a share of the commission as possible. These interests do conflict or compete, despite all good intentions. As a result, it is often unclear, especially without the benefit of clear, written disclosures, exactly whose agent a broker or his or her associates may be.

Identification Problems

One source of the problem is that there is no accepted procedure by which one can readily identify the correct agent-principal relationship in a real estate transaction. There usually is no problem in identifying the agent and the principal in other businesses, for example, in negotiations between management and an union's representative, a baseball owner and the representative of the league's home-run king or an insurance company and the attorney for an injured pedestrian. But the lines of agency in real estate transactions are sometimes blurred because neither the existence of a listing agreement nor the fact that one person completely pays the broker's commission determines who is the principal. This identification problem is compounded by the fact that after a buyer locates a broker to help in the search for a property, the buyer often believes that the broker is working for him or her. And in some cases the buyer actually works with several real estate brokers or their sales associates in the search for the right property.

SOME BASIC AGENCY RELATIONSHIPS

Some agency relationships that exist in the typical real estate transaction are shown in Figure 2.2. The most common agency relationship is that between the seller and the listing broker. Usually, sellers list their property with a broker under a written exclusive listing agreement. The broker agrees to perform diligently to find a ready, willing and able buyer and to act in the best interests of the seller at all times. Even if the listing agreement does not enumerate the fiduciary duties owed by common law and the TREC Rules, they are considered, by Texas law, to be contained in the listing agreement. As the courts found in *Kinnard v. Homann*, 750 S.W.2d 30 (Tex App.-Austin 1988), "that law, existing at the time a contract is formed, becomes a part of the contract." The listing broker is the agent of the seller or landlord, and the seller or landlord is the principal of the broker. In the case of buyer or tenant representation by the broker, the broker is the agent of the buyer or tenant and the buyer or tenant is the principal of the broker. In a dual agency situation, both parties are principals (clients) relative to their shared broker/agent.

The broker frequently retains licensed salespeople and licensed broker associates to help in locating, listing and marketing property. Under the law, the salesman or broker associate is the agent of the broker, even though, for tax purposes, the salesperson

Figure 2.2 Diagram of Agency Relationships

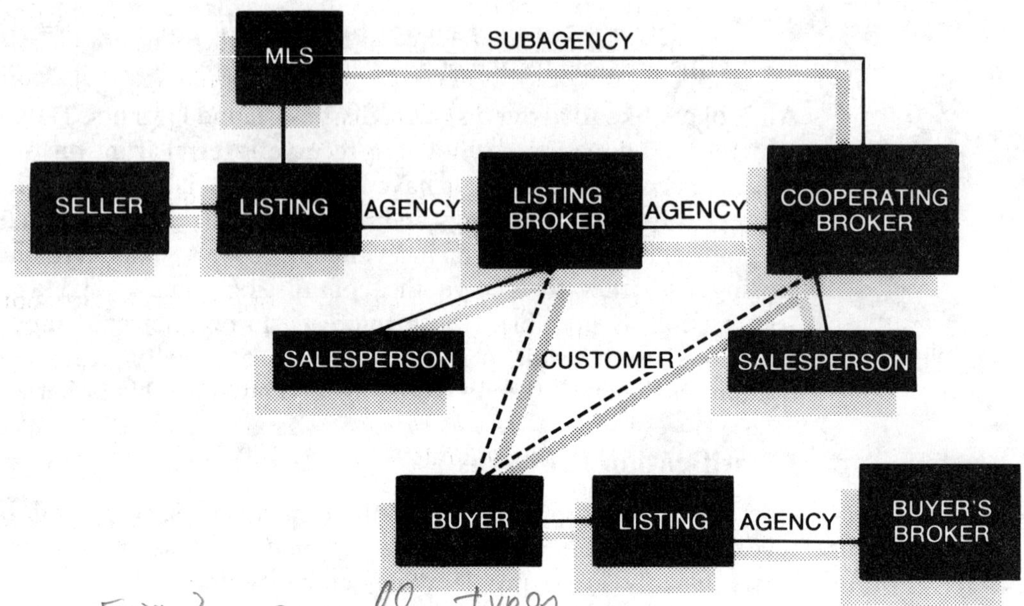

1. The agency relationship with the seller typically is created with a listing agreement or seller representation agreement.
2. The listing broker by law must supervise his or her licensed associates, who are agents of the broker and, by extension, agents of the seller.
3. The buyer may be a customer of the listing broker but not a client (unless the broker is a dual agent). There is no agency relationship with the buyer.
4. The listing broker may be authorized by the seller to offer subagency to other brokerage companies, through custom and practice or through an MLS. The other broker, if he or she has accepted the offer of subagency, is the agent of the listing broker and the subagent of the seller who offers subagency in the MLS. In Texas, the cooperating broker or selling agent is now referred to as the *other broker.* The term *other broker* provides an agency-neutral term to be used in the Texas TREC contract forms. The licensed associates working for the other broker also are subagents of the seller if the listing broker has offered subagency and if the other broker has accepted the offer of subagency.
5. The buyer may be a customer of an other broker. There is no express agency relationship, but the other broker must be careful not to create an implied agency relationship with the buyer.
6. A buyer and a broker may create an express agency relationship by express contract. This agreement is typically referred to as a buyer representation agreement. In this case, the buyer is the client and the seller is a customer of the buyer's broker.

salesperson may be an "independent contractor." [22 TAC 535.2 (g)] Because the sponsoring or principal broker is the primary agent of the seller, the salesperson or broker associate owes the full compliment of fiduciary duties to both the seller and the sponsoring broker. Thus, the salesperson or broker associate has two principals in two related agency relationships: (1) the broker and (2) the seller. The primary agency relationship exists between the client and the broker; the secondary agency relationship exists between the client and the broker's licensed associate. The sponsoring or principal broker is the responsible person, acting either directly or indirectly through a salesman or broker associate. The listing is taken in the sponsoring broker's name and, under state law [TRELA Sec. 1(b)], is subject to the control and supervision of the broker. This is true regardless of how the listing was obtained.

A few states have attempted to change the common law and permit the client to designate a particular salesperson to be the only licensed associate in the firm to represent the client. However, this is not legal in Texas. Texas licensees should exercise caution before implementing recommendations or options pertaining to marketing and agency relationships in other states that may not be permitted in Texas.

The seller's broker's job is to market the seller's property. To do this, the seller's broker constantly deals with prospective buyers, buyer's brokers, subagents and finders in an effort to cultivate a list of qualified buyers for properties available through the broker.

To do a good job for the seller, the seller's broker must develop skills that will attract buyers. Buyers are attracted to brokers who communicate well, who have quick access to the market and who are able to help the buyer through the complex process of buying a property. Because brokers who represent sellers often have several properties listed at the same time, prospects usually will be shown a number of properties before one is selected.

In the majority of real estate transactions in the past, it was not the listing broker but another broker who found the buyer. In the past, the listing broker commonly appointed other brokers as subagents, called *cooperating brokers* or *selling brokers* (now called the *other broker*), to procure a buyer for the property. If the other broker did not reject the blanket unilateral offer of subagency made through the MLS and merely acted by showing the house, the other broker became the agent of the listing broker and subagent of the seller. This was true by virtue of the MLS blanket unilateral offer of subagency from the listing broker and the other broker's acceptance in the form of acting upon it. The buyer was still a customer, not a client. If the seller authorized the use of agents other than the listing to broker to work in his or her behalf, whether by custom, express contract or implication, these other brokers, typically known as *selling brokers,* were then referred to as—and became—*subagents.* They were agents of the listing broker and subagents of the seller. They owed the same level of fiduciary duty to the seller as did the listing broker; likewise, they could bind their principals—the seller and the listing broker—by their conduct and representations. The cooperating or other brokers acted either directly or indirectly through their licensed associates.

With the passage of Senate Bill 314 in Texas regarding the practice of brokers representing more than one party to a real estate transaction, listing agreements began to change. After September 1, 1993, typical Texas listing agreements began to appear with a box which, if checked, allows the seller's agent to also represent a buyer or tenant. The listing agreement allows the broker to also be the agent of a buyer/client who might wish to negotiate to purchase or lease the broker's seller-client's property. With this change, some brokerages began immediately to adopt the practice of refusing to offer subagency under the MLS system, resulting in formerly cooperating subagents having to choose to be buyer's brokers or non-agent finders or middlemen.

In some brokerages, however, these new policies appear to be being implemented on a case by case basis, thus allowing the seller and listing broker to grant some exceptions and allow subagency. Companies who elect to offer "subagency by exception" should carefully analyze their criteria for the exceptions and see that they are rigidly adhered to. Otherwise, they could unintentionally find themselves on the wrong end of a federal fair housing complaint without an adequate defense.

One way to create a subagency is to list a property in a multiple listing service (MLS) and to make an offer of subagency on a blanket basis to all MLS members with arrangements for a commission split. The offer of subagency may be accepted when a cooperating member broker produces a ready, willing and able buyer. If the other broker rejects the offer of subagency, then the other broker will not have a fiduciary relationship with either the listing broker or the seller but will still generally have the right to share in the listing broker's commission based on the amount noted in the MLS listing.

The other broker who rejects the offer of subagency with the seller most frequently acts as the agent of the buyer. Some other brokers or purchasing brokers operate under a formal written buyer representation agreement with a buyer. Some purchasing brokers act as the buyer's agent under an express or implied oral arrangement. It is not a wise business practice to operate under an oral agency agreement, whether acting as a buyer or seller agent, particularly in light of TRELA §15C. Those brokers wishing to operate in a non-agent finder or middleman role should express all agreements in writing. In a middleman or finder agreement, it should be clarified in writing that neither principal will consider the broker as an agent for anyone in the transaction. In Texas, TRELA §20(b) will not permit a licensee to bring a court action for the recovery of a commission "unless the promise or agreement on which the action is brought, or some memorandum thereof, is in writing and signed by the party to be charged or signed by a person lawfully authorized by him [her] to sign it."

THE LICENSEE'S ROLE: AGENT? DUAL AGENT? NON-AGENT?

Once an agent's agency or non-agency role is established, confusion can occur as to what the licensee's role as agent or non-agent entails. Is the licensee's role a non-agency one to both parties? One of facilitator, mediator or arbitrator of differences? Is the licensee's role a true agent role as an advisor, negotiator and advocate for his or her principal's best interest? Some licensees confuse their roles in transactions with those of practicing law, arranging financing or warranting structural soundness. Other licensees confuse the relationships created by exclusive agency, subagency and buyer agency. Even more commonly, others confuse the fiduciary duties to their clients with the general duties of good faith, fairness, honesty and competence owed to all parties in the transaction, without regard to whether they are clients or customers.

No profession can afford to have clients who are uncertain of their relationship with the professionals to whom they entrust their personal and business affairs. Such uncertainty puts the real estate licensee acting as an agent in a tenuous position. Everyone will benefit from positive steps taken to clarify existing agency relationships. In this way real estate licensees acting as agents can greatly minimize misunderstandings, false expectations and feelings of unfair treatment.

FIDUCIARY DUTIES AND RESPONSIBILITIES

If an agency relationship exists, the real estate agent is held to be a fiduciary. In classic terms, a fiduciary responsibility implies a position of trust or confidence in which one person (the *fiduciary*) is usually entrusted to hold or manage the assets (in real estate, the property) of another (the *principal* or *client*). Common examples of fiduciaries are trustees, executors and guardians. In modern real estate terms, the client relies on the real estate agent, as a fiduciary, to give skilled and knowledgeable advice and to help negotiate the best transaction for the client in dealings with a third person (the *customer*).

Section 13a of the Restatement (Second) of Agency, a widely accepted legal authority on the law of agency, states that:

> Fiduciaries are held to the highest amount of good faith, are required to exclude all selfish interest, are prohibited from putting themselves in positions where personal interest and representative interest will conflict and must, in any direct dealing with the principal, make full disclosure of all relevant facts and give the latter an opportunity to obtain independent advice.

In lay terms, the fiduciary has special skills and expertise that place him or her in a position of advantage over the principal. An important aspect of this relationship is that the trust and confidence are on one side (the principal's) and the superiority and influence are on the other (the agent's). This is why the fiduciary has special obligations to the principal. The most important obligations a fiduciary owes to a principal are:

- loyalty;
- confidentiality;
- full disclosure;
- obedience;
- the duty to investigate and to use skill, care and due diligence; and
- the duty to account for all monies.

It is important to note that the real estate licensee, when acting as an agent for either party in the transaction, owes these fiduciary duties in addition to whatever duties are specified in the listing contract, the buyer representation agreement, the Texas Real Estate License Act and the TREC Rules. In addition, if the licensee is a REALTOR®, he or she owes the duties outlined in the REALTOR®'s Code of Ethics. In fact, because the NAR®'s Code of Ethics is generally recognized as representing the required and accepted standard of conduct for any real estate licensee, even a non-REALTOR® may be held liable to the standards of the Code at bench trial.

The Fiduciary Duty of Loyalty

The real estate licensee acting as an agent must act in the best interests of his or her principal. The agent owes allegiance to the client. After a broker obtains a listing or seller representation agreement from a seller, the listing broker and all his or her sales associates, whether licensed as salesperson or broker, become agents for the seller and are duty-bound to represent the best interests of the seller. This means striving to obtain a combination of the best price and terms possible to satisfy the seller's needs; investigating and explaining to the seller all offers received; obtaining as much relevant information about the buyer as possible; and, above all, exerting maximum efforts for the seller's benefit. The broker who acts otherwise is not acting in the best interests of his or her client. This is a requirement not only of Texas common law but a requirement under the laws of Texas known as the Texas Administrative Code, especially that section of the Code known as the Rules of the Texas Real Estate Commission and, in particular, 22 TAC 535.2(f), 535.16(c), 535.150, and 535.156(a),(b) and (c).

In other words, disloyalty of an agent to his or her principal or client is not only unethical and unprofessional, it is forbidden and illegal. Disloyalty is the cardinal sin of the agent and is grounds for forfeiture of commission without proof of damages, a loss of license, a law suit for damages and even possible recision of the sales or lease contract itself.

Example:

Broker Sally owned a home in a subdivision. Sally listed George's home down the street. Sally showed George's home to Betty, who expressed an immediate desire to purchase it for cash. Sally then persuaded Betty to purchase her own home instead. Sally has breached her fiduciary duty of loyalty to George.

The common violation of loyalty is the undisclosed or inadequately disclosed representation of both the buyer and the seller, known as *undisclosed dual agency.*

Example:

Sally, a real estate licensee, is hired by Bob to sell his house. Sally brings her sister to see the house and begins negotiations but fails to tell Bob that the buyer is her sister.

Example:

Betty hires real estate licensee Sally to be her agent and asks Sally to find a home for her. Sally sees a suitable property, which is for sale by owner (FSBO). Sally persuades the owner to list the home with her for one day, thus becoming the owner's agent. Unknown to either Betty or the owner, Sally collects a commission from both. If Sally receives payment from one party only but fails to make clear to either or both parties the nature of her relationship, she has still violated her promise of loyalty.

Example:

Broker Sally represents several buyers looking for an industrial property. Sally locates an excellent property at low price and has her brother buy the property before the buyers find out about it. Had Sally merely been working with the buyers instead of for them as their agent she could legally have competed with them for the property.

The Fiduciary Duty of Confidentiality

Related to the duty of loyalty is the duty to keep confidential any discussions, facts or information about the principal that should not be revealed to others. This is similar to the privileged-information concept of a lawyer-client or doctor-patient relationship. The duty of confidentiality owed to a client extends to an affirmative responsibility to withhold from a non-represented party such confidential information as: the client's bargaining position; motivations for selling or buying; opinions of value; marketing and negotiating strategies; the client's lowest acceptable price; the existence or non-existence of other offers or competing properties; and the client's financial position (unless the client is aware of and consents to the disclosure of such information). The NAR® Code of Ethics & Standard of Practice 7-8 obligates the REALTOR® to preserve confidential information provided by his or her clients even after the termination of the agency relationship (*see* Appendix B.)

However, there are limits to this duty to maintain confidentiality. The duty of confidentiality may be modified by a greater duty to the general public. For example, the duty of confidentiality does not extend to permit the broker to withhold material facts that should be disclosed to the buyer under the general legal requirements of honesty and fairness. For instance, the broker would be obligated to reveal to the buyer any known hazardous conditions.

The Fiduciary Duty of Full Disclosure

A key point related to loyalty is the obligation of the agent to make a full, fair and timely disclosure to his or her client or principal of all known facts relevant to the transaction. A *relevant* fact is one that a reasonable person might feel is important in choosing a course of action. Important disclosures by a listing agent to a seller client include such things as:

- the relationship between the client's agent and other parties to the transaction [TRELA §15(a)(6)(V) and 22 TAC §535.156];
- the existence of other offers and the status of the earnest money deposit [TRELA §15(a)(6)(V) and 22 TAC §535.156];
- the buyer's financial condition, the property's true worth and the agent's true opinion of the property's value [TRELA §15(a)(6)(V); 22 TAC §535.156; 22 TAC §535.16(d)];
- the commission split between a listing broker and another broker;
- the meaning of factual statements and business details contained in the contract [TRELA §15(a)(6)(V); 22 TAC §535.156]; and
- all known facts that might affect the status or title to real estate. [TRELA §15(a)(6)(V); 22 TAC §535.156; 22 TAC §537.11(c)(d)]

Liability may exist even for failure to disclose facts that the broker "should" have known within the range of expertise expected of a broker. For example, Texas courts have held that the real estate broker is not liable for physical inspection of the property for defects. This is the realm of the licensed inspector, not brokers and salesmen. [*Kubinski v. Van Zandt Realtors,* 811 S.W.2d 711 (Tex. 1991)] However, if the broker has actual knowledge of the defect, then he or she is liable both to the client/principal and to the non-client/customer for failure to disclose. Thus, in addition to disclosure, there is a duty of discovery and to investigate the many aspects of the transaction as they affect the client's decision-making. In one case the court held the listing broker negligent because the listing broker had failed to verify the appraised value of a property that the buyer was using as part of the downpayment.

Full disclosure. Full disclosure is required, regardless of whether the fact is favorable or unfavorable, is found before or after the purchase contract is signed or even if disclosure might prevent the deal. The principal is not only entitled to know the same facts that his or her agent knows, but the principal is generally assumed by law to know what his or her agent knows. The duty of disclosure is greater to a client than to a customer. A customer must be told material facts about that affect the property itself, not facts about the seller or the broker's opinion of value.

Full disclosure of relationships. The real estate broker who has the listing (i.e., the seller's agent) must disclose to the seller any special relationship that may exist between the broker and any of his or her sales associates and the buyer. Because the seller may be relying on his or her broker's loyal advice and counsel, it is important to know what interest the listing broker may have in the buyer's decision. The listing broker must disclose, for example, that the prospective buyer is a relative or close friend of one of the broker's salespeople, if a broker has an agreement with the buyer to be compensated if and when the buyer resells the seller's property or if the broker is loaning money to the buyer for the downpayment. The licensee must also obtain permission to receive compensation from the referral of business to companies controlled by the broker or others, such as appraisal, termite control, lender, title, escrow and property inspection services.

Full disclosure of other offers. As a matter of top priority, the listing broker should continue to present all offers to the seller or landlord until the sales contract is agreed to by all parties and closed. For rental property, the agent should continue to submit offers until the parties sign or orally agree to a lease and may want to consider presenting offers until the tenant's possession of the premises. The broker must submit, or at least communicate, all offers and counteroffers to his or her client, even those that he or she believes are too low or high to warrant serious consideration, whether the offers are oral or in writing or have any earnest money with them. If the broker is a REALTOR®, the NAR® Code of Ethics & Standard of Practice 7-1 requires the timely submission of all offers and counteroffers until closing, unless waived in writing. If there is any question as to whether a pre-existing contract has been terminated, or even if it is clear that there is already an existing contract agreed to by all parties, the broker is required by law to recommend to both the client and the customer that they obtain legal advice before signing the document [22 TAC 537.11(e)].

The listing agent should disclose any offers presented after the acceptance of an offer because the seller or landlord may want to accept these offers as secondary. This decision is for the seller or landlord to make. Although TREC Rule 22 TAC 535.156(a) states that, "The licensee shall have no duty to submit offers to the principal after the principal has accepted an offer," this rule is primarily permissive in nature and is aimed at allowing the licensee to not lose his or her license for failure to submit offers. However, it is recommended that the broker warn the client to handle all subsequent offers strictly as secondary contracts with the appropriate clarifying addenda so as to avoid the dangers of lawsuits for breach of contract and tortious interference with contract lawsuits.

The seller's broker must disclose all information that would help the seller develop the best selling strategy (unless the broker is a dual agent), which means disclosing information the broker has about a buyer's level of price resistance. For instance, the listing broker should encourage a buyer to submit the highest and best offer the first time and, in the interest of confidentiality and fairness, not disclose to the buyer, without the seller's consent, the terms of any other current offer or those previously rejected or countered. TREC considers "shopping" offers a violation of TRELA § 15(a)(6)(V), which states that "conduct which constitutes dishonest dealings, bad faith or untrustworthiness" is ground for loss of license. What bad faith conduct is involved in shopping offers? It is considered bad faith when a licensee does not tell a first offeror that his or her offer will be made known to competing bidders or, conversely, when the licensee does not give the first offeror an equal opportunity to learn the same details about a second offer. If each offeror is continually allowed to have knowledge of all competing offers, an auction has been introduced. It is best, regardless of the client's consent, to not disclose even the existence or non-existence of other offers, much less the price, terms or conditions. There is always the possibility that the second buyer or tenant will pay more if he or she doesn't know what the seller or landlord was willing to settle for in the first offer or contract.

Also, saying there is another offer when no other offer exists is *misrepresentation.* If it is said in order to induce the consumer into a transaction that he or she otherwise might not have entered into or to achieve a higher price than otherwise might have been paid, it is a deceptive trade practice under Texas law. Likewise, even disclosing the price, terms or conditions of previously negotiated or non-accepted offers could easily breach a fiduciary duty to the seller.

Full disclosure regarding status of earnest money deposits. Many listing agreements authorize the seller's broker to accept an earnest money deposit from the buyer. If the deposit is in the form of a postdated check or a promissory note, the broker must inform the seller. Otherwise, if the buyer defaults and the seller cannot collect on the note, the broker could be liable to the seller for the amount of the deposit to which the seller would normally be entitled. With the 1994 TREC-promulgated contract forms, the buyer, not the broker, is responsible for depositing the earnest money with an escrow agent upon final signing of the contract by all parties. It is incumbent on the seller's agent to check periodically with the escrow agent named in the contract to determine the status of the earnest money check and to keep the seller informed as to all findings. If the buyer asks the seller's agent if the agent can postpone the deposit of the earnest money check, the seller's agent should obtain written agreement between the parties to delay deposit. Otherwise, the licensee holding the money has one of two choices: (1) to deposit it according to the contract or (2) to deposit it within a reasonable time, which is defined as "the close of business of the second working day after the execution of the contract by the principals." [22 TAC 535.159(i) and 535.2(g)(h)]

Full disclosure of buyer's financial condition. The seller's broker takes a risk in advising the seller that the buyer is financially sound. He or she takes an even greater risk when, if knowing information that might indicate the buyer is financially unsound, the listing broker or subagent neglects to communicate that information to the seller. Buyer's brokers have no such duty to communicate negative information concerning the buyer's financial strength to the seller. Instead, buyer's brokers have a duty of confidentiality **not** to communicate to the seller the financial strength of buyer's position unless given permission or direction to do so from his or her buyer-client.

This does not mean the buyer's broker can misrepresent the buyer's financial strength by giving false or misleading information. Normally, the seller should make an independent evaluation of the buyer's finances on the basis of the data the broker collects from the buyer. The prudent seller's agent or subagent will point out to the seller that he or she is not a lender nor an arranger of credit and is not in a position to verify the financial information supplied by the prospective buyer, but will nonetheless use all possible skill to ascertain such information. Because of the fiduciary relationship between the listing broker, any subagents and the seller, the listing broker and/or subagents from other cooperating brokerages must disclose any negative information that the broker has concerning the prospective buyer's financial situation. This is especially true when the seller is being asked to carryback financing or allow an assumption of an existing loan. The listing agent or subagents must disclose to the seller such facts that the buyer states or that the broker has learned independently, for instance, that the buyer has a condominium in Oklahoma City that he must sell before he can close on the seller's house in Houston. The seller's agents and subagents cannot remain silent in the face of information that affects the buyer's ability to obtain financing or gives the buyer an option to terminate the offer [22 TAC 535.156(a)&(c) and 535.2(f)], and the liability of a broker and the right to a commission does not depend on whether the seller was damaged but, rather, on whether the broker breached the duty to disclose.

Full disclosure of property value. Because property value is a matter of opinion, the broker must, under Texas law, disclose to his or her client, *not a customer*, his or her true "opinion of the market value of a property when negotiating a listing or offering to purchase the property for the licensee's own account as a result of contact made while acting as a real estate agent." [TRELA 2(2)(D); 22 TAC 535.16(c)&(d)] The broker's fiduciary duty for full disclosure of property value to his or her client includes disclosure of all known sales of comparable property, whether at higher or lower prices. The broker is also liable for disclosure of all those comparables that the broker should have known through a reasonable review. A broker can be held liable to his or her client and customer for rendering a false opinion of value. A broker is also liable for giving a wrong opinion of value to a client or customer if the opinion was negligently based on inaccurate comparisons or inaccurate application of appraisal methods. [TRELA § 15(a)(6)(W); 22 TAC 535.157; 22 TAC 535.156(d); DTPA § 17.46(b)(5), (6) and (7)] These duties and the law are especially relevant in cases in which the listing broker deliberately underprices or overprices a property when obtaining a listing. When a broker learns of factors that change the value of the property after the listing is signed, he or she must disclose such factors as soon as possible and certainly before the client decides to accept an offer. The price and terms of the listing may have to be adjusted in accordance with such changed conditions. [TRELA 15(a)(6)(V); 22 TAC 535.156(c)&(d)]

Full disclosure of commission split. The listing broker must disclose to the seller the existence of any fee-sharing arrangement with a cooperating broker. Although the exact amount of any split does not have to be revealed, it is better to disclose fully to the client the amounts to be split, with the rationale for doing so. This disclosure should be in writing, preferably in the listing agreement. Under the NAR® Code of Ethics & Standards of Practice 9-10, the listing broker must disclose the general company policy regarding cooperation with subagents, buyer agents or both, and it is better to disclose, discuss and deal with that issue before it becomes a point of dispute. Some sellers would be angry to find out that part of the commission money they paid their listing agent was split with a buyer's broker who was negotiating for a lower sales price.

There are good arguments for a seller to allow the policy of splitting commissions with buyer's brokers, not the least of which are the reduced liability the seller has for the actions of a buyer's broker as opposed to a subagent and the potential increased exposure of his or her property to buyers. [**Note:** It is a violation of TRELA 15(a)(6)(F) for a broker to pay a commission or fees to or divide a commission or fees with anyone not licensed as a real estate broker or salesman for compensation for services as a real estate agent.]

Full disclosure of contract provisions. The broker must discuss with the client each provision of a contract that the client is being asked to sign; alternatively, the broker should suggest that the client obtain competent legal advice. In fact, where it appears that there is an unusual matter that should be resolved by legal counsel or that the instrument is to be acknowledged and filed of record, the licensee is required by

Texas law to advise both parties in the transaction to seek legal counsel. Failure to do so is grounds for loss of license. [22 TAC 537.11(e)]

The similar general warning in a TREC-promulgated contract form does not meet this specific requirement. Although licensees should not practice law or give legal advice, nothing in the TREC Rules or the License Act is "deemed to limit the licensee's fiduciary obligation to disclose to his or her principals all pertinent facts which are within the knowledge of the licensee, including such facts which might affect the status of or title to real estate." [22 TAC 537.11(b),(c),(d), (e),(f),(g)] The Rules further state that "Nothing herein shall be deemed to prevent the licensee from explaining to the principals the meaning of factual statements and business details contained in the said instrument so long as the licensee does not offer or give legal advice."

The Fiduciary Duty of Obedience

Brokers must follow the lawful instructions of their clients. They must obtain a survey or appraisal if their clients so direct and may not extend closing dates or loan approval dates contrary to sellers' instructions. However, brokers may not violate the law, for example, by refusing to show a seller's property to a member of a minority group or withholding information about structural damage, even if directed to do so by a seller. In other words, a client's instructions to his or her agent to break a law cannot be obeyed.

The Fiduciary Duty of Reasonable Skill and Care

A broker is hired to do more than merely locate a property or find a ready, willing and able buyer, and a broker's obligations extend beyond simply selling or locating a property. The real estate broker is held to a standard of care that requires, among other things, that he or she be knowledgeable concerning the land, the title and the physical characteristics of the property being sold.

The broker for the seller must use reasonable skill and care in:

- guiding the seller to arrive at a reasonable listing price in light of the current market value and advising as to an adequate purchase price;
- affirmatively discovering relevant facts and disclosing the facts to the seller;
- investigating the material facts related to the sale and asking the seller questions (the duty to interrogate) that will clarify the seller's needs and protect his or her best interests (e.g., "Does your roof leak?");
- preparing and/or explaining portions of the listing form, purchase contract and other relevant legal documents;
- recommending that the seller seek independent expert advisers when appropriate;
- meeting deadlines and closing dates; and
- making reasonable efforts to sell the property, such as holding open houses, advertising and listing with an MLS, if customary.

Suppose a broker sells a home one week after the listing is signed. Initially, the seller is thrilled. Later, however, the seller may complain that the broker lacked skill and care because the broker set the listing price too low or failed to obtain better financing terms. The seller may be angry because he or she discovered that the agent had assisted the buyer in obtaining financing with higher discount points when lower discount point options were available. Likewise, a seller who unwittingly closes a transaction a few days before being eligible for favorable tax benefits could well complain that the broker's failure to exercise reasonable skill in allowing an early close cost the seller thousands of dollars in avoidable taxes.

Likewise, a broker who undertakes to represent a buyer must exercise reasonable skill and care on the buyer's behalf. This duty extends beyond giving honest information to a customer—it extends to rendering sound advice and advising the buyer to obtain assistance from experts when appropriate. At the very essence of the fiduciary concept is the fact that a true agent is an "equity preserver" for his or her client. A buyer's agent preserves equity for his or her buyer-client by using all of the broker's specialized skills and knowledge in negotiating the least possible price with the best terms.

Brokers do not have to meet the high standard of legal knowledge required of attorneys; however, brokers do need a basic knowledge of real estate law to qualify for state licenses. Courts impose on brokers a duty to know and to explain in basic terms the practical effect of key financing terms, contingency clauses, holding title, restrictions and routine contract provisions. In short, brokers must spot common problem areas and direct their clients to expert help when the client requires specific advice.

Unlike attorneys, brokers' responsibilities are more than acting as fiduciaries. Typically, brokers are hired to market property. Sometimes these dual responsibilities—that of marketing and that of advising—create practical and ethical dilemmas not normally experienced by other fiduciaries. Recognizing that his or her income depends on a sale, the nonprofessional broker could easily justify holding back information, based on the likelihood that the sale will proceed and that certain information would only cloud the seller's decision. Nevertheless, the broker must disclose information to the seller as part of the fiduciary duty required by law and ethics.

A practical test applied by courts to decide whether a broker used reasonable skill and care in a given case is: Would a reasonably efficient broker in the community in a like situation use more care to protect the best interests of the client? If the answer by the trier of fact is yes, then the broker has been negligent.

The Fiduciary Duty of Accounting

Monies received by the broker as a result of a purchase contract are trust funds and must be held for the benefit of the principal. A broker may not normally deposit these funds into an account with interest accruing to the benefit of either the broker or the seller. However, with the written agreement of both the buyer and the seller, the broker may do so. Trust funds must be delivered to the principal within a reasonable time. Brokers are required to maintain client trust fund accounts separate from their general accounts. To lessen the risk of unintended commingling, brokers should have separate trust accounts for sales and for rentals.

State licensing law prohibits commingling of funds. In some states the law contains strict rules on trust fund accounting. TREC can suspend or revoke a broker's license if the broker does not properly account for client funds. As a general practice in Texas, most brokers in residential real estate sales do not hold earnest money in their own trust accounts but instead insist that the principals in the transaction agree on a neutral escrow agent to hold the earnest money. Generally the escrow agent is the same title company that will also close the transaction and provide the title insurance.

SCOPE OF AUTHORITY

The agent is authorized to perform only those acts permitted by the principal. Real estate agents are referred to as limited or special agents; their scope of authority does not usually extend beyond the terms of the listing agreement. The listing broker is authorized to find a ready, willing and able buyer, but generally has no authority to sign contracts for the seller, initial changes to an offer, receive the full purchase price on behalf of the seller or permit early occupancy. Typically, a real estate property manager is a general agent with powers to sign contracts on behalf of the owner within certain dollar or other limits.

The authority granted to a broker should be stated expressly in the listing agreement. In a typical listing contract, the seller specifically authorizes the broker to place a sign on the property, advertise, show property, cooperate with other brokers, including buyer's brokers, use a MLS and accept earnest money deposits. Usually, the broker is not given the right to sign contracts, although in exceptional cases, the broker may be appointed as attorney-in-fact under a separately granted power of attorney. Under the "equal dignities rule," if the document to be signed by the agent is to be recorded, then a power-of-attorney must also be in recordable form.

In addition to express authority, the broker is often granted that authority that is customary or incidental to accomplish the stated purposes of the agency. Incidental authority may include the use of salespeople to staff open houses or even to enter the property for purpose of posting a for-sale sign.

DUTIES TO OTHERS

Although a broker owes specific fiduciary duties to the client, the broker also owes a general duty, under Texas law, of honesty and fairness to all parties in a transaction. There is a great deal of confusion concerning the use of the word *fairly,* which remains in the Texas law. Remember, *fairly* does not mean *equally* in the context of comparative duties owed to a client versus those owed to a customer. However, when *fair* or *fairly* is used in discussing the comparative duties owed to or treatment of one customer versus another customer, then the concept of equality of treatment is much more appropriate.

Likewise, the listing broker has responsibilities to both the seller and the buyer, although it is clear that the responsibilities to each are different. The listing broker owes the buyer (the customer) duties of honesty, competency, good faith and disclosure of all material facts. Additionally, the listing broker and seller's subagent broker owe the buyer certain statutory duties and other duties under TREC Rules of fairness, such as prompt presentation of all offers, not shopping the buyer's offer to other competing buyers and avoidance of misrepresentation and false promises. If the buyer is represented by a broker, that fact does not diminish the duties of the listing broker to the buyer through the buyer's broker.

AVOID MISREPRESENTATION

The most common complaint of buyers against listing brokers is based on misrepresentation by the brokers. Listing brokers have a duty to disclose material facts concerning the value and desirability of a property. Brokers are frequently asked by buyers to describe a property and to make representations in connection with a sale. A common complaint involves concealment by the listing broker of material defects about which the broker knew or should have known. In California, for instance, court rulings have identified "red flags"—things that should put the broker on notice that a problem exists—and which should be brought to the buyer's attention. Such red flags include evidence of recent mudslides, obvious building code violations and drainage and soil settlement problems. However, in Texas, the licensee, even if licensed as a real estate inspector, is not expected nor even allowed to function as a broker and a inspector in the same transaction. The broker is always responsible for revealing what he or she knows or had good reason to know but is not responsible for functioning as an inspector.

Section 5.008 of the Texas Property Code now requires a seller's disclosure notice for most residential resales occurring on or after January 1, 1994. TREC has produced a form for licensees to help sellers meet their requirement under the property code. (*See* Figure 2.3.) The form is called *Seller's Disclosure of Property Condition* and should not be confused with the *Property Condition Addendum* in the sales contract. According to TREC, "This new form provides a vehicle for disclosure of defects or items in need of repair. Conditions such as the presence of lead-based paint, termite damage and flooding are also addressed. If the notice is not given prior to the effective date of the contract, the purchaser may terminate the contract for any reason within seven days after receiving the notice. New TREC contract forms have been modified to facilitate compliance with the law." Consistent and proper use of this form could prevent Deceptive Trade Practices lawsuits against the broker.

When is information considered to be a material fact that should be disclosed? The broker must be careful not to go too far in volunteering information to the buyer that could harm the seller's negotiating position. Suppose there are general discussions in the City Council about down-zoning an area in which the listing broker is selling a property. If the broker discloses this future possibility and the buyer chooses not to buy, can the seller claim that the listing broker acted contrary to the seller's best interest and cancel the listing? The buyer would obviously like to know that the seller is considering a price reduction, but the buyer is not entitled to disclosure of this information.

Suppose the seller orders the listing broker not to disclose a material fact, such as a basement that floods. If such an order is given early in the listing period, the broker should decline the listing and refuse to work with this seller. But if the order comes two days before closing, after the broker has fully performed his or her obligations, should the broker disregard the instruction, make the disclosure and protect the earned commission, even if the disclosure prevents the sale? Whenever full and fair disclosure of a material fact is not made, the real estate agent is at risk. The broker has an independent duty to the buyer to take reasonable steps to avoid giving the buyer false information or concealing material facts. Seek legal counsel on these situations immediately. It is not a good idea to continue to market the property until you have resolved the problem.

To have a successful misrepresentation claim against a broker, the plaintiff must prove that:

Figure 2.3 Seller's Disclosure of Property Condition

APPROVED BY THE TEXAS REAL ESTATE COMMISSION (TREC) 10-25-93

SELLER'S DISCLOSURE OF PROPERTY CONDITION

(SECTION 5.008, TEXAS PROPERTY CODE)

CONCERNING THE PROPERTY AT____
(Street Address and City)

THIS NOTICE IS A DISCLOSURE OF SELLER'S KNOWLEDGE OF THE CONDITION OF THE PROPERTY AS OF THE DATE SIGNED BY SELLER AND IS NOT A SUBSTITUTE FOR ANY INSPECTIONS OR WARRANTIES THE PURCHASER MAY WISH TO OBTAIN. IT IS NOT A WARRANTY OF ANY KIND BY SELLER OR SELLER'S AGENTS.

Seller ☐ is ☐ is not occupying the Property. If unoccupied, how long since Seller has occupied the Property? ______________

1. The Property has the items checked below [Write Yes (Y), No (N), or Unknown (U)]:

___Range	___Oven	___Microwave
___Dishwasher	___Trash Compactor	___Disposal
___Washer/Dryer Hookups	___Window Screens	___Rain Gutters
___Security System	___Fire Detection Equipment	___Intercom System
___TV Antenna	___Cable TV Wiring	___Satellite Dish
___Ceiling Fan(s)	___Attic Fan(s)	___Exhaust Fan(s)
___Central A/C	___Central Heating	___Wall/Window Air Conditioning
___Plumbing System	___Septic System	___Public Sewer System
___Patio/Decking	___Outdoor Grill	___Fences
___Pool	___Sauna	___Spa___Hot Tub
___Pool Equipment	___Pool Heater	___Automatic Lawn Sprinkler System
___Fireplace(s) & Chimney(Woodburning)	___Fireplace(s) & Chimney (Mock)	___Gas Lines (Nat./LP)
___Gas Fixtures	Garage:___Attached ___Not Attached	___Carport
Garage Door Opener(s):	___Electronic	___Control(s)
Water Heater:	___Gas	___Electric

Water Supply: ___City ___Well ___MUD ___Co-op

Roof Type:______________________ Age:______________________(approx)

Are you (Seller) aware of any of the above items that are not in working condition, that have known defects, or that are in need of repair? ☐ Yes ☐ No ☐ Unknown. If yes, then describe. (Attach additional sheets if necessary):______________________

2. Are you (Seller) aware of any known defects/malfunctions in any of the following? Write Yes (Y) if you are aware, write No (N) if you are not aware.

___Interior Walls	___Ceilings	___Floors
___Exterior Walls	___Doors	___Windows
___Roof	___Foundation/Slab(s)	___Basement
___Walls/Fences	___Driveways	___Sidewalks
___Plumbing/Sewers/Septics	___Electrical Systems	___Lighting Fixtures

___Other Structural Components (Describe):______________________

№ 000

Figure 2.3 continued

Seller's Disclosure Notice Concerning the Property at ______________________ Page 2 10-25-93
(Street Address and City)

If the answer to any of the above is yes, explain. (Attach additional sheets if necessary): ______________________

3. Are you (Seller) aware of any of the following conditions? Write Yes (Y) if you are aware, write No (N) if you are not aware.

___Active Termites (includes wood-destroying insects)
___Termite or Wood Rot Damage Needing Repair
___Previous Termite Damage
___Previous Termite Treatment
___Previous Flooding
___Improper Drainage
___Water Penetration
___Located in 100-Year Floodplain
___Present Flood Insurance Coverage
___Previous Structural or Roof Repair
___Hazardous or Toxic Waste
___Asbestos Components
___Urea-formaldehyde Insulation
___Radon Gas
___Lead Based Paint
___Aluminum Wiring
___Previous Fires
___Unplatted Easements
___Landfill, Settling, Soil Movement, Fault Lines
___Subsurface Structure or Pits

If the answer to any of the above is yes, explain. (Attach additional sheets if necessary): ______________________

4. Are you (Seller) aware of any item, equipment, or system in or on the Property that is in need of repair? ☐ Yes (if you are aware) ☐ No (if you are not aware). If yes, explain (attach additional sheets as necessary). ______________________

5. Are you (Seller) aware of any of the following? Write Yes (Y) if you are aware, write No (N) if you are not aware.

___ Room additions, structural modifications, or other alterations or repairs made without necessary permits or not in compliance with building codes in effect at that time.

___ Homeowners' Association or maintenance fees or assessments.

___ Any "common area" (facilities such as pools, tennis courts, walkways, or other areas) co-owned in undivided interest with others.

___ Any notices of violations of deed restrictions or governmental ordinances affecting the condition or use of the Property.

___ Any lawsuits directly or indirectly affecting the Property.

___ Any condition on the Property which materially affects the physical health or safety of an individual.

If the answer to any of the above is yes, explain. (Attach additional sheets if necessary): ______________________

______________________ ______________________
Date Signature of Seller Date Signature of Seller

The undersigned purchaser hereby acknowledges receipt of the foregoing notice.

______________________ ______________________
Date Signature of Purchaser Date Signature of Purchaser

№ 000

- the broker made a misstatement (oral or written) to the buyer or failed to disclose a material fact to the buyer;
- the broker either knew or should have known that the statement was not accurate or that the information should have been disclosed;
- the buyer reasonably relied on such statements; and
- the buyer was damaged as a result.

Element of reliance. Courts have held that the buyer is entitled to relief if the representations were a material inducement to the contract, even though the buyer may have made efforts to discover the truth and did not rely wholly on the representations. Also, "agency is no defense;" that is, it is generally no defense that the broker was merely passing along information that the seller had provided, for example, the amount of taxes or the connection to the sewer system. The seller has a duty not to misrepresent, and the broker's duty stems from the seller's duty.

In fixing liability or in applying remedies it makes no difference whether the misrepresentation was intentional or negligent. The most common remedies available include monetary damages, rescission and forfeiture of the broker's commission.

Buyer Beware. Although the trend is full disclosure to the buyer of material defects in the property condition, a few states continue to hold on to the doctrine of "buyer beware." Texas is **not** one of these. In these states the seller's agent or subagent is often found not liable for failure to disclose material facts. Not surprisingly, some brokers in these states are reluctant to become buyer's agents for fear of the potential liability related to the increased duty of disclosure as a fiduciary to the buyer-client.

Watch What Is Said

Brokers must carefully consider their statements to buyers and sellers. The broker is considered the real estate expert; therefore, the consumer relies on what the broker says, even when the broker is not acting as the buyer's agent. Here is a short list of broker statements that never should be made:

- "No need to get a title search. I sold this same property last year and there was no title problem."
- "Don't worry, the seller told me by phone I could sign the contract for her."
- "If it helps you make up your mind about the price to offer on my listing, the seller countered a $130,000 offer last week for $135,000."
- "I won't be able to present your offer until the seller decides on the offer submitted yesterday."
- "I can't present your offer yet. We have a contract working."
- "I can't/won't present your offer with that type of contingency clause in there."
- "Go ahead and make an offer. If you can't get financing, you don't have to buy anyway and you'll still get your earnest money back."
- "I can't submit your offer without earnest money. It's not legal."
- "Trust me. I can word a contingency clause in such a way that you can back out whenever you want."

SUMMARY

In any given transaction, the decision to represent the seller exclusively, the buyer exclusively or both of them at the same time is a serious matter. Brokers must understand their fiduciary responsibilities to clients and their general duties of fairness, honesty and good faith to customers. It is easy for salespeople in an automobile showroom to know who they work for (client-employer) and who they work with (customer). It is a more complex question in real estate when the salesperson can show a buyer in one day an in-house listing, MLS listing, a FSBO property or even the salesperson's own home. The various relationships must be understood by all participants in the transaction. One way to understand is to see how agency relationships are created.

KEY POINTS

- As a fiduciary, a real estate agent owes greater duties to a client than to a customer and thus the risk of liability is greater.
- There are a variety of agency relationships for brokers, buyers and sellers to consider in every transaction.
- The most important characteristic of an agency relationship for the consumer is the agent's duty of undivided loyalty and total allegiance.
- A fiduciary for one party still owes a duty of fairness and honesty to the party for which the agent is not a fiduciary.

SUGGESTIONS FOR BROKERS

Develop a policy for the proper handling of offers to purchase, to include:

1. **Multiple Offers.** Inform sellers promptly of all offers, even after acceptance. Consider an open bid auction approach to handling multiple offers on a property, with the buyers openly bidding against each other. However, remember that in Texas auctioning real property requires a license. Check with TREC before adopting such a policy.
2. **Confidentiality.** If there is doubt as to whether licensees in your firm will shop your offers, do not reveal to in-house staff the dollar amount of offers or even the existence or non-existence of other offers, whether from buyers working directly with members of your firm or received from cooperating brokers. Do not disclose to prospective buyers or agents in your firm the dollar amount of previous counteroffers made by the seller.
3. **Personal Offers.** Make appropriate disclosures to the seller and to cooperating brokers if one of your salespeople is making a personal bid on an in-house listing. This is an exception to the shopping of offers prohibition because your agents will likely know of the offers of other buyers while the other buyers will not know about the agent's offer. Each of the other buyers should be told of your agent's offer but not about any other offer. To avoid this dilemma, many brokers make an office policy prohibiting the purchase of any of the firm's listings by any of its employees. This limits lawsuits, unpleasant disputes, accusations of not dealing fairly with the public and complaints of conflict of interest with the seller/client.

QUIZ

1. A broker can buy a property listed with him or her under which of the following conditions?
   a. A family member secretly purchases the property for more than the asking price.
   b. Under no circumstance.
   c. Only if the property is listed by an open listing.
   d. Only if full disclosure is made to the seller of the broker's involvement as a purchaser.
2. The listing broker:
   a. may refuse to present an offer if it is too low.
   b. must tell the buyer the seller's lowest acceptable price.
   c. must present every written offer to the seller.
   d. may tell the buyer the terms of a counteroffer the seller made yesterday.
3. A salesperson owes all of the following fiduciary duties *except*:
   a. to inform the broker and the seller of material facts.
   b. to be loyal to the best interests of the principal.
   c. to prepare a power of attorney for the buyer.
   d. to obey the lawful instructions of the broker.
4. A listing broker tells a buyer-customer that the seller is under pressure to sell because of a pending divorce and possible foreclosure. Such disclosure is:
   a. acceptable if it results in a sale.
   b. acceptable if none of the details of the foreclosure are disclosed.
   c. unacceptable because the listing broker is the agent of the buyer.
   d. unacceptable because of the fiduciary duty owed the owner.
5. Sally listed and sold George's townhouse. She did not tell George that there was a major zoning change in process that would allow business use in the area, thus increasing property values. Which is true?
   a. Sally did not have to disclose the change because George never asked her.
   b. Sally did not have to disclose the change if George received his full asking price.
   c. Sally had to disclose the change because it was a material and pertinent fact.
   d. Sally had to disclose the change because the zoning laws require notice to all interested persons.

DISCUSSION QUESTIONS

1. What are the main duties a fiduciary owes to the principal?
2. What is the best procedure to use to present multiple offers? Suppose you have two written offers and a buyer telephones that she will better any offer. Do you tell the buyer the amount of the highest offer?
3. Why should you tell the seller about offers received after the seller has already accepted an offer?
4. In the typical residential real estate transaction in Texas prior to September 1, 1993, who did the brokers usually represent?

5. If you are acting for the listing broker or as a subagent of the listing broker, how far do you go in disclosing facts to the buyer before you begin to act contrary to the best interests of your seller?

6. If you are acting for the buyer as a buyer's broker, how far do you go in disclosing facts to the seller or his or her agents before you begin to act contrary to the best interests of your buyer?

* TREC requires Form 3 disclosure on all type of transaction

CHAPTER

3

CREATION AND TERMINATION OF AGENCY

In general, an agency relationship is created when one person authorizes another to act on his or her behalf and to exercise some degree of authority and discretion while so acting. The agent may be empowered to do many of the things the principal could do but has chosen not to do. Typically, the agency is created by express or implied agreement and consent is required.

All parties to a real estate transaction must understand the rules that distinguish agency from the other two types of working relationships relative to agency (non-agency and dual agency) and also must be able to identify exactly when an agency or dual agency relationship is created so that they know when their responsibilities begin and which set of legal duties they owe. Additionally, often real estate licensees are not clear on the question of a how a lawful or unlawful dual agency is created. Few people, licensees included, know the acts, conditions, expectations, statements and reliances that can turn an ordinary broker into an agent or dual agent unintentionally. Most textbooks, the REALTOR® Code of Ethics and state licensing laws focus on the strict fulfillment of the rules of conduct for an agent but offer few guidelines, however, as to how and when an agency is created and to whom fiduciary duties are owed. They assume that agency relationships are understood and apparent when, in fact, such relationships are not always clear.

This chapter discusses the following:

- How Agency Is Created
    - Compensation
    - Express Agency
    - Implied Agency
    - Agency Ratification and Estoppel
- Important to Decide
    - Legal Effect
    - Imputed Notice
    - Professional and Ethical Responsibility
    - Quality of Representation
- How Agency is Terminated
- Understanding Relationships
    - Single Agency
    - Seller Agency

Buyer Agency
Subagency
Dual Agency

HOW AGENCY IS CREATED

The fact that a person licensed as a real estate broker or salesman performs a service for a consumer is not, by itself, sufficient to create an agency. A real estate licensee's stock in trade is to give valuable service both to clients and to customers. The creation of an agency requires more than just giving benefits and services. It requires consent and control. Once created, agency requires the subordination of the agent's interest in the transaction to the interests of the party he or her represents, the principal. This subordination of interests coupled with rendered services manifests itself in representation of the client served. The licensee turned agent becomes an advocate of the party he or she serves and no one else and is, in fact, obligated to protect the interests of the person he or she represents.

Technically, an agency relationship results from mutual consent between the principal and the agent to the effect that the agent will act on the principal's behalf, subject to the principal's control. Formalities are not required to create an agency. An agent does not need a license, written contract or commission or fee for an agency relationship to exist (*see* Figure 3.1).

It is commonly thought that no agency exists unless there is a written agreement. An agreement in writing is not required to create an agency relationship, although most states, including Texas, require a written agreement if the broker wants to sue for a commission or to perform a specific act, such as advertising or placing the broker's sign on the property. (Even though an agency may be created by oral agreement, the prudent broker will, at a minimum, send the principal a letter, confirming the existence of the agency relationship and spelling out the amount and expected source of any fee.)

Figure 3.1 Elements *Not* Essential to Create an Agency

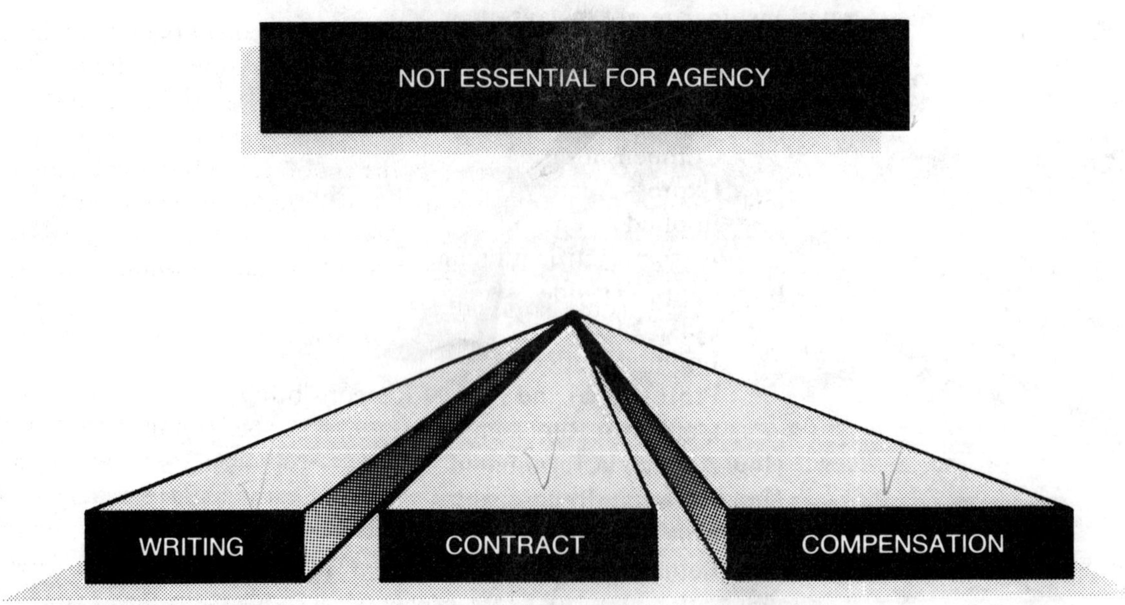

What is needed is specific authorization from the principal that permits the agent to perform acts on behalf of the principal in dealing with others. The principal must delegate authority to act to the agent and the agent must consent to act, or there is no agency. Ask this question: "Is the agent acting on behalf of the principal in a contractual relationship, be it express or implied, oral or written?"

Compensation

The most common notion of agency is frequently expressed as "You are the agent of the person who pays you." When asked what the determining factor is in creating an agency, most real estate licensees answer that it is payment of the fee. However, the payment of a commission is not the sole factor in creating an agency relationship. In fact, by contract, the seller could agree to pay the buyer's broker's fee, just like the seller sometimes agrees to pay the points on the buyer's loan or the cost of the professional home inspection. Also, by contract, the buyer could agree to pay the buyer's broker's fee, the listing broker's fee or any or all of the seller's closing expenses. An agency relationship can be created regardless of whether the seller pays the fee, the buyer pays the fee, each pays or neither pays. Most state agency disclosure laws confirm the common law rule that payment of the fee does not determine agency.

An agency can be created even if the agent charges no fee. Thus, a gratuitous agent giving free advice, perhaps to build goodwill, could be held liable if he or she gives wrong advice. For example, an agent working without charge could be liable for bad advice on the effect of a "risk of loss" provision in a contract in regard to obtaining property insurance if it were relied upon and resulted in injury to the principal.

Despite the fact that payment of the commission does not necessarily determine agency, prudent brokers should discuss and document who they represent and who is paying who. A clear disclosure can dispel any notion that the broker represented the person who paid the broker's commission. If no agency documentation exists, courts will probably use the commission payment as evidence of the intended agency relationship, especially if the person paying the fee is the one claiming that an agency existed. Without clear evidence to the contrary, the broker then will have a difficult burden to prove no agency existed.

Express Agency

An agency is frequently created by express agreement between principal and agent. Some states require such an agreement of representation to be in writing under both the licensing law and the Statute of Frauds. However, Texas only requires that an agreement or some note or memorandum of an agreement to compensate be in writing for one reason: in order to bring a court action for collection of the fee. Oral listing agreements, buyer or tenant representation agreements and management agreements do not have to be in writing in Texas. The major exception to this general rule is dual agency agreements. If a dual agency exists without a written agreement conforming to TRELA §15C, then it is illegal.

Implied Agency

Brokers are not accustomed to discussing and confirming who they represent. As a result, buyers often rely on "their" broker to represent them, ignorant of the fact that the broker might legally represent the seller. Courts will frequently look to the actions of the broker and to the reliance by the buyer; based on these, courts may find an implied agency between the broker and the buyer. Because formalities are not required, courts may hold that an agency arrangement was implied, based on the intentions of the agent and the alleged principal, as shown by their outward conduct and words. Even though a broker is the seller's agent, the broker could be held to be functioning as the buyer's agent as well. Courts will ask the question: Did the broker act under the alleged principal's direction and control?

Example:

Betty contacts Bay Realty, seeking a four-unit rental building. Sally, a salesperson with Bay Realty, agrees to work with Betty. After showing Betty ten properties and negotiating unsuccessfully on two of those properties, Sally finds a four-unit rental building that suits Betty's needs and qualifications. Sally then obtains the listing on the four-unit building from owner Harry on behalf of Bay Realty. If a judge had to rule on the agency issue, he or she would probably hold that Bay Realty was a dual agent, a ruling based on an express agency with the seller and an implied agency with Betty.

Disclosure and clarification should lessen findings of an implied agency. However, a broker who behaves like a buyer's agent, even though bound to an express written agreement to represent the seller, will nevertheless be deemed an implied agent of the buyer. Brokers must be careful how they act, even after they put their agency arrangements in writing, because the conduct of the parties can result in the creation of an agency even though a written agreement asserts that there is no agency or that the parties never intended an agency.

Agency Ratification and Estoppel

An agency relationship may also be created by *ratification* or by *estoppel.* Under the ratification theory, the principal may be held to have approved the agency if he or she accepted the benefits of an agent's previously unauthorized act. This is *agency after the fact.*

Example:

Sally from Bay Realty tried unsuccessfully to obtain a listing on a warehouse from Harry. Sally went to Harry one day and told him she had a number of interested buyers, but Harry would not give her a listing. Nevertheless, Sally showed several buyers the property. When Sally brought in an acceptable offer from a buyer, Harry accepted the offer, which contained a provision for him to pay Sally. Harry asked Sally to monitor the closing. Subsequently, the buyer brought a lawsuit against Harry to cancel the purchase contract because of a misrepresentation made by Sally. Harry argued that Sally was not his agent because he did not sign a listing agreement. A court will likely hold that Harry ratified or affirmed the agency by his conduct and is thus bound by Sally's misrepresentation.

Even if a listing expires, if the seller still allows his or her agent broker to show and advertise the property, the agency will continue. If a buyer later sues the seller because of a misrepresentation made by the agent broker and the seller claims that the agency had ended, the court is likely to hold that, based on the doctrine of estoppel, the seller cannot deny the agency. This is also called *ostensible agency* ("for all appearances") because the seller allowed others to believe that an agency relationship continued to exist between him or her and the agent broker, and potential buyers were justified in relying on that belief.

IMPORTANT TO DECIDE

Why is it so important to determine—in every case—whether an agency relationship has, in fact, been created? The main reasons are: legal effect, imputed notice, professional and ethical responsibility and the quality of representation.

Legal Effect

The agent stands in the shoes of the principal. The agent speaks, listens and acts for the principal. This is the very essence of the word represents when used in the context of the agency relationship.

Because the agent acts in behalf of the principal, the principal is bound to the agent's statements intended to be taken as true and the agent's conduct performed during the scope of the agency; that is, anything done to further the principal's objective to sell or purchase is assumed to be done with the knowledge and approval of the principal. This is true whether the actions are fraudulent, negligent or innocent. The statements, omissions, admissions and misrepresentations made by the agent or subagent will be attributed to the principal, even though the principal may be unaware of them. For this reason alone, the principal should make an informed choice of his or her agent.

Example:

Bob asks Sally of Bay Realty, the selling broker, whether it is permissible to build a second story onto a property Sally found listed in the MLS. No one asks the seller or Sam of Main Realty, who is the listing broker. Sally checks the zoning and responds, "There is no problem." Sally, however, has failed to discover recorded private deed restrictions that limit structures to one story. If Sally and Bay Realty are deemed the subagent of the seller (i.e., the agent of Main Realty, the seller's agent), then the buyer can assert Sally's negligent misrepresentation as a legal basis to cancel the contract with the seller (rescission). Of course, the seller can seek to recover damages (based on indemnification) against Sally and Bay Realty, but the sale will have been lost nonetheless. On the other hand, if Sally is deemed the agent of the buyer, then Bob will not be able to assert Sally's misrepresentation as a ground to rescind the contract with the seller. Bob will have to perform the contract with the seller and then seek monetary damages directly against his own agent, Sally and Bay Realty.

Principals are also bound by the negligence of their agents. The reasoning behind this ruling is that principals should not be allowed to benefit from the negligent acts of their agents and subagents. A recent judicial trend is to expand broker liability in the area of negligence. Courts often base decisions on the fact that an agent knew or should have known certain information, such as that the sewer wasn't connected, the roof leaked or the property was located in a slide area. The listing broker's failure to discover defects and disclose such obvious defects to the buyer may be termed negligence. Not only may the listing broker and subagents be liable for this negligence, but the seller may also be liable.

However, in Texas, the courts have found that agents who did not know of latent defects were not bound to the extent of duties as real estate inspectors and are, in fact, prohibited from acting as inspectors and brokers in the same transaction. Thus, in *Kubinsky v. Van Zandt,* the broker was appropriately not found to be in a should-have-known situation.

A few courts in the United States have held that brokers—and their principals—are liable for the brokers' innocent misrepresentations.

Example:

Sally checked the prior survey map of a lot and then reported that the area of the lot was 10,000 square feet. In fact, the survey was in error. The lot, a corner lot and not a perfect rectangle, was 9,950 square feet in area. As a result, Betty and Bob Brown must obtain a variance to build a second dwelling on the property because it is less than the 10,000 square-foot minimum lot size. Both the seller and Bay Realty may be liable for Sally's innocent misrepresentation. In order to better protect herself and her company, Sally should have said, "The survey says the lot area is 10,000 square feet but I have no personal knowledge that the lot is exactly 10,000 square feet or that the survey is accurate in other ways. If the total square footage or precise boundaries are a matter of importance to you, then you should have these figures and measurements verified by your own surveyor or have the calculations on this survey verified."

If a licensee is going to quote sources, he or she should quote the source exactly, state who or what the source is, disclaim personal knowledge or responsibility for the accuracy of the information and caution the party not to rely on the accuracy but to seek independent verification if the information is material to his or her decision or course of action. None of the above, however, will spare a licensee from liability if the licensee knows or has reason to know that the information is inaccurate and uses it anyway in order to influence another party's decisions in a transaction, which is a deceptive trade practice.

Imputed Notice

Many agents erroneously believe that they have to actually tell their principal before notice is effective. In reality, the knowledge of, or notice to, the agent is attributed to and binding on the principal, even if the information is never conveyed to the principal. Notifying the agent is regarded as actually notifying the principal. This is called *constructive* or *imputed notice.*

Sometimes it is critical to prove that notice was given by a certain date. This is especially true in connection with giving notice of the exercise of an option, the revocation of an offer or the satisfaction of a contingency, such as obtaining a title report or loan approval by a certain date. A question that sometimes arises is whether notice to the cooperating broker ought to be notice to the buyer or notice to the seller.

The answer depends on whether the cooperating broker is the agent of the buyer or the subagent of the seller. Much depends on the facts of each transaction and whether there was any disclosure of agency. One of the more difficult and interesting problems regarding the legal construct of imputed notice is what will the courts in Texas decide regarding the efficacy of notice to a broker who is a dual agent or a non-agent in the transaction. There is Texas case law that implies that, in the situation of a dual agent being told something by one of his two principals, knowledge of that information would not be imputed to the other principal. Instead, the dual agent will have to actually communicate the information to his or her other principal and the concept of constructive notice will not apply. For a broker acting as a non-agent, notice to him or her by one party in the transaction is not notice to the other party because neither party is the broker's principal or client. That is one way an intended licensed middleman or facilitator made be adjudged an agent, regardless of the licensee's intent.

Professional and Ethical Responsibility

Real estate agents licensees acting as agents owe general duties of good faith, fairness and honesty to all with whom they deal. But when acting as agents and subagents, licensees owe a far greater degree of care and loyalty to their principal than they do to a third person. In general, a customer is entitled to honesty, fairness, accurate information and material facts concerning a property. [22 TAC 53.156 (d)] A client is entitled to accurate information and advice about the significance of facts and information, the alternative courses of action that are available and the recommendations of the agent. The best interests of the client must be kept in mind at all times. [22 TAC 531.1 (a),(b) and (c); 535.2 (f) and 535.156(a)(b)(c)]

The following lists some of the distinctions between duties that a broker, acting as an agent for only one party in a transaction, has to her or her client versus duties to a customer:

- To a customer, the seller's agent points out the remedies on default by the seller in the purchase contract. To his or her client, the buyer's agent might suggest that the buyer deposit a minimal amount of earnest money and make the forfeiture of that liquidated damage money the seller's sole remedy in the event of the buyer's default or the use of a specially prepared offer form with provisions more protective of the buyer's interest than those of the standard, seller-oriented offer forms. A dual agent has two clients and no customers and, therefore, under the TRELA §15C, can probably make no such suggestions or recommendations to either party without shifting the risk or costs from one party to the other party. However, if it would save them both money and reduce both their risks, then it would be appropriate, in fact mandatory, that the suggestion be made. A non-agent has two customers and no clients and should in fact be careful not to make any recommendations or engage in any advocacy or negotiations, lest he or she be declared an agent by conduct.
- When the seller is carrying back financing, the seller's agent negotiates or attempts to negotiate into the original offer coverage of many contract provisions differently than the buyer's agent does. Such provisions include prepayment, due on sale, right to make improvements, nonrecourse (no personal liability), reinstatement prior to foreclosure sale, grace periods, late charges, etc. A dual agent could likely not negotiate one way or the other on these critical matters without making the dual agency unlawful. A non-agent could not negotiate one way or the other unless he or she wanted to run the risk of being called an agent.
- To a customer, the seller's agent discloses the existence of an underground water easement. To his or her client, the buyer's agent goes an extra step and reviews a copy of the grant of easement, just in case there were any restrictions affecting the buyer's expected use of the property, such as a prohibition against constructing any improvement within a certain distance of the easement. A dual agent's role becomes very murky at this point.
- To a customer, the seller's agent emphasizes the attractive features of the seller's property. To his or her client, the buyer's agent points out the negative features and shows why the property might be overpriced. The buyer's agent would be more willing to show the buyer other properties for comparison purposes, even properties not listed in a MLS. If a dual agent attempted either of these courses of action one of his or her clients would likely file suit.

- A seller's agent or subagent, working directly with the buyer who is unrepresented or working with the buyer's broker, negotiates to the best of his or her ability for everything to be structured in favor of the seller, using skill, without fraud or deceit. A buyer's agent, on the other hand, reduces his or her buyer-client's risk and financial exposure in the offer, shifting as much of the cost and risk burden to the seller as possible. A dual agent could do neither legally. A non-agent hopes for the swiftest deal.

The more sophisticated and complex a transaction, the more likely it is that the buyer will expect to be treated as a client rather than a customer and the more care the agent will have to take to make a clear distinction between client and customer. Correspondingly, the less educated one of the parties is, the more likely they will be to have erroneous expectations and therefore have a recognizable need for professional representation. All other factors being equal, the courts are more likely to side with the less knowledgeable party and hold the better educated, licensed expert responsible for not recognizing the parties' need for professional counsel.

Quality of Representation

Buyers and real estate licensees are gradually becoming aware of the different levels of service the seller's broker may offer a buyer. A seller's broker may offer a buyer a wide range of services and pertinent information without any conflict with his or her primary allegiance to the seller. But increasing number of buyers desire more than accurate and honest information about the property. These buyers, once they understand the difference between a customer and a client, want to be treated as clients. They want the same treatment they would receive if they were selling property. Most buyers, when fully informed, want full fiduciary duties and undivided loyalty in their behalf. It is important to ask buyers, sellers, tenants or landlords what they want in the way of fiduciary services and to discuss the choices available. Texas law makes it mandatory, at least to a minimal extent, by the requirement of presenting TREC Information and Disclosure Form Number 3 to all consumers of real estate services.

The professional real estate licensee feels great pride and satisfaction when advising clients, be they buyers or sellers, landlords or tenants. The recent trend to buyer representation is nothing more than a reevaluation of the role of the broker and a recognition that more buyers are seeking client-level services from the broker. A buyer or tenant who wants to be treated as a client should consider employing a broker under a written agreement. Such an agreement is commonly referred to as a *Buyer (Tenant) Representation Agreement* (*see* Appendix E).

Real estate licensees who do not wish to represent buyers or tenants should develop and practice so that they are comfortable in explaining to these prospective consumers the types of services they can render to buyers and tenants as customers for their in-house listings or as customers for the listings of other brokers when their own company is acting as a subagent of the listing broker. Similarly, licensees who have chosen to represent only buyers and tenants can provide valuable services to landlords and sellers without becoming their agents. These brokers should hone their presentation skills in order to build a ready pool of seller and landlord customers with properties for their buyer and tenant clients to inspect. Sellers and landlords who are capable of representing themselves may rather have direct access to more buyers without the commitment of tying up their property on an exclusive-right-to-sell contract with a broker who may or may not use best efforts to attempt to sell it.

HOW AGENCY IS TERMINATED

Except in the case of an agency coupled with an interest, an agency relationship may be terminated at any time for any of the following reasons:

- Lapse of a reasonable time if no time is specified
- Lapse of the time specified in the agreement
- Completion of the purpose of the agency
- Mutual recision
- Revocation by the principal
- Agent's renunciation
- Abandonment of the agreement by the agent
- Incapacity or death of either the agent or the principal
- Bankruptcy of the owner if title transferred to receiver
- Condemnation or destruction of the premises

If the principal revokes the agency unilaterally, without just cause, he or she may be liable to the agent for compensation. However, if the agent breaches any of the agent's fiduciary duties to the principal, there will typically be just cause for the principal to terminate the agency without liability to the agent. Even if the completion of the agency purpose has already been achieved the principal may be legally allowed to withhold compensation for breach of fiduciary duty by the agent during the agency period.

An agency agreement cannot be assigned by the agent without the consent of the principal. The agency relationship is in the nature of a personal service, which is generally unassignable. Agency can be terminated wrongfully but liability for damages caused by the wrongful termination may be produced as a result. In an agency coupled with an interest, the agent is given or acquires an interest in the property being sold. This type agency cannot be terminated by the death of the principal or by revocation by the principal.

The question of when an agency relationship ends can be as important as how the agency ends. In most cases written notice helps to eliminate doubt.

Example:

Sally from Bay Realty listed and sold Harry's home. Three weeks after closing, Harry shows up at one of Sally's open houses. Is Harry still Sally's client? Once a client always a client? Not necessarily, but Sally needs to clarify to her former client Harry that he is no longer her client. Because it is sometimes difficult to treat a former client as a customer, some firms in these situations are prepared to obtain dual agency consent agreements from the buyer and seller. Even if Bay Realty is unwilling to represent a former client in a new transaction, Sally is not permitted to disclose to a new client information obtained in confidence from a former client during the previous agency relationship. The agency may have terminated, but not the duty of confidentiality. (*See* NAR® Code of Ethics & Standard of Practice 7-8 in Appendix D.)

UNDERSTANDING RELATIONSHIPS

The law is relatively clear as to the responsibilities an agent owes to his or her principal and to the general public (*see* Figure 3.2). What is not commonly understood are the various working relationships that can exist when brokers work with both buyers and sellers in the marketplace.

Example:

Sally and Bay Realty have numerous agency relationships from which to choose. For example, Sally could show Bob and Betty Buyer:

- listings that Sally personally had obtained for Bay Realty;
- listings that another agent in Bay Realty had obtained for Bay Realty;
- listings from another brokerage firm that commonly cooperates with Bay Realty in which Bay Realty agents act as subagents of the other firm and therefore represents the other firm's sellers;
- listings from another firm published in a MLS book where the other firm may or may not be offering subagency as a choice; or
- properties not listed but available, such as for sale by owner, foreclosure sale, government-owned or probate sale properties.

Sally and Bay Realty could have been involved in some of these variations of agency relationships: seller agency, seller subagency, buyer agency or buyer subagency. They could have chosen one of the alternatives to true agency: consensual dual agency, undisclosed dual agency, facilitator or non-agency.

Single Agency

The primary alternative to dual agency and non-agency (facilitator/finder/transaction broker) is *single agency.* The single agency broker represents only one client in any one transaction, either the buyer or the seller, and works with other parties only on a customer basis.

Some brokers only act as sellers' agents exclusively; that is, they never represent buyers. Some brokers only act as buyers' agents exclusively, that is they never take listings or represent sellers. Other brokers will represent either sellers wanting to sell or buyers wanting to buy, but never represent both in the same transaction. These broker-agents will represent one party only on a principal-agent basis and usually under an exclusive right-to-sell agency agreement or an exclusive right-to-purchase agency agreement. The broker who practices single agency prefers to work with the client, regardless of whether the client is buying or selling. If the client is buying, then the broker must understand the application of his or her agency duties in the buyer-client relationship; if the client is selling, then the broker must understand the application of agency duties in the seller-client relationship. Likewise for a broker who represents landlords or one who represents tenants.

Seller Agency

Seller or landlord exclusive representation was, until very recently, the most common form of agency relationship. In seller agency, the real estate licensee represents the seller on a client basis and treats the buyer as a customer. These brokers and their salespeople are clear about the identity of their clients, regardless of whether they are listing brokers or cooperating brokers on other brokers' listings. The seller's or

Figure 3.2
Agent's Roles and Responsibilities

AGENT

Listing Agent, Seller's Subagent, Buyer's Broker, Buyer's Subagent

(1) A real estate licensee, when acting as an agent in a real estate transaction, must by law, ethics and custom be a (an):

(a) Equity Preserver for his/her client/principal;

(b) Risk Benefit Analyst for his/her client/principal;

(c) Skilled Negotiator for his/her client/principal; and

(d) Transaction Catalyst to secure a contract for his/her client/principal in a:

- reasonable time;
- with best possible price;
- under most favorable; terms; and
- with minimum legal, financial and personal risk to client/principal.

(2) He/she is not allowed to advance his/her interests over the client's interests.

(3) The agent owes loyalty only to his/her client in the transaction and no one else.

(4) Is allowed to place personal interests over the non-client party's interest. May compete against non-client in bidding for properties.

(5) If the agent's conduct is such that it can be shown he/she is a dual agent, then commission, license and transaction may be forfeited and could face DTPA suit.

DUAL AGENT

Consensual, Disclosed, Un- or Underdisclosed

A real estate agent may not act as a dual agent in Texas unless the licensee follows specific state laws and obtains the fully informed, written consent of both parties.

(1) Cannot act as Equity Preserver for either client.

(2) Cannot act as Risk Benefit Analyst for either client.

(3) Cannot use negotiation skills against one client to accomplish the other's aim.

(4) Liable to both parties for fiduciary breach.

(5) Cannot offer opinions of value or CMA unless giving the same to both sides. Must disclose before becoming dual agent.

(6) Cannot attempt to reduce one client's legal or financial risk if it increases the other client's risk.

(7) Place both clients' interest above personal interest in the transaction.

(8) Undisclosed and under- disclosed both illegal. May face loss of license and, commission, lawsuit for fraud and rescission of contract.

NON-AGENT

Finder, Facilitator or Transaction-Broker

In order to keep from being declared an agent by his/her actions, a real estate licen- see is required by law to be:

(1) Neutral as to the interests between the parties.

(2) Held to the standard of good faith and fair dealing.

(3) Operating at arm's length, not a position of trust and confidence. Should not negotiate for either party.

(4) Parties should not and are not entitled to rely on a finder's opinions or advice.

(5) Is allowed to advance his/her own interests above either party to the transaction. May compete against either party in bidding.

(6) Should not prepare CMA for either party or in anyway present self as representing the interests of either party.

Proving that a person is merely a finder is extremely difficult in Texas because one's conduct frequently leads a court to conclude that the person is an agent.

KEY TERMS

Expectations • Reliance • Agent • Reasonable • Fiduciary • Safety • Negotiator • Mediator • Arbitrator • Price • Terms • Certainty • Client • Customer • Self • Dealing • Equity • Full Disclosure • Informed Consent landlord's broker is free to work with the buyer or tenant, provided the broker's agency is clearly disclosed. The buyer must understand that the broker is not acting in a representative capacity; that is, the buyer or tenant must understand that he or she is a customer receiving various services from the broker, who primarily is acting on behalf of and in the best interests of the seller.

Buyer Agency

In Texas, exclusive buyer or tenant representation is agency in which the broker's client base is limited to buyers and/or tenants only. The agency duties are identical to those owed in a listing situation, only now the client is buying real estate rather than selling. Therefore, the duties will manifest themselves in a different set of activities and different negotiation framework. The buyer's broker is not attempting to sell a buyer a house but rather he or she is attempting to help the buyer buy a house. Buyer-brokers are not procuring a buyer for a seller. They are procuring a property for a purchaser. The buyer's broker should never be referred to as the selling agent or even the cooperating agent and especially not subagent. The agent for the buyer is in every sense of the term a purchasing agent, buying agent, buyer's agent, buyer's broker or even other broker. Similarly, a tenant rep should never be referred to as a leasing agent.

Many listing brokers, commercial as well as residential, are not yet accustomed to dealing with offers presented by buyer's or tenant's agents. Thus, there is sometimes confusion over rights and privileges of showing properties, sources of fees, sharing or adjusting fees, procuring cause disputes, loan approval and contract preparation. Chapter 6 on buyer agency is designed to clarify some of this confusion. It is important that listing brokers understand how buyers' brokers work, even though the listing broker has personally decided to represent sellers only. To best serve the interest of the seller or landlord, the listing broker should encourage all offers, including those coming from buyers' brokers or tenant reps. If a former customer, who has previously been shown a house or commercial property by a listing broker or leasing agent, comes back to see the same property with a buyer's broker representing the buyer or a tenant rep, then procuring cause issues go out the window. There is no basis in Texas for a "procuring cause" claim on the part of a listing broker against a buyer's broker or tenant rep.

Subagency

Subagency occurs when the subagent broker's client base is another broker's clients. Brokers routinely use other agents to market a seller's property. A subagency results when the seller expressly or implicitly authorizes the broker to use these other agents. While sellers often carefully select their listing broker, they usually don't think much about formally appointing subagents or about discussing the customary practice of using subagents. In many cases, there is no clear understanding of the relationship between the listing broker and the selling broker, other than the fact that the commission will be shared.

Likewise, selling brokers work closely with buyers to find the best property. Rarely is subagency discussed, and buyers often think the selling brokers represent them. Buyers might be surprised to discover that selling brokers are frequently the sellers' subagents. Naturally, a clear disclosure of subagency coupled with appropriate conduct could dispel any notion that selling brokers represent buyers.

Seller subagents are agents of the agents and, therefore, owe the same degree of fiduciary duties to sellers as do listing brokers. Likewise, buyer subagents are agents of the agents and owe the same degree of fiduciary duties to the buyers as do buyer's brokers. The same is true of sales associates or broker associates working for brokers and cooperating brokers. When properly appointed by authority of the principal, a subagent has the capability to bind a principal to the same extent as does a listing broker. In addition, a listing broker is also liable for the conduct and representations of subagents.

Is the selling broker the subagent of the seller or the agent of the buyer? The outcome of a lawsuit will often answer this question. Because subagencies usually arise without full discussion of the relationship, the answer is often difficult to ascertain and dual agency problems can arise even when a selling broker declares a subagency to the seller, if he or she outwardly acts in the best interests of the buyer rather than the seller.

Dual Agency

A real estate broker who attempts to represent both the seller or landlord and the buyer or tenant in the same transaction is a *dual agent* and, in Texas, owes a greatly limited set of fiduciary duties to both. Because the seller and the buyer have diverse interests and, in effect, compete with one another, the dual agent has an inherent conflict of interest. Thus, the duties are more severely limited than when only one side is represented. In fact, in Texas these duties are limited by law and any act that goes beyond those limits is likely to cause the entire dual agency to be unlawful. Dual agency is very different from subagency. In dual agency, one agent represents two principals. In subagency, two agents represent one principal.

The broker must clearly disclose any conflicts of interest to both the seller and the buyer and obtain informed, written consent from each to act on his or her behalf. Failure to obtain informed written consent will result in an unlawful representation and can be the basis for rescission of the transaction, money damages, forfeiture of commission or disciplinary action, including loss of license for the sponsoring broker.

Often, the broker becomes a dual agent and is not even aware of it. Thus, the accidental or unintended dual agency may arise from a variety of situations. For instance, a dual agency could arise:

- when the listing broker accepts future employment from the buyer;
- when the cooperating broker is a disclosed subagent yet is also acting as the buyer's agent;
- when the listing broker is asked to represent the seller in the purchase of another property listed with the broker;
- when a buyer's agent is paid by the listing broker without proper notice to all sides;
- when the broker purchases property listed with the broker; or
- when one salesperson from the listing office acts on the buyer's behalf and another salesperson from the same office acts on the seller's behalf.

The main problem with an unintended dual agency is that the broker has no awareness of the need to obtain the required consents. With a disclosed dual agency, the broker has the opportunity to develop the types of full disclosure required by law and minimize the risks of conflicts of interest.

SUMMARY

Real estate licensees need to be aware of the variety of positions that a broker can have in a real estate transaction relative to agency. Because there are no formalities required to create an agency relationship, an agency can be found to exist when none was ever intended. The existence of an agency relationship can have significant impact on issues of liability, notice, responsibility and quality of representation. By becoming more aware of agency issues, the real estate agent can better define and control agency relationships, thus ensuring that working relationships that are intentionally created are the ones that will be the most effective and successful.

Subsequent chapters will examine in depth each of the agency alternatives. Brokers will have to evaluate which alternative is best. There are many factors to consider in developing the company's agency policy. One thing is certain: there is no perfect solution.

KEY POINTS

- The payment of a fee does not determine agency.
- An agency can be created expressly or by implication, with or without a written agreement.
- A customer is entitled to accurate information and material facts; a client is entitled to accurate information and advice.
- The duty of confidentiality continues after the termination of an agency.
- Courts look not only at the documents creating agency, but also the acts of the agent and the parties.
- The alternatives to agency are non-exclusive client agency, exclusive seller or landlord agency, subagency or exclusive buyer or tenant agency.
- A real estate licensee, acting as an agent, owes a much greater duty of disclosure and loyalty to a client than to a customer.

SUGGESTIONS FOR BROKERS

Develop a company policy covering which agency alternative the company prefers and what services the broker or sales and broker associates may extend to customers and must or must not provide to clients. Any variations must be reported to the managing broker, such as when a salesperson in a large exclusive seller agency-oriented firm attempts to represent a buyer in locating a property.

QUIZ

1. Which term best describes the relationship of a listing broker to a property owner?

   a. Attorney-in-fact
   b. Fiduciary
   c. Subagent
   d. Ostensible agent

2. Which of the following statements is true regarding the determination of whom the broker represents?

   a. Whoever pays the commission is the principal.
   b. The principal must sign a written agreement for there to be an agency.
   c. It is important to decide whether the buyer or the seller is the broker's principal because the broker will owe the principal a higher standard of care and more extensive duties.
   d. The broker must be paid a commission for there to be an agency.

3. The rule that notice to an agent is attributable to the principal is known as:

   a. ostensible notice.
   b. implied notice.
   c. imputed notice.
   d. unintended notice.

4. A salesperson's relationship to his or her broker may be all of the following *except:*

   a. independent contractor.
   b. principal.
   c. employee.
   d. agent.

5. A seller may be liable for the acts and representations of all of the following *except:*

   a. cooperating broker acting as a subagent.
   b. listing broker.
   c. salesperson of the listing broker.
   d. buyer's broker.

DISCUSSION QUESTIONS

1. What are two essential elements to create an agency?
2. What are the four reasons why it is important to disclose in each transaction who represents who?
3. What kinds of services can a seller's agent provide to a buyer without necessarily becoming the agent of the buyer?
4. What are some of the actions of a real estate broker that might lead a buyer to think the broker represents the buyer?
5. Name several examples of how the imputed notice rule can affect the outcome of a real estate lawsuit.

CHAPTER

4

SELLER AGENCY

The traditional viewpoint in real estate brokerage has been that the real estate licensee, when acting as an agent in the transaction, represents the seller. Despite the agency relationship with the seller, the broker can still provide some valuable services to a buyer customer on behalf of and for the benefit of the seller. This is as true when the broker is the listing agent as when the broker is acting in a subagent capacity. This chapter discusses the following:

- Express and Implied
- Use of Licensed Associates
- In-House Sales
- Example Situations
  - How to Handle In-House Sales
- Cooperative Sales
  - Loyalty

EXPRESS AND IMPLIED

The most common and easily recognized agency relationship in real estate is that between the seller (client) and the listing broker (agent). The relationship is usually evidenced by a written agreement called a *listing,* typically an exclusive right to sell listing. In Texas, the License Act states that "an action may not be brought in a court in this state for the recovery of a commission for the sale or purchase of real estate unless the promise or agreement on which the action is brought, or some note or memorandum thereof, is in writing and signed by the party to be charged or signed by a person lawfully authorized by him [her] to sign it." [TRELA §20(b)] This is not to say that a listing agreement must be in writing. Properties may be listed orally, but if the seller refuses to pay an orally agreed-upon commission, the broker cannot find redress in the courts to compel the seller to pay. (An oral listing agreement and commission entitlement may, however, be good against third parties who attempt to tortiously interfere with it.) However, neither a written contract or an oral agreement to pay a fee is a prerequisite to creating an agency relationship with the seller; an agency relationship may be created by the words and conduct of the parties. The agency relationship with the seller may continue after the stated expiration date of the agency agreement. As discussed previously, this is called an *implied agency,* and brokers may be surprised when courts find an agency when none was intended by the broker.

Once an agency is created with the seller, the law imposes a number of fiduciary duties on the seller's agent, the most important one being that the agent must protect and promote the best interest of the seller. The interest of the seller must be placed above that of anyone else, including that of the agent. The seller's agent owes absolute allegiance to the seller.

USE OF LICENSED ASSOCIATES AS SALESPERSON OR BROKER

In Texas, approximately two thirds of all brokers work for the remaining third. The broker who is held responsible to the state and the public for the conduct of other licensees who are either licensed under him or her or working as independent contractors or employees is frequently referred to as a *sponsoring broker, principal broker* or *designated broker.* The employed, associated or sponsored licensee is either licensed as a salesperson or as a broker. If the associate is a broker instead of a salesperson, he or she is generally referred to as a *broker associate.* There is no associate broker license in Texas. An individual licensed as salesperson is required to work under the direction and supervision of a principal or sponsoring broker. The broker may be a corporation or an individual. A person licensed as a broker may work independently or enter into an agency relationship with another principal broker to represent the other broker in dealings with the public.

Based on the state licensing law and the doctrine of *respondeat superior* ("Let the master answer"), the broker is responsible for the acts and conduct of all salesperson associates and broker associates during the ordinary course of employment. [22 TAC §§535.2(c), (g) and 535.141(c)] Under general agency concepts, each of these licensed associates is the agent of the broker. Listings are made in the name of the broker, not the salesperson or broker associate. The broker is the party responsible to the public and to clients, whether acting directly or indirectly through agents. If a broker has a listing (open or exclusive), then that broker and all the licensed associates in that firm represent the seller in a fiduciary capacity. This is true of all licensed associates working in each of the listing broker's offices. (This rule, however, does not apply to franchise organizations in which each franchised brokerage firm is independently owned.)

It is worth noting here that to the general public outside the individual brokerage, such broker's agent licensees and even the sponsoring broker should not be referred to as real estate "agents." Until they are in an actual agency relationship they are real estate licensees. At the point a member of public hires a licensed broker to be his or her agent, he or she becomes a client or principal of the broker. Simultaneously, all the broker's agents, when acting in transactions involving their broker's client, act as agents of the broker and for the client.

Example:

Sally, an associate for Bay Realty, licensed as a salesperson, finds a buyer for a property listed with Bay Realty. The property was actually listed by Tom, a licensed broker associate of Bay Realty. Sally, acting on behalf of Bay Realty, must act in the best interest of the seller. Many licensees in this circumstance erroneously assume that Sally represents the buyer and Tom represents the seller.

> Even if Sally works out of a different branch office than Tom, the law still requires that the listing broker (Bay Realty) and all licensed associates (Sally and Tom) represent the seller.

It is very important to understand that a licensed salesperson cannot lawfully sell his or her services directly to the public. He must perform all tasks under the direct supervision of a broker. This is true even if the salesperson may, for tax purposes, be an independent contractor. Under agency and licensing law and for purposes of supervision, the salesperson who is licensed with the broker is an agent and employee of the broker and is acting for his broker. The terminology *acting for,* as used in TREC Rules cited here, is equivalent to the description of an agency relationship. [TRELA §1(b) and (c)]

A licensed salesperson cannot legally:

- list property in his or her own name [22 TAC §535.154(d)];
- enter into buyer agency or dual agency agreements in his or her own name, either orally or in writing;
- generally directly sue sellers, buyers, landlords or tenants for unpaid commissions [TRELA §20(b)];
- open his or her own office without hiring a broker to be responsible for all the licensees in the office;
- work independently without having a licensed broker to shelter or hold the salesperson's license;
- be licensed at the same time under more than one broker;
- take listings or buyer/tenant representation agreements when he or she moves to a new brokerage office with or without the current broker's consent (although the broker may release the represented owner or buyer from their agreement and allow the salesperson's new broker to attempt to contract with the owner, buyer or tenant);
- advertise in his or her own name unless the broker's name also appears and it is clear to the public which one is the broker [TRELA §15(a)(6)(P); 22 TAC §535.154(d) & (e)];
- open his or her own client trust accounts for sales or rentals [22 TAC §§535.159(f) and 535.2(h)];
- accept compensation directly from clients or other brokers for real estate sales and transactions without the broker's consent [TRELA §1(d); 22 TAC §535.3]; or
- pay a commission to any person except through the broker under whom he or she is licensed or with the broker's knowledge and consent [TRELA §1(e); 22 TAC §535.4].

Broker associates, on the other hand, because they have exactly the same state license the principal broker does, may be allowed to do virtually any of those things if the broker they work for does not prohibit them from running another brokerage operation. This practice is not the norm however, and any broker associate attempting any of the above listed items without his or her broker's knowledge and consent would likely be at risk. TREC, however, does not regulate the broker's contractual arrangements with other brokers. [22 TAC §535.2(a)] The principal broker of a broker associate should keep in mind—and make the associate aware—that the License Act holds the principal broker responsible for the acts of his or her broker associates. [22 TAC §535.2(g)] In addition, in any lawsuit against the associate broker, if the plaintiff believes the associate was acting in the name of the principal broker, the principal broker will most likely be named in the lawsuit and may be held liable for the damages caused by an associate broker.

Unless permitted by state law, as currently in Illinois or Maine, it is not legally possible to construct an internal wall within a brokerage firm and argue that because there are different licensed associates acting for the buyer and the seller there is no dual agency. In Texas, such an attempt would likely not hold up in court or at a TREC disciplinary hearing. By analogy, a large law firm could not have one of its associates on the tenth floor represent the seller of a commercial warehouse and another associate on the eleventh floor represent the buyer without first obtaining from the buyer and the seller very complete and detailed consent to such dual representation and agreement to receive a very limited form of fiduciary representation.

Some brokerage firms advertise that they have salespeople who represent buyers and other salespeople who represent sellers. For example, Tom from Bay Realty, as the listing agent, innocently might tell an interested buyer who has expressed a desire to obtain her own agent that "I can't be your agent, but Sally in our other office is very knowledgeable, loves to represent buyers and can give you the type of representation you want."

Tom's firm must be careful to develop its company policies within the bounds of agency law. It is the firm, not the associates, that by law represents the buyer or the seller. Listing brokers should set up internal management controls to ensure that their associates understand these basic agency principles.

Example:

Sally decides to help her best friend Betty buy some investment property. The ideal property is listed with Sally's firm, Bay Realty. Sally not only provides Betty with helpful information but negotiates on Betty's behalf. Bay Realty has now unknowingly become a dual agent for both the buyer and the seller. To make this lawful, Bay Realty must obtain the written informed consent of Betty and the seller in accordance with the exacting provisions of TRELA §15C and then make sure all its agents conduct themselves differently in the role of dual agent than they normally would when only representing the seller.

IN-HOUSE SALES

The majority of residential real estate transactions involve the services of two brokers in a cooperative sale. However, a significant portion of sales are in-house sales, especially in those real estate offices with a large share of the market. In these sales, there is only one broker, although several associates from the same brokerage firm may participate.

When a seller lists a property with a broker, the seller expects—and Texas law demands—that everyone associated with the brokerage firm use their best efforts to produce a ready, willing and able buyer, assuming an individual associate is involved with the property in any way. The associate taking the listing, as well as all associates in the firm, will be working for the seller to find a buyer.

Most brokers prefer to sell their own listings in-house because of the control they maintain over the transaction and because of the prospect of earning a full commission. Some firms offer the selling salesperson a higher share of the commission as an incentive for producing an in-house sale. This incentive may motivate some salespeople to look primarily toward in-house listings, something that may not be in the best interest of every prospective buyer.

Example Situations

There are a variety of situations that can arise in an in-house sale, as illustrated in the following examples. Let's assume that Sally is a top salesperson for Bay Realty, a 150-person multi-office brokerage firm.

Sally as listing agent: Sally is successful in acquiring for Bay Realty an exclusive listing of a three-bedroom townhouse from her friend George. As is the custom, Bay Realty submits the listing to a multiple listing service (MLS) for greater exposure. At the first open house, Betty, a prospective buyer, discusses the property with Sally, who gives Betty TREC Agency Disclosure Form Number 3 and tells Betty that she, Sally, represents the seller and not Betty. Later that night, Sally writes up the offer according to Betty's instructions. The offer is then accepted by the seller.

In this case, Bay Realty clearly represents George only. There are no facts to indicate that Bay Realty has become an implied agent of Betty because of any of Sally's actions. There is no law prohibiting in-house sales nor requiring Sally to suggest that the buyer hire another broker to write the offer. Sally can show the property, explain its features and deliver the buyer's offer without creating any implied agency with the buyer—in fact, that's her job. However, Sally must tell Betty that she is the agent of the seller and that she does not represent Betty. Also, Sally must present Betty with TREC Information and Disclosure Form Number 3, signed by Sally, indicating that she represents the seller only, and she must present the form early enough to preclude Betty giving her any information that Betty might not want the seller to know. Otherwise, the disclosure is not timely and may fail to protect Sally in a lawsuit later.

Sally as listing agent but Bay Realty also representing the buyer in another transaction: Sally of Bay Realty's main office is sitting open house on her listing of George's condominium unit. Betty walks through the unit and decides to make an offer on the spot. The offer is contingent on Betty's obtaining loan approval in 45 days. Betty mentions that she'll be able to qualify for the loan once the sale of her home closes, which should be in about three weeks. Tom from another Bay Realty office is the broker associate that listed Betty's home for Bay Realty. Betty tells Sally she does not want to make her offer contingent on the closing of her home sale because that may make her offer seem less attractive to the seller, George.

Should Sally advise Betty of the significance of not including a financing contingency clause, especially as it relates to not being entitled to a return of her earnest money? If Sally were Betty's agent, it would be clear that she would have to advise Betty either of the effect of not inserting a contingency clause or to consult an attorney. Such a duty to advise is less clear because Sally is George's agent and Betty appears to be merely her customer in the purchase of the condominium unit. The problem is compounded by the fact that Bay Realty owes fiduciary duties to Betty, even though such duties arise from a separate transaction.

Does Sally have an affirmative duty to explain to George that Betty will not be able to qualify for the loan if the sale of her home becomes delayed or does not close? Yes. As the seller's agent, Sally, on behalf of Bay Realty, must disclose to the seller all pertinent facts that are relevant to the seller's decision to sell. There is no question that George would want to know that Betty's loan qualification depends on the sale

of a property that has not yet closed. George would want to know that his broker, Bay Realty, is also representing the buyer in that other sale.

Does Bay Realty have a duty to disclose to Betty that they are going to have to tell George about the necessity to sell Betty's house? Yes. What if Sally and Tom get George and Betty to sign a dual agency agreement with Bay Realty? Then, in Texas, they will have to keep the fact of Betty's home sale contingency confidential by law. Further, they must clearly explain to both Betty and George, before getting their consent to the dual agency, that they would have to keep any such information confidential or they would violate TRELA §15C and face loss of the firm's broker license along with Sally's and/or Tom's license.

Sally as selling agent with no prior relationship with buyer: Sally is sitting office floor duty when Bob Brown walks in and asks about available properties. Sally checks Bay Realty's listings and finds a property on Main Street listed by Carol in Sally's office and one on King Street listed by Tom from a branch office on the other side of town.

Sally must remember that Bay Realty is the agent of the sellers of both the Main Street and the King Street properties. Even though a salesperson other than Sally took the listing, Sally is bound to act in the best interests of the seller. Because Carol or Tom is representing the seller on behalf of Bay Realty, Sally should be careful not to convey to Bob the impression that she can represent him. This can be done by giving him the current TREC agency disclosure form and discussing it with him. In an exclusive seller agency firm Sally should treat Bob as a customer, not as a client. Sally is the agent of Bay Realty and must act on behalf of Bay Realty's clients. This is true even though the property is listed with a different Bay Realty office. If Sally worked for a dual agency firm, Sally might be able to work with Bob as a client on Bay Realty listings, provided she obtains the informed written consent of both Bob and the seller and fully discloses to them all the potential conflicts and subsequent reduction of services.

Sally as selling agent with prior relationship with buyer: Sally, as listing agent, has just negotiated a completed sales contract on George's townhouse. She has opened escrow by placing the contract and earnest money with the escrow agent named in the contract. George is extremely pleased with Sally's professional attitude and skills and asks her to find a suitable replacement property. Sally is well aware of George's needs and wants, as well as his financial resources and favorite bargaining techniques. Sally knows a perfect property for George and it happens to be listed with Bay Realty through Tom, a salesperson.

Sally knows from experience that when a satisfied client like George sells his home and then buys a replacement property in the same locality, the client typically uses the same listing agent (Sally). It is natural for George to think he is still Sally's client. Sally recognizes that the seller of the new home might find it useful in negotiations to know how much cash the prospective buyer (George) will receive from his recent sale and when George's pending move date will be. Sellers often want to learn from their agent as much information as possible about the buyer, especially if the offer is contingent on financing. If Sally is now to represent the new seller on behalf of Bay Realty, shouldn't Sally disclose these useful facts to the seller? Would such disclosure surprise George or violate any fiduciary duty to him?

This in-house turnaround sale, so common in today's market, can present some confusing agency relationship questions. Is Bay Realty a disclosed dual agent? Is George a client as to his townhouse and a customer as to the replacement property?

Is it understandable for George to expect he'll continue to receive client-level services, even though his status has changed from a seller to a buyer?

It would be the path of least resistance for Sally to keep quiet, avoid raising any of these questions, simply proceed to do the best job for both parties and hope all goes well. This too often happens in the real world of real estate, especially with real estate agents who regard themselves primarily as facilitators whose job it is to help work out differences between the buyer and the seller and bring the transaction to a successful close. The correct approach, though, is to clarify each relationship through discussion and disclosure to the buyer and the seller. This might very well be the type of situation in which both buyer and seller would give their informed consent to dual representation by Bay Realty, with both parties seeing no practical need to halt the transaction to obtain outside assistance.

Example:

Sally has helped Alice on all six of Alice's prior real estate purchases as a buyer's broker. Alice has offered to pay Sally $1,000 finder fee if Sally hears of any property available on Nob Hill that Alice subsequently purchases. Bay Realty just signed a listing on a nice mansion on Nob Hill through Salesperson Tom. Alice wants Sally to show her the property to see if it fits her investment plans.

Sally must recognize that she and Bay Realty represent the seller of the Nob Hill property, even though Sally has never met the seller. Without disclosure to the seller and consent, Sally can neither accept the $1,000 nor act on behalf of Alice. If she does, she has created a dual agency. Sally can certainly provide Alice with helpful information and show the property, but she must be careful to clarify to Alice that she and Bay Realty represent the seller. She must avoid any appearance of acting contrary to the best interests of the seller. Perhaps Sally should consider advising Alice to retain an outside consultant, especially if the purchase decision involves independent financial and investment analysis. Sally should also consider the risks involved in acting as a dual agent, even after obtaining the informed consent of both Alice and the seller.

How to Handle In-House Sales

There is no law that prohibits the in-house sale of a broker's own listing to a buyer, provided the buyer understands that the salesperson's brokerage firm is, in fact, employed by and is a fiduciary for the seller. By law, the broker must treat the buyer customer honestly, fairly (not equally with seller client) and ethically, make full disclosure of material facts about the condition of the property and present all offers to the seller. In other words, the salesperson can provide the buyer with a great deal of customer service, although not in a representative, fiduciary capacity. The agent or subagent of the seller client can discuss with the buyer customer all factual data and public information available about the property and answer the buyer customer's questions honestly and accurately. This includes refusing to answer questions in the way the buyer customer expects when it would breach the agent's or subagent's fiduciary duty to the seller client to do so. For example, in response to a buyer customer's question as to why the seller is selling, the seller's agent or subagent might respond honestly, fairly and accurately in the following manner:

"As I discussed with you yesterday when you consented to allow me to show you homes without becoming your agent, I represent sellers. I am prohibited by law and my fiduciary duty from discussing matters such as the seller's reason for moving or motivations to sell. As I'm sure you can appreciate, those are private considerations and do not effect the value of the home. If you were the seller you would probably expect the same kind of loyalty and confidentiality from me as your agent. If there are any material defects in the property of which the seller or I am aware and that are not readily visible from your own inspection it is our obligation to reveal those to you." [See 22 TAC §535.156]

Remember, the licensee dealing with a buyer cannot provide advice regarding the purchase decision that may be considered adverse to the seller's best interest unless it is information that the licensee is required by law to supply.

The seller client's agent should also make clear to the buyer customer that the broker works on behalf of the seller on all negotiable issues. It is very important to note at this point that almost every term or condition in any potential sales contract is fully negotiable between the buyer and the seller. The fact that there are TREC-promulgated forms for contracts that call for certain costs to be borne by the buyer and others costs by the seller in no way bars principals in the transaction from reallocating those costs to the other party through negotiation. It is the licensee's legal obligation to conform the instrument (contract) to the intent of the principals by adding factual statements and business details desired by the principals and striking only such matter as is desired by the principals. [22 TAC §537.11(d)] There is a fine line here between modifying the contract to "conform the instrument to the intent of the parties" and engaging in the unauthorized practice of law. All Texas licensees should be thoroughly familiar with the provisions and implications of TRELA §16 and 22 TAC §537.11 before attempting to assist in contract negotiations.

Under these circumstances, the buyer should deal with the seller's agent or subagent as though the buyer were dealing or negotiating directly with the seller. The buyer should be told, in the initial interview, not to disclose anything to the seller's agents or subagents that the buyer would not tell the seller, and told not to expect to receive any information from the seller's agent or subagents that the seller would not want to tell the buyer directly. The seller's agent or subagent must be careful in responding to questions such as: "How low will the seller go?" "Will he take less?" or "How can I get the seller to compromise on terms and come down in price?" Questions like those and the ones that follow should have carefully rehearsed answers so that the agent can appear professional and competent, reply honestly and fairly, and not be disloyal to the client or misleading to the customer.

Disclosure. To avoid a supposed or feared negative effect on a buyer by giving a direct explanation of the agency relationship with the seller, some brokers, especially a mediator or facilitator-type broker, purposefully and illegally fails to raise the issue of who represents who. This is not the case with a broker who understands and practices his or her agency correctly. A broker with the listing, practicing agency properly, might suggest that the buyer obtain outside representation, perhaps on an hourly consulting basis, from another broker, appraiser or from an attorney. Interestingly enough, when asked to make a choice of representation, many buyers decide that they can represent themselves and do not need an outside consultant or their own real estate agent. Such buyers prefer to work with the listing broker on a customer basis, even though the broker has made it clear that the broker does not work for them on a client basis.

If, on the other hand, the buyer wants to be or expects to be treated as a client and have one of the listing firm's licensed associates represent him or her, then one choice for the listing broker is to prepare appropriate dual agency disclosures to the seller and the buyer and obtain the written, informed consent of both. The law is not clear as to what kind of service the disclosed dual agent can do for either principal, beyond acting as a messenger and conduit of non-confidential information and proposals. In Texas, both the buyer and the seller should be told about and agree to the type of limited services to be provided and the specific, limited role of the dual agent as well as apprised of the types of potential conflicts that may arise. This must be done before consents are obtained. The licensee attempting to create a dual agency is required under Texas law to use due diligence to assist the prospective multiple clients to understand consents, agreements or instructions under Section 15C of the License Act. Failure to do so results in:

1. a violation of the statutory prohibition against the broker acting as a dual agent in the transaction;
2. subjection of the broker and offending associate to possible revocation or suspension of license;
3. potential liability for damages resulting from the failure to make proper disclosures;
4. possible loss of a commission; and
5. potential recision of the contract by either party.

Example:

Sally of Bay Realty, an exclusive seller agency firm, recently listed and sold Betty's home. Betty has $35,000 net cash proceeds from the now closed sale to do with as she pleases. Sally gained this information as a result of her agency in the transaction. Betty now wants to buy George's house, one of Bay Realty's listings, and is willing to make a $15,000 downpayment and sign a seller-financed first lien note for $90,000 for six years with interest payments deferred during the first year. Sally fails to tell Bay Realty or George that Betty has $35,000 cash. What does Sally say when George asks her the simple question: "Sally, is this the best offer I can get from Betty?"

Because Sally is currently an agent only for the seller, she would normally have to reveal to the seller everything she knew about Betty's cash position. The dilemma is that even if Betty is no longer Sally's client, the information that Sally learned about Betty while Betty was Sally's client must remain confidential even after the agency relationship terminated. Sally has no duty to protect information that Sally learns about Betty after the agency termination. However, in protecting previous client confidences, Sally must disclose to George, her current client, that she will not be able to disclose previous client confidences to him. George's respect for Sally's professionalism will probably be enhanced and he will feel more secure in the notion that he can trust his own confidential information safely with Sally. If George wants Sally to continue to represent him after this limitation is explained, he may simply reaffirm the agency or imply his consent for her continued representation by not revoking the relationship.

Accommodating Buyers' Needs. Because in-house sales can be an important part of real estate brokerage business (for some firms more than half their business), brokers should exercise great care with in-house sales to ensure that both the buyer and the seller understand the type of representation and service they can expect. Primary emphasis should be placed on the fact that a real estate agent can represent a seller in a fiduciary capacity and still accommodate a buyer's need for some very important services without automatically developing a secondary fiduciary relationship with that buyer. (*See* the Customer Letter in Appendix E.)

In initial discussions, a listing broker's salesperson or broker associate may find that many buyers actually do not want representation as clients. What many buyers want is to work with someone with ready access to inventory who will competently gather the relevant data, accurately describe the property and act as a conduit to the seller. The fact that the licensee's firm represents the seller in a fiduciary capacity may not discourage such buyers from working with the seller's representative and negotiating for themselves against the seller and his agent or subagent. These buyers understand what is involved in a transaction in which they seek services as a customer to help them make their purchase decision. Such buyers typically do not want to be contractually obligated to a buyer's broker, thus frequently being directly obligated to pay the buyer's broker and sometimes even resist committing themselves in writing to deal with only one broker. However, they may change their minds after the benefits of such written buyer representation agreements are carefully explained.

COOPERATIVE SALES

While many properties are sold in-house, in the majority of sales the buyer is found by a cooperating broker, also called a *selling broker.* Since the advent of buyer representation as an important force in the market, TREC-promulgated contract forms refer to this second broker as the *other broker,* finding, according to The Texas Broker-Lawyer Committee, that the terms *cooperating, selling* and *purchasing* broker were somewhat presumptive. Another series of boxes to mark were introduced to the contract form to allow the parties to distinguish whether the other broker was the agent of the buyer, subagent of the seller or a dual agent. It is important to clarify and/or gain the necessary consents early in the transaction as to whether the other broker is or expects to be a subagent of the seller, an agent of the buyer, a dual agent or a licensee working with a customer but not in an agency relationship to either the seller or the buyer (i.e., facilitator, finder or middleman). There is no box to check in the TREC contract form for middleman; therefore, that clarification would need to be written in.

To whom does the other broker owe fiduciary responsibilities? If the listing broker and other broker do not clarify the role of the other broker, a court may find an agency relationship even where one was not consciously intended by anyone in the transaction. Courts have been known to impose an agency relationship in order to provide a remedy for an injured consumer.

Example:

Betty was referred to Sally by their mutual friend George. George talked about how helpful and knowledgeable Sally had been in listing and selling his townhouse. Sally talked with Betty about her real estate needs, her criteria and her qualifications. Sally then reviewed all her in-house Bay Realty listings, but nothing seemed to fit. Bay Realty belonged to a traditional MLS that accepted listings that offered subagency and compensation to members who found buyers for its listings. Sally went to her MLS book and selected ten homes to inspect. Betty liked the one on South Street. Sally met with the listing broker, Jeff from South Side Realty. Sally then assisted Betty in preparing an offer, which was presented to the seller by Jeff. The seller accepted. At closing, South Side Realty paid half its commission to Bay Realty, which, in turn, paid a portion to Sally.

What are the agency relationships in the above example?

- South Side Realty is the exclusive listing broker and represents the seller.

- Jeff is an agent of South Side Realty (broker) and owes allegiance to South Side Realty and the seller through South Side Realty.
- Bay Realty, the other or cooperating broker, is the subagent of the seller and the agent of South Side Realty.
- Sally is the agent of Bay Realty, which, in turn, is the subagent of the seller through South Side Realty. Sally owes allegiance to the seller, although she must treat Betty honestly and fairly and disclose any adverse factors about the property. TREC Rule 22 TAC 535.156(b), in part, states, "a licensee must deal honestly and fairly with all parties." TRELA § 15(a)(6)(D) states, in part, that a licensee's license may be revoked for "failing to make clear, to all parties of a transaction, which party he [or she] is acting for."

Let's assume that Bay Realty prefers the traditional approach to real estate sales and regards its prospective buyers as customers. No agreements are signed with buyers. Bay Realty treats buyers fairly and honestly relative to its seller clients and offers buyer customers a variety of free services in the hopes the buyers will decide to purchase property from or through Bay Realty. If Betty decides to submit an offer through a broker other than Bay Realty, then neither Bay Realty nor Sally will receive anything for their previous non-contracted, voluntary services to Betty. As far as agency relationships are concerned, Bay Realty, as a subagent, represents the seller client and not the buyer customer.

Loyalty

The other broker acting in a subagency capacity is the subagent of the seller. Brokers should be aware that their natural inclination to do a good job for the buyer may sometimes result in a conflict with their fiduciary duties owed to their client, the seller.

Example:

Charlie, a licensed associate with East Side Realty, an exclusive seller representation firm, helped the Smiths sell their home and then buy another. East Side Realty recently received this letter from the Smiths:

> *We want to thank your salesperson, Charlie Smith, for the superb job in selling our home and helping us buy an even better one. Charlie protected us in the sale of our home, refusing to allow other brokers to coax us into a situation not in our best interest. And when Charlie found us the perfect house through the MLS system, Charlie was at his best in negotiating for us the lowest possible price and best carryback financing terms. Charlie was especially helpful in persuading the seller to lower the interest rate and increase the term of the loan and in suggesting we ask for a non-recourse loan. The real estate industry needs more people like Charlie.*

Are Charlie's actions consistent with East Side Realty's policy of accepting an offer of subagency under the MLS system? Charlie's actions toward the Smiths as sellers and his role as a seller's agent were acceptable. However, his actions toward them when they became buyers were only acceptable if he was functioning as their broker agent. If he was going to help them buy a home he should have asked his broker first. His broker then should have said, "Tell the Smiths, 'Thanks, but no thanks. We don't represent buyers; we only represent sellers. And, because we now know so much about your confidential situation, it would not be appropriate to work with you as subagents of other sellers. We must refer you.'" Otherwise, Charlie and East Side Realty might find themselves in an undisclosed dual agency, with resulting conflict of interest problems.

Seller Agent's Disclosures To Seller

Before signing the listing agreement the listing broker should make several disclosures concerning agency relationships, carefully following 22 TAC §535.164. To ensure that licensees make these disclosures, TREC, under TRELA §15C, promulgated an agency disclosure form "that defines common agency relationships, duties of the broker, and potential conflicts that may develop." These same disclosures are required of every licensee dealing with consumers of real estate services, that is, prospective buyers, sellers, landlords and tenants. This form, TREC Agency Disclosure Form Number 3, is to be furnished to the prospective client or customer at the first face-to-face meeting with the licensee or first written communication from the licensee, whichever event occurs first. [22 TAC §535.164]

In addition, the NAR® Code of Ethics and Standards of Practice 9-10(a) requires the listing agent to advise sellers of:

- general company policies regarding cooperating with subagents, buyer/tenant agents or both;
- the fact that buyer/tenant agents represent the buyer/tenant even if paid by the listing broker or the seller; and
- the potential, if any, of the listing broker agent acting as a disclosed dual agent.

The listing agent should also discuss with the seller whether a multiple listing service will be used and whether a blanket offer of subagency will be made to other brokers.

TREC rules require a real estate licensee to give the seller the licensee's opinion of market value of the property at the time of negotiating a listing. If the licensee expects to receive compensation from more than one party or to be a dual of agent in the transaction, the source of compensation and consent to the arrangement must be expressed in writing or the dual agency will be illegal. [22 TAC §535.16(d); TRELA §§15(a)(6)(d) and 15C(a)(3)]

These and other disclosures can be made in the listing agreement or in a special addendum to the listing agreement.

Seller Agent's Disclosures To Buyer

The seller's agent must disclose to the buyer that the brokerage represents the seller, not the buyer. To facilitate this TREC-mandated disclosure, some firms have the buyer read and acknowledge a customer letter that outlines what the sales agent can and cannot do for the buyer. This letter could soften the tone of the disclosure but should not blunt the intent.

NAR® Code of Ethics & Standard of Practice 21-14 requires seller's agents to disclose their relationship with the seller to the buyer/tenant as *soon as practicable* and provide written confirmation not later than signing any purchase or lease agreement. Early disclosure is the best policy. But remember, state law prevails. TREC Rule §535.164 requires disclosure to all prospects at the first face-to-face meeting with or written communication from the licensee, whichever occurs first.

Exclusive Seller Agency

Some real estate brokerage firms represent only sellers. The seller is always the client, the buyer is always the customer. Until the recent acceptance of buyer agency, exclusive seller agency was the traditional and predominate type of practice. Many firms today find that it is their business to represent people generally rather than people classified by their relationship to the property in question, that is, whether that person is selling, buying or leasing. As a result, exclusive seller agency is no longer the majority practice. However, in Texas, while some traditional brokerages have made the switch to dual agency/seller agency/buyer agency, other firms are staying with their commitment to represent sellers exclusively. These brokerages encourage buyers and tenants, who want representation, to seek a buyer's broker, an appraiser or an attorney while offering to work with them in the purchase or lease of property as long as the buyers realize the broker and all their licensed associates will be representing the interests of the sellers and landlords.

Some advantages to exclusive seller agency are:

- It reduces chances of conflict of interest that arise by mixing dual agency or buyer agency in the same firm, especially if the brokerage has a considerable number of licensed associates and listings.
- The seller receives 100 percent loyalty and confidentiality, with someone advocating his or her best interests and providing expert advice.
- It may be more comfortable and familiar to those licensees trained this way.
- It is a proven method of compensation in cooperating sales transactions.
- Agency lines are clarified in the in-house sale.

Some disadvantages of exclusive seller agency are:

- It does not satisfy needs of qualified buyers seeking representation.
- There is an increased potential for undisclosed dual agency (may be an implied buyer agency).
- The seller and seller's agent are liable for acts of a subagent.

SUMMARY

The broker who consistently acts in the capacity of a seller's agent has little trouble distinguishing the client from the customer. Up until the end of 1993, firms with a large share of the market often chose this type of relationship to lessen the risks of conflicts of loyalty in selling their own listings. However, with the passing into law of the new TRELA §15C, many of the larger Texas firms are experimenting with a variety of policies. Some firms have a clearly stated policy of not offering subagency except on an individual, case by case situation. Great care should be exercised, both with in-house sales and cooperative sales, to avoid conduct that could be interpreted to create an implied agency with the buyer if none is intended. Supervising brokers can and should develop policies and procedures and competently train licensed associates to act consistently with company policy.

KEY POINTS

- The fact the listing agent is the only broker in the transaction does not mean there is a dual agency, so long as there is no conduct or words to indicate otherwise.
- Early disclosure of seller agency helps lessen the chance the buyer will claim later that the broker also represented the buyer.

- Written disclosures and brochures help to clarify that the buyer is the customer and the seller is the client. Warning: Do not substitute the words *impartially* or *equally* for their sometime synonym *fairly* in the context of how an agent for the seller client will treat the buyer customer. The customer must be treated fairly by law, but not impartially or equally relative to the client.
- A licensed associate of a broker is an agent of his or her broker, regardless of whether the associate is licensed as a broker or salesperson and even if the associate is an independent contractor for tax purposes. It is the principal broker who owns the listing; not the associate. Licensed salespersons cannot lawfully sell their services directly to the public—they must perform tasks under the direct supervision of a broker. Under agency and licensing law and for purposes of supervision, the salesperson who is licensed with the broker is an agent and employee of the broker. A licensed salesperson or broker associate is acting for his broker. The terminology *acting for,* as used in TREC Rules cited here, is the description of an agency relationship. [TRELA §1(b) and (c)]
- It is sometimes tempting for an exclusive seller agency broker to represent the buyer; for instance when a seller client decides to buy an in-house listing. In addition to disclosure, the broker and all associates need to act like the seller's agent throughout the transaction.

SUGGESTIONS FOR BROKERS

Review with your licensed associates the types of services they can provide to accommodate at least some of the needs of the buyer while remembering the fact that they are acting as agents or subagents of the seller. To ensure that your licensed associates do not accidentally create an implied or accidental agency with the buyer, require that the associates have the buyer acknowledge in writing that the buyer is on notice that your company and your associate are acting as agents of the seller and not as agents of the buyer.

QUIZ

1. A listing broker owes which of the following duties to the prospective buyer customer?

   a. Loyalty
   b. Obedience
   c. Disclosure of material defects
   d. All of the above

2. All licensed associates (broker or salesperson) of a listing brokerage firm are best described as:

   a. agents of the seller.
   b. principals.
   c. subagents of the seller.
   d. agents of the buyer.

3. A listing broker can normally do all of the following *except:*

   a. sell the listing broker's own listings.
   b. advertise listed properties.
   c. hold open houses.
   d. split fees with a buyer's broker without the seller's knowledge.

4. Which of the following statements is true concerning a licensed associate who is an independent contractor working for the listing broker in an exclusive seller representation type brokerage?

   a. The associate can tell a buyer that the seller will accept $10,000 less than asking price.
   b. The associate owes legal duties only to the seller, not the buyer.
   c. The associate is, by law, the agent of the listing broker.
   d. The associate can take the listings when he or she quits.

5. The relationship of the licensed associate of a listing broker to his or her seller is best described as that of:

   a. an independent contractor.
   b. an agent.
   c. an employee.
   d. a subagent.

DISCUSSION QUESTIONS

1. Why can't licensed associates take listings with them when they transfer to a new firm?
2. In exclusive seller representation brokerage firm, what is the best way to handle a turnaround transaction in which your seller wants you to help find a replacement property?
3. Should a brokerage firm be prohibited by law from selling its own listings? Why or why not?
4. How would you offer to help a prospective buyer you meet at an open house and still remain loyal to the seller?

5. Why can't a salesperson in a branch office represent a buyer purchasing a property listed in the firm's main office without a dual agency problem being created?
6. What should the listing broker say when the buyer asks common questions such as: How low will the seller go? Do you think the property is worth what the seller is asking? Are there any other offers on the property? Have you had any contracts that fell through?

CHAPTER

5

SUBAGENCY

One of the least understood agency relationships is subagency. A *subagent* is a person appointed by an agent, with the informed consent of the agent's principal, to perform functions undertaken by the agent for the principal and for whose conduct both the agent and principal are responsible. Typically, a subagent is a real estate broker appointed by a listing broker, under authority granted by the seller, to perform functions on the seller's behalf. Less frequently, a buyer's broker or tenant's representative will appoint a subagent to perform functions on the buyer's or tenant's behalf, especially in the area of opinions of value. On other occasions, the buyer-broker will utilize buyer's brokers located in different geographic areas or buyer's brokers or tenant "reps" who specialize in certain properties.

This chapter focuses on the relationship between the listing broker and the cooperating or other broker, also called the *selling* broker, the one who actually finds the ready, willing and able buyer. Remember a buyer's broker should not be referred to as a selling broker, cooperating broker or subagent of the listing broker. Buyer's brokers do not procure ready, willing and able buyers for sellers. Instead they procure suitable properties for buyer clients. Buyer's brokers should not be the target of procuring cause grievances of listing agents or subagents because buyer's brokers are under separate contract to a buyer, not the seller or his or her agents.

This chapter discusses the following:

- Establishing Status: Subagent or Buyer's Broker?
- Creation of Subagency
    - Selective Offers of Subagency
    - Blanket Unilateral Offers of Subagency (MLS)
    - Rejecting Subagency
    - No Offer of Subagency
    - Subagency Optional
    - Sellers and Subagency
- Subagent's Liability and Ethics
    - Liability to Seller
    - Ethical Concerns
- Deciding on Subagency
    - Level of Service

ESTABLISHING STATUS: SUBAGENT OR BUYER'S BROKER?

Transactions usually start from two positions quite independent of each other. A buyer begins to think about buying and then starts taking action to buy. Meanwhile, a seller starts thinking about selling and later starts taking action to sell. A transaction is the result of these two independent forces meeting. During the marketing of a property by the seller's broker, the buyer frequently visits the property with another broker or licensed associate of a broker, who is called the other broker, cooperating broker, selling broker, buyer's broker or finder. Who is this other broker? Who does the other broker represent?

The status of the other broker should be established as early as possible. Whether the other broker is a seller's subagent or a buyer's broker can be of critical importance.

- If held to be a seller's subagent, then the other broker owes fiduciary duties and primary allegiance to the seller and the seller may vicariously liable for the his or her subagent's conduct toward third parties.
- If held to be a buyer's broker, then the other broker owes fiduciary duties and primary allegiance to the buyer.
- If held to be a dual agent, the other broker owes a set of highly statutorily modified fiduciary duties.
- If held to be a finder, middleman or facilitator, the other broker owes no allegiance to anyone but him- or herself and neither party is liable for the middleman's conduct toward the other party.

CREATION OF SUBAGENCY

Like any agency relationship, the subagency relationship is created by the consent of those involved. Only when the subagency is validly created does the law impose fiduciary duties and liabilities on the subagent. Subagency may be created expressly by agreement or implicitly by words, conduct or custom. Subagency may be created within or apart from the framework of a multiple listing service (MLS). Even within an MLS, subagency is not automatic. The seller has the option to offer subagency. On the other hand, the listing broker has the option to condition his or her taking of the listing on whether the seller will allow and/or insist on subagency or dual agency. Also, any other broker in the transaction can reject any offer of subagency that is made and elect to work with the buyer on a client basis or to attempt to remain a finder or middleman and represent no one.

Selective Offers of Subagency

Subagency can be created outside the framework of a MLS. While many listing brokers are members of a multiple listing service, there are thousands of listings in the small towns and rural areas of Texas that have no MLS systems. Further, MLS systems do not require that certain types of properties be listed. Commercial properties, new project sales, business opportunities, long-term leases and vacant land typically fall into this voluntary category. Still, the listing broker may decide to work with other brokers on a selective basis to help in the search for buyers for these types of property. Rather than talk in terms of a formal offer of subagency, however, the

Figure 5.1 Subagency Relationship Chart

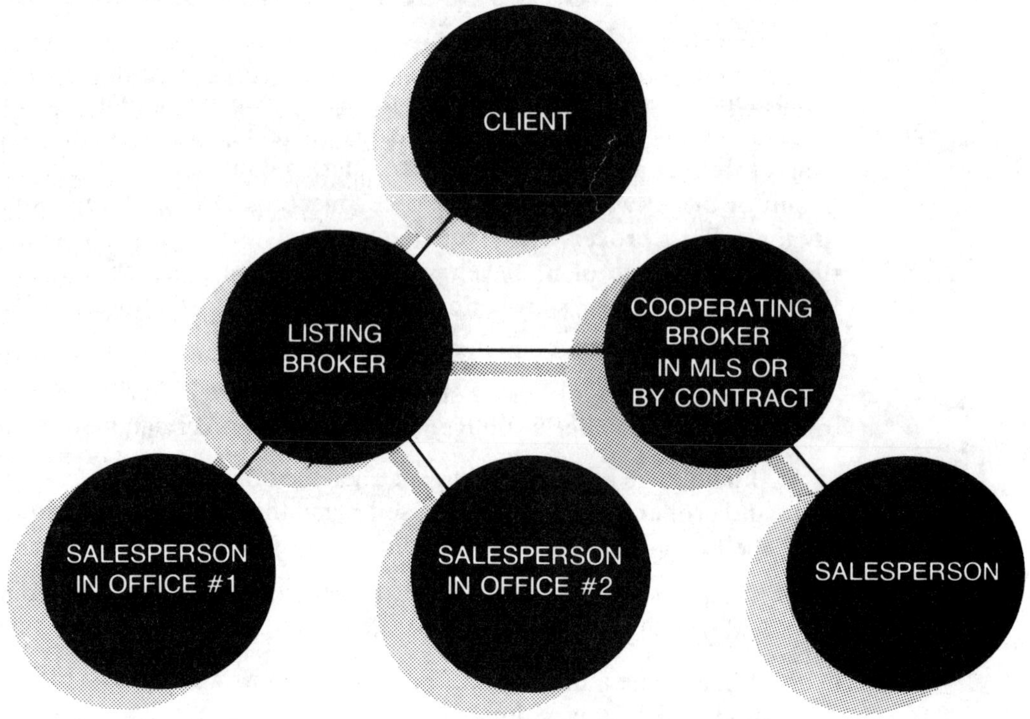

AGENCY RELATIONSHIP = ANY ONE STEP BETWEEN CIRCLES

SUBAGENCY RELATIONSHIP = MORE THAN ONE STEP

brokers talk of cooperating in the transaction and sharing or splitting the commission. This type of informal understanding is particularly dangerous because it is often completely unclear as to who the other broker represents or who is responsible for payment. In a recent case, an honorable Texas commercial broker failed to recover a commission in a $9 million transaction because he was unable to convincingly establish whose agent he was, whose best interests he acted in and who was supposed to pay him. Instead of the $270,000 commission he sued for, he ended up settling for $40,000. Had the commercial broker known and practiced the principles set out by law there may have been a decidedly different outcome.

Listing brokers and the other brokers involved in the transaction often have separate commission agreements between themselves that serve as a basis for the subagency relationship. Such agreements are often silent as to the agency duties and tend to cover only how the commission is to be split. Brokers who deal with each other frequently operate without any specific written or oral agreement; however, a written arrangement is preferable.

The listing broker usually appoints a number of subagents, yet only the subagent who procures the sale is entitled to a share of the commission as the procuring cause. This arrangement is similar to an open listing. As in any situation where more than one broker works with a single buyer, there is the possibility that procuring cause disputes may arise between different selling, cooperating or other brokers, with two or more of the other brokers each claiming a right to share the commission with the listing broker.

Example:

Broker Jeff of South Side Realty tells brokers Bob and Aileen, each from different companies, about a commercial office building listed for sale with South Side Realty. The seller had authorized Jeff in the listing agreement to use subagents. Bob and Aileen each separately agree to help market the property. Both Bob and Aileen are now subagents of the seller and agents of Jeff's South Side Realty. If Bob finds the buyer who eventually buys the building, then Bob is entitled to a previously agreed-upon share of South Side's listing commission and Aileen receives nothing for her efforts. However, if Aileen had originally shown the building to the buyer but the buyer utilized Bob to write up the offer, both Aileen and Bob might involve South Side Realty in a dispute over who, between Bob and Aileen, was the procuring cause of the sale and thus entitled to share in the commission. On the other hand, if Bob was a buyer's broker in this situation, any claims by Aileen as being the procuring cause would be directed to the listing broker and would not effect Bob or his compensation because Bob's agency relationship is with the buyer. Bob's right to a commission would come from his buyer client negotiating Bob's payment as a part of the negotiated contract with the seller and would be independent of the listing agent's listing agreement or offers of compensation or cooperation to other brokers.

Blanket Unilateral Offer of Subagency (MLS)

Residential properties are typically listed in an area-wide MLS. A seller often lists property with a licensed associate of a broker who is a member of the local MLS. The seller expects that the property will receive the widest possible exposure to potential buyers through the efforts of hundreds of local real estate licensees. A MLS is a convenient way to offer subagency and arrange to share commissions.

Until the late 1970s, the MLS was defined as a system created for the orderly dissemination and correlation of listing information. MLS regulations, written under guidelines formulated by the National Association of REALTORS®, were modified to provide that by submitting a property to the MLS through the broker, the seller authorizes the broker to make a blanket unilateral offer of subagency to the other members of the MLS.

The cooperating broker accepted the unilateral blanket offer by showing the property to the buyer and by procuring an offer to purchase. There is no established rule as to exactly when the subagency offer is accepted, other than acceptance is based on performance. If no written acceptance of the subagency offer exists, there may be a question as to whether the subagency offer is accepted at the time a property is shown or only when an offer is produced.

One uncertainty is the effect of the other broker accepting subagency from a listing broker while showing one of that broker's listings to a buyer-customer, then later returning with a second buyer who is already a buyer-client.

Example:

Suppose Sally, a subagent of the seller, shows a customer, Alice, a property listed in the MLS. Alice decides she does not like the house. The next week, Sally is looking for a home for her buyer client, Betty, with whom she and Bay Realty have a written buyer-agency agreement. Can Sally be a buyer's agent to Betty with respect to this home or will her earlier subagency to the seller, with Alice as a prospective customer, make her a dual agent? Can Sally tell Betty that the seller had agreed to reduce the asking price for Alice?

It would seem that subagency applies to the *person,* not the *property.* Thus, the earlier subagency does not apply to a later transaction. If it did, then after Sally showed Alice the property, all of Bay Realty's salespeople would become subagents of the seller until that property was sold. On the other hand, the argument can be made that once Sally showed the home the first time, she may have learned confidential information from the listing agent who believed Sally to be accepting the blanket unilateral offer of subagency. The listing agent would have had good reason to believe Sally was accepting subagency by acting in showing the house without clearly rejecting the offer of subagency. Therefore, the listing agent would have been within the proper scope of her duty if she conveyed to Sally confidential information with regard to the seller's motivations and negotiating position. The latter, in point of fact, occurs regularly by comments from listing agents who believe the other broker is accepting subagency. Having once been entrusted with the information about the seller, actually or constructively, intentionally or accidentally, while in a subagency capacity and having made the entire brokerage the subagent of the listing broker, the question is whether a licensee—or anyone in her entire brokerage—could now represent a buyer without full disclosure of the potential conflicts and consent of all the parties.

By accepting the offer of subagency, the cooperating broker owes complete fiduciary duties and loyalty to the seller. Real estate brokers who are subagents of the seller must relate to buyers and sellers exactly as if the listing had been taken by the subagent's company. The cooperating broker must be careful not to act for the buyer in any manner adverse to the seller's best interest. This may be a problem if the cooperating broker has developed close ties with the buyer. By the same token, the cooperating broker rarely meets the seller and usually knows little about the seller's needs. The broker's main source of information will be what is revealed in the MLS or what is discussed with the listing broker.

Rejecting Subagency

What some brokers fail to realize is that it is not mandatory that an other broker accept the offer of subagency or that the listing broker even extend an offer of subagency. Listing a property in a MLS may permit subagency, but does not automatically create it or require it. Unless otherwise noted, it is assumed that the listing broker is offering subagency on behalf of the seller and those cooperating members who attempt to find a buyer for a listed property are subagents of the seller. However, these are only presumptions. Therefore, all brokers would do well to clarify agency relationships before acting, not after. Other brokers and buyers are free to arrange their legal relationships as they see fit, so long as adequate disclosure is made. Under the new MLS systems, the seller can direct the broker to offer subagency on a blanket basis or not allow them to offer subagency at all. The broker, with the consent of the seller, may offer compensation to subagents or buyer's agents.

The other broker may reject the offer of subagency and work as a buyer's broker. A common example of this is when other brokers decide to buy property listed in an MLS for their own account. If the other broker wishes to reject subagency, then it is extremely important that the other broker notify the listing broker and the seller that the other broker is not a subagent of the seller (i.e., to immediately disclaim any subagency in the transaction) and obtain a clear understanding with the listing broker and seller handling the commission of the other broker.

No Offer of Subagency

Just as some MLS brokers decide not to accept the offer of subagency, there are some sellers who decide not to authorize subagency on a blanket basis. Sellers often carefully select their own listing broker. They may not want other brokers representing them in the transaction, especially brokers who they do not know. While these sellers want the market exposure of a MLS, they feel that cooperating subagents do not actively work to obtain the most favorable terms for them but are, instead, trying to get the best deal for buyers. The common perception is that the cooperating broker represents the buyer.

In the past, listings in which the seller did not want other brokers or a MLS involved were called *office exclusives.* Today, many sellers want their brokers to submit these listings to a MLS so they can benefit from the wide exposure of their property. These sellers prefer the use of a blanket unilateral offer of cooperation (in the form of a commission split) but no subagency.

Subagency Optional

As of July 1, 1993, all Board of REALTORS® MLSs are required to amend their regulations to delete mandatory offers of subagency and to make offers of subagency optional. Participants submitting listings to the MLS must, however, offer cooperation to other MLS participants in the form of a subagency or cooperation with buyer agents or other legally recognized licensees (transaction broker, coordinator or finder). All offers of subagency or cooperation made through a MLS must include an offer of compensation. Sellers are now free to have their listing brokers submit the listing to the MLS and offer cooperation and fee splitting as always, but now they are also free *not* to offer subagency. A seller can always direct the broker to make a blanket offer of subagency as was the customary practice, and if the listing broker chooses to take the listing under that condition, the listing broker must offer subagency.

The other broker who brings a buyer to a listing where no subagency is offered has to be clear about his or her agency status. An offer of subagency that is not made cannot be accepted. However, when an other broker comes to a property with a buyer customer in hand and has not clarified the relationships, the other broker may find him- or herself in the middle of the transaction as an agent for no one. In many such cases, other brokers would be buyer's agents. There is the possibility, however, that a buyer might want a broker to help the buyer search for a property but will refuse to allow the cooperating broker to act as a buyer's agent. If the buyer does refuse, then the cooperating broker will be neither the agent of the buyer nor the subagent of the seller but a non-agent. The other broker will still be subject to the provisions of the state licensing law but will be acting in the particular transaction more in the capacity of a finder, middleman or facilitator than in the representative or advocate capacity of an authorized agent or subagent. In Texas, this role for the broker is generally referred to as *finder* or *middleman.* The compensation between the listing broker and the other broker must be specified within the MLS framework if offered through a MLS. Keep in mind however, that in Texas approximately two-thirds of all real estate licensees are **not** REALTORS® and many that are REALTORS® are not members of any formal or NAR®-sanctioned MLS system. Therefore, they are not subject to MLS rules on listings. Brokers bringing buyers to such homes as builder or FSBO homes need to have a very clear understanding of the agency relationships and compensation agreements with all the parties before any work begins.

Sellers and Subagency

There are some benefits for the seller in authorizing the use of subagents when the subagency is carried out properly. Theoretically, in addition to the listing broker, the seller will have the benefit of all members of the MLS acting on his or her behalf to find and qualify buyers. All brokers will owe the seller their fiduciary duties and professional skills. Further, this increased exposure may hasten the sale of the property. The seller can direct the listing broker to exert better control by imposing on subagents special requirements for showing, presenting offers, depositing earnest money, registering buyers and opening escrow.

For example, the listing on George's house by Sally's firm, Bay Realty, recently expired. George then listed the home with Main Realty, who submitted the listing to the local MLS. Sally meets Betty, and the home is perfect for Betty. Because of Sally's prior client relationship with George, it would be advisable for Sally to treat the buyer, Betty, as a customer and work on this property as a subagent of the seller, George, with the express consent of George and Main Realty.

Despite its benefits, subagency may not be right for every seller. Although subagency increases the number of agents working on the seller's behalf, it also increases the seller's exposure to potential liability caused by the subagents. Others will argue that, in Texas, the seller is not liable for the acts of subagents appointed by the seller's agent. Licensees should get legal advice concerning this matter and suggest their seller clients seek their own legal counsel in this regard. Until clarified, listing brokers should be alert that their clients may possibly be bound by and responsible for the conduct and representations of authorized subagents, most of whom they have never met and over whom they have no practical control.

LIABILITY AND ETHICS

No one can make an informed decision to choose or not to choose subagency without first becoming aware of the legal and practical consequences of a subagency relationship. Often the outcome of a case will turn on whether the other broker is found to be a subagent of the seller or an agent of the buyer. Following are some examples that should help clarify the role of the subagent and the importance of promptly disclosing agency status.

SITUATION: *Betty Buyer submits an offer for $100,000 through Sally of Bay Realty on a property listed by Jeff of South Side Realty. The seller counters at $105,000. Betty Buyer accepts the counteroffer in the presence of Sally only. One hour later, before Sally has told Jeff or the seller of Betty's acceptance of the offer, Jeff delivers to Betty a written revocation of the counteroffer. Meanwhile, the seller accepts an offer from another buyer for $110,000.*

QUESTION: *Did Betty accept the counteroffer before the seller revoked it? Must the seller sell to Betty?*

DISCUSSION: *The general rule is that notice to an agent is the same as notice to the principal. Therefore, if Sally is the subagent of the seller, then the seller is bound by Betty's notice of acceptance given to Sally. If Sally is Betty's agent, however, then the seller's revocation is effective because it was delivered to Betty before Betty's notice of acceptance was delivered to the seller or to Jeff.*

SITUATION: *Jeff, the listing agent, tells Sally that the roof leaks. Sally fails to tell Betty, who doesn't discover this fact until the first rainy spell after closing.*

QUESTION: *Who is potentially liable for failing to disclose a known material fact?*

DISCUSSION: *The seller, Jeff, South Side Realty, Sally and Bay Realty are all potentially liable. If Jeff, South Side Realty and the seller were all held liable for Sally's negligence, then they would have claims for indemnification against Sally and Bay Realty. The general rule is that the listing broker and the seller may be liable for the faults of their authorized subagent, even if the error occurred without the knowledge or consent of the listing broker or seller. The result would be different if Sally and Bay Realty had been Betty Buyer's agents because Betty would then have bought with the constructive or imputed notice that the roof leaked, because Betty's own buyer's agent, Sally, had been told of the leak. Also, Sally's negligence would not then be imputed to South Side Realty because Bay Realty was not their agent, although Betty would have a claim against Bay Realty on account of Sally's negligence.*

SITUATION: *Jeff tells Sally that the sewer is connected and Sally passes on this information to Betty. The fact is that every house in the subdivision is connected to the sewer except the one Jeff listed.*

QUESTION: *Who is liable to Betty for this misrepresentation?*

DISCUSSION: *The seller, Jeff, South Side Realty, Sally and Bay Realty are all potentially liable. Sally and Bay Realty may be able to seek indemnity from Jeff and South Side Realty, although a court might hold that they had an equal duty to verify the information received from the listing broker by consulting the public records.*

SITUATION: *Betty asks Sally for advice on making an offer before obtaining loan approval. Sally says not to worry because Betty can cancel the contract if she doesn't get the loan. No financing contingency clause is written into the contract.*

QUESTION: *Can Betty cancel if she doesn't qualify for the loan?*

DISCUSSION: *If Sally is a subagent of the seller, then Betty can cancel, based on improper advice. The seller cannot benefit by the negligence of one of the seller's subagents. If Sally is Betty's agent, a buyer's broker, the result is different. Betty must perform her obligations under the contract or face the consequences in the contract under the default paragraph. She can later seek money damages against Sally and Bay Realty, her agent.*

Subagent's Liability to Seller

Subagents need to consider their legal and ethical responsibilities to the seller. For example, as a buyer's broker presenting an offer on a Veteran's Administration (VA) loan assumption, a broker is under no legal duty to suggest that the seller require from the buyer a substitution of eligibility or release of liability (from both VA and the lender). A subagent, however, would be legally obligated to point out to the seller the risks involved in accepting such an offer. Likewise, the subagent, as well as the listing broker, could be liable to the seller of a dilapidated old house for failure to advise (or recommend that an attorney be consulted) on the appropriate use of an as-is clause or the fact that the seller may have to make repairs if a Federal Housing Administration (FHA) loan is involved.

Similarly, a buyer's broker has no duty to point out the risks to the seller of accepting a wraparound mortgage or an installment land contract of sale in which the buyer does not agree to pay at satisfaction any prepayment penalties on the seller's underlying loan. As a subagent of the seller, however, a broker would be obligated to point out any risks to the seller that are evident to the ordinary broker, even if the buyer instructed the broker to remain silent regarding such risks. Likewise, as a seller's subagent, a broker would be remiss if he or she failed to point out to the seller the risks involved in accepting as partial payment a note from a recently formed corporation without any personal guaranty from the principals of the corporation. A buyer's broker is under no similar duty toward the seller.

Ethical Concerns

Other brokers or cooperating brokers who serve as subagents are sometimes confronted with difficult ethical questions. Consider the following examples, in which Sally and Bay Realty are acting as the seller's subagents on a property listed in the MLS by Jeff of South Side Realty.

SITUATION: *Sally learns that Betty Buyer has an option on the two parcels on both sides of the listed property. Betty is trying to consolidate and subdivide the three lots, hoping to double their value. The seller asks Sally: Is the buyer's offer her best offer or should I hold out for more?*

QUESTION: *What does Sally tell the seller?*

DISCUSSION: *As a seller's subagent, Sally has a fiduciary duty of full disclosure to the seller of all material facts. She is also obligated under 22 TAC §535.156 (a) and (c) to "convey to [her] principal all known information which would affect the principal's decision on whether or not to accept or reject offers" and Sally "has an affirmative duty to keep [her] principal informed at all times of significant information applicable to the transaction or transactions in which the licensee is acting as an agent for the principal." She is further required under 22 TAC §535.16(c) to "make diligent efforts to obtain the best possible price for the principal" and under 22 TAC §535.2(f) to "negotiate the best possible transaction for [her] principal, the person she has agreed to represent." Armed with Sally's information about Betty's consolidation plans, the seller might well decide to hold out for a better offer, especially if the seller is not under great pressure to sell. This example is also useful in understanding the dilemma of a disclosed dual agent.*

SITUATION: *Betty makes an offer through Sally with the seller to carryback a large purchase money note. To save the transaction, Sally lends Betty $5,000 at closing to help make the down payment.*

QUESTION: *Must Sally tell the seller about the loan?*

DISCUSSION: *Yes. The fact that Betty needs a loan to close may be relevant to her creditworthiness. Sally should disclose this fact to the seller and obtain the seller's permission, especially if Sally is to earn interest on the loan. In addition, Sally should disclose all compensation she is receiving, including any rebates. Note that if Sally was a* *buyer's broker, she would have no duty to disclose to the seller that she was making the loan.*

SITUATION: *Jeff listed Carol's home for sale. Carol asks Jeff to find a suitable replacement home. Jeff finds the perfect home owned by George listed in the MLS by Sally from Bay Realty. Jeff helps Carol, who is now in the role of a buyer, to prepare an offer that involves George's carrying back a second purchase money note. Carol's offer is also contingent on the sale of her home, presently under a signed contract with Betty Buyer. Betty's offer to buy Carol's home is contingent on the sale of Betty's home.*

QUESTION: *Jeff finds out that Carol has lost her job and is contemplating filing bankruptcy. Should this information be disclosed? If so, to whom?*

DISCUSSION: *It is not uncommon to find several transactions dependent on each other. If one of the transactions falls apart, this domino effect may result in ill feelings and lawsuits, even when agency relationships are clearly defined. Unless Jeff disclaims subagency, Jeff is the subagent of George. Jeff is thus caught in the dilemma of representing Carol in the sale of her home but not representing her in her purchase of a new home. Jeff has the duty to disclose Carol's financial problems to George and, at the same time, the duty to Carol not to disclose. Jeff could have avoided this conflict if he had disclaimed subagency to George, and worked as a buyer's agent for Carol. That is, of course, if Jeff's broker allowed buyer agency.*

SITUATION: *Betty has Sally, on Betty's behalf, prepare an offer to buy a property listed with South Side Realty. Betty agrees to assume the seller's loan and asks Sally to review the seller's note and mortgage.*

QUESTION: *Must Sally explain to Betty the consequences of negative amortization or an excessive prepayment penalty clause in the note or a due-on-sale clause in the mortgage?*

DISCUSSION: *Even as a seller's subagent, Sally must be honest with Betty and treat her fairly. [22 TAC §535.156(b)] If there is anything unfair in the mortgage or note, Sally must point it out or encourage Betty to seek legal help. However, Sally is not required to explain all of the provisions in the mortgage to see if they meet with Betty's expectations. If Sally were to give erroneous advice about the mortgage, then Sally's principal, the seller, would be liable for such negligence. As a buyer's agent, though, Sally would have a greater duty of exploring the problem areas in the mortgage or, alternatively, of advising strongly that Betty, her client, obtain expert assistance. Sally would not only point out the proposed due-on-sale clause but perhaps advise Betty to avoid it or negotiate around it.*

DECIDING ON SUBAGENCY

While brokers outside the listing brokerage or other brokers should recognize the potential liability of being a subagent, the more important question for the other broker working with a buyer is: How effective am I when I act in the capacity of a subagent? Often the answer depends on how real estate licensees perceive their roles: whether as facilitators and marketing specialists or as negotiators and representatives of a client. Some brokers and salespeople, as subagents of the seller in a cooperative sale transaction, feel very comfortable in limiting their roles with buyers to providing accurate and honest customer-level service and actually negotiating for the seller's best interests. They also feel assured of having an enforceable right to get paid, once the listing brokers are paid by the sellers, that is, of course, if they have made the appropriate agreements.

Other licensees feel less comfortable and less effective as subagents. They often sense a hesitation or resistance on the part of buyers or tenants to trust or rely on them as professionals, especially when they point out that they represent the owner or that they cannot give the buyer or tenant true or full representation because they intend to operate only as dual agents. These brokers feel they can demonstrate more of their talents and creative skills when they represent and negotiate on behalf of the buyer as client. This is especially true if prospective buyers or tenants are unsophisticated investors or business owners with plenty of disposable income but little negotiating ability or experience as far as real estate is concerned. These brokers find success in carefully screening prospective buyers and tenants and electing to work for a few on a client/agent basis.

There are several factors to consider in deciding whether to be a subagent.

- Some brokers find difficulty in explaining subagency to buyers, especially if a buyer expects the broker to protect and promote the buyer's best interest.
- A subagent can't be too aggressive in furthering the buyer's interest for fear of being disloyal to the seller. The subagent would feel an ethical discomfort if, in his or her opinion, the seller's listing was overpriced, the seller's terms were unreasonable or there were better properties available. Should seller's subagents withhold their opinion because of the duty of loyalty to the seller?
- Under the NAR® Code of Ethics & Standard of Practice 22-1, a subagent of the seller must immediately disclose all pertinent facts to the listing broker both before and after the contract is signed. TREC Rules require full disclosure of all material information to a client. This includes information about the buyer's ability to pay, the buyer's plans to resell for a profit or the buyer's willingness to offer a higher price. This can have a chilling effect on the working relationship with the buyer.
- Seller's subagents know there is a likelihood that they may not be told all the pertinent facts about the property or a seller. Because the subagent is potentially liable for errors of the listing broker, the subagent either accepts this liability or conducts an independent investigation to try to verify the information received from the listing office. The competent listing broker and seller are unlikely to tell the subagent anything that they do not want the buyer to hear.
- The subagent has no contractual relationship with the seller and cannot sue the seller if the seller cancels the sale and the listing broker elects not to pursue the seller for the commission. Nor is he or she protected if the listing agent breaches his or her fiduciary duties to the seller and the seller refuses to pay the listing broker. If the listing broker's listing is invalid or unenforceable and the seller refuses to pay, then the subagent will get part of nothing.

Level of Service

To make an informed decision to act as a subagent, the real estate licensee must understand the different levels of services rendered to a client and to a customer. A real estate licensee often decides to treat the buyer as a customer, in which case a subagency relationship with the seller may be appropriate. Occasionally, however, a licensee may want to represent and negotiate for a particular buyer as a client, in which case subagency with the seller is not appropriate. This is more likely when the buyer is a former client or a quality prospect, one whom the licensee wants to represent and does not want to lose. To gain a better understanding of the key concept of client-level service as compared to customer-level service, compare the following two situations.

SITUATION 1: *George, a former client, refers Harry to Sally of Bay Realty. Harry is interested in looking at expensive homes. Bay Realty has no high-priced listings, but there are several expensive homes listed in the local MLS. Harry mentions that he has talked to five other brokers and will be talking to several others. Sally decides to work with Harry on a customer basis. Sally shows Harry a property listed in the MLS with Sam of Main Realty and Harry decides to buy it.*

QUESTION: *In the course of negotiations, Sally deals with a number of important items, such as (1) price and appraised value; (2) seller carryback financing; (3) earnest money, amount and default remedies; (4) condition of property; (5) contingencies; (6) fixtures; and (7) inventory. How should Sally deal with each item, recognizing that her primary allegiance is to the seller?*

DISCUSSION: *Sally must be honest with Harry and make appropriate disclosures; as a subagent of the seller, however, Sally owes a duty of loyalty only to the seller and a much higher degree of skill, care and disclosure to the seller than to the buyer. Sally should handle each item as follows:*

1. Price and appraised value. *Sally must try to obtain the highest price and best terms for the seller consistent with the seller's preferred terms. Sally should not show Harry a competitive market analysis (CMA) and probably is not obligated to disclose any previous lower appraised value. Sally should not suggest nor encourage starting with a low offer to test the seller. She has a legal and ethical obligation to attempt to get the best transaction possible for the seller.*
2. Seller carryback financing. *While Sally can mention the types of provisions commonly found in mortgages, she should not encourage terms unfavorable to the seller. Sally should encourage the seller to request a financial statement and credit report on Harry and point out any negative features of the buyer's qualifications to the seller, such as repeated late payments.*
3. Earnest money. *Sally should try to obtain a sufficient amount of earnest deposit to protect the seller in case of default. The seller should have the choice of remedies in the event of the buyer's default and should not be limited only to retention of earnest money. As mentioned previously, in Texas, under the most recent TREC residential earnest money contract form it is now the buyer's duty, not the real estate licensee's duty, to deposit the earnest money with the escrow agent.*
4. Condition of property. *Sally should disclose all known and reasonably discoverable material defects and inform Harry that he is responsible for inspecting the property to make sure it meets his specifications. If appropriate, Sally might be obligated to suggest that the seller use a detailed and properly worded as-is clause to limit the seller's exposure to liability for obvious defects in a run-down property. Sally should suggest that the*

seller get the exact wording from his attorney. As-is is not a defense against deceptive trade practices or not revealing defects that are known by either the seller or the seller's agents.

5. Contingencies. *Sally should make certain that contingencies are worded clearly. If Harry insists on language unfavorable to the seller, such as an unlimited right to extend the closing date pending loan approval, Sally must point this out to the seller. In fact, Sally has a duty to the seller equal to that of Sam, the listing broker, to point out any known problem areas in the offer. Sally must advise the seller, usually through the listing broker, her opinion as to the reasonableness of the offer. Any doubts should be shared with Sally's client, the seller. Sally may need to advise the seller, through Sam or with Sam present, to consider making a counteroffer with time limits for performance of the contingency or with a 72-hour right of first refusal, in case the seller receives another offer during the contingency period. However, to avoid a charge of unauthorized practice of law, neither Sam nor Sally should draft any language regarding contingencies or conditions in contracts that affect the legal rights of the parties to the contract. They should stick to using TREC-promulgated addenda or recommend the parties get legal counsel on the wording. [*See 22 *TAC §537.11(b),(c) and (d) for more detail on this issue.]*

6. Fixtures. *Sally must point out to the seller any personal property included in Harry's offer that is not included in the listing, such as a portable microwave oven or a satellite dish.*

7. Other items. *Sally must be careful not to disclose facts that may compromise the seller's position (e.g., that the seller is near foreclosure or bankruptcy or that the property is overpriced). However, Sally must disclose to Harry any material conditions that may affect value or desirability, such as building code violations or lack of legal access, about which Sally actually knows or reasonably should know.*

Sally, as well as Sam, must disclose to the seller such pertinent facts as a proposed favorable rezoning that may increase the value of the property, that Harry has a resale buyer lined up once the property has been subdivided, that Harry is the brother of Sally, that Harry is willing to pay higher than the offering price or that the undisclosed buyer is a business competitor of the seller and is using Harry as a straw man to make the offer to buy.

Sally cannot agree to accept bonus money from Harry for obtaining a reduction in the listed price. Nor can she consider offers of future listings of Harry's five rental properties if she'll treat him right on this deal.

Sally must respond as accurately as she can to Harry's questions about easements, loans or restrictions on the property. Sally might give Harry copies of all relevant documents, such as loan assumption papers, declaration of restrictions, title reports, easements and deeds. Sally should be careful not to act as Harry's adviser in interpreting such documents, although Sally can suggest that Harry have other experts review these documents on his behalf. Sally should be careful to follow through on promises she or the seller makes, such as promises to obtain adequate insurance coverage for Harry or to make necessary repairs. Failure to do as promised could result in the seller being liable for Sally's carelessness (for example, if the uninsured home were to burn to the ground two days after closing).

SITUATION 2: *George refers Betty to Sally of Bay Realty. Betty is interested in looking at expensive homes. Betty says she wants someone to represent her best interests and, if she works well with Sally, Betty will purchase other expensive homes through Sally. Sally decides to work with Betty on a client basis. Betty indicates she is willing to pay Sally for her help and advice or to see that she is paid by the seller as a condition of any subsequent contract. She signs an exclusive buyer representation agreement. Sally shows Betty a country property listed in the MLS with Sam of Main Realty and Betty decides to buy it. Sally properly notifies Sam that she disclaims any subagency to Sam and that she and Bay Realty represent the buyer and not the seller.*

QUESTION: *In the course of negotiations, Sally deals with a number of important items, such as: (1) price and appraised value; (2) seller carryback financing; (3) earnest money; amount and default remedies; (4) condition of property; (5) contingencies; and (6) fixtures and inventory. How should Sally deal with each item, recognizing that her primary allegiance is to Betty?*

DISCUSSION: *Sally must be honest and make appropriate disclosure to the seller; as an agent of Betty, however, she owes a greater duty of skill, care and disclosure to protect Betty's best interests. Sally can advise Betty how to persuade the seller to modify the terms and reduce the selling price and what Betty's alternative courses of action are. Sally should handle each item as follows:*

1. Price and appraised value. *Sally should analyze the property and the seller's position so as to obtain the lowest realistic price for Betty. She should do a CMA on the property and should consider getting Betty's permission to submit the CMA along with any lower offer on the property. She may ask to see any appraisals and may suggest obtaining another appraisal to support a lower price offer. Sally, as a buyer's broker, is legally negotiating with the seller for a lower price. She would not be as a subagent. In a buyer's market, Sally might suggest that Betty prepare two offers and not reveal the higher offer unless and until the seller rejects the first offer. A subagent who did that would breach his or her fiduciary duties.*

2. Seller carryback financing. *Sally need not suggest that Betty submit tax returns and a credit report unless these are requested by the seller. Sally can suggest the following financing terms, all of which favor Betty: no due on sale clause; no prepayment penalty; liberal grace periods and minimal late charges; default remedies limited to judicial foreclosure with no deficiency against Betty (non-recourse); deferred interest; and reinstatement of the loan any time up to the foreclosure sale by payment of past due amounts (no acceleration).*

3. Earnest money. *Sally can suggest that the standard purchase contract be changed so that retention of the earnest money is the seller's sole remedy in the event of Betty's default, but she should have Betty consult an attorney to draft such language. Sally can also suggest that the earnest money be relatively modest or be reflected in an unsecured note.*

4. Condition of property. *Sally might suggest the use of a property inspection clause that makes the purchase contingent on Betty's satisfaction, using, of course, the TREC-required forms. Sally could suggest a clause requiring*

that the seller pay for a home protection plan; give written warranties regarding roofing, plumbing and termites; or warrant the information on a comprehensive property condition form that covers significant property features.

5. Contingencies. *Sally can suggest that contingencies be worded in such a way that Betty can waive the contingency and proceed to close, even though the contingency cannot be met (for example, loan not approved or rezoning not obtained). Sally can provide that Betty be given a generous time in which to perform any obligations leading up to closing. She should, however, be very careful not to engage in the unauthorized practice of law when dealing with contingencies and use TREC-promulgated addenda when appropriate.*
6. Fixtures. *Sally may advise Betty to include in Betty's offer additional personal property for the same purchase price, such as paintings and Oriental rugs. Sally should review any written inventory list before the offer is prepared and check to see that no substitution of items occurs.*
7. Other items. *As a buyer's broker, Sally must be careful not to reveal to the seller or listing broker facts regarding Betty's bargaining position, such as plans to buy adjoining parcels or adjoining condominium apartment units or that there is a resale buyer in the wings. There is no duty to disclose the name of the buyer or the fact that Sally is lending Betty money to make the down payment. However, in Texas, if Sally is being paid by Betty and expects to also be paid by Sam, that fact must be clearly disclosed and consented to by all parties or Sally or Bay Realty could face TREC Disciplinary Hearings and loss of license. [TRELA §15(a)(6)(D)]*

Sally must use her skill to research and investigate the contemplated acquisition and must advise Betty of any facts relevant to the purchase decision that can be used to negotiate better terms (for example, the seller is near foreclosure, is filing for divorce or has already bought a new home; the property is about to be rezoned; the neighbors are unruly; or the house was burglarized four times last year).

Sally can accept an incentive fee for obtaining a reduction in the listed price. But again, if Sally is receiving compensation from more than one party in the transaction, that fact must be consented to by all parties.

Sally must do more than produce copies of relevant documents for Betty. She must be sure Betty understands the impact on her purchase decision of key provisions in the documents. If she feels it is necessary, Sally should recommend that Betty obtain legal, title or property inspection advice from outside experts.

Sally has a duty to express any doubts she may have about the suitability of the property for Betty, especially if she feels that the property is, in Sally's opinion, overpriced.

In general, Sally may be more comfortable with Betty as a client than she is with Harry as a customer in disclosing to Betty every bit of information known to her. Sally does not decide which fact may or may not be important to Betty in making a decision to buy. With Harry, on the other hand, she may face difficult disclosure decisions. For instance, must she tell Harry about the opera singer next door who practices at 5 A.M., the poorly designed traffic flow of the house, the inadequate storage or that there have been newspaper articles about a new highway to be located nearby? Would disclosure of these negative features to Harry violate Sally's fiduciary duty to act in the best interests of the seller? This is Sally's dilemma when working with a customer. How far can she go in making disclosures and still not act contrary to the best interest of the seller?

The distinction between providing customer-level service and client-level service is further illustrated by the comparison chart shown as Figure 5.2. Imagine that you are working with two buyers on separate types of property. One buyer, your customer, is taking a great deal of your time and effort, but isn't sure about buying at the present time and insists on working with other brokers as well. You are giving a considerable amount of free service, hoping, of course, that he or she will eventually buy through you. The other buyer, your client, has agreed to work with you exclusively. Do you provide the same level of service to each buyer?

Subagency Advantages and Disadvantages

Some of the advantages of subagency are:

- Subagency established the traditional basis for a cooperating broker to be compensated.
- With subagency there is no need to obtain written agreement from buyer as is required by law in a dual agency.
- The customer may be advantaged by not being contractually bound to use only one broker to assist him or her or to have to pay for assistance the customer may never utilize.

Some of the disadvantages of subagency are:

- The seller's subagent must give a disclosure notice to buyer customers, potentially causing them to seek someone who can legally represent their interests. Less frequently, any buyer's subagent must also give any seller customer the same required notice.
- A subagent may find it too easy to act like the customer's agent, misleading the customer that he or she is a client, thus risking the creation of an undisclosed dual agency.
- The seller and listing broker might be liable for acts of seller's subagent.
- The subagent owes fiduciary duties to the listing broker and an unknown seller.
- Confusing relationships, disclosures and conflicts arise if the licensee acts as subagent with one buyer and buyer's agent with another buyer on the same property.

SUMMARY

In the majority of residential real estate transactions, the buyer is produced by a broker other than the listing broker. It is important to make an early decision about whether this other broker is a subagent of the seller or an agent of the buyer or expects to be a dual agent. This will depend on whether subagency was offered and whether it was accepted. If accepted, then the subagent owes client-level services to the seller and customer-level services to the buyer.

Figure 5.2 Customer-Level vs. Client-Level Service

THE SELLING BROKER

Customer-Level Service as Subagent	*Client-Level Service as Buyer's Broker*
RESPONSIBILITIES	
Be honest with buyer but owe greater responsibility to seller, including duty of skill and care to promote and safeguard seller's best interest.	Be honest with seller but owe greater responsibility to buyer, including duty of skill and care to promote and safeguard buyer's best interest.
EARNEST MONEY DEPOSIT	
Collect amount sufficient to protect seller.	Suggest minimum amount, perhaps a note; put money in interest-bearing account; suggest that forfeiture of earnest money be sole remedy if buyer defaults.
SELLER FINANCING	
Can discuss, but should not encourage, financing terms and contract provisions unfavorable to seller, such as (1) no due-on-sale clause, (2) no deficiency judgment (nonrecourse), (3) unsecured note. If a corporate buyer, suggest seller require personal guaranty.	Suggest terms in best interest of buyer, such as low down payment, deferred interest, long maturity dates, no due-on-sale clause, long grace period, nonrecourse.
DISCLOSURE	
Disclose to seller pertinent facts (which might not be able to disclose if a buyer's broker) such as (1) buyer's willingness to offer higher price and/or better terms, (2) buyer's urgency to buy, (3) buyer's plans to resell at profit or resubdivide to increase value, (4) buyer is a relative of broker.	Disclose to buyer pertinent facts (which might not be able to disclose if subagent of seller) such as (1) seller near bankruptcy or foreclosure, (2) property overpriced, (3) other properties available at a better buy, (4) negative features, such as poor traffic flow, (5) construction of chemical plant (for example) down street that may affect property value.
NONDISCLOSURE	
Refrain from disclosing to buyer facts that may compromise seller's position (seller's pending divorce, for example) unless under a legal duty to disclose (zoning violation, for example).	Refrain from disclosing to seller facts regarding buyer's position, such as buyer has options on three adjoining parcels. No duty to disclose name of buyer or that broker is loaning buyer money to make down payment.
PROPERTY CONDITION	
Suggest use of as-is clause, if appropriate, to protect seller (still must specify hidden defects).	Require that seller sign property condition statement and confirm representations of condition; require soil, termite inspections, if appropriate; look for negative features and use them to negotiate better price and terms.
DOCUMENTS	
Give buyer a copy of important documents, such as mortgage to be assumed, declaration of restrictions, title report, condominium bylaws and house rules.	Research and explain significant portions of important documents affecting transaction, such as prepayment penalties, subordination, right of first refusal; refer buyer to expert advisers when appropriate.
NEGOTIATION	
Use negotiating strategy and bargaining talents in seller's best interest.	Use negotiating strategy and bargaining talents in buyer's best interest.

Figure 5.2 (Continued)

Customer-Level Service as Subagent	*Client-Level Service as Buyer's Broker*
SHOWING	
Show buyer properties in which broker's commission is protected, such as in-house or MLS-listed properties. Pick best times to show property. Emphasize attributes and amenities.	Search for best properties for buyer to inspect, widening marketplace to for sale by owner, lender-owned (REO), probate sales and unlisted properties. View property at different times to find negative features, such as evening noise, afternoon sun, traffic congestion.
PROPERTY GOALS	
Find buyer the type of property buyer seeks; more concerned with *sale* of seller's property that fits buyer's stated objectives.	Counsel buyer as to developing accurate objectives; may find that buyer who wants apartment building might be better with duplex at half the price or that buyer looking for vacant lot would benefit more from an investment in improved property.
OFFERS	
Can help prepare and transmit buyer's offer on behalf of seller; must reveal to seller that buyer has prepared two offers, in case first offer not accepted.	Help buyer prepare strongest offer; can suggest buyer prepare two offers and have broker submit lower offer first without revealing fact of second offer.
POSSESSION DATES	
Consider what is best date for seller in terms of moving out, notice to existing tenants, impact on insurance and risk of loss provision.	Consider what is best date for buyer in terms of moving in, storage and favorable risk of loss provision if fire destroys property prior to closing.
DEFAULT	
Discuss remedies upon default by either party. Point out to seller any attempt by buyer to limit liability (nonrecourse, deposit money is sole liquidated damages).	Suggest seller's remedy be limited to retention of deposit money; consider having seller pay buyer's expenses and cancellation charges if seller defaults.
BIDDING	
Can bid for own account against buyer/customer but should disclose to buyer and seller.	Cannot bid for own account against buyer/client.
EFFICIENCY	
Don't expend much time and effort, as in an open listing, because in competition with the listing broker, seller and other brokers to sell buyer a property before someone else does.	Work at an exclusive listing efficiency, realizing that broker's role is to assist buyer in locating and acquiring best property, not to sell buyer any *one* property.
APPRAISAL	
Unless asked, no duty to disclose low appraisal or fact broker sold similar unit yesterday for $10,000 less.	Suggest independent appraisal be used to negotiate lower price offer; review seller's comparables from buyer's perspective.
BONUS	
Cannot agree to accept bonus from buyer for obtaining reduction in listed price.	Can receive incentive fee for negotiating reduction in listed price.
TERMINATION	
Easier to terminate a subagency relationship (as when broker decides to bid on property).	Legal and ethical implications of agency relationship and certain duties may continue even after clearly documented termination.

SUGGESTIONS FOR BROKERS

When acting as the non-listing or other broker, decide if you prefer to represent the buyer or to represent the seller as a subagent or want to try to be a dual agent or non-agent middleman. Choose what works best for you and, to be safe, get the informed written consent of all parties to act in that manner. Note that the offer of subagency is no longer automatic and, even if given, offers of subagency can be rejected. Because principals may incur some liability by the acts of their subagents, listing brokers should tell sellers of the risks, as well as the benefits, of using subagents.

KEY POINTS

- A seller's subagent owes a general duty of fairness and honesty to the buyer (customer) but owes full fiduciary duties to the seller (client).
- Under MLS, subagency is no longer automatic; it is optional whether subagency is offered and a buyer's agent is free to reject an offer of subagency.
- As a matter of routine, the listing office should clarify subagency status of any other broker.
- Some brokers don't feel very effective as a subagent, especially if they favor the buyer in the transaction.
- Some cooperating brokers will prefer to treat certain buyers as customers and thus subagency to the seller is the appropriate relationship.
- It is easy to appear to treat the buyer as a client, leading the buyer to believe he or she is a client, and thus create an accidental undisclosed dual agency.

QUIZ

1. The listing broker can direct a cooperating broker acting as a subagent to do all of the following *except:*

   a. register buyers to lessen procuring cause problems for the listing broker.
   b. show the property only in the evening.
   c. obtain earnest deposits only in the form of cashier's or certified checks.
   d. act as a fiduciary to the buyer.

2. In the typical MLS transaction, prior to January 1, 1994, which agent owed primary loyalty to the buyer?

   a. Selling agent
   b. Listing agent
   c. Both a and b
   d. Neither a nor b

3. George lists his house with Sally of Bay Realty, a member of the local Board of REALTORS® MLS. Subagency is offered and not disclaimed. Betty arrives in town and goes to Jeff of South Side Realty for help in buying a home. Jeff shows her George's house and helps Betty with an offer, which is accepted by George. Who does Jeff primarily represent?

   a. George
   b. Betty
   c. Sally
   d. The MLS

4. Using the facts in Question 3, who does the MLS represent?

   a. Betty
   b. George
   c. Bay Realty
   d. No one

5. A buyer asks a cooperating broker, who is the subagent of the listing broker, whether the seller would accept $4,000 less than the asking price. The listing broker already has told the cooperating broker subagent that the seller will take $5,000 less. Which is the best response for the cooperating broker?

   a. "Go ahead and make the offer, because the seller needs to sell fast before the bank forecloses."
   b. "Go ahead and make the offer and we'll see what the seller says. But remember, you may want to make your very best offer the first time because we don't discuss the existence or non-existence of other offers."
   c. "I can't present an offer less than the asking price."
   d. "If I get the seller to accept this low offer, I want a $1,000 bonus. But remember, you may want to make your very best offer the first time because we don't discuss the existence or non existence of other offers."

DISCUSSION QUESTIONS

1. Does a subagent owe the seller any different fiduciary duties than those owed by the listing broker?
2. Can the subagent sue the seller for a commission if the seller defaults and the listing broker elects not to sue? Why or why not?
3. What are the pros and cons of a seller offering subagency to cooperating brokers?
4. What are some of the differences between client-level services and customer-level services?
5. Do you feel more effective as a real estate agent working with a buyer when you are a subagent or a buyer's broker?

CHAPTER

6

BUYER AGENCY

Buyer agency exists when the broker represents the buyer exclusively in the real estate transaction. Buyer agency is not a revolutionary business practice. Brokers have for decades been employed to represent buyers. Buyer representation has been practiced in commercial real estate transactions regularly for the better part of this century. Brokers also have represented themselves, their business ventures, their relatives and undisclosed principals in the acquisition of real estate. Still, the buyer usually does not employ a broker under written contract to represent the buyer in the selection, negotiation or acquisition of real estate. However, for the most part, brokers have generally treated, theoretically at least, buyers as customers, not as clients.

Consumers often see that they can benefit from client-quality representation, whether they are buyers or sellers. In the 1970s and 1980s, some residential brokers began to offer their services to buyers. To this rapidly growing market segment, many brokers now offer client-level service to the right buyer. Other brokers continue to offer only customer-level service to buyers. Many licensees do not understand the basic differences relative to conduct and duties in agency and dual agency. This chapter explores the factors that affect the broker's decision to treat certain buyers as clients rather than as customers or as one of two clients in a dual agency situation.

The contents of the chapter include:

Gross Sales Price
Procuring Cause
Purchase Agreement
Buyer's Broker Disclosures
To Buyer
To Seller or Listing Broker

DECIDING TO REPRESENT THE BUYER

Just because a prospective buyer enters a broker's office asking to see homes for sale, the broker does not necessarily have to represent the buyer in an agency capacity, even if the broker specializes in representing buyers. A seller's broker spends a considerable amount of time leading up to the listing of the seller's property. Likewise, a buyer's broker spends time discussing the buyer's preferences and qualifications.

In some cases, a broker may not feel comfortable in a fiduciary relationship with a particular buyer. This may be because of pre-existing agency relationships the company has with sellers or because of an analysis of this particular buyer in terms of his or her cash, credit or capacity to buy, seriousness in buying or incompatible personality traits. Nevertheless, the broker may still want to show that same buyer, as a customer, properties listed in-house. In addition, some brokers choose to spend time showing a buyer properties listed in the MLS in which the broker accepts the offer to act as a subagent of the seller. It is not necessary that a broker create an agency relationship to help a buyer locate a property.

The professional broker recognizes that adequately representing a buyer is an enormous responsibility. The broker is held to a higher standard of care in working with a client than with a customer. If the buyer feels the broker has given poor advice, the buyer may threaten to sue the broker for breach of fiduciary duty. The buyer might ask, "Who was it that got me into this deal, anyway?" Deciding to offer client-level services, whether the client is the seller or the buyer, is a serious business decision with significant legal and economic consequences. It is for this reason that many brokers work with most buyer prospects on a customer-level basis and chose to work with only select buyers on a client-level basis.

Factors to Consider

There is nothing to stop brokers from showing properties to buyers as clients, provided the brokers clarify their role early in the transaction. The broker should decide, disclose and obtain necessary consents to act whether he or she is an agent of the buyer, a subagent of the seller or a licensee not acting in an agency capacity for either party yet rendering specified services to one or both (in a finder or transaction broker capacity).

In deciding whether to represent the buyer, the broker should keep several points in mind:

- The broker, not the licensed associate of the broker, is the primary agent of the buyer. If the broker represents the seller, dual agency questions will arise if a broker's licensed associate acts in such a way as to give the impression that he or she represents the buyer. As with seller's listings, if the salesperson who obtained a buyer's representation agreement leaves the brokerage firm, the agreement remains with the firm. A buyer's representation agreement can't be automatically transferred to a new employing broker of the former associate.

- The real estate agent can, with proper disclosures, provide valuable services to a buyer without creating an agency relationship. This is especially true in the in-house sale situation. Real estate firms that wish to avoid dual agency develop ways to accommodate some of the needs of buyers in a seller-oriented service business without crossing into agency representation of buyers.
- Few brokers are exclusively buyer's brokers. Even though some brokers start out representing buyers only, they often find that satisfied buyers eventually turn into sellers and want the broker to list their property for sale. One reason that single agency brokerage practice developed was to enable the agent to represent either the buyer or the seller in a given transaction.
- Out of ten unlisted or uncontracted prospective buyer customers working with a real estate licensee, only one or two may actually buy through the licensee. The percentage of buyers signed up under exclusive buyer representation agreements who actually buy, using the license's services as an agent, is reportedly much greater. While the real estate licensee may work with fewer buyers in a given time period under this contractual agency scenario, the time spent is often more productive.
- Buyer's brokers can, with proper authority, appoint subagents to help in the search for the right property. This is especially useful in long-distance transactions, such as with employees of nationwide companies who frequently are transferred and relocated.

MYTHS ABOUT BUYER AGENCY

Early on, there were certain myths that created obstacles to the widespread acceptance of representing buyers as clients. Exclusive buyer's brokers and single agency practitioners recognized that these myths were unfounded. Recognition of buyer brokerage as a viable business arrangement by the NAR® has helped to dispel these myths, but some survive, such as:

- Buyer agency is illegal.
- Buyer agency is prohibited by MLS rules.
- Buyer agency does not permit the seller to pay the commission nor does it allow the listing broker to split commissions with the buyer's agent.
- Buyer agency is not recognized by lenders.
- Buyer agency increases the risk of procuring cause disputes.
- Buyer agency is too complicated for the average buyer or seller to understand.
- Buyer agency must be created by written agreement in order to be lawful.

THE CREATION OF BUYER AGENCY

A buyer agency relationship can be created by verbal agreement or by implication and may be expressed orally or in writing. Texas does not require any real estate agency agreement to be in writing, except dual agency agreements, which must conform at least minimally to Section 15C of the License Act. The requirement that some note or memorandum of an agreement to pay a commission be in writing is a limiting requirement only if the Texas broker wishes to pursue legal action for the recovery of any agreed-upon commission. While a written agreement is certainly preferable for any type of agency agreement, many express buyer agency and listing agreements are oral with written confirmation noted in the sales contract.

Listing (Representation) Agreements

Most states require that an agreement to compensation be in writing before the broker can sue to collect from the principal for services rendered in connection with the sale or purchase of real estate. However, no other part of the agency or listing agreement has to be in writing. There is no legal requirement of the law for two or more brokers who want to split a fee to have to put the agreement in writing.

Even in those states that do not require a written listing agreement, it is good business practice for a broker to obtain a written understanding that the broker is entitled to a commission and have the agreement signed by both the buyer and the broker. A written buyer's broker agreement or buyer representation agreement could be important when a seller refuses to permit a fee split or in a transaction such as a FSBO. A written agreement between the buyer broker and buyer client is quite helpful to the buyer's broker in the event a listing broker or seller subagent raises a procuring cause issue. It can also be quite helpful if two brokers execute an Agreement Between Brokers prior to the submission of the offer to purchase. The agreement between such brokers that appears at the bottom of a standard TREC contract form should spell out under what conditions and in what amounts any compensation will be paid from the listing broker to the other broker.

A buyer's broker should clarify the types of services to be offered to the buyer client (in addition to the traditional services rendered by real estate licensees to buyers as customers). These could include such tasks as the structuring of the transaction, investment analysis, assistance in development, assistance in planning and financing and negotiations for the acquisition. The buyer's broker should point out to his or her buyer client the possible need for the buyer to consult legal, tax and other expert advisers.

Buyer representation agreements can take many forms, depending on what the buyer and the buyer's broker want and are able to negotiate. Even if a broker decided not to work as an agent with the buyer, the broker and the buyer may enter into a general written understanding of their working relationship. This can be especially useful in large real estate firms that have many listings and need to avoid dual agency claims. Under one arrangement, the buyer agrees to work exclusively with the broker and recognizes that the broker is rendering various specified services to the buyer/customer as an agent or subagent of the seller and that the broker will be paid by the seller (see Appendix B).

Single Property. A broker may also wish to contractually represent a buyer with respect to a single property only. This is similar to obtaining a single party listing (One-time Listing Agreement) from a seller for the sale of an otherwise unlisted property to a specific buyer. To contractually represent (list) a buyer in this case, the broker should prepare a brief letter agreement after first determining that the buyer is unaware of any similar property in the general location. For example, the broker might ask whether the buyer had previously been shown any large apartment buildings in the midtown area. If not, then the buyer agrees to pay a fee to the broker if the buyer purchases a specific property. The broker does not reveal the exact location of this property until the agreement is signed. This technique has proved helpful when the seller refuses to list a particular commercial property and the buyer does not want client status in regard to any other property except the one to be shown.

Buyer's brokers frequently develop their own buyer representation agreement forms. Brokers who drafts their working agreements without good legal counsel may be taking unnecessary risks, but they are not considered to be engaged in the unauthorized practice of law by so doing. In commercial transactions that involve large commissions, brokers often have their attorney prepare a comprehensive listing agreement. TREC has no state-approved or promulgated form for agency agreements, listing agreements, buyer representation agreements or dual agency agreements. However, TAR® and local REALTOR® associations do have such forms for their members only.

In some residential real estate transactions, the buyer's broker's form is not comprehensive, such as may be found in big commercial transactions or the more carefully crafted agreements of the exclusive buyer's broker firms. These more generalized agreements are designed to encourage trust and understanding but typically do not to enable the real estate agent to prevail in a lawsuit. The control of the client arises from the trust relationship itself, not from a supposedly ironclad agreement. Still, it should be specific on essential items to minimize misunderstandings and disputes. Some of the key points to consider in any buyer's broker listing agreement are exclusivity, termination date, conflicts of interest, role of the broker and fees. More comprehensive buyer representation agreements are as protective as well written exclusive-right-to-sell listing agreements. In fact, most have an enforceable exclusive-right-to-purchase clause that allows the broker to sue the buyer for compensation if the buyer buys a property without compensating the broker during the period of the agreement, even if the broker did not show the buyer the property. A sample is shown in Figure 6.1.

Exclusive-Right-to-Purchase. Novice buyer brokers are sometimes uncomfortable asking buyers to sign an exclusive representation agreement. Some develop a non-exclusive agreement containing an automatic right-to-terminate provision. More experienced buyer's brokers have already developed their counseling skills to a point where they are as comfortable in securing a buyer's broker exclusive representation agreement as seller's agents are in securing from sellers an exclusive-right-to-sell listing. Brokers know that an exclusive-right-to-sell or exclusive-right-to-buy listing means better control over the transaction and provides a better means for the buyer's broker to protect his or her investment of time, energy and skill. They also know that a buyer broker's open buyer agency agreement can lead to the same type of procuring cause disagreements between themselves and buyers as in seller open-listing situations. The buyer has to make the same choice as the seller in an open listing: Does the buyer client want more brokers working on his or her behalf but with less commitment, motivation or knowledge of the buyer's needs? It is also much more important for the broker to have exclusive agency rights when the broker is compensated by a contingent fee rather than by a hourly fee.

Termination Date. Both the broker and the buyer should be clear as to when the agency relationship will be terminated. A specific termination date on any listing contract is required by Texas state licensing law. The expiration period is fully negotiable and can be longer or shorter than in a listing agreement with a seller. If the broker wants to be covered for a sale that takes place on a certain property after the listing expires, then an extending carryover clause should be inserted to specify the protection period and the procedures for registering prospects. The agreement may be terminated by mutual consent.

Figure 6.1 Buyer Representation Agreement

EQUAL HOUSING OPPORTUNITY

TEXAS ASSOCIATION OF REALTORS®

BUYER/TENANT REPRESENTATION AGREEMENT
EXCLUSIVE RIGHT TO BUY(LEASE)

REALTOR®

THIS FORM IS FURNISHED BY THE TEXAS ASSOCIATION OF REALTORS® FOR USE BY ITS MEMBERS. USE OF THIS FORM BY PERSONS NOT MEMBERS OF THE TEXAS ASSOCIATION OF REALTORS® IS NOT AUTHORIZED.

1. **PARTIES:** The parties to this agreement are ____________________________ (Buyer/Tenant, hereafter referred to as Buyer) and ____________________________ (Broker). In consideration of services to be performed by Broker, Buyer appoints Broker as Buyer's sole and exclusive agent and grants to Broker the irrevocable and exclusive right to represent and assist Buyer in locating suitable real property to buy within the Market Area and negotiating the purchase, rental, lease, or acquisition of an ownership or equitable interest in real property within the Market Area. For the purpose of this agreement: (a) "Buyer" means buyer or tenant; (b) "buy", "purchase", or "acquire" means to buy, purchase, acquire, lease, or rent; (c) "purchase or acquisition" means a purchase, acquisition, lease, or rental; (d) "seller" means seller or landlord; and (e) "gross purchase or sales price" means gross purchase price, gross sales price, or total gross rentals to be paid during a lease term.

2. **MARKET AREA:** Market Area is defined as that area located within the perimeter boundaries of the following areas or counties: ____________________________ all within the State of Texas.

3. **TERM:** This agreement shall commence on the _______ day of ____________________, 19____ and shall terminate at 11:59 p.m. on the ______ day of ____________________, 19 ____ (termination date). However, if on the termination date there is a pending contract for the purchase of real property within the Market Area in effect between Buyer and a seller of such property and the transaction described in such a contract has not closed and funded, this agreement shall continue in effect until such time as the transaction has closed and funded or the transaction has otherwise terminated or within __________ days after the termination date of this agreement, whichever is earlier.

4. **BROKER'S OBLIGATIONS:** Broker shall: (a) use diligence in locating suitable real property within the Market Area; (b) represent and assist Buyer in negotiating the purchase or acquisition of suitable real property within the Market Area; and (c) use Broker's best efforts to procure the purchase or acquisition of suitable real property within the Market Area on terms acceptable to Buyer. Broker's duties to Buyer include loyalty, obedience, disclosure, confidentiality, due diligence and reasonable care, and accounting, subject to the terms, restrictions, or limitations as set forth in this agreement.

5. **BUYER'S OBLIGATIONS:** Buyer shall during the term of this agreement, including any renewals or extensions, conduct all negotiations and efforts to locate real property within the Market Area through Broker only, and shall refer to Broker all inquiries received from real estate brokers, salesmen, prospective sellers, or any other source. Buyer represents that Buyer is not now a party to a Buyer Representation Agreement with another broker for the purchase or acquisition of real property in the Market Area. Buyer represents that all information relating to Buyer's ability to purchase or acquire a property in the Market Area given by Buyer to Broker is true and correct.

6. **RETAINER:** Upon final execution of this agreement Buyer shall pay to Broker a non-refundable retainer for Broker's services in the amount of $________________________. THE RETAINER IS NOT REFUNDABLE with the exception that Broker shall refund the retainer to Buyer upon Broker's receipt of Broker's Compensation set forth in paragraph 7.

7. **BROKER'S COMPENSATION:** Broker's Compensation shall be paid as follows:

❑ (a) Fee or Commission paid by Buyer: Upon Buyer's purchase or acquisition of any real property in the Market Area during the term of this agreement, including any renewal or extension, Buyer shall pay Broker a fee of $___________________ or ________% (select only one) of the gross purchase or sales price of the purchased or acquired property in cash at closing or as otherwise specified herein: ____________________________ in the county in which the purchase or acquisition is closed. Broker's Compensation is earned when Buyer enters into a binding written contract for the purchase of real property within the Market Area and is payable upon closing or as otherwise specified or upon Buyer's default of such written contract.

❑ (b) Fee or Commission paid by Seller or Seller's Broker: Upon Buyer's purchase or acquisition of any real property in the Market Area during the term of this agreement, including any renewal or extension, Broker shall seek compensation in the amount of $_____________ or ______% (select only one) of the gross purchase or sales price of the real

Figure 6.1 (Continued)

property purchased or acquired from the seller or seller's broker. However, if a seller or seller's broker of a property Buyer desires to purchase or acquire refuses to compensate Broker in the amount specified in this paragraph, and Buyer agrees to purchase or acquire the property, Buyer shall pay Broker in cash at closing in the county in which the purchase or acquisition is closed the amount of compensation specified in this paragraph less any amounts received from the seller or seller's broker. Broker's Compensation is earned when Buyer enters into a binding written contract for the purchase of real property within the Market Area and is payable upon closing or upon Buyer's default of such written contract.

☐ (c) Other: ____
____.

Buyer shall pay Broker compensation at the rate of $____________ per hour (Broker's hourly rate) for Broker's services pursuant to this agreement payable when billed to Buyer. Compensation is earned when Broker's services are rendered. Any amounts paid to Broker prior to closing for Broker's hourly rate ☐ shall ☐ shall not be refunded to Buyer upon Broker's receipt of Broker's Compensation specified in subparagraph 7(a), (b), or (c). In the event Broker is to receive compensation greater than the amount specified in this agreement from any source, Broker shall retain the excess compensation. **NOTICE: §15(a)(6)(D) of the Real Estate License Act prohibits Broker from receiving compensation from more than one party except with the full knowledge and consent of all parties.**

8. **PROTECTION PERIOD:** If within _________ days after the termination date of this agreement (the Protection Period), Buyer enters into a contract to purchase or acquire a legal or equitable interest of real property within the Market Area which was called to the attention of Buyer by Broker, any other broker, or Buyer, during the term of this agreement Buyer shall pay Broker's Compensation specified in paragraph 7 in cash at closing, provided Broker, prior to or within five (5) days after the termination of this agreement, has sent to Buyer written notice specifying the addresses or locations of the properties which were called to the attention of Buyer by Broker, any other broker, or Buyer. If during the term of the Protection Period, Buyer has entered into another Buyer Represenation Agreement with another Texas-licensed real estate broker at the time the purchase or acquisition is negotiated, this paragraph shall not apply and Buyer shall not be obligated to pay Broker's Compensation.

9. **COOPERATING BROKER:** Buyer authorizes Broker to share or divide Broker's Compensation, on terms and conditions as Broker determines, with any licensed real estate broker or brokers who assist Broker in locating or acquiring real property for Buyer within the Market Area.

10. **BUYER'S IDENTITY:** Unless otherwise agreed in writing, Broker may disclose the identity of Buyer to a prospective seller or a seller's agent.

11. **COMPETING BUYERS:** Buyer acknowledges that Broker may represent other prospective buyers seeking to purchase properties that may meet Buyer's criteria. Buyer agrees that Broker may, during the term of this agreement or after its termination, represent such other prospective buyers, show the same properties to other prospective buyers shown to Buyer, and represent other prospective buyers in negotiations for the purchase of the same properties Buyer may seek to purchase. In the event Broker submits offers by competing buyers for the purchase or acquisition of the same property Buyer has offered or wishes to offer to purchase, Broker shall notify Buyer of the conflicting offers, but shall not disclose any material terms or conditions of any offers made by competing buyers. Buyer may object to the conflict and terminate this agreement in writing or waive any objections to any conflict by reason of competing buyers.

12. **CONFLICTS OF INTEREST AND MULTIPLE REPRESENTATION:** During the term of this agreement, Broker is Buyer's agent and shall represent the interests of Buyer in any negotiations for the purchase or acquisition of real property in the Market Area, unless Buyer authorizes Broker as set forth below, to represent both Buyer and a prospective seller of real property in the Market Area, in which event certain restrictions and limitations apply to Broker's representation of Buyer's interests.

Discussion of Agency Relationships: Buyer is advised that real estate brokers who hold themselves out as buyer brokers or buyer agents represent buyers. Real estate brokers who hold themselves out as listing brokers or listing agents represent sellers. Real estate brokers who hold themselves out as subagents represent sellers through cooperation with the listing broker. Buyer should know that Broker, as part of Broker's business, may work with both buyers and sellers and Broker may enter into buyer representation agreements to represent buyers and listing agreements to represent sellers. In the event Broker does work with both buyers and sellers, it is possible that one or more of the properties Broker has listed for sale, which are owned by persons Broker has agreed to represent, will meet Buyer's criteria and Buyer may be interested in looking at such properties. In such an event, Broker may be faced with a potential conflict of interest. The law in the State of Texas states that a broker may not act as an agent for more than one party to a transaction unless both parties consent to and authorize the broker to represent more than one party.

(TAR- 039) Rev. 9/7/93-SUB Initialed for Indentification by: ______, ______ Buyer ______Broker or Agent Page 2 of 4

Figure 6.1 (Continued)

To resolve potential conflicts of interests, Buyer and Broker agree to the following (choose either (a) or (b)):

☐ (a) Buyer Agency Only: Broker shall represent Buyer exclusively in any negotiations for the purchase or acquisition of property Buyer wishes to purchase. Buyer understands that (choose either (1) or (2)):

☐ (1) Broker exclusively represents buyers of real property and does not represent sellers of real property.

☐ (2) Broker does represent both buyers and sellers of real property, however, Broker shall not show to Buyer any properties Broker lists for sale. If Buyer desires to purchase a property Broker has listed for sale, Broker shall refer Buyer to another broker.

☐ (b) Dual Agency: Buyer authorizes Broker to show to Buyer properties which Broker has listed for sale. If Buyer wishes to purchase any property Broker has listed for sale, Buyer authorizes Broker to present to the seller any offers Buyer may wish to make, to assist in negotiations for the sale of property, and to act as an agent for both Buyer and the seller of any property Broker has listed for sale. Broker's Compensation shall be paid in accordance with the terms of this agreement. **In the event Broker acts as an agent for both the Buyer and the seller in the purchase or acquisition of real property within the Market Area, Broker (or any associates of Broker) shall:**

(1) not disclose to Buyer that the seller will accept a price less than the asking price unless otherwise instructed in a separate writing by the seller;

(2) not disclose to the seller that Buyer will pay a price greater than the price submitted in a written offer to the seller unless otherwise instructed in a separate writing from Buyer;

(3) not disclose any confidential information or any information the seller or Buyer specifically instructs Broker in writing not to disclose unless otherwise instructed in a separate writing by the respective party or required to disclose such information by law; and

(4) treat all parties to the transaction honestly and impartially so as not to favor one party or work to the disadvantage of any party.

Broker shall not knowingly, during the term of this agreement or after its termination, disclose information obtained in confidence from Buyer except as authorized by Buyer or as required by law. Broker shall not disclose to Buyer any information obtained in confidence regarding any other person Broker represents or may have represented except as required by law.

13. **SPECIAL PROVISIONS:**

14. **ESCROW AUTHORIZATION:** Buyer authorizes any escrow or closing agent authorized to close a transaction for the purchase or acquisition of real property contemplated in this agreement to collect and disburse to Broker the Broker's Compensation due under this agreement.

15. **DEFAULT:** Failure by either party to comply with this agreement shall be a default, and the non-defaulting party may seek any relief as provided by law. In the event of Buyer's default, Buyer shall be liable for any compensation Broker is entitled to receive under this agreement or the fair value of Broker's services rendered to the time of default.

16. **ATTORNEYS' FEES:** If Buyer or Broker is a prevailing party in any legal proceeding brought as a result of a dispute under this agreement, such party shall be entitled to recover from the non-prevailing party all costs of such proceeding and reasonable attorneys' fees. **NOTICE TO BUYER: It is the policy of the state of Texas to encourage the peaceable resolution of disputes through alternative dispute resolution procedures. The parties are encouraged to submit to mediation or arbitration (services which are provided by most Associations of REALTORS® and others) disputes which cannot be resolved in good faith through informal discussion.**

(TAR-039) Rev. 9/7/93 Initialed for Indentification by: ______, ______ Buyer ______ Broker or Agent Page 3 of 4

Figure 6.1 (Continued)

17. ACKNOWLEDGMENT, ENTIRE AGREEMENT, ASSIGNABILITY, BINDING EFFECT, AND SAVING CLAUSE: Buyer acknowledges that Buyer has read this agreement and understands its contents. This agreement contains the entire agreement between Buyer and Broker and cannot be changed except by written agreement. This agreement is binding upon the parties, their heirs, administrators, executors, successors, and assigns. This agreement may not be assigned by either party without the written approval of the other party. Should any clause in this agreement be found invalid or unenforceable by a court of law, the remainder of this agreement shall not be affected and all other provisions of this agreement shall remain valid and enforceable to the fullest extent permitted by law.

18. ADDITIONAL NOTICES TO BUYER:

(a) Fair housing laws require the Broker and Buyer to perform under this agreement without regard to race, color, religion, national origin, marital status, sex, handicap, or familial status.

(b) In the event Buyer agrees to purchase property, Buyer should have an abstract covering the property examined by an attorney of Buyer's choice or obtain a policy of title insurance.

(c) Broker Fees or commission rates are not fixed, controlled, recommended, suggested, or maintained by the Association of REALTORS®. The amount a Broker is paid is negotiable between the Broker and Buyer.

(d) Broker advises Buyer that residential service contracts (home warranties) are available from Residential Service Companies licensed under Article 6573b, Texas Civil Statutes. A residential service contract is an agreement whereby the residential service company may, under the terms of the agreement, repair or replace all or any part of the appliances, or electrical, plumbing, heating, cooling, or other systems of a property.

(e) Broker cannot give legal advice. This is intended to be a legally binding agreement. READ IT CAREFULLY. If you do not understand the effect of this agreement, consult your attorney BEFORE signing.

AGREED BETWEEN:

Broker ______ License No.	Buyer ______ Date
By: ______ Date	Buyer ______ Date
Address ______	Address ______
Phone: ______	Phone: ______

(TAR-039) Rev. 9/7/93 Page 4 of 4

Conflicts of Interest. A problem exists if the buyer wants to purchase a property already listed by the broker or another associate in the same office. If the broker has a buyer's representation agreement with the buyer, then under Texas law, all licensees associated with that broker also represent the buyer and must act in that buyer's best interest in any transaction. To attempt to avoid dual agency conflicts, the buyer's listing agreement may contain a withdrawal provision in which the buyer's listing agreement becomes, in effect, inapplicable to any such transaction in which a conflict arises. The buyer is free to seek outside counsel in making the offer and is not obligated to pay any fee to the broker who, in this case, is compensated by the seller. Another method to consider is renouncing one or the other agency relationship. Some brokers use the "LIFO" approach (last in, first out), in which the broker represents, for this transaction only, the buyer or the seller, depending on who signed the representation agreement first. The last one in can choose self-representation or find outside representation and is not obligated to pay the broker any fee. All of these approaches have risks in that once agency is begun is not simple to disengage one part of the relationship or its consequences.

Some brokerage firms have developed a practice of representing buyers in the purchase of all properties except those listed with the firm. In this fashion, the in-house listings are excluded first before buyer representation begins and dual agency problems are lessened. Other firms specializing in representing buyers take the position that they will not actively solicit listings to sell. They will, however, occasionally list a property for one of their satisfied buyer clients who now wants to sell a property. They will also register a seller's property with the understanding that these properties will be exposed to the broker's buyer clients. There is a clear disclaimer of agency with the seller and no fee is required to register the property.

Another conflict may arise when more than one buyer client is interested in the same property. This is the reverse of the situation of a listing broker working with a customer who is interested in more than one of the broker's listings in the same location. Some buyer representation agreements contain a disclosure that the buyer's agent may enter into agreements with other buyers to locate property and that it is possible for two or more buyers to be interested in the same property. If this should occur, the buyer's agent might first offer the property to the buyer with the earlier representation agreement. If the first buyer does not make an offer on the property, the opportunity will then be offered to the next buyer. Alternatively, the agreement could authorize the broker to show the property to all buyer clients with the agreement that: (1) none of the buyer clients will consider that to be a conflict of interest and (2) that all such multiple interest will be strictly confidential to the broker. Remember, in the real estate business there are no forms of agency so pure that potential conflicts of interest cannot arise. If recognized before they arise and agreed to as to how to handle the conflicts, serious problems might be avoided.

WORKING RELATIONSHIPS WITH BUYERS

Buyers as Customers

Not every buyer wants to be represented by an agent. Some buyers appreciate the flexibility of dealing with several brokers and avoiding commitments and loyalties to any one of the them. Such buyers work with brokers acquire enough facts to enable them to make a decision, such as information about property values and seller motivation. They may be unaware of any fiduciary duties owed to the seller or landlord by the broker, unless TREC Agency Disclosure Notice Number 3 has been clearly discussed and explained to them. Others enjoy the "free ride" given by many brokers, who each hope that the buyer will make an offer to purchase through him or her. Still other buyers prefer to deal directly with the listing broker, either because they hope to obtain some inside information that they can use to make the best deal or because they fear they may lose the opportunity to buy the house they really want if they make an offer through their own broker. This fear of missed opportunity may be based on the time factor involved in presenting an offer in a seller's market. Another concern is that the unprofessional listing broker might produce an equivalent or better offer in-house after having first seen the buyer's offer submitted by the buyer's broker.

Buyers as Clients

Some buyers and tenants want more than customer service. They need and want advice, something the listing broker, seller's subagent or dual agent ethically and legally cannot provide. Some want client-level service and they are willing to pay for it.

Agency Benefits to Buyer or Tenant

Some of the benefits to the buyer/tenant receiving client-level services are:

Tailored buyer representation contract. In a buyer/tenant representation agreement with the broker, the buyer can tailor the broker's services to meet the buyer's needs and adjust the compensation accordingly. This applies not only to large national companies seeking housing for relocated employees or sites for chainstores or restaurants, but also to purchasers seeking a residence or an investment opportunity. In some cases, the buyer has already identified the property and the financing and wants the broker to handle the negotiations.

Access to larger marketplace. In practice, traditional brokers frequently limit their search of properties to those properties in which the broker's commission is protected. This means that they limit their search to properties listed in-house or in the MLS. The buyer's broker whose guarantee of commission is protected, not necessarily paid, by a buyer client is motivated to show the buyer all available properties that meet his or her requirements, including:

- open listing properties;
- properties exclusively listed with other brokers;
- for-sale-by-owner properties;
- foreclosure and probate sales;
- sales by lenders of real estate owned properties;
- sales by trusts and pension plans;
- properties owned by a governmental agency; and
- properties not yet on market.

Stronger negotiating strategy. The buyer's broker views the entire transaction from the buyer's perspective, without the divided and diminished loyalty that would be demanded of a dual agent. The buyer is in a stronger negotiating position. Also, the buyer may want the protection of a broker in dealing with an unrepresented owner. Some buyers fear that the reason the owner did not list with a broker is because something is wrong with the property.

Fiduciary responsibility of broker. Under both state licensing and the common law, the buyer's broker is held to a higher standard of skill and care in dealing with the buyer than is a subagent of the seller or the seller's listing agent who works with the buyer on a customer basis. Buyer's brokers have an affirmative duty to their client to thoroughly investigate and completely disclose all facts that bear on the buyer's decision to buy. On the other hand, buyer brokers have a duty to be honest and deal fairly—not equally or impartially—with sellers but owe no duty to advise and counsel sellers. For example, if the buyer offers to pay a portion of the down payment by way of a note secured by a California property, the buyer broker would breach no duty by failing to advise the seller that California law does not permit a deficiency judgment on residential mortgages.

The buyer's broker is held to the same standard of performance in dealing with the buyer that the listing broker owes to the seller. There is nothing unique about the responsibility and duties of the buyer's broker. There is no new fiduciary duty or ethical responsibility that the buyer's broker must learn. What is different is the broker owes conventional common, statutory and administrative law fiduciary duties to a different group of participants, namely buyers. The quantity and quality of client-level service is at least the same that a listing broker would give sellers. It is simply the other side of the representation coin. Buyers are quite simply not legally entitled to this level of service unless they retain their own real estate broker. By Texas statute, no licensee is allowed to give this level of service if the licensee is attempting to be or becomes a dual agent. This is true regardless of whether the licensee began the relationship representing the buyer exclusively.

Confidentiality. Confidentiality can be especially important when the buyer wishes to remain anonymous.

Example:

Sarah, a famous movie star, considers purchasing a new mansion. If the seller learns the identity of the intended buyer, the seller may likely hold firm or increase the asking price. A buyer's broker acting for an undisclosed principal may be able to negotiate a better price and terms for an such anonymous buyer.

More counseling, less selling. The buyer can expect to receive more counseling, expert opinion, advocacy and advice regarding the acquisition decision as opposed to persuasion to buy. When a broker is hired by the seller under an exclusive-right-to-sell listing, the broker's emphasis is on selling the property. When a broker is hired by the buyer under an exclusive-right-to-represent agreement, the broker is not selling a house, he or she is assisting a buyer in purchasing a house. In a very real sense he or she is a purchasing agent, not a selling agent. The buyer's broker's emphasis is on assisting the client to evaluate different properties and alternative courses of action, then get the best deal possible once having elected to go forward with negotiations on a property.

A buyer's broker might recommend inspection of a home at random times of the day and perhaps check with the neighbors to gain more complete information about the property or the seller. Buyer's brokers do their best to find out things about the property that the seller or the listing broker might not want to disclose or might feel obligated to disclose, such as excess noise, sewage odors, high energy costs, traffic congestion or unauthorized seller improvements. Buyers also expect their broker to review any proposed contract to determine if there are any unfavorable provisions that could necessitate hiring a real estate attorney.

Benefits to Broker

The buyer's broker can expect certain benefits from an agency relationship with the buyers:

Greater client loyalty. Traditionally, real estate agents work with a "wandering" buyer on the chance of earning a fee, sometimes even if the chances are remote. With an exclusive-right-to-purchase representation agreement, the broker has greater control and little fear of losing the buyer to an owner or to another broker. Traditional brokers seldom take an open listing with the seller (oral or written).

Avoid conflict of loyalty. The buyer's broker should feel no ethical discomfort or hesitancy in withholding from the seller information on the buyer's future plans for the property, including immediate resale or obtaining options on adjoining properties. Nor should the buyer's broker be reluctant to disclose to the buyer the broker's opinion that the property is overpriced or that the seller's terms are unrealistic. As a matter of fact, he or she is duty-bound to express such opinions to a buyer client.

Within the bounds of honesty and fairness to the seller, the buyer's broker can develop with the buyer a negotiating strategy that promotes the buyer's best interest at all times and seeks to obtain reasonable concessions from the seller. Healthy and complete negotiations are not as likely in a traditional real estate transaction where one or both agents represent the seller's interests only. While the buyer and seller are not hostile in the sense of a plaintiff and defendant in a lawsuit, they do have competing interests. The buyer's broker will be able to represent the buyer's best interest in this spirit of competition while negotiating honestly to arrive at a transaction agreeable to both the buyer and the seller.

In addition to price, there are many other items to be negotiated in every transaction. These include initial and additional earnest money deposits, downpayment, seller financing, interest rate, due date, sales price, commissions, terms, home warranty, termite report, assessments, appraisal, closing costs, title report, possession date, impound, reserve or escrow accounts on the seller's loan in assumption situations, title and escrow agent, personal property and inventory, points, repairs, inspection contingencies, hazard insurance, default remedies, extensions and more. During the offer and counteroffer stage of the transaction, any one of these items can provide an opportunity for a conflict between the buyer and the seller or deal-making compromise. The buyer's broker is able to negotiate all of these items on the buyer's behalf. A listing agent, a cooperating broker acting as the seller's subagent or a dual agent do not have the legal ability to negotiate on the buyer's behalf.

No liability for acts of the listing broker. Because a buyer's broker has no agency relationship with either the seller or the listing broker, the buyer's broker is not vicariously liable for their acts. In addition, buyer's brokers tend either to verify information about the property given by the listing broker or require that the seller give certain warranties or representations concerning such conditions of a property as roof, plumbing and boundaries. This reduces the broker's exposure to claims for misrepresentation, for concealment of material defects or for failure to ascertain material facts. There is less chance of the buyer's broker being sued for things that are not the broker's fault. However, in Texas, the buyer's broker does have an increased responsibility to his or her buyer client to use due diligence to discover problems that may adversely affect the client.

FEE ARRANGEMENTS

An entire book could be written on all the possible methods of compensating a buyer's broker. It is important to keep in mind that the broker's first concern is to become comfortable with understanding the agency relationship that exists and the type of service to be provided. The mechanics of compensation seem to fall into place once the agency relationships are clearly understood. Often, the buyer's broker fee is paid out of the sales proceeds, either through an authorized commission split or through a credit from the seller to the buyer at closing.

Seller-oriented brokers can still benefit from understanding the methods by which buyer's brokers structure their compensation arrangements. Listing brokers will be receiving offers from buyers represented by their own brokers, so the listing broker should become acquainted with how the offers may be structured and how fees are handled. The following is a summary of how buyer's brokers can be paid for their services. The way in which fees are to be paid should be stated in writing and clearly understood well in advance to avoid potential conflict between the buyer and the broker.

Retainer Fee

Regardless of how the broker is compensated, some brokers feel more comfortable in obtaining advance payments. This can serve as a screening device for determining whether a buyer is serious about buying. However, some states have extensive restrictions on advance fees. (For example, in California the broker cannot withdraw monies from retainer trust accounts to cover hourly fees until several days after an accounting has been made to a client for services performed and statements must be sent every calendar quarter and upon termination.) In Texas, no such requirement exists, although TREC does caution against taking retainer fees. If a retainer fee is to be taken, some benefit or service must accrue to the person paying the fee, otherwise it may be considered as one of the two unconscionable acts under the Texas Deceptive Trade Practices and Consumer Protection Act. If no research is done for the client, no houses shown, no counseling and advising nor any other service performed, and the client cancels the agreement, then TREC recommends the refunding of the retainer fee.

If the retainer fee from the buyer is retained by the broker and the transaction closes with the buyer's broker being compensated from the seller's side of the transaction, the broker is technically receiving compensation from both parties, a fact which must be disclosed and consented to by all parties. Some broker's choose to refund the retainer fee upon closing to avoid this problem and make as much cash available for the buyer as possible. Tax counsel should be consulted regarding the deductibility of the retainer portion as a professional fee.

Seller-Paid Fee

There is no legal or ethical barrier to the seller paying the buyer's broker's fee or authorizing the listing broker to share fees with the buyer's broker. Either way is a matter of contract and may be handled in advance by appropriate language in both the seller's listing agreement and the buyer's representation agreement. There is substantial legal authority for the proposition that the payment of fees does not determine who an agent represents (see Appendix C). As long as the agency relationship is clear and explicit, it does not matter legally whether the buyer or the seller pays the fee. If, however, the agency is unclear, a court will likely consider the question of who paid the fee as an important factor in determining who is the principal of the agent.

There will be a period, especially in residential sales, in which the traditional commission-sharing arrangement between listing broker and other broker will likely be the accepted mode of compensation for the buyer's broker. In essence, the seller is notified of the arrangement and agrees that the other broker represents the buyer and that the commission may be split between the listing broker and the buyer's agent. This tends to keep the transaction simple. However, this practice sets up some unnecessary conflicts of interest and misunderstandings, especially regarding procuring cause issues.

In Texas, a new practice is emerging: the practice of the buyer inserting a condition in the sales contract that requires the seller to pay the buyer's broker on behalf of the buyer or reimburse the buyer for brokerage expenses at closing so that the buyer may pay his or her own broker. These conditional terms should not be drafted by the broker.

To the traditional agent, the buyer broker receives a share of the commission from the listing broker out of the sales proceeds. However, there are two alternative methods of providing compensation. In the first method, the listing broker agrees to reduce the commission by the amount of the usual split with the cooperating broker so that the seller either can reduce the price by a like amount (the net offer approach) or can give an offsetting credit on the buyer's closing statement in the amount of the cooperating broker's share. In the second method, the buyer's broker receives the amount of the fee negotiated with the buyer. If the amount offered by the seller to the cooperating broker exceeds the fee that the buyer is obligated to pay, any difference is credited to the buyer. If the amount is not sufficient to pay the fee, then the buyer pays the difference to the broker. In Texas, as a result of cases such as *LA&N Interests, Inc. v. Fish,* 864 S.W.2d 745 (Tex. App. Houston [14th Dist.]), experienced buyer brokers are more often asking that the buyer be responsible for payment of their commission. Cover letters should be drafted to accompany the offer to explain this arrangement to both the listing agent and the seller.

Commission Split

In a number of states, real estate agents do not use formal written agreements to represent buyers. Commissions are normally paid out of an authorized commission split with the listing broker or by way of the seller crediting the buyer a specified amount out of the sales proceeds. There is usually a written acknowledgment of buyer representation in the state-required agency disclosure form with a written confirmation also included in the purchase agreement. The preferred practice is to use a formal written buyer representation agreement that addresses the issues of exclusivity, compensation, scope of services, termination and conflicts of interest.

In Texas there is no state-approved or promulgated form for buyer representation, seller representation, dual agency representation nor middleman participation. The Texas Association of REALTORS® (TAR®), however, produces such forms for their membership. Some of the larger local REALTOR® associations have also developed separate forms for their own local membership.

Buyer's brokers, if planning on a traditional split method, must ascertain from the listing broker, at initial contact, whether the listing broker is authorized and willing to split the commission with a buyer's broker (as opposed to a subagent of the seller). If the listing broker is not authorized to split the commission, the buyer's broker should advise the buyer of that fact. The buyer may then decide to reduce the offering price to a net amount that reflects that the buyer is to pay his or her broker's fee. The seller and the listing broker will have to reach their own agreement on whether to reduce the listing broker's commission. The Colorado listing form, for example, contains a paragraph in which the seller and the listing broker agree on the adjustment, if any, to be made to their listing commission in the event the buyer is produced by an outside buyer's broker to whom the buyer is obligated to pay a commission.

Now that most MLSs accept listings in which sellers can offer cooperation regarding commissions but not subagency, there will be an increased general acceptance by sellers, buyers and brokers of such a commission-splitting arrangement. Sellers are primarily concerned with selling their property and netting a certain amount of money from the sales proceeds. Most sellers are much less concerned about whether their broker splits commissions with someone labeled a buyer's broker or a subagent of the seller. In fact, sellers often feel that the other broker, even if described as a subagent, actually works for the buyer. Some sellers feel that compensation for both the listing broker and the selling broker is already part of the listing and purchase price; that is, they may feel there really are two fees, the listing fee and the selling fee.

In the previously mentioned case, *LA & N Interests, Inc. v. Fish,* a buyer's broker and his licensed associate felt that they had been unjustly deprived of a commission in a transaction and sued their client and the competing broker to recover their commission and/or damages for interference with their buyer's brokerage agreement. The buyer client bought a property with the assistance of another broker and the buyer's broker was paid nothing, even though the buyer's broker had an exclusive agency representation agreement with the buyer. The buyer's brokerage agreement with the buyer client clearly stated that the client "shall have no liability or obligation to pay a Professional Service Fee to [the buyer broker]" but that rather the seller would pay the buyer's broker's fee. This flaw—to assume that some party other than the client would pay the commission—led to the broker not being able to recover from his client. Neither was he able to recover from the subsequent seller, who had never agreed to pay him in the first place.

Although listing brokers typically voluntarily reduce their share of the commission if another broker, as subagent, finds the buyer, a few listing brokers adamantly resist such a reduction. In the first instance, why should a seller or a listing broker consent to a split? Simply because it is more likely to lead to a sale of the listed property. The listing broker, some sellers reason, should not be paid twice as much just because the buyer has an agent instead of working with the seller's subagent. Assume that the seller signs an exclusive listing agreement at 7 percent. Most of the transaction participants expect that the 7 percent will cover all the sales commissions involved, with both the listing broker and the other broker each earning 3.5 percent. Most sellers would refuse to sign if the total commissions were 10.5 percent, with the listing broker receiving 7 percent.

Why would a seller not consent to a split commission? When the listing broker sees an opportunity to obtain a full rather than a reduced commission. If the listing agreement contains a clause permitting such a split with a buyer's broker, listing brokers who are REALTORS® should reconsider this refusal in view of the ethical restrictions in Articles 7 and 22 of the NAR® Code of Ethics. These articles require that the broker cooperate with other brokers and act in the best interests of the client at all times. If the listing broker's refusal to share commissions results in too low an offer, or no offer at all, the seller may have grounds for complaint, especially if it appears the broker's sole motivation was to receive a greater fee than usual in a cooperative sale. In any event, an agent's fiduciary duty of full disclosure to his or her client under TREC Rules, as well as NAR® Code of Ethics & Standard of Practice 9-10(a), require the listing broker to advise the seller of the general company policy regarding cooperation with buyer's agents. In brief, listing brokers should do everything possible to make it easy for the broker who has the buyer to show the seller's property and make an offer.

Buyer-Paid Fee

The buyer may elect to pay the commission directly to his or her buyer broker. This may avoid any implication of seller agency or conflict of interest that may be present when the seller pays the brokerage fee. An experienced buyer's broker may prefer to be paid directly by the buyer, rather than receiving a commission split from the listing broker or being paid directly by the seller at closing, not wanting a non-client to control payment.

Example:

Sam, the listing broker, and Carol, the other broker acting as a subagent of the seller, agree on a 50-50 commission split. The property is a commercial warehouse not listed in the MLS. The listing commission is 5 percent. The offer is submitted at $1 million on a $1.2 million listing. The seller accepts the offer, provided that Sam reduces his fee to 4 percent. Sam agrees to do so but fails to inform Carol. Carol now receives $24,000 instead of $30,000.

Buyer-paid compensation can take several forms, such as an hourly rate, a percentage fee or a flat fee.

Hourly Rate. Under this arrangement, the broker is, in essence, a consultant, charging a non-contingent hourly rate. It is payable regardless of whether a title transfer is contemplated, such as when a consultant advises on whether to develop a shopping center or a commercial office building. A variation may be an hourly fee that is applied against an incentive fee if the broker finds the right property for the buyer. This requires brokers to keep time sheets and become diligent in their recordkeeping and billing practices.

Percentage Fee. Buyer's brokers may charge a percentage fee based on the selling price of the property bought by their client just as most listing agents do. The obvious problem the percentage fee creates is the appearance of a potential conflict of interest because the higher the purchase price the greater the fee, making the percentage fee appear to be seller-oriented. The prime benefit of the percentage fee is that real estate agents and clients are accustomed to this arrangement. Many buyer's agents begin by charging buyers on a percentage basis and later progress into charging flat fees (discussed below). Other brokers combine an hourly rate with a percentage of the purchase price. Rates may vary when the seller is not represented by a listing broker, because the buyer's broker may have to do more of the background work and handle negotiations with the seller.

Flat Fees (Contingent or Non-Contingent). Some buyer's brokers are compensated on a flat fee that is payable if the buyer purchases a property located through the broker. The amount of the flat fee is based on the estimate by the broker of the work and skills involved, the potential fee that will be paid by the seller and the risk of success. A contingent flat fee often is based on what the buyer will pay for the agent's services based on a price range of the home or an estimate of the amount of work involved.

Example:

Betty is looking for a property in the $175,000 to $225,000 range. A cooperating broker might expect to receive a fee of $6,000 on a $200,000 sale. Carol, a buyer's broker, charges the buyer a $6,000 flat contingent fee. Whether Betty selects a property for $175,000 or for $225,000, the fee to Carol remains $6,000.

Another method of compensation is a non-contingent flat fee. The broker predicts the amount of work necessary to accomplish the client's objectives and then sets a flat fee. This approach is seldom used unless the broker has gained a great deal of experience in representing buyers.

Some buyer representation agreements provide that the buyer is obligated to pay the fee but is entitled to a credit for any amounts the seller agrees to pay. Thus, the buyer would not pay the buyer's broker's fee in the usual MLS sale, although the buyer might pay the fee directly if the broker located an unlisted property, builder-owned home or a for sale-by-owner property. An experienced buyer broker might encourage his or her client to make such a stipulation, just as he or she might base a sale on the condition the seller fix the roof.

Disclosure of Fee. Some buyer's brokers paid directly by their buyer disclose the exact amount of their fee on the offer to purchase. In this way, the seller and the listing broker have a clear understanding of what fees are being paid. It is easier for the seller to see that the seller's net proceeds will be about the same, whether the seller accepts a gross price offer, with the seller paying both brokers or a net price offer with the buyer paying the buyer's broker's commission and the seller paying the listing broker a reduced commission.

There is an argument for not disclosing the amount of fees on the offer to purchase based on confidentiality. If, in fact, the buyer's broker has contracted to receive less than the typical commission split, the amount of the difference will accrue to the buyer's benefit.

Net Purchase Price

The net purchase price is the sales price reduced by the buyer's broker's fee.

Example:

Betty makes a full price offer to the seller on a $100,000 listing in the following way: a net purchase price of $97,300, plus Betty agrees to pay Carol, her buyer's broker, a cash fee of $2,700. The seller acknowledges that the buyer's broker represents the buyer and not the seller in this transaction. Carol inserts a provision in the sales contract that the buyer agrees to pay the sum of $97,300 to the seller and $2,700 to her for services rendered.

A theory of the net price method is that the buyer has only a certain amount for the down payment. A portion of that money no longer will be deducted from the seller's proceeds to pay the cooperating broker. Rather, that money will now be used to pay the buyer's broker. The restructured brokerage fees will not increase the acquisition costs. The overall transaction will not change, even if a loan is involved. If accepted, a net offer may result in lower title and closing costs, which are now based on the lower purchase price.

Lenders. The amount of a maximum loan is based on a percentage of the purchase price plus the buyer broker's commission. The buyer broker's commission is thus paid from the loan proceeds, rather than from the buyer's personal cash. A different approach is used in a net offer situation. So that lenders will add to the sales price the buyer broker's commission as an acquisition cost, some brokers provide the lender with a copy of the purchase contract in the buyer acknowledges the buyer broker's commission. This makes it easier for lenders to visualize the economic adjustments made in the transaction.

Federal Housing Administration (FHA) regulations specifically authorize an add-back to the purchase price of the buyer's broker's fee under Section 532 of the National Housing Act. The notable exception is a Veteran's Administration (VA) loan. The VA does not allow lenders to include buyer's broker's fees in the loan to be paid by the veteran purchaser; their position is based on the belief that (1) the buyer broker's fee may increase the acquisition cost; (2) that buyers are adequately protected by the requirement to furnish a Certificate of Reasonable Value and reasonable closing costs and by access to many properties through general advertising; and (3) that selling brokers, although representing the seller, do not ignore the buyer's interests. Note that there is no VA prohibition against the buyer's broker receiving a seller-approved commission split from the listing broker. Thus, there can be a buyer's broker in a VA transaction, but the broker must be compensated by or through the seller. This is similar to the seller paying the points on the buyer's loan.

Gross Price

An alternative method of buyer's broker compensation that is gaining acceptance in residential sales transactions is the gross price method. The buyer pays the gross purchase price. The purchase contract provides that the seller pays the buyer's broker's commission. The seller acknowledges and accepts that the buyer's broker solely represents the buyer and not the seller, despite the payment of the fee by the seller. To ease the listing broker's and seller's concerns, some brokers add that this fee is the buyer broker's sole compensation in the transaction. Sellers and listing brokers might resent that the buyer broker is getting paid twice. Texas licensees should recall that it is grounds for loss of license to be paid by more than one party to a transaction without the full knowledge and consent of all parties.

This method satisfies all outside participants in the transaction, such as appraisers, lenders and insurers and it is easier to finance the contract amount. This method helps reduce the concerns over excess commission expense and double charging, and it seems easier for the seller to understand and respond to a customary sales price offer. The seller's main difficulty is psychological: The seller and the listing broker may feel that while they are paying the buyer's broker fee, the buyer is receiving the service. This flaw is less serious here than when using the gross price method of fee payment, where a buyer broker's commission can be built into the contract price through the terms of the buyer's offer. As a consequence, the cash required, the mortgage amount, the net proceeds to the seller and the sales price are approximately the same as they would be in the traditional sale in which both brokers represent the seller and both commissions are included in the contract price. To avoid loan underwriting problems, some brokers include the following language in the purchase contract: "Seller credits $[dollar amount] toward buyer's expenses listed on the closing statement."

Some advantages of the seller paying the commission are it:

1. clears up questions of who works for who and who pays who;

2. protects the buyer's broker from the listing agent's breaches and other disentitlements to commissions because of badly crafted listing agreements;
3. protects the buyer client from having to pay the broker's commission at closing if the seller refuses to pay but with the option to do so should the situation require;
4. allows no basis for procuring cause disputes;
5. does not present any suggestion of interfering with the listing broker's commission agreements with the seller;
6. works just as well for listed, unlisted, builder, MLS or non-MLS properties;
7. places responsibility for securing the buyer broker's compensation directly on the shoulders of the client whose interests were served by the broker; and
8. does not trigger the TRELA §15(a)(6)(D) prohibition concerning payment from more than one party in the transaction without knowledge and consent of both, even if the buyer's broker has collected a retainer fee from the buyer in advance.

Some disadvantages are:

1. it is relatively untested in the courts in Texas;
2. it may change expected tax advantages for the parties; and
3. it may cause some confusion among lenders until it is widely recognized, thus impeding some transactions.

It is important for brokers to understand compensation alternatives when they consider representing buyers. Many brokers working with a buyer prospect now realize that they do not need to give away their time and expertise. Brokers should study the different methods of representation and develop their skills so that they can comfortably discuss with buyers and listing brokers the amounts and various methods of compensation. For assistance in this area, there are buyer's broker books and seminars that are helpful. [An excellent source is *Buyer Agency, 2nd Edition,* by Gail Lyons and Don Harlan, Dearborn 1993.]

PROCURING CAUSE

Occasionally, more than one real estate agent works with a buyer in locating a property. Without clear written agreement, disputes may arise over which agent was the procuring cause of the sale and thus entitled to a share of commission. These disputes are sometimes resolved in arbitration using guidelines developed by the NAR®. [*See* Appendix D for sample guidelines.] In Texas, when a buyer or tenant, commercial or residential, decides that he or she needs or wants representation by their own agent and contracts with a buyer's broker or tenant representative, procuring cause will generally become a legal non-issue, even if the buyer or tenant was first shown a property by the listing or leasing agents or their subagents and even if negotiations have begun.

PURCHASE AGREEMENT

Attorneys representing buyers often view TREC-promulgated earnest money contract forms for residential sales as being seller-oriented or at least as containing some buyer compromises. Therefore, some buyer's brokers prefer to work with their own attorneys to develop an acceptable purchase agreement. This agreement could be similar in format to the standard purchase contract except that it is prepared from the buyer's perspective. Other brokers prefer to use a special buyer's addendum, which can be attached to the standard form of purchase agreement.

When assisting a buyer with the preparation of an offer to purchase, the buyer's broker should keep in mind that:

- the broker is not an attorney and must avoid the unauthorized practice of law;
- any complicated drafting should be left to an attorney, although it may be appropriate for the broker to suggest various negotiating strategies and certain contingencies and financing techniques that should be incorporated into the offer;
- the offer should not be so one-sided as to be unfair or unrealistic; and
- although the broker should help the buyer in evaluating key contract terms, the broker should not decide what is best for the buyer.

What follows is a list of important items for the buyer's broker to consider before preparing an offer to purchase. Some of the items will influence price negotiations. Some states require the use of pre-approved forms, and this requirement may affect the ability of a buyer's broker to use some of these suggestions. Again, keep in mind that the TREC contract forms are to be conformed to the intent of the principals, not rigidly copied.

[Also remember that we are looking at these contract terms from the buyer and buyer broker's point of view in this chapter. Many of these statements would be reversed in the negotiating strategy of the seller's agent or subagent.]

Earnest Money Deposit

In Texas, earnest money is not essential to the validity of a contract. A real estate contract in Texas is just as valid without earnest money as it is with earnest money. Earnest money is not the consideration necessary to make the contract valid. Earnest money is money or something of value, usually to be held in escrow by a third party, to be given to the seller in the event of the buyer's default on the contract before closing in order to provide a non-judicial remedy for damages incurred by the seller because of the buyer's default. It is an alternative remedy to a lawsuit for damages, specific performance, injunction or other legal action. However, its major significance is that a seller does not have to go to court to get the earnest money; that is why earnest money is referred to as a non-judicial remedy. Until very recently, the buyer gave the earnest money check to the broker to accompany the offer and to be deposited by the broker. Since 1992, TREC-promulgated forms do not indicate that necessity, only that the buyer shall deposit the earnest money with the escrow agent named in the contract "upon execution of this contract by both parties."

Buyers' brokers should keep the following in mind when their clients agree to deposit earnest money in the course of a transaction:

- Discuss with the buyer client the strategy of depositing a large amount of earnest money as a negotiation tool to drive down the sales price, giving an offer, in the eyes of the seller, an advantage over competing offers without such security. Remember, though, that a large deposit increases the buyer client's potential financial loss. If the buyer client is risk-averse, then he or she might want to keep the initial deposit low, with any additional deposit to be made 10 to 15 days after the seller accepts the offer. If a substantial deposit is made, have the client consider the use of an interest-bearing account to the benefit of the buyer.
- Avoid giving the deposit directly to the seller. As stated earlier, the new TREC contract forms do not provide for sellers nor seller's agents or subagents to deposit the earnest money. Nor does it provide for the earnest money check to be carried back and forth with the contract documents. It is to be deposited by the buyer or designated agent upon execution of the contract by both parties unless otherwise agreed. If done differently the contract should specify exactly how it will be handled. Remember, the selection of the stakeholder in the contract is a fully negotiable item; however, the issue must be agreed upon by the parties or there is no enforceable contract.
- Provide that forfeiture of the buyer's earnest money be deemed liquidated damages and that such forfeiture shall be the seller's sole remedy in the event of the buyer's default. This may avoid a potential personal judgment for money damages against the defaulting buyer, especially if the property's value declines.
- Where appropriate, request that the seller deposit a sufficient sum of earnest money to cover any closing and title cancellation charges, buyer's moving and storage expenses and some money for the buyer broker if the contract is terminated due to the seller's default. If the buyer representation agreement calls for the broker to get half of any earnest money put up by and forfeited by the seller, then the amount requested must be doubled or else the buyer will not receive enough to cover reasonable potential damages.

Assignability

Most standard contracts are unclear whether the buyer may assign the rights in a purchase contract. Buyers, therefore, may want to expressly state that their rights can be assigned.

Seller Financing

If the buyer is asking the seller to carryback a note and mortgage or similar security instrument, such as a deed of trust or installment sales contract, the buyer should specify in the purchase agreement the key provisions to be inserted in the financing document for the buyer's benefit. These might include the following: no prepayment penalty; no due-on-sale clause; the liability is non-recourse (i.e., the seller's remedy is to foreclose on the property without the buyer being personally liable for any deficiency); extended grace periods; and possible deferral of interest. Depending on the terms of the seller-provided financing (i.e., maturity date, interest rate and amount of down payment), the buyer should be flexible in selecting the offering price. These provisions are provided for in a TREC-promulgated addendum for seller financing that should be the only form used unless the buyer's or seller's attorney draft another addendum. Don't try to create them in the Special Provisions paragraph of the contract. That is grounds for loss of license and basis for lawsuit by the client if the terms are drafted incorrectly and lead to damage to the buyer.

Contract Acceptance

The seller's acceptance of the offer could be effective only if delivered in writing to the buyer or the buyer's broker. This gives the buyer the longest time possible in which to revoke the offer if the buyer subsequently so chooses for whatever reason.

Extended Closing

For their own protection, buyers should consider whether they want to be given the contractual right to extend closing dates, beyond those in the TREC form, if they have difficulty arranging financing or otherwise meeting the closing dates.

Inspection

The buyer's offer could be made contingent on one or more professional inspections. If there are problems with the condition of the property, the buyer may be justified in canceling, based on the results of the inspection. The seller could be required to agree to pay for any major repairs or repairs up to a certain dollar amount. In the case of rental property, the buyer should be given sufficient time to inspect all units, review all of the leases and verify the income and expense statements. Texas now has a new contract addendum form, promulgated by TREC, entitled "Addendum for Inspection with Right To Terminate" (Form Number 27-0), to be used in these situations. This new addendum is not suitable for commercial transactions, but is an excellent form for buyer's brokers in residential real estate. A buyer's broker or seller's agent/subagent attempting to create his or her own version of this provision will be engaging in the unauthorized practice of law.

Property Condition

The seller should submit a property condition disclosure report for the buyer's approval (*see* Appendix E). A buyer's broker may counsel his or her buyer client to require the seller to agree not to substitute any personal property items for those at the property when it was shown and that were expected, by the buyer, to be included in the purchase price; that the property is in the same or required improved condition at the time of possession by the buyer as so contracted; the property is clear of debris; that the appliances, plumbing, heating and electrical systems should be in good working condition; and that present use is lawful.

TREC contract forms already include most of these concerns. Texas law requires the delivery of a Seller's Disclosure of Property Condition in accordance with Section 5.008 of the Texas Property Code. TREC has produced an approved but not promulgated form that licensees may use to meet this Property Code requirement. There must be a seller's disclosure of property condition made to the buyer by the time specified in the Property Code or the transaction may be subject to recision by the buyer. A licensee who fails to make his or her client aware of the necessity and availability of this form for use could face a lawsuit from a damaged client and loss of license under TRELA §15(a)(6)(W).

Pests

The buyer may want to require the seller to agree to pay for a pest-clearance report from a licensed exterminator chosen by the buyer and the seller should agree to repair all pest damage or to treat the home if necessary. The seller should treat for fleas, termites and other wood-infesting organisms, using care not to use chemicals that may make the dwelling unsafe after use.

Assessments

The seller should agree to pay all assessments at closing on the theory that the enhanced value of these improvements has been reflected in the sales price. Suppose that an assessment is outstanding at a low interest rate ($20,000 sewer assessment payable ten years at 6 percent). Rather than have the seller pay off the assessment, consider having the buyer assume the assessment and lower the purchase price accordingly or credit this amount against the downpayment.

Title Matters

The seller should agree to correct any title defect by a certain date; in fact, the closing can be postponed at the buyer's election to allow the defect to be cleared. The buyer may want to consider paying for the owner's title insurance policy (not necessarily the title company where it closes or who holds the earnest money, but the title insurance company that underwrites the insurance) in order to have the non-negotiable right under RESPA Chapter 9 to choose the title insurer. Under RESPA, if the buyer pays for the title insurance, the seller cannot make the choice of title insurer a subject of negotiations in the contract.

Financing and Other Contingencies

Financing contingencies should be structured so that the buyer has a sufficient time period to perform. It would be appropriate to make the contract subject to the review and approval of the buyer's attorney or tax advisor. If the buyer cannot meet a contingency, such as obtaining loan approval, the buyer should have the choice to cancel, extend or waive the condition and proceed to close, perhaps obtaining funds from another source. If the property increases in value after the offer is accepted and before title transfers, the buyer (who didn't qualify for financing) could benefit by waiving the contingency and assigning his or her rights in the contract to another buyer for a profit. The buyer should use reasonable efforts to meet the contingency and not use the contingency clause as a bad-faith means to tie up the seller's property.

Miscellaneous Checklist

In a seller's market the buyer may not be in a good position to demand too many concessions from the seller.

The buyer's broker should consider covering some of the following items with his or her client for possible inclusion in a purchase contract for the buyer's benefit:

- The buyer may be permitted occupancy prior to closing.
- The buyer should be granted a right of first refusal to acquire any adjoining property owned by the seller.
- The buyer should be given credit for any impound accounts on assumed mortgages.
- The buyer should be given the right to lock in points on a loan.
- The seller should pay the appraisal fees and points on the loan.
- The buyer should be able to extend the satisfaction date of any seller-provided financing.

- The buyer/borrower should be given the right of first refusal if the seller discounts the sale of any purchase money mortgage that the seller carried back.
- The seller should agree to allow the buyer/borrower to substitute collateral on any seller-provided financing.
- The seller should provide a corporate resolution, if the seller is a corporation, indicating, among other things, who is duly authorized by the corporation to sign all necessary documents on behalf of the corporation.
- The seller should cover the buyer's expenses if the seller refuses to close on time.
- The seller should permit the buyer to show the property to prospective tenants prior to closing.
- The seller should allow the buyer reasonable access to the property to permit inspection by the buyer's representatives, such as interior designers and architects.

A seller's agent or subagent should urge the seller to consider resisting any or all of these concessions unless his or her seller client gains some exceptional benefit in return.

BUYER'S BROKER DISCLOSURES

Disclosures to Buyer

Before entering into a buyer representation agreement, the real estate agent is required by 22 TAC §535.164 to discuss the types of working relationships available to the buyer and to present the buyer with TREC Agency Disclosure Form Number 3. The broker should attempt to have the buyer read and sign the broker's copy to prove compliance with the state law and, then, to prevent later misunderstandings, discuss it and answer the buyer's questions. Keep in mind that the consumer is not required by state law to sign the form, although the licensee is. The NAR® Code of Ethics & Standard of Practice 9-10(b) requires a buyer's agent to inform the buyer about (1) the company's policy regarding cooperation with other firms, (2) the potential for the buyer's agent to act as a disclosed dual agent and (3) the procedure for handling an in-house transaction. If the buyer's broker's or tenant rep's firm represents buyers or tenants exclusively there will be no in-house transactions.

Disclosures to Seller or Listing Broker

TREC 22 TAC §535.164 does not require a buyer's broker to submit TREC Form Number 3 to the seller's agent, but he or she must make at least oral (although preferably written) disclosure of buyer representation to the listing broker. The form must be presented at either the first face-to-face meeting or first written communication from the buyer's broker to seller, whichever occurs first. This does not include the offer itself because the offer is a written communication from the buyer to the seller, not from the buyer's agent to the seller. If the first face-to-face meeting occurs after the parties to the transaction have signed a contract to buy, sell, rent or lease the real property, then the licensee is not required to provide a copy of the form to the seller or landlord.

NAR® Code of Ethics & Standard of Practice 21-12 requires the buyer's agent to disclose that relationship to the listing agent at first contact and to provide written confirmation of that disclosure no later than signing the purchase agreement. As soon as the buyer's agent calls for an appointment, the buyer's broker should inform the listing broker that he or she represents the buyer and rejects any offer of subagency that might have been made. If the property is not listed, the buyer agent should disclose the relationship to the seller at first contact and make any requests for compensation from the seller at first contact (NAR® Code of Ethics & Standard of Practice 21-13).

ADVANTAGES/DISADVANTAGES

Some of the advantages of exclusive buyer agency are it:

- reduces the possibility of dual agency because exclusive buyer's brokers do not take listings;
- gives buyers greater confidence that they will see all the properties available from any source;
- gives buyers greater confidence that they will have 100% undivided loyalty and expert advice on all property negotiations;
- increases buyer loyalty under an exclusive buyer's representation agreement;
- tends to prevent lapses or mistakes in negotiating objectives and styles that often occur when switching back and forth from one type role to the other as do brokers who practice non-exclusive agency; and
- more likely to be able to charge and collect retainer fees because buyer is sure of 100 percent commitment from buyer's broker.

Some of the disadvantages of buyer agency exclusively are:

- buyers sometimes want to sell, yet company does not take listing;
- potential conflict of interest if two buyer clients want to make offers on same property; and
- raises compensation issues, such as who pays the fee or whether listing broker will cooperate and split fees.

SUMMARY

In Texas, before 1994, in the majority of real estate transactions, the seller was represented by a real estate agent, but the buyer was not. Many buyers, however, now seek the same level of client service that they typically receive from brokers when they are sellers. The decision to represent a buyer is a serious one because the broker will be held to a high standard of care and will owe fiduciary duties to the buyer. Both the broker and the buyer will want to weigh the various benefits of buyer representation. It is strongly recommended that brokers use a written buyer agency agreement and carefully discuss alternative methods of compensation. In assisting the buyer or the buyer's attorney to prepare the purchase agreement, the broker should consider the negotiable aspects of the transaction from the buyer's perspective.

KEY POINTS

- Whether to represent the buyer is an important decision because the agent owes the full range of fiduciary responsibilities. The real estate licensee may want to be selective and not represent every buyer who walks in the front door.
- Buyer brokerage does not mean that the broker is in the business of representing buyers only. Most buyer's agents regard buyer agency as one of the choices available to them in a single agency or non-exclusive agency practice.
- Not every buyer wants or needs representation. Some prefer to represent themselves, especially those not wanting to risk a missed opportunity in a fast moving seller's market.
- Written buyer representation agreements are preferable over oral ones.
- In showing buyers in-house listings, care must be taken to avoid unintentional and unauthorized dual agency. If dual agency is to be authorized, the broker must make full disclosure of the potential conflicts of interest to both buyer and seller.
- Buyer's agents must disclose to the listing broker at initial contact that they are buyer's agents and clearly reject any offer of subagency. Frequently the listing broker will be authorized to share fees with buyer's agents and allow them equal access to the property for showing.
- Buyer's brokers in Texas should seriously consider not approaching listing agents, sellers or landlords with the intention of negotiating their compensation directly from these parties.

SUGGESTIONS FOR BROKERS

Establish an office policy on how to handle an offer received from a buyer's broker on one of your listings. Discuss with the seller the possibility that you will be receiving offers from buyer's brokers and that these offers may require a commission split or an adjustment in the offering price when the buyer will pay the buyer's broker directly. Discuss the net effect these offers will have on the seller's position and advise the seller accordingly.

QUIZ

1. Which of the following factors might a court consider in deciding whether a broker represented a buyer?
   a. Whether the buyer paid the commission
   b. Whether the buyer signed an exclusive representation agreement
   c. Whether the buyer asked the broker to help negotiate the purchase of an already identified property
   d. All of the above
2. In a traditional real estate transaction, a fiduciary relationship most likely exists between which of the following?
   a. Seller and buyer
   b. Broker and buyer
   c. Listing broker and buyer's broker
   d. Seller and broker
3. When a cooperating broker accepts an MLS offer of subagency, the broker becomes the fiduciary of which of the following?
   a. Buyer
   b. Buyer's broker
   c. Seller
   d. MLS
4. In a multiple listing situation, a salesperson who negotiates the sale of a property listed with another company is directly responsible to:
   a. the listing broker.
   b. the seller.
   c. the employing broker.
   d. the buyer.
5. In which of the following cases must a real estate broker obtain a written agreement with a buyer?
   a. The broker is to act as a buyer's agent
   b. The broker is to be paid a commission by the seller
   c. Both of the above
   d. Neither of the above

DISCUSSION QUESTIONS

1. Can a buyer's broker participate in the MLS and receive a share of the listing broker's commission?
2. Why would a listing broker reduce a portion of the sales commission so the seller could credit that portion to the buyer for payment of the buyer's broker's commission?
3. How could a buyer's broker handle conflicts of interest situations involving in-house sales?

4. Name at least four important elements of a well-drafted buyer's broker representation agreement.
5. Name at least five important points for a buyer's broker to cover in a purchase contract.

CHAPTER

7

DUAL AGENCY

The year 1994 began in Texas with a number of real estate firms altering their business practices, moving away from the traditional exclusive seller agency and subagency combination of the past several decades. These new brokerage practices are the economic and political responses to the perceived competition and business pressure put on traditional brokerages by the advent of exclusive buyer representation. One of these responses is the move toward disclosed or consensual dual agency.

A dual agency exists when one broker, by express or implied agreement, represents both the buyer and the seller in the same transaction. Because the dual agent owes the same fiduciary duties to both principals, the dual agent must avoid situations where he or she unintentionally compromises one principal in favor of the other. Actually, dual agency is a misnomer because, by definition, an agent can have only one master. Although divided representation, multiple representation or limited agency may be more accurate terms, this book will use the more common term *dual agency.*

This chapter will discuss the following:

- Creation of Dual Agency
- Effect of Dual Agency
- Duties of Dual Agent
- Intended or Unintended Dual Agency
    - Prior Relationships
    - In-House Sale
    - Cooperative or Other Broker
    - Broker as Principal
    - Adopting the Buyer
- Dual Agency Disclosures
    - Informed Consent
    - Timing of Disclosure
    - Different Approaches
- Role of Dual Agent
- Limited or Statutory Agency
- Consensual Dual Agency
- Non-Agents
- Nonresidential Dual Agency

CREATION OF DUAL AGENCY

Brokers do not intend to create conflicts of interest or be disloyal to their clients. Often, dual agency is unintended and subtly arises when the conduct of a listing broker creates an implied agency with a buyer. In some cases, a real estate agent backs into a dual agency situation without being aware of it.

Example:

Sally is trying to sell one of her listed properties at 10 Main Street. Sally has several meetings over the next few weeks with a prospective buyer, Betty. Sally shows Betty a number of properties. Because of Sally's sincere efforts to find the right property, Betty tends to rely on Sally's judgment and advice. Betty shows an interest in making an offer on the property, but first asks Sally to find a resale buyer so Betty can sell the property within 90 days of her buying it.

The nature of the real estate brokerage business is such that a broker cannot always give 100 percent undivided loyalty to a client. Even a single agency or non-exclusive agency broker has to modify the level of representation in such cases as an expired listing, in which the former listing broker now represents a buyer client or a turnaround sale in which the listed seller now wants to buy a replacement property listed with the same company. A conflict exists between the duty of confidentiality and the duty of full disclosure.

Dual agency situations can arise with in-house sales, cooperative sales, exchanges, syndications and purchases by real estate agents for their own accounts. Sellers have been known to raise the defense of dual agency in suits by a broker for a commission that the seller now refuses to pay. A buyer may raise dual agency as a defense in a foreclosure action by the seller, who carried back a mortgage to secure a deferred portion of the purchase price. Many reported cases of dual agency arise in "self-dealing" where brokers place their own personal gain above the best interests of their client.

EFFECT OF DUAL AGENCY

If a broker is willing to bear the risk of acting as a dual agent, it is imperative that he or she provide full written disclosure to both the buyer and the seller and obtain the written consent of each. In Texas, these writings must contain all the requirements contained in TRELA §15C or the multiple representation will be considered an undisclosed dual agency, which violates both state licensing and general agency law. Such a broker is also likely to jeopardize any right to a commission in the transaction and may cause either the seller or the buyer to rescind the transaction. The broker is then potentially liable for monetary damages. This right of rescission exists regardless of whether there is injury, even if the transaction is fair or the agent acts in good faith. Even though the dual agent obtains the required consents, the agent must still be extremely careful to act as a dual agent within the rules of TRELA 15C and not favor one side over the other. The cautious dual agent will also encourage both parties to consult with their own legal counsel. Rather than "let the buyer beware," the dual agent's motto should be, "let the broker, buyer and seller be aware!"

Dual agency raises some very tough questions. In performing conflicting duties, the dual agent may do a disservice to one or both principals. The broker may be privy to confidential information from each side that could affect the other side's position. Must the dual agent broker tell the seller if any part of the offer is unreasonable or unsound for the seller client? If he or she only represented the seller the answer would obviously be yes; if functioning only as a buyer's broker the answer is no. But as a dual agent in Texas, there are no such obvious answers. TRELA §15C(c) and (d) state in part: "(c) A real estate broker who acts as an agent for more than one party to a transaction shall . . . (3) not disclose any confidential information or any information a party specifically instructs the real estate broker in writing not to disclose unless otherwise instructed in a separate writing by the respective party or required to disclose such information by law; and (4) treat all parties to the transaction honestly and impartially so as not to favor one party or work to the disadvantage of any party. (d) The real estate broker shall use due diligence to assist the parties in understanding the consents, agreements or instructions under this section."

Comparables. One of the toughest questions in Texas for the licensee attempting to be a lawful dual agent broker is the question concerning the use of comparables and CMAs for clients. Nearly all real estate licensees are willing to take listings at least a few thousand dollars more than their own competitive market analysis indicates. This willingness to take the overpriced listing, especially when only slightly above the broker's opinion of value, is generally expressed in terms of one or a combination of at least seven reasons:

1. Overpricing leaves room to negotiate.
2. The seller won't list the house for less.
3. The broker's competition will list it for that price if the broker refuses the listing.
4. Having the listing and the sign in the yard will make the phone ring and the broker will sell other properties from the calls.
5. It will give the broker something to advertise.
6. No one really knows what any property is truly worth.
7. It is not the broker's job to price the property. Just take the listing at whatever the seller wants and don't offer opinions.

Remember, Texas law requires that "a real estate licensee is obligated to advise a property owner as to the licensee's opinion of the market value of a property when negotiating a listing or offering to purchase the property for the licensee's own account as a result of contact made while acting as a real estate agent." [22 TAC §535.16(d)]

DUTIES OF A DUAL AGENT

In general, the dual agent owes to each principal the duties of good faith, disclosure, loyalty, competence and confidentiality. Because the broker cannot possibly provide full client-level service to both, each client must be alerted that he or she will receive less than full representation. The broker simply cannot presume that each client will be satisfied just because the transaction closes and the broker is helpful and honest. Each client must understand what level of service each will waive and will not receive when consenting to a dual agency.

It is difficult to define in specific terms the responsibilities that a dual agent owes to a buyer and to a seller. Much depends on the type of dual agency disclosure given to the buyer and the seller. For example, if a seller client consents to his or her listing broker's acting as an intermediary between the seller and a buyer client of the broker, then the seller might challenge the broker's behavior in suggesting tactics that seem to favor only the buyer. On the other hand, if the seller and buyer give their informed consent to have a broker negotiate on the seller's behalf and another agent from the same brokerage negotiate on the buyer's behalf, then, arguably, the seller and buyer have agreed to a limited agency and waive any challenge to the brokerage's dual representation. Nevertheless, dual agents must be careful to act in a manner consistent with the dual agency disclosure.

Conflicting Positions

The very positions of buyer and seller are inherently in conflict. The two of them may be very friendly and they have a common goal of making a transaction work; in law, however, their interests are considered to be distinct and each needs protection. Transactions seldom exist in which the objectives of the buyer and the seller are identical. The broker is placed in the delicate position of utilizing any knowledge about either side in such a way as to please both sides and complete the transaction. There is a good chance that at least one side will not receive full representation because the broker will find it impossible to remain totally neutral. If forced to decide, the dual agent broker probably will favor a seller who is a long-standing client over a first-time buyer.

A disgruntled buyer or seller may decide, at any time, to challenge the broker's actions. In hindsight, either client may later assert that the dual agent violated the trust given him or her because the representation scale tipped in favor of the other client. The provisions in a contract that benefit one side may burden the other. If desirous of attempting to represent the interests of more than one party in a transaction, the broker is expected and required to maintain a delicate balance and avoid the risk of sacrificing the interest of one client for another.

Conflicting expectations may make the dual agent's job difficult, especially because the real estate market is characterized by the negotiation of price within a reasonable range. The process of negotiation is an expected and usual part of consummating a transaction. The ultimate issue is whether the buyer and the seller can benefit best by having only one broker represent both clients in the negotiations. If yes, the dual agency is lawful, provided both clients give their written informed consent, and all the requirements of TRELA §15C, as to the terms that must be included in such a written agreement, are met precisely.

Explosive Issue

As long as the buyer and the seller are happy with their transaction, the question of dual agency might never arise. But if either party becomes unhappy, for whatever reason, even months after closing, dual agency may provide the mechanism to undo the transaction, recover commissions from the offending broker, seek money damages and cause the revocation of broker licensure. It is no legal defense that the dual agency was unintended or was performed with all good intentions to help both the buyer and the seller. Buyers and sellers generally neither care nor know about the subject of dual agency until one of them wants to back out of the deal and consult an attorney. It is then the principals often find out that they did not receive the level of service they should have. Dual agency cases have a high rate of success for plaintiffs and a high value for settlement purposes.

By itself, dual agency, even when disclosed and intended, is risky. This is true despite the fact that in some cases neither party loses and both, perhaps, gain. This might occur, for example, if the dual agent discloses the seller's urgency to sell and also discloses the buyer's recent profitable cash sale of another property. These and other confidential disclosures may actually speed up acceptance of an agreement with respect to price and terms fully acceptable to both parties. Nevertheless, dual agents take a calculated risk whenever they conceal or reveal information that potentially compromises the position of one of their principals. The principal may later be heard to argue in court that the agent's loyalty was improperly to the transaction itself and the compensation to be derived from it, and not to the clients' best interests.

For years, the National Association of REALTORS® took the position that dual agency is a totally inappropriate agency relationship. As buyer representation increased in popularity during the mid 1980s, it soon became evident that brokerages would find themselves with buyer clients who were interested in negotiating on company listings. How to handle this new type of in-house sale while fighting off the exclusive buyer's broker's appeal to the traditional broker's customers became a key issue for most firms to resolve. After extensive study, the 1992 NAR® Presidential Advisory Group on Agency recommended that:

> While dual agency is permitted, it should be limited to unique transactions and only when there is full and complete disclosure of the kinds of services the dual agent can provide, followed by written consent of both parties.

Likewise, TREC has now officially published its position that the Commission does not encourage the practice of dual agency. [*See* TREC *Advisor,* Col. 3, Pg. 3, Vol. 5, No. 1 1994 and 22 TAC 535.16 (c).]

Occasionally, it is a buyer or tenant, or possibly a landlord or seller, who suggests to the broker that the broker be the dual agent. The buyer might say, "Why complicate this by bringing in another broker?" One client is the primary client, with whom the broker has an existing agency; the other client is the secondary client, who comes in contact with the broker as a result of the transaction itself. The primary and secondary clients may feel that using one broker will expedite the transaction and reduce costs. They may not be aware that each party will receive less than full representation by the very nature of dual agency itself.

Single agency brokers or non-exclusive client agency brokers typically refuse to represent both the buyer/tenant and the seller/landlord in the same transaction. Their feeling is that there is a high probability that conflicts of interest will develop at some point during the course of the transaction, even if everyone is friendly and in agreement when the lease or purchase contract is signed. They question the dual agent's ability to effectively and comfortably handle the variety of problems that generally arise prior to closing. These may include such problems as removal of tenants and disclosure of potential negative aspects of the property.

Ethically, the broker will have to consider the real test: Can the dual broker make compatible recommendations beneficial to each client? Brokers should ask themselves, "If another broker was acting separately for the client, would that broker be likely to make the same recommendations, point out the same facts and negotiate for the same safeguards as I would as a dual agent?" If the broker cannot comfortably answer this question affirmatively, then the broker should make certain clients understand the limited role of the broker before acting as a dual agent.

INTENDED VERSUS UNINTENDED DUAL AGENCY

In considering dual agency, one must distinguish between intended dual agency and unintended or *accidental dual agency,* which occurs because the broker is unaware of the dual agency until after the fact. An intended dual agency presents some serious business risks, but it does provide the broker with an opportunity to discuss dual agency and to obtain written consents designed to minimize risk. If a broker doesn't know that a dual agency exists, there is no contractual way to minimize the risks inherent in the dual representation. Some common dual agency situations are outlined on the chart shown as Figure 7.1.

More commonly, unintended dual agency occurs in one of these contexts:

1. The listing broker or licensed associate represents both the buyer and the seller.
2. Separate associates from the listing office (an in-house sale) represent the buyer and the seller.
3. A cooperating broker represents the buyer and is also a subagent of the seller.
4. The real estate licensee is acting as a buyer or a seller.

One Agent

The conduct of the listing broker's licensed associate may be such that the buyer is led to believe that the associate represents the buyer. In his or her zeal to develop rapport with the buyer prospect, the salesperson sometimes gives the buyer that impression. In its handbook *Who Is My Client?,* the NAR® lists the following examples of words or phrases often used by real estate brokers that can create implied agency relationships with buyers:

- "I'll take care of everything. I'll handle the sale for you."
- "I'll see if I can get the seller to come down on the price."
- "This listing has been on the market for six months. That tells me it's overpriced. Let's offer $80,000 and see what they say."
- "I'll get you the best deal I possibly can."
- "Trust me. I'm sure the seller won't counter at that price."
- "If the seller is going to insist on a full price sale, I think you should tell him no. Then we can try an offer on that house your wife liked so much. I'm sure those sellers will be more realistic."
- "If they insist on the full $100,000, I'll remind them that the furnace is 15 years old and the carpet is fraying. That should justify at least a $3,000 reduction."

Prior Relationships

Sometimes a dual agency arises based on the prior relationship between the listing broker and the buyer.

Figure 7.1 Dual Agency Chart

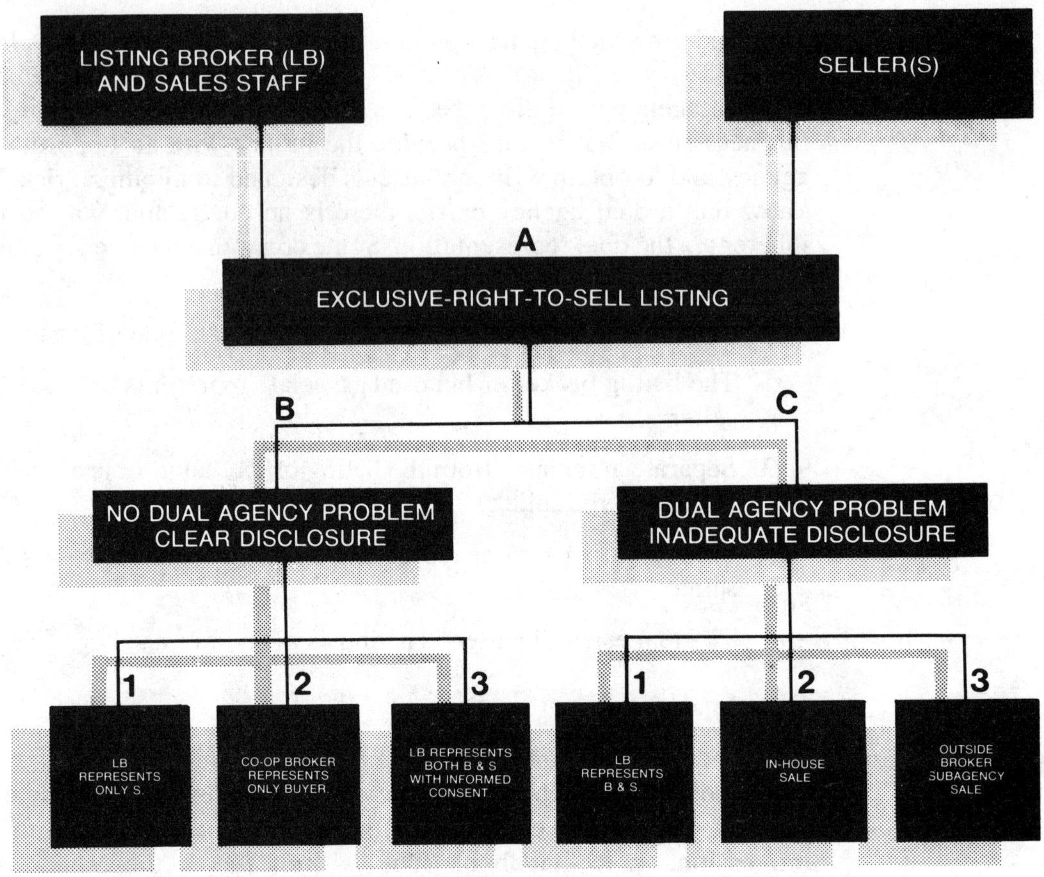

A. Sellers often list property with a listing broker under an exclusive-right-to-sell listing. The listing broker and his or her entire staff represent the seller.

B. There is no dual agency problem if there is clear disclosure, consent and conduct that: (1) the listing broker represents only the seller. The buyer is a customer and the seller is a client; (2) the cooperating broker is a buyer's broker. The seller is a customer and the buyer is a client; or (3) the broker represents both buyer and seller as a dual agent after full disclosure, informed written consent and adherence to TRELA §15C.

C. There is a dual agency problem if the dual agency arises because of inadequate or no disclosure that: (1) the listing broker represents both buyer and seller; (2) two licensed associates from the same brokerage are attempting to represent the buyer and seller separately; (3) the cooperating broker is thought to be a subagent of the seller but his or her conduct is that of a buyer's agent; (4) the conduct of the disclosed dual agent broker doesn't comply with TRELA §15C; or (5) the written contract required by TRELA §15C is either not in writing, does not contain the precise wording required by the act or the required language is not in conspicuous bold or underlined print.

SITUATION: *Sally of Bay Realty listed George's house. Sally has previously represented Betty on several sales and purchases of property. Sally tells Betty about the house and Betty wants Sally to prepare an offer 10 percent below the asking price. Betty mentions she'll pay near the asking price, if necessary.*

QUESTION: *Who does Sally represent?*

DISCUSSION: *As the listing salesperson, Sally's primary allegiance is to George, the seller. Based on her prior relationship with Betty, Sally may, under implied agency principles, also be held to represent Betty. This could put Sally's firm, Bay Realty, into an unintended dual agency role.*

Sally's choices are either to disclose the dual agency and obtain written consents from Betty, George and Bay Realty or to disclaim any agency to Betty and clarify to Betty that she can work with Betty but only on a customer basis, as the agent of the seller.

If Sally is a lawful dual agent, under Texas law, she has no duty to tell George about Betty's willingness to make a higher offer as she would have to if she were his agent only. In fact, as a lawful dual agent, she has an affirmative duty to not do so. She has a duty to her client, Betty, not to reveal Betty's bargaining intentions. Neither can she tell Betty that her other client, George, will take $10,000 less than list or reveal any of his other bargaining intentions. These normally inappropriate duties are the norm of dual agency and mutually exclusive duties are the dilemma of the dual agent. With clear disclosure and consents, Sally, under the first choice, may be authorized to keep confidential her discussions regarding price and terms. On the other hand, if Sally disclaims an agency relationship with Betty, under the second choice, she would have to tell George that Betty has expressed a willingness to increase her first offer. Sally should, in either event, tell George about her prior business relationship with Betty.

In-House Sale

Even though the selling salesperson in an in-house sale is someone other than the listing salesperson, there is still a dual agency because the employing broker has become a dual agent through the conduct of the two salespeople.

SITUATION: *Tom, a salesperson with Bay Realty, listed Harry's house. Sally, also of Bay Realty, has been looking for two months to find the right home for her client, Betty. She shows Betty the house that Tom listed. Betty loves it and wants Sally to negotiate on her behalf for a lower price, a long closing period and favorable financing terms. Betty wants Sally secretly to look for a resale buyer at a quick profit, hopefully in a back-to-back closing.*

QUESTION: *Who represents whom?*

DISCUSSION: *Bay Realty represents both the seller and the buyer as a dual agent. The knowledge possessed by both Tom and Sally will be imputed to Bay Realty and to each other. In Texas, even with proper disclosure, it is questionable whether Betty or Harry are able to give a meaningful consent (from a legal standpoint) to work with their respective agent, with each agent bargaining for the best interest of their respective client and agreeing not to divulge confidential information. The primary danger here is that Texas law simply does not allow dual agency unless the broker and all his or her agents forego the advocacy role for both clients. Bay Realty is still the broker and would therefore be advocating for both sides against each other. The only logical conclusion that seems possible is that Bay Realty would be an unlawful dual agent. The danger here is of actually trading inside information within the same office.*

Some brokers are not aware that this two-salesperson situation in an in-house sale creates a dual agency conflict and therefore will not attempt to obtain proper consents. The broker believes that both the buyer and the seller will be treated fairly and that each will receive full representation from their respective associates.

The broker is often made aware of the conflict for the first time when he or she is served with a lawsuit. It is then, for example, that the listing broker discovers the salesperson never told the seller that the real reason for extending the closing date was to close the sale of the buyer's home, which was also listed by the broker. The seller then claims a breach of fiduciary duty because the broker failed to point out the seller's choices in agreeing to an extension. For example, as a condition for extending, the seller possibly could have asked for compensating concessions. Disclosure of dual agency at the point of a lawsuit is too late to protect the broker.

Cooperating or Other Broker

The cooperating broker often acts as the agent of the buyer in negotiations to acquire a property listed in a multiple listing service (MLS). If subagency is offered and the broker fails to disclaim the offer of subagency, the cooperating broker may be deemed to be the subagent of the seller and the implied agent of the buyer.

SITUATION: *Sally checks the MLS book in her search of homes for Betty. She sees an interesting home and calls Jeff from South Side Realty about his listing. She makes arrangements to see the property and submits Betty's offer. The negotiations are long and hard, but after a series of four different offers and counteroffers, the seller agrees to Betty's offer. Before closing, Betty gets cold feet and asks for a return of her deposit money.*

QUESTION: *Does Betty have a valid claim for rescission of the contract based on dual agency?*

DISCUSSION: *Even though it may have no relevance to the true reason why Betty wants to back out, she might assert that she relied upon the fact that Sally was her agent. Later, Betty alleges she discovered that Sally and Bay Realty were really subagents of the seller. Because Bay Realty acted as an undisclosed dual agent, she argues, either the buyer or the seller can legally refuse to close, even though no damages are proven. Sally should have clarified her agency status to both Betty and Jeff when she first contacted Jeff to view the property. Under typical MLS rules, if subagency is offered, according to current Texas common law, Sally will probably be presumed to be the subagent of the seller unless she rejects the offer of subagency and declares that she is a buyer's agent. As a subagent, Sally has to act as a subagent. In this case, she negotiated hard for her client Betty, and it may very well be that Sally and Bay Realty were unintended agents of Betty as well as intended agents of the seller.*

Real estate licensees should note that professional liability is often based on the law of agency and the failure of the licensee to live up to the duties of an agent when held to be acting as one. Subagency may complicate this problem by creating an unintended dual agency with an inherent conflict of interest.

Broker as Principal

Brokers should be especially alert to dual agency problems when they or their associates or employees, licensed or otherwise, buy or sell property for their own accounts. This can happen in several contexts.

Buying an In-House Listing. On occasion, a broker or one of his or her associates decides to make an offer on one of the broker's own listings. As a general rule, brokers should not purchase one of their own listings, especially if the price is a real bargain. The risks to the professional image of the broker are too great, not to mention the risks of loss of commission for breach of the duties of good faith and loyalty and loss of license under TRELA §15(a)(6)(J) and/or (V) and 22 TAC §535.150 and §535.156. To minimize exposure to liability, brokers desiring to purchase in-house listings should recommend that sellers obtain confirming appraisals and retain other consultants or advisers.

SITUATION: *Debra lists her home with Broker Sid for $100,000. After six months of marketing, Debra has received only one offer, for $75,000. Sid offers to pay $95,000 by way of an assumption of the $80,000 first mortgage and further agrees to reduce the 7 percent listing fee to 3½ percent. Five days before closing, Sid meets Betty, a recent arrival, who buys the home from Sid for $110,000 five days after closing.*

QUESTION: *Did Sid breach a fiduciary duty to Debra?*

DISCUSSION: *Probably, if Sid did not inform Debra immediately upon learning of the Betty's offer. TREC Rule 22 TAC §535.156 requires that a broker "must put the interest of his [or her] principal above his [or her] own interest" and that he or she has "an affirmative duty to keep his [or her] principal informed at all times of significant information applicable to the transaction." TREC Rules 22 TAC §535.2(f) and §535.16 require Sid to obtain the best possible transaction and the best possible price. Even if technically Sid was found to have breached no fiduciary duty, the appearance of wrong is there. Sid may have a difficult time proving to a jury that he acted in Debra's best interest, particularly if the home's appraised value exceeded the listing price. At best, there will always be a doubt in the mind of Debra as to whether Sid stole a profit opportunity away from her. Even if Betty had not appeared until a few days after closing, Sid would have a tough time convincing a jury that he didn't knowingly underprice the house at the time of the listing, which would be an additional breach of fiduciary duty and a deceptive trade practice. Sid should offer to return to Debra all or a fair portion of the quick profit or allow Debra the opportunity to sell direct to Betty. Such an attitude enhances the broker's professional standing in the community. It may enhance the broker's reputation so much that it more than makes up for the temporary loss of revenue. However, the fact that it is more profitable is not an appropriate standard by which to measure moral conduct. It is easy for brokers to say they promote the client's best interests above anyone else's, including their own. It is much more effective to demonstrate these qualities. [*See Wilson v. Donze, *692 S.W.2d 735 (Tex. App. 2 Dist. 1985). Broker had a duty to obtain the best price possible, even above the asking price. Even though seller ultimately determines the list price, broker's duty is still to obtain best possible price.]*

The risks of a lawsuit increase if the broker buying an in-house listing is competing against offers submitted by cooperating brokers on behalf of the buyers or by buyer's brokers on behalf of their clients. The listing broker has an unfair competitive advantage over other buyers because the broker knows all the bids. Section 15(a)(6)(V) of the License Act, concerning dealing in bad faith and dishonest dealings, will also apply. The listing broker should reveal to other buyers the price and terms of any prior or subsequent offer submitted by the listing broker (*see* Article 12, NAR® Code of Ethics). The broker risks possible action by the buyer for breach of the general duty of fairness and/or honesty. Such an action could be based on failure to present the buyer's offer in a timely manner, failure to notify a buyer after the broker outbid the buyer or failure to reveal information the buyer might have used to justify a more attractive offering price, such as a pending beneficial zoning change.

State licensing law often requires that real estate licensees disclose in writing their true positions when offering to buy property listed with the broker. Although TRELA §15(a)(6)(J) requires this disclosure, it does not require that it be in writing. However, coupled with TRELA 15C it may be possible to convincingly demonstrate that it must also be in writing because self-dealing might be characterized by the plaintiff seller's lawyer as the most dangerous of all forms of dual agency. The necessity for this disclosure also applies when the buyer is related to the listing broker in some way, for example, as a family member, member of a corporation or a business partner. As the buyer, the listing broker must remember that unless the agency is terminated, the broker is still a fiduciary of the seller, must act primarily for the benefit of the seller and owes the seller the standard duties of full disclosure, skill and care, in addition to honesty and fairness.

Buying Property Listed in a MLS. A broker may decide to purchase a property listed in the MLS by another firm. The broker should disclaim any subagency to the seller. Otherwise, the seller may claim that the buyer/broker owed fiduciary duties to the seller under any MLS offer of subagency. Note that brokers are not normal consumers and may be required, under agency law, to disclose their opinion of value or of the likelihood of future appreciation. [22 TAC 535.16(d)]

Sellers have won cases against cooperating brokers who bought for their own accounts. The successes of these suits have been based on failure by brokers to disclose the true market value (one week after purchase of a property, for example, a broker listed it on its financial statement at a $20,000 greater value) or to disclose that a simple subdivision of the property would increase its market value by 25 percent. The sellers won because the cooperating brokers owed fiduciary duties to the sellers based on the rules of subagency. These cases might have turned out differently had the brokers rejected subagency from the beginning, made all proper disclosures and documented them before proceeding.

If there is to be a commission split, the listing broker should fully disclose so. This amount is often used as part of the down payment. The cooperating broker should disclose in the purchase contract that the receipt of such split does not create an agency relationship between the other broker (i.e., the buyer) and the seller. It is much safer for the broker/buyer to disclaim subagency, deduct the fee from the offering price and not participate in the fee paid by the seller.

Buying from a FSBO Owner. Brokers buying properties for sale by owner (FSBO) should disclaim any agency relationship with the sellers and should not approach the seller under the guise of representing the seller's best interests and/or listing the property. Otherwise, they may be deemed to be agents of the sellers. If the brokers are deemed to be agents, the effect will be to hold them to a higher standard of care with a greater duty to sellers as to disclosure. [22 TAC &535.16(c) and (d)]

The FSBO seller often agrees to pay a reduced commission amount to the broker/buyer as a "courtesy fee." The seller may later argue that the payment of a fee to the broker/buyer was enough to create an agency relationship. At a minimum, the broker/buyer should insert disclaimer language, such as: "Seller understands that buyer is a licensed real estate broker buying for the broker's own account and is not acting as an agent of the seller. Seller is not relying on broker for any advice or counsel regarding the sale. Broker has advised seller that seller is free to obtain an independent consultant."

Licensed Associates Buying. The same principles discussed above for brokers apply equally to licensed associates buying for their own accounts. Some realty firms have a policy that prohibits or limits the right of its associates to buy properties listed with the firm. In some cases the property must be offered to the public for at least 45 days before anyone in-house is allowed to make an offer on the property. These firms believe that the risks of alienating clients and prospective buyers outweigh any benefits to the brokerage firm.

If the associate does offer to buy property listed with the broker, the contract should clearly state that the seller understands that the buyer is employed by the listing broker.

If the associate is buying property listed in a MLS (offering subagency) and is receiving a commission split, both the associate and the broker are considered subagents of the seller unless they clearly disclaim any agency relationship. As subagents, they would both owe complete fiduciary duties to the seller. Another approach, thought by some to be a somewhat safer for the buyer/associate, would be to take a buyer's broker position, offer a lower net price, and not participate in any fee paid by the seller. The salesperson will have to discuss compensation with the cooperating broker, who normally expects to receive a portion of the commission split from the listing broker. If, for example, the cooperating broker normally would have received $1,000 from the sales proceeds (from a higher gross price), perhaps the salesperson can compensate by paying the cooperating broker $1,000 directly and reducing the offering price accordingly. The seller may not care, provided his or her net proceeds are not less than they would be in a gross price sale.

Selling Broker's Own Property. Brokers who sell their own property must disclose to a prospective purchaser that the seller is a licensed broker. For the protection of both the broker and buyer, brokers should also make clear to buyers that they are not acting as agents for the buyers and that buyers are free to seek independent representation. This is true regardless of whether the broker has a full or a partial ownership, as when he or she is part of an investment group that owns the property. [TRELA §15(a)(3) and 22 TAC §535.144]

Some brokers limit the number of properties, owned by a associate, that can be sold at reduced commission rates. Brokers fear that associates will create the impression of spending valuable time competing for qualified buyers with sellers who have listed properties with the broker. Other brokers prohibit their associates from marketing their personally owned property to past or present clients to avoid any impression of impropriety. Associates should always inform their broker of any intention to sell any personal property.

Adopting the Buyer

If there is no cooperating broker involved, the listing broker often spends a good deal of time with the buyer both before and after the contract is signed. A clear conflict arises in the back-to-back sale if the broker, before the offer is made, signs a listing with the buyer to resell the property. More likely, however, is a situation in which a broker "adopts" a buyer during the closing process, agreeing, for example, to list other properties of the buyer, to cooperatively develop the property or otherwise create an implied or express conflict of interest and/or representation agreement with the buyer.

Suppose the listing broker is asked by a buyer prior to closing to look for a resale buyer at $10,000 more than the contract price. While there is nothing illegal about taking a listing from a buyer after the contract is signed, the listing broker ethically and legally must disclose the dual agency to the seller. The seller might feel, in retrospect, that the broker, before the contract was signed, failed to disclose the existence of a resale buyer and possible higher selling price so that the broker could make a double commission.

DUAL AGENCY DISCLOSURES

If a broker intends to be a dual agent, the prudent way to explain the agency role of the broker is to deliver separate disclosure statements to both the buyer and the seller. The disclosure statements should be tailored specifically to the particular facts and clients in that specific transaction. They should clearly point out the potential for conflict of interest and the advantages and risks of a dual agency. This will alert the clients to the fact that they should assume more responsibility in making decisions than would be the case if each client had his or her own independent broker. Figures 7.2, 7.3 and 7.4 show sample TAR® disclosures.

Informed Consent

Comprehensive and separate disclosures, consented to by both the buyer and the seller, have a much better chance to withstand an informed-consent challenge than would preprinted boilerplate language or an one-line statement in the sales contract to the effect that buyer and seller understand the brokerage represents both. Informed consent is more than just knowing that one and the same agent represents both the buyer and the seller. The broker is obligated to disclose all facts relevant to the buyer's and the seller's decisions of whether or not to consent to the common representation. Not, of course, the precise set of those facts that would be confidential under 15C if a dual agency were consented to, but rather, in that case, the categories of facts or types of fact situations that could not be disclosed.

Unlike some professions, the real estate industry does not have extensive conflict of interest guidelines or suggested dual agency disclosure forms to help brokers. This explains why real estate agents in the field are confused on how best to handle the disclosure of dual agency. The medical profession, for example, has stressed the need to explain to patients in plain language, prior to obtaining their written consent, the nature of the medical operation or service to be performed. The emphasis is on the patient's informed consent.

Under the legal profession's disciplinary rules, a lawyer may represent both the buyer and the seller only if it is obvious that the lawyer can adequately represent the interests of each and only if each consents to the representation after full disclosure of the possible effect of such representation on the exercise of the lawyer's independent professional judgment on behalf of each. Like real estate agents, attorneys have the same arguments among themselves whether, despite such guidelines, an attorney can timely and adequately represent both sides of a real estate transaction.

Unlike the attorney, a real estate broker is hired to market and sell a property, not just to act as a fiduciary. The buyer and seller are not generally adversarial to the same degree as are the plaintiff and defendant in a lawsuit. They each have a goal to effect a transfer of the property on terms satisfactory to themselves.

It is not sufficient that brokers simply make up their own minds to assume the role of fair and honest intermediaries with both buyers and sellers. Both buyers and sellers must fully understand that dual agent brokers are also brokers for the other parties

Figure 7.2 Sample Dual Agency Consent Request Letter

John Blair
200 Dayton
Dallas, Texas

Dear Mr. Blair:

Bob Chaillet of our downtown office listed your residence under an exclusive authorization to sell contract.

John Delfino of our main office has been hired by a prospective buyer to find suitable property. Mr. Delfino has discussed your property with the buyer who has expressed an interest in finding out more about the property. It appears this qualified buyer is a serious prospect for your property.

Mr. Chaillet and Mr. Delfino are both licensed associates with Bay Realty. Bay Realty is, therefore, an agent for both you and the prospective buyer. It is a potential conflict of interest for our firm to represent both buyer and seller in the same transaction, even though separate licensed associates are involved. The conflict could arise because both you and the prospective buyer may rely upon the advice of associates within the same company. The advice may, in some instances, favor the position of one side over the other. For a dual agency to be lawful in Texas, neither of our associates, acting for Bay Realty, is allowed to give either you or the buyer the benefit of our advice, opinions or counsel on matters that could violate our legal duty to remain impartial.

Before any such dual representation takes place, we want to disclose to you the existence of this potential conflict of interest. It is our policy, and state law, not to undertake this dual representation without your written consent, as well as that of the buyer.

By signing this letter you are acknowledging that Bay Realty represents both buyer and seller, subject to the attached dual agency agreement, drawn up in accordance with TRELA §15C of the Texas Real Estate License Act, and that Bay Realty and all its associates will serve in a limited agency capacity to bring both buyer and seller together. If you consent to this common representation, you should understand that Bay Realty must be impartial to both sides, as required by law in a dual agency. It should be understood that, unless express permission has been given and the attached dual agency agreement is signed by both parties, Bay Realty may not continue with this potential transaction as a representative or agent for both buyer and seller.

Any agreement between buyer and seller as to a final contract price and other terms is a result of negotiations between buyer and seller acting in their own best interests and on their own behalf. By signing this letter and contract, you acknowledge that Bay Realty has explained the risks and implications of dual representations, including the fact that opinions of market value and all other significant professional opinions, given to you at the time of listing, must be given to the buyer in a dual agency situation.

Please call me if you have any questions.

Very truly yours,

GEORGE DRUGER, Principal Broker
Bay Realty

I have read the explanation above and acknowledge that I have been afforded the opportunity to discuss this letter and the attached dual agency agreement with my own advisers. I consent to the dual representation by Bay Realty, as outlined by the terms of the attached dual agency agreement. Bay Realty will be acting through Bob Chaillet and John Delfino, licensed associates of Bay Realty.

____________________________ ____________
Signature Date

Figure 7.3 Sample Notification of Dual Agency to Sellers or Landlords

EQUAL HOUSING OPPORTUNITY

TEXAS ASSOCIATION OF REALTORS®

SAMPLE NOTIFICATION OF DUAL AGENCY TO BUYERS OR TENANTS

To be used only if dual agency was previously authorized in buyer representation agreement

REALTOR®

__________ *(Date)*

________________ *(Buyer's or Tenant's Name)*
________________ *(Address)*
________________ *(City, State, Zip)*

Re: ______________ *(Property Address)*

Dear ______________: *(Buyer's or Tenant's Name)*

In accordance with paragraph _____ *(insert appropriate paragraph #)* of the ________ *(buyer or tenant)* representation agreement you entered into with this firm, we are notifying you that the property located at ________________________________ *(property address)* is a listing of this firm. This firm agreed to represent the ____________ *(seller or landlord)* of that property, ________________________ ________________________ *(name of seller or landlord)* through a listing agreement.

Since this firm represents both you and the prospective ______________ *(seller or landlord)*, this firm now faces a potential conflict of interest. Please recall that paragraph _____ *(insert appropriate paragraph #)* of the __________ *(buyer or tenant)* representation agreement discussed how we would resolve any potential conflict. When this firm presents an offer from you to ________________________ *(name of seller or landlord)* this firm will treat both parties honestly and impartially so as not to favor one party over the other. During the negotiations regarding the offer, this firm will act in accordance with the provisions of paragraph _____ *(insert appropriate paragraph #)* of the __________ *(buyer or tenant)* representation agreement.

(If applicable insert the following paragraph): This firm also wishes to inform you of the following additional information regarding a potential conflict of interest: ________________________
____
(disclose any relevant information that may affect a person's decision to authorize dual agency; e.g., existence of personal relationships, prior business relationships, or contemplated future business relationships).

If you have any questions about this situation or if you have any objections to this firm representing both you and ____________________________ *(name of seller or landlord)* during the negotiations please notify this firm immediately. We would appreciate your acknowledgment of this letter by signing below.

Sincerely,

______________________ *(Name of Firm)*
By: ____________________ *(Broker's or Agent's Name)*

ACKNOWLEDGMENT AND CONSENT: I/we acknowledge receipt of this letter and understand its contents. I/we do not object to ____________________________ *(name of brokerage firm)* representing both me/us and the named prospective ___________ *(seller(s) or landlord(s))* in any negotiations for the __________ *(purchase or lease)* of the property.

____________________________ ______________
(Buyer's or Tenant's Signature) Date

____________________________ ______________
(Buyer's or Tenant's Signature) Date

(TAR-027A) Rev. 9-7-93 Page 1 of 1

Figure 7.4 Sample Notification of Dual Agency to Buyers or Tenants

TEXAS ASSOCIATION OF REALTORS®

SAMPLE NOTIFICATION OF DUAL AGENCY TO SELLERS OR LANDLORDS

To be used only if dual agency was previously authorized in listing agreement

EQUAL HOUSING OPPORTUNITY

REALTOR®

__________ *(Date)*

__________________ *(Seller's or Landlord's Name)*
__________________ *(Address)*
__________________ *(City, State, Zip)*

Re: ______________ *(Property Address)*

Dear ______________ *(Seller's or Landlord's Name)*

In accordance with paragraph ______ *(insert appropriate paragraph #)* of the listing agreement you entered into with this firm for the ___________ *(sale or lease)* of your property, this firm is notifying you that a __________ *(buyer or tenant)*, ________________________, *(name of buyer or tenant)* who this firm has agreed to represent is interested in making an offer to __________ *(purchase or lease)* your property.

Since this firm represents both you and the prospective ___________ *(buyer or tenant)*, this firm now faces a potential conflict of interest. Please recall that paragraph ______ *(insert appropriate paragraph #)* of the listing agreement discussed how we would resolve any potential conflict. When this firm presents an offer from ______________________________ *(name of buyer or tenant)* to you this firm will treat both parties honestly and impartially so as not to favor one party over the other. During the negotiations regarding the offer from ______________________________ *(name of buyer or tenant)*, this firm will act in accordance with the provisions of paragraph ______ *(insert appropriate paragraph #)* of the listing agreement.

(If applicable insert the following paragraph): This firm also wishes to inform you of the following additional information regarding a potential conflict of interest: ______________________________
____
(disclose any relevant information that may affect a person's decision to authorize dual agency; e.g., existence of personal relationships, prior business relationships, or contemplated future business relationships).

If you have any questions about this situation or if you have any objections to this firm representing both you and ______________________________ *(name of buyer or tenant)* during the negotiations please notify this firm immediately. We would appreciate your acknowledgment of this letter by signing below.

Sincerely,

______________________ *(Name of Firm)*
By: ___________________ *(Broker's or Agent's Name)*

ACKNOWLEDGMENT AND CONSENT: I/we acknowledge receipt of this letter and understand its contents. I/we do not object to ______________________ *(name of brokerage firm)* representing both me/us and the named prospective ___________ *(buyer(s) or tenant(s))* in any negotiations for the __________ *(sale or lease)* of my/our property.

______________________________ ______________
(Seller's or Landlord's Signature) Date

______________________________ ______________
(Seller's or Landlord's Signature) Date

(TAR-027) Rev. 9-7-93

Page 1 of 1

and that brokers, to avoid conflicts of loyalty, may, in effect, be acting as facilitators or mediators so as not to favor one side over the other. In a few situations, it is unlawful to represent both the buyer and the seller, even with their consent. For example, the Federal Bankruptcy Act forbids a real estate broker from representing both the debtor/seller and the prospective buyer.

Extent of Disclosure. The State of Texas (i.e., TREC or the legislature) has not developed a dual agency contract form. Various, state and local trade associations and individual brokers have originated their own dual agency agreements, incorporating the state-mandated TRELA §15C explanations and terminology. TREC Agency Disclosure Form Number 3 is **not** a consent form but rather a combination information form and a disclosure of who the agent currently represents. Even by signing, the consumer has not evidenced consent nor have the requirements of TRELA § 15C been met. The consumer signing the form is merely acknowledging that he or she has been given the form. TREC does not develop listing agreements or any form that purports to spell out the relationship or agreements that licensees may have with their customers and clients. TAR® does produce them, however, and so do local associations.

However, TREC and the state legislature do put a few limitations on the agency agreements as to a few specific provisions and wording. For instance, in TRELA §15(a)(6)(G) we find that it is grounds for loss of license for "failing to specify in a listing contract a definite termination date which is not subject to prior notice." TREC Rule 22 TAC § 535.148(a) clarifies the statute by stating,

> (a) Every listing contract shall have a definite termination date, upon which date the listing will automatically expire without any requirement of notice to the real estate licensee.

Brokers need to give careful thought to the extent of dual agency agreement. It needs to be legally sufficient, and it needs to be something the licensed associates can work with in the field. The initial draft of the dual agency agreement should be reviewed by the company attorney, as well as the company management team. Extensive training should be given in the appropriate use of the agreement. At a minimum, the agreement should describe the limited agency role the dual agent must play, the role of buyer and seller in handling all of their own negotiating and the specific types of actions the broker can and cannot do for both clients, such as how disclosures or non-disclosures of comparables and the preparation of CMAs for both parties will be handled. In addition, each client should review the agreement and the transaction with their own attorney and other advisors.

Timing of Disclosure

In addition to being meaningful, the disclosures must be made in a timely manner. Early identification of a dual agency situation will permit the renegotiation of any existing agency relationship with the seller or the buyer. A consent signed at the closing table is too late to be effective. Because, in Texas, it is now statutorily against the law to be a dual agent without the proper prior written agreements, operating as a dual agent prior to the writings being executed will very likely be a violation of the License Act. Likewise, in a case where negotiations have gone on for several months, a one-line dual agency statement on the final purchase contract is insufficient. At the time of signing the contract, the buyer and the seller may be excited or nervous about entering into the transaction. Typically, each side is optimistic and believes that nothing is going to go wrong. Given these pressures, the buyer and the seller may be quick to sign anything, including dual agency consents. Later, if the deal sours or they find another property or tenant they like better, they may challenge the effectiveness of such consents.

Disclosures and consents should occur as early in the transaction as is practicable to help maximize the broker's protection against dual agency claims. When dual agency becomes an issue in a lawsuit, the broker has the burden of proving that the disclosures were made, that they were timely and adequate and that the broker used "due diligence to assist the parties in understanding the consents, agreements or instructions" under Section 15C of the License Act, which permits him or her "to represent more than one party to a transaction." [TRELA §15C(d)]

Different Approaches

Brokers are beginning to experiment with new disclosure practices to reduce their exposure to dual agency claims. For example, South Side Realty may have recently adopted a policy under which any buyer client must agree in the buyer agency agreement that South Side Realty will not represent the buyer on any in-house listing. The buyers can represent themselves or find an appraiser, broker or attorney to advise them on the purchase of an in-house listed property. A different approach may be that of North Side Realty, a brokerage firm that emphasizes prospecting for buyers who are relocating to its area (large corporate transfers or military personnel). North Side Realty might advise its seller clients, in the listing agreement, that the firm searches for, cultivates and qualifies buyers moving to the area; that the firm treats these buyers as clients; that many of these buyers would be ideal buyers for the seller's property; that the firm intends to represent both these buyers and the sellers; and that to reduce the conflict, the firm will assign separate salespeople to help negotiate on behalf of each. While this approach still does not insulate North Side Realty from dual agency claims, it at least attempts to clarify the situation through early disclosure to the seller and the buyer.

East Side Realty may take yet another position. This position might be to show its in-house listings to all buyers, whether clients or customers. If a buyer customer decides to make an offer, there is no dual agency problem because the broker has earlier clarified to the customer that the broker represents the seller. If a buyer client decides to make an offer, then an in-house dual agency arises. In this case, the broker, the seller and the buyer all consider whether to enter into a new agreement that will terminate the earlier agency agreements among the parties. This new agreement will set forth the fiduciary relationship among the parties, delineate the responsibilities of each party and determine how negotiations are to be handled.

In the event that the buyer, the seller or both parties refuse to sign an informed consent disclosure letter and the dual agency agreement required by TRELA §15C, then the broker might renounce one of the agencies and withdraw from the transaction as a dual agent. However, the realities may be that he or she will have to withdraw from the transaction altogether. For example, the listing broker may withdraw from representing the buyer, as to this particular property, although the broker may agree to continue representing the buyer in the acquisition of other properties.

ROLE OF DUAL AGENT

After full disclosure of the representation alternatives, the buyer and the seller might agree that the broker will be a collector of information and a messenger of positions rather than a broker who will investigate, disclose, advise, negotiate and fully protect a principal's best interests. If the buyer and the seller, after having been informed as to what the law requires, still want to complete the transaction using only the single broker, it is possible that they are not legally prevented from restructuring the agency relationship and changing or limiting the type of representation expected from the agent by state law.

The buyer and the seller might place the real estate agent in the same category as an escrow agent. An escrow agent acts as the agent of the buyer for holding the money and the agent of the seller for holding the transfer documents. For other purposes, the escrow agent acts as an impartial facilitator or messenger. By the very nature of its role, escrow cannot favor one side over the other.

The buyer and the seller might agree that an agent from one brokerage can act as the buyer's representative while another agent from the same brokerage can represent the seller; however, such an arrangement runs counter to TRELA §15C. Both the buyer and the seller should be told—and consent to—the type of service they can expect from their agent. This approach is not risk-free, however, as it is difficult to prevent potentially compromising information from being exchanged between associates.

Some would recommend another approach, which is to point out that the dual agent may be making recommendations for one side that may not, at that time, necessarily favor the other side. Still, this argument goes, the task of the dual agent is to reach a negotiated agreement generally acceptable, but not necessarily favorable, to both the buyer and the seller. In the course of negotiations, the dual agent might suggest that the seller, who has been asked to carry back a second loan, require a higher down payment, a shorter term and a higher interest rate than proposed by the buyer. The agent might point out to the buyer that it is not in the buyer's best interests to accept a due on sale clause, but it is advisable to request a non-recourse loan. The balancing act is not always comfortable and any such advice should be clearly documented in writing and made available to all parties during the negotiating process. Another approach is to encourage the buyer and seller to directly negotiate significant price and term matters between themselves with the dual agent looking on to clarify problems and facilitate dialogue until agreement is reached.

LIMITED OR STATUTORY AGENCY

There is a trend to pass legislation that will authorize the listing broker to designate one licensed associate to represent a seller or landlord and a different associate in the same firm to represent the buyer or tenant in the same transaction. Maine has recently passed just such legislation, LD 1714, which creates, by statute, a new class of statutory agent entitled an *appointed agent.* This type of legislation is designed to create an invisible wall, permitting two associates of the same broker to actively advocate for their respective clients, just as if the transaction involved separate companies or brokers. This type of legislation, as first adopted in Illinois, will have to pass the scrutiny of the courts in every state (which is the recommendation of the NAR®).

CONSENSUAL DUAL AGENCY

Real estate companies with a large market share often find themselves advising their buyer clients interested in company listings. Recognizing the likelihood of a dual agency situation arising, these companies insert a provision into their listing agreements covering the possibility of dual agency. This clause points out that, because the company represents buyers as well as sellers, it is likely that a qualified buyer client might become interested in the seller client's listed property (if the seller lists with this type company). If so, the broker would be a dual agent. In most cases, it is argued, the broker would be able to represent them to reach a mutually acceptable transaction.

Some advantages of consensual dual agency are:

- For the broker:
    - Lessens the risks associated with the completely undisclosed dual agency
    - Enables one broker to control entire transaction and receive full commission
- For the buyer:
    - Allows a knowledgeable buyer to neutralize the effectiveness of the seller's agent to negotiate for the best possible transaction for his or her seller client, a duty the seller's agent, who was not a dual agent, would otherwise be required by law to undertake
    - Allows a buyer to see homes he or she might not otherwise get to see if working with a broker who has a substantial number of listings but won't show them without consensual dual agency
- For the seller:
    - Allows a knowledgeable seller to neutralize the effectiveness of the buyer's agent to negotiate for the best possible transaction for his or her buyer client, a duty the buyer's agent, who was not a dual agent, would otherwise be required to undertake by law
    - Allows a seller to have more prospective buyers see his or her home than might otherwise get to see it if working with a broker who has a substantial number of buyer clients but won't show them the seller's home unless the seller consents to the dual agency

Some disadvantages of consensual dual agency are:

- For the buyer and seller:
    - Neither buyer/tenant nor seller/landlord receive full representation, expert advice or advocacy
- For the broker:
    - Confusion over proper role and conduct of broker, licensed associate, buyer or tenant and landlord or seller
    - Unlawful in Texas if not in writing prior to commencement of the dual representation, with complete disclosures and consents required by TRELA § 15C.

NON-AGENTS

As an alternative to dual agency, some states have introduced the concept of facilitator into their law. For our purposes, a *facilitator* may be defined as one who assists a buyer and a seller in reaching an agreement in a real estate transaction without being an advocate for the interests of any one party but instead for the mutual interest of all parties. As such, the facilitator is an agent of neither the seller or buyer individually nor both simultaneously. In some states, the facilitator is labeled a *transaction broker* (Colorado), *transaction coordinator* (Michigan) or a *limited dual agent* (Georgia). The courts in Texas frequently refer to a non-agent, non-principal licensee in a real estate transaction as a *middleman* or *finder.*

Some of the situations in which a facilitator or middleman approach could apply are when the consumer does not want to retain an agent, when the consumer does not want to have vicarious liability for an agency relationship or when the seller does not allow his or her broker to offer subagency and the buyer does not want to sign an agency agreement.

Texas law has never favored real estate licensees functioning as middlemen or facilitators, and the courts usually find a way to hold that they were in fact agents of one or more parties to the transaction. The Rules of the Commission clarify that the "License Act is an agency law." [22 TAC 535.1(c)] The act's purpose is to protect the public from fraud, negligence and incompetence on the part of real estate licensees. Holding licensees to a fiduciary standard produces accountability and possibility for legal remedies for the damages caused by that trio of wrongs. The facilitator role could weaken those remedies because of the lessening of accountability, leaving the public defenseless against specially licensed and trained experts.

Statutes regarding facilitators, in those states which have them, usually specify the duties of the real estate licensee. In general, the facilitator must use reasonable skill and care, present all offers, disclose known material facts, account for monies received and assist in closing the transaction. The critical difference is that a facilitator cannot act as an advocate, market analyst, advisor or risk benefit analyst for the buyer or seller and must, by law, make that fact clear.

It is interesting to observe whether consumers are willing to pay equal amounts for a facilitator as for an agent (with duties of loyalty and advocacy). The 1993 Report of the NAR® Presidential Advisory Group on the Facilitator/Non-Agency Concept recommended that "NAR® should not further develop or promote the pure non-agency facilitator concept" but instead suggested elements for a legislative framework that clarifies the common law by creating a statutorily defined limited agency relationship unless the licensee and the client enter into an agreement specifically providing for a different type of relationship. Importantly, the legislation should provide for the ability on the part of a broker in an in-company transaction to designate an individual licensee within the broker's company to represent the seller and to designate another individual licensee within the company to represent the buyer without creating a dual agency relationship. Also, the legislation should eliminate or modify the consumer's vicarious liability for the acts of the licensee. Finally, the report recommended, the legislation specifically should state that it overrules the common law of agency as it applies to real estate brokerage relationships.

NONRESIDENTIAL DUAL AGENCY

Dual agency is not confined to residential transactions, and brokers should be especially aware of dual agency issues arising in real estate exchanges, syndications, farm and ranch, industrial, special use properties and commercial transactions.

Exchanges

Some brokers help owners exchange property under the Internal Revenue Code of 1986 Section 1031 Tax-Deferred Exchange Provisions. Clear disclosures must be made when only one broker is involved with more than one party to an exchange. With one agent and two commissions at stake, there is ample temptation for the nonprofessional broker to compromise the interests of either or both parties. There is often more than one broker involved in an exchange. Until recently, exchange brokers would pool their fees and split them equally to avoid arguments over fair compensation in cases in which the market values of the exchanged properties were very different. This practice has been generally discontinued.

Syndications

Dual agency problems may arise in several situations in which the general partner of a limited partnership syndication is also a broker; for example, if:

- the general partner sells or leases partnership property for a fee to be paid by the partnership;
- the general partner sells his or her own property to the partnership for a fee;
- the general partner, on behalf of the partnership, buys property listed with another firm and seeks a commission split; or
- the general partner, on behalf of the partnership, buys unlisted property and seeks compensation from the seller/owner.

The general partner has a primary fiduciary obligation to other general partners and limited partners. The broker should represent and be paid by the partnership only, unless full disclosures are made and written consent is obtained from all principals and brokers involved.

Commercial Leasing Agent

Brokers involved in commercial real estate leasing may find themselves in potential dual agency situations. Leasing agents often work under exclusive-right-to-lease listings from developers or building owners. Usually, a MLS does not require the listing of commercial leases. In commercial leasing, there frequently is a great deal of negotiation between the owner and lessee regarding lease terms and concessions. The leasing agent is usually at the center of such negotiations and should be careful to assure that both the owner and the lessee understand the role of the leasing agent.

In many cases the lessee is sophisticated and is represented by an attorney and/or accountant, in which case the lessee probably will not look to the owner's leasing agent for advice of a legal or financial nature. Often the principals do their own negotiations and look to the broker as an effective go-between. The lessee looks to the leasing agent more for accurate information and figures, especially about market trends and economic factors, which typically are not within the attorney's field of expertise.

For those cases when the lessee has no advisor and looks to the leasing agent for negotiating advice, a cautious leasing agent will have the owner and lessee consent to a dual agency agreement and further recommend that the lessor or lessee obtain his or her own legal counsel.

Leasing agents may work with lessees to locate and evaluate specific sites. It is not unusual for a leasing agent to approach the owner of an unlisted building. In these no-listing transactions, there should be a clear written understanding as to whom the leasing agent represents, especially when the owner is being asked to pay the commission.

SUMMARY

Undisclosed dual agency is a clear breach of the agent's fiduciary duty of loyalty. Even when the agent intends to act as a dual agent, such representation is unlawful if adequate disclosure is not given to both the buyer and the seller and unless consents are obtained from both in the form of a written contract meeting the requirements of the License Act. Most dual agencies, however, are accidental and arise because of the conduct of the parties. Brokers need to establish internal management controls to lessen the risks of unintended dual agency and underdisclosed dual agency. While the risks of a dual agency must be recognized, there are several excellent alternatives.

KEY POINTS

- In Texas, disclosure and consent for a dual agency must be accomplished before it can arise lawfully. It cannot be delayed until the sales contract is prepared. If disclosure of a dual agency occurs after the dual agency comes into being, the dual agency is unlawful.
- If properly entered into and conducted, consensual dual agency is lawful; however, undisclosed or underdisclosed dual agency is illegal.
- It is possible to sell your own listing without becoming a dual agent, provided the buyer remains a customer.
- The dual agency agreement must outline what it is the dual agent can and cannot do as a limited representative. Merely providing the statutory minimums may not be enough, but they must be included.
- If a broker plans on being a dual agent then he or she should lay a foundation early by discussing the possibility of dual agency with in-house sales at the listing stage. The possibility of dual agency should never be sprung on a client. Attempting to get blanket consent to a dual agency in advance at the time of listing or signing with a buyer broker or tenant rep is not advisable, even if permitted by statute.

SUGGESTIONS FOR BROKERS

Brokers who purchase listed properties for themselves or in joint ventures with buyer clients should at least consider buying them net without commission (lower the offering price) and disclosing in writing that the properties are purchased for the brokers' own accounts. Brokers should consider formally terminating the agency and perhaps recommending that the sellers retain real estate consultants for advice. Read and discuss 22 TAC 535.16(d) and TRELA §15(a)(6)(J) before writing this section of your company policy manual.

Brokers should consider not accepting a commission in a purchase from a FSBO. Brokers may be held to have a fiduciary duty to the seller. Brokers who do take the risk should use full and understandable disclaimer language.

QUIZ

1. A broker can accept compensation from both the buyer and the seller under what conditions?

   a. Under no circumstances
   b. Only if there is a written listing from both
   c. Only if both consent after full disclosure of the dual compensation
   d. Only if the total amount is reasonable

2. What are some of the remedies available in the event a broker acts as a dual agent without disclosure or consent?

   a. Rescission of the contract
   b. Forfeiture of commission
   c. Loss of license
   d. All of the above

3. George listed his home with Sally. Alice asked Jeff to help her find a home. Jeff contacted Sally as a result of Sally's listing in the MLS, which offered subagency. Which statement best describes Jeff's status upon showing George's home to Betty?

   a. Jeff is the agent of Sally.
   b. Jeff is the subagent of George.
   c. Jeff is Betty's agent.
   d. Jeff may be the agent of George or Betty or both, depending on his actions.

4. Undisclosed dual agency is permitted in:

   a. commercial transactions.
   b. residential transactions.
   c. syndications.
   d. None of the above

5. State licensing laws prohibit which of the following?

   a. Dual agency
   b. Dual escrows
   c. Dual commissions
   d. Dual contracts

DISCUSSION QUESTIONS

1. What should be covered in an informed consent disclosure to a dual agency?
2. Is there a dual agency problem if two salespeople from the same office represent the buyer and the seller separately?
3. What are some ways brokers can reduce their exposure to dual agency claims on in-house sales where no dual agency is intended?
4. What should you do if you decide to purchase one of your company's listings? Suppose the property is listed in the MLS by another broker?
5. In what ways is representation by a dual agent more limited than representation by a single agent?

CHAPTER

8

SINGLE AGENCY

By many within the real estate industry, the term *agency* is now being modified with the adjective *single.* Single agency is not a recognized legal term; it is a descriptive term that, on the surface, appears to attempt to distinguish dual agency from agency. The broker practicing *single agency* or *non-specific client-based agency* must understand the specific procedural and position features of both representing sellers and representing buyers.

This chapter presents an overview of the following agency practice issues applied to a broker who has decided to practice single agency without limiting his or her client base to only one category of clients:

Practicing Single Agency
Counseling Sessions Prior to Engagement
Conflicts of Interest
Hybrid Approach
Advantages and Disadvantages

PRACTICING SINGLE AGENCY

A single agency broker represents either the buyer or seller, tenant or landlord or only one party to an exchange, but never both in the same transaction. The single agency broker is a person-oriented agent rather than a position-oriented agent, meaning that his or her client target market is not related to the client's relationship to the property, as is an exclusively buyer's or seller's agent, but rather to the needs of an individual person, whether that person is buying, selling, leasing, developing or building real estate. The single agency type of brokerage practice appeals to those real estate professionals who are interested in long-term broker-client relationships in which the agent becomes part of the family advisory team, just as the family doctor, lawyer and accountant are.

In some cases, the single agency broker is paid directly by the broker's client, be it the buyer, seller, tenant or landlord. In other cases, the single agency broker is compensated indirectly by the another party as a term of the contract or is paid by an authorized commission split from the broker representing the other side in the transaction.

James B. Warkentin, in *Buyer Brokering: How to Represent and Get Paid by the Buyer,* describes single agency as follows:

> Single agency means that each principal can choose to be represented by their own broker or to represent themselves. Since all listed sellers have their own broker, this area is not a problem. It is the buyer who needs the choice of being a client of his own broker or representing himself. At this time, the vast majority of buyers are customers and are not given a choice. In essence, this means that client quality services are available to sellers and customer quality services are available to buyers. Client quality services are always greater than customer quality services. This is in the nature of the relationship. For example, you are a client with your attorney, a customer with a new car salesperson.

The NAR®'s handbook, *Who Is My Client?,* states:

> The obvious alternative to dual agency is single agency: A real estate broker should have one and only one principal per transaction; he [or she] should loyally and diligently pursue the legitimate interests of his [or her] principal and should scrupulously avoid accepting or exercising any authority on behalf of the other party to the transaction.

Being a single agency broker does not mean, however, that there must be two brokers in every transaction. While a single agency broker often works with both sides, he or she will not work for both sides. The dedicated single agency broker will not, in any given transaction, act in a representative capacity for both the buyer and the seller or both the landlord and the tenant. The dedicated single agency broker will also not represent different parties in multiple transactions involving a common party.

Example:

Sara is buying a property from Sam. Sarah is also selling her own property to Bob in another, but concurrent, transaction. There is only one broker per transaction.

A single agency broker would likely represent Sara in both transactions. A careful exclusive buyer's broker would only represent Sara in the buying Sam's property **or** represent Bob in buying Sarah's property. Likewise, a careful exclusive seller's broker would represent either Sam and Sara in selling their properties (as separate transactions). The advantage then of single agency for the broker, in this example, is that the broker practicing single agency can have a client in each transaction and two commissions. The advantage to the consumer being represented is true representation with undivided loyalty in both the sale and the purchase.

COUNSELING SESSIONS PRIOR TO ENGAGEMENT

Usually, the single agency practitioner does not agree to represent a client without first conducting a counseling session. Modern real estate practice is much more than just listing and selling. It differs from buying, say, an expensive car, for which the title, specifications, and warranties are relatively consistent and clear. The real estate client's objectives, criteria and limitations must be clearly understood. The broker's job is to help develop this information before attempting to market or locate a property for a client. Then the property must be diligently investigated and the interests of others in the property ascertained. Most important, both broker and client must be comfortable in working together to meet the client's objectives.

Single agency brokers represent clients, not just buyers or sellers. Some brokers specialize in representing buyers; however, they realize that in certain cases their satisfied buyer clients will someday want to employ them to sell their property. In those cases, when a seller lists property with a single agency broker, the broker will make full disclosure at the outset to buyer prospects that the broker represents the seller only. In Texas, the broker must deliver to the buyer a current TREC Agency Disclosure Form Number 3 detailing the different representation alternatives available (*see* Figure 8.1). If the buyer makes an informed decision to continue in the transaction without representation, then the broker may commence working with the buyer to provide customer service, but not client representation.

Conflicts of Interest

Because the broker practicing single agency never acts as a dual agent, the broker may have to withdraw from representing one or both of the clients if a buyer-client becomes interested in a seller-client's property. Typically, the broker will inform the buyer of the need to terminate the agency relationship for that particular transaction. If the buyer decides to continue with the transaction without representation, the broker will work with the buyer as a customer in this purchase from the seller client. Caution is advised if the seller asks the broker to disclose information about the buyer that was obtained in the earlier confidential agency relationship. Confidential information remains confidential even after the agency relationship is terminated. The broker should disclose to the remaining seller client that the buyer was, until recently, a client and the broker is prohibited from disclosing confidential information about the buyer that was learned in the previous relationship. However, the broker is not prohibited from revealing information about the former client that has been learned since the termination of the previous agency.

Some single agency brokers will first show all their listings to a buyer customer before agreeing to represent that buyer as a client. While this lessens the chances of a conflict of interest, it doesn't eliminate the possibility that the buyer client may later decide to buy a company listing previously shown when the buyer was a customer but after confidential matters and motives were disclosed. Nor does it preclude the ideal house for the buyer from coming into the company listing inventory after the buyer customer has been converted to a buyer client.

Hybrid Approach

Many Texas real estate companies have adopted a policy that combines single agency and consensual dual agency. This policy requires single agency representation in all transactions except those in which a buyer client is interested in a company listing. With full disclosure and the informed consent of the buyer and seller, the company will act as a dual agent. A traditional single agency broker would not use this hybrid approach.

ADVANTAGES AND DISADVANTAGES

Some advantages of single agency are:

- For the broker:
    - Brokers can represent sellers and buyers but in different transactions; therefore, the broker has a wider potential client base and can participate in more transactions with any given client, reducing the time and money required to produce new clients;

Figure 8.1 TREC Agency Disclosure Form Number 3

INFORMATION and DISCLOSURE REGARDING REAL ESTATE AGENCY RELATIONSHIPS

08-31-93

● WHO WILL THE BROKER REPRESENT IN THIS TRANSACTION? ●

Before working with a real estate broker you should know that the duties of the broker to you depend upon whom the broker represents. If you are a prospective seller or landlord (Owner) or a prospective buyer or tenant (Buyer), you should know that the broker who lists the property for sale or lease is the Owner's agent. A broker who acts as subagent represents the Owner through the listing broker, and a broker who acts as a buyer's agent represents the Buyer. A broker may not represent both an Owner and a Buyer in the same transaction unless both Owner and Buyer consent in writing to the representation. A broker can assist in locating a property, preparing a contract or lease, or obtaining financing without representing you. Brokers are obligated by law to treat you honestly and fairly.

● WHAT WILL BE THE BROKER'S DUTIES TO YOU? ●

IF THE BROKER REPRESENTS THE OWNER: The broker typically becomes the Owner's agent by entering into a listing agreement with the Owner or by agreeing to act as a subagent through a listing broker. A subagent may work in a different real estate office. A listing agent or subagent can assist the Buyer but does not represent the Buyer. A listing agent or subagent must place the interests of the Owner first. The Buyer should not tell a listing agent or subagent anything the Buyer would not want the Owner to know, because a listing agent or subagent must disclose to the Owner any material information he or she knows.

IF THE BROKER REPRESENTS THE BUYER: The broker typically becomes the Buyer's agent by entering into an agreement to represent the Buyer. A Buyer's agent can assist the Owner but does not represent the Owner. A Buyer's agent must place the interests of the Buyer first. The Owner should not tell a Buyer's agent anything the Owner would not want the Buyer to know, because a Buyer's agent must disclose to the Buyer any material information he or she knows.

IF THE BROKER REPRESENTS BOTH: A broker may not act as an agent for more than one party to a transaction unless the broker complies with specific requirements established by law. In addition to providing the parties with this form, the broker must enter into a written agreement with each party which authorizes the broker to represent more than one party and sets forth who will pay the broker's fee. The broker is required to treat both parties honestly and impartially so as not to favor one party or work to the disadvantage of any party. Unless written permission from the appropriate party is obtained, the broker is prohibited from disclosing: (a) that the Owner will accept a price less than the asking price; (b) that the Buyer will pay a price greater than the price submitted in a written offer; (c) any confidential information; or (d) any other information a party specifically instructs the broker in writing not to disclose, unless disclosure is required by law. The broker's duties are more limited if he or she represents both parties. There are potential conflicts of interest when a broker represents more than one party. The broker is obligated to inform each party of all facts the broker knows which would affect the party's decision to permit the broker to represent both the Owner and the Buyer. For example, the broker would inform the Owner if the broker expects to represent the Buyer in purchasing additional properties in the near future.

If you choose to have a broker represent you, you should enter a written contract that clearly establishes the obligations of both you and the broker and that sets out how and by whom your broker will be paid. You have the right to choose the type of representation you wish to receive. Payment of a fee to a broker does not necessarily establish that the broker represents you. If you have any questions regarding the duties and responsibilities of the broker, you should resolve those questions before going further. Regardless of the agency relationships which may be established, you have the responsibility to protect your own interests. Once you have read and discussed this information with the broker, please acknowledge your receipt of a copy of this form. Your cooperation will help the broker to comply with the rules of the Texas Real Estate Commission. The broker is required to provide this form to you and disclose below who the broker represents. This form is to be used in residential, commercial and other types of real estate transactions.

DISCLOSURE OF AGENCY, IF ANY: The Broker named below represents: ☐ Owner ☐ Buyer ☐ Owner and Buyer

______________________ By: ______________________ Date: __________
Brokerage Company Name — Broker or Sales Associate

ACKNOWLEDGMENT OF RECEIPT OF AGENCY DISCLOSURE FORM: I acknowledge I have received a copy of this form. I understand that agreements I may sign may affect or change agency relationships and that the broker may only represent both the Owner and the Buyer with their full knowledge and consent.

______________________ Date: __________
Owner (Landlord) or Buyer (Tenant) or Authorized Representative

______________________ Date: __________
Owner (Landlord) or Buyer (Tenant) or Authorized Representative

This form is promulgated by the Texas Real Estate Commission for mandatory use by real estate licensees. Brokers must conduct transactions without regard to race, color, sex, religion, handicap, familial status or national origin. TREC AGENCY DISCLOSURE FORM NO. 3 (08-93).

- reduces broker liability for undisclosed or consensual dual agency;
- increases client loyalty for professionalism, resulting in more referrals; and
- allows broker to have a long-term, continuing client-level relationship with an individual, regardless of whether the individual is buying or selling, without concern whether the broker's client is positioned in the transaction as a landlord or tenant.

- For buyers and sellers:
  - clients receive full representation and undivided loyalty; and
  - allows individual to have a long-term, continuing client-level agency relationship with a specific and trusted broker, regardless of whether the individual is buying or selling or acting as a landlord or tenant.

Some disadvantages of single agency are:

- For the broker:
  - reduces the possibility of double-ending commissions in any given transaction. However, as long as only one of the parties has representation, a broker practicing single agency might receive an undivided commission amount that otherwise would have been split with a subagent or the broker representing the other party;
  - may lose a buyer-client interested in company listing; and
  - difficult to switch back and forth from client to customer.
- For buyers and sellers:
  - brokers may not be able to show their company's listings to buyer clients without creating a dual agency, thereby reducing a seller-client's access to potential buyers.

SUMMARY

A single agency practice enables a broker to represent buyers or sellers. Brokers must be careful to avoid conflicts of interest caused by selling listed property to buyer clients. The use of a clear agency disclosure statement is helpful.

An organization greatly responsible for raising public awareness of single agency and professional practices in real estate is Who's Who in Creative Real Estate, Inc., P.O. Box 23275, Ventura, California 93002-3275, 805/643-2337. This organization publishes the quarterly newsletter *Agency Advocate* and maintains a unique buyer's broker registry that identifies brokers who have been trained in representing buyers and/or are committed to the practice of single agency. It also markets single agency communication tools, including a *Representation Alternatives* pamphlet and a consumer disclosure form, found in Appendix C (however, this form is not a legal substitute for TREC Agency Disclosure Form 3).

SUGGESTIONS FOR BROKERS

If you choose the single agency type of practice, decide how to handle the situation in which a prospective buyer wants you to locate property but does not want to sign a buyer's agency agreement. Most single agency practitioners will not help a buyer investigate properties listed by other brokers in MLS if the buyer intends that broker to act as a subagent of the seller.

KEY POINTS

- The single agency broker represents either buyer or seller, but never both in same transaction.
- Clients receive full representation but may have to switch to customer status if a conflict arises or the broker may have to withdraw from transaction altogether.

QUIZ

1. The single agency broker represents all of the following *except:*

   a. tenant or landlord.
   b. buyer or seller.
   c. vendee or vendor.
   d. both parties to a transaction.

2. The single agency broker is least likely to act as a:

   a. seller's agent.
   b. buyer's agent.
   c. subagent of the seller.
   d. listing agent.

3. Betty wants to make an offer on a property listed by Sally, a single agency broker. Who can help Betty submit an offer to buy?

   a. Another broker
   b. Betty herself
   c. Sally
   d. All of the above

4. All of the following are advantages of single agency *except:*

   a. broker has a wider potential client base.
   b. reduces dual agency liability.
   c. allows broker and client to have a long-term professional relationship.
   d. it increases the possibility of double-ending commissions.

5. Which of the following best describes the single agency broker's initial meeting with a prospective buyer or seller?

   a. Signing listing agreement
   b. Counseling
   c. Consulting
   d. Advance retainer fee

DISCUSSION QUESTIONS

1. How does the single agency broker normally handle the situation when both the buyer and the seller want the broker to represent them?
2. Why does single agency practice not result in two brokers being required for every transaction?
3. What relation does buyer brokerage have to single agency practice?
4. What is the difference between working with a buyer and working for a buyer?

CHAPTER 9

CLARIFYING AGENCY RELATIONSHIPS

Most real estate licensees operate on the basis of high ethical standards that require that they be fair and honest to customers and clients. Disclosure of their agency relationship to the buyer or seller in a real estate transaction has been required for decades, but only since September 1, 1988, have real estate licensees in Texas been required to disclose these agency relationships in writing. There is no consensus among real estate professionals on the best way to discuss and to document agency relationships. However, there are Texas agency disclosure laws that apply to commercial brokers as well as residential brokers and to leases as well as sales.

In many transactions, at least one person is under the wrong impression of who represents who. While there are no easy solutions, there are steps the broker can—and must by law—take to eliminate any confusion, which often results from a lack of discussion of the true agency role of the broker. This chapter helps the broker develop workable strategies to reduce complaints and possible lawsuits while enhancing professional reputation.

The following subjects are discussed:

- Disclosure Policy:
  - Decide
  - Disclose
  - Document
  - Do As You Say
- Developing a Company Policy

DISCLOSURE POLICY

Much of the present confusion could be eliminated if the broker would

- *decide* in each particular transaction whether he or she intends to represent the buyer or the seller;
- *disclose* to the buyer and the seller who he or she represents as soon as there is agreement on the representation;
- *document* the disclosure with an adequate and timely written confirmation; and

- *do* as he or she has declared, acting consistently with the disclosed decision.

Decide

Each transaction is different. Brokers must be prepared to decide in each transaction who they intend to represent and what their relationship is to the other participants. However, the broker must take care not to decide unilaterally. Because agency is a consensual relationship, the broker may decide who he or she wants to represent but cannot without the party's informed (and possibly written) consent.

The identification of the principal is sometimes difficult when only one real estate agent is involved or only one principal pays the fee. Each of these facts, though, does not necessarily determine who an agent represents. The key for the broker is flexibility in approaching the wide variety of situations that may develop. Before deciding on the appropriate working relationship, the broker must *define* what role to play in each transaction. For example, a broker may handle new project sales differently than resales, commercial property differently than residential property and first-time buyers differently than sophisticated buyers.

In any single transaction or relationship with a particular individual in multiple transactions, the real estate broker can choose from a number of basic working relationships:

- Agent for either seller (or landlord) or buyer (or tenant) but not both (single agency)
- Agent for both buyer and seller (dual agency)
- Agent for another agent, who is working for either buyer or seller (subagency)
- Agent only for buyers (exclusive buyer representation)
- Agent only for sellers (exclusive seller representation)
- Fiduciary consultant or counselor not representing clients in direct talks or negotiations with third parties
- Finder, middleman or facilitator

Some relevant questions from the listing broker's perspective are:

- Is only the listing salesperson involved or is this an in-house sale of another salesperson's listing or one from another branch office?
- If a cooperating or other broker is presenting an offer, is that broker a subagent of the seller or an agent of the buyer? Or is the other broker attempting to act only as a facilitator?
- Does the listing broker have any prior or current relationship with the buyer, such as having previously listed the buyer's home, having previously acted as the property manager on one of the buyer's rental properties or having agreed to act as the buyer's agent in future transactions?
- Is the broker working with a buyer who is only a customer and not a client?

Some relevant questions from the cooperating broker's perspective are:

- Is this a multiple listing service (MLS) sale?
- Is subagency being offered to other brokers?

- Is there a prior or present business relationship with the buyer? This would be the case if, for example, the cooperating broker, who has listed the buyer's two-bedroom home, helps the buyer submit an offer on a three-bedroom home that is contingent on the sale of the buyer's two-bedroom home.

It is not always easy to decide who the real estate broker and his or her associates represent. When in doubt, ask:

- Who is my client and what services must I perform?
- Who is my customer and what services can I perform?

Disclose

It is not enough for the broker to decide who to represent. Real estate agents must discuss with buyers and sellers (or landlords and tenants) all proposed agency relationships so that the principals can make an informed choice. Agency is a consensual relationship that requires a delegation of authority by the principal and a consent by the agent. It is equally important for the buyer and the seller to know who will **not** be their agent. Buyers and sellers who are alerted to the fact that they are not represented by an agent will recognize that they must take greater responsibility throughout the transaction to protect their own interests. Timing of disclosure is critical and should occur before anyone can claim that an agency relationship already has been formed. At the time of closing or even the preparation of offer is generally too late because expectations have been created, actions taken in reliance on those expectations and confidences shared.

Disclosure of information about agency relationships in general and whom the licensee currently represents, if anyone, relative to the contemplated transaction, must take place according to Texas law:

> **22 TAC §535.164** (Rules for use of TREC Agency Disclosure Form Number 3)
>
> **(a)** The Texas Real Estate Commission adopts by reference Agency Disclosure Form 3, approved by the Texas Real Estate Commission in 1993. This document is published by and available from the Texas Real Estate Commission, P.O. Box 12188, Austin, Texas 78711-2188.
>
> **(b)** Except as provided by subsection (e), a real estate licensee shall furnish a prospective buyer, seller, landlord or tenant with a copy of TREC Agency Disclosure Form 3 ("the form") at the time of the first of the following events regarding a real estate transaction:
>
> **(1)** a face-to-face meeting with the licensee; or
>
> **(2)** a written communication from the licensee.
>
> **(c)** The licensee shall complete the appropriate portion of the form relating to disclosure of agency and shall sign the form.
>
> **(d)** For the purposes of this section, the terms "buyer," "seller," "landlord" or "tenant" include an authorized representative such as an attorney, trustee or attorney in fact but do not include a real estate licensee representing the buyer, seller, landlord or tenant. The term "licensee" includes the licensed associates of a licensee.

(e) A real estate licensee is not required to provide a copy of the form to a prospective buyer, seller, landlord or tenant in the following instances:

(1) the licensee is acting solely as a principal and not as an agent;

(2) the proposed transaction is for a residential lease for one year or less and no sale is involved;

(3) the licensee is representing the buyer, seller, landlord or tenant with whom the licensee is meeting or communicating, by a prior agreement with another real estate licensee who represents the same person;

(4) the written communication from the licensee is a solicitation of business or an initial response to a request for information;

(5) the face-to-face meeting with a licensee occurs at a property which is being held open for prospective purchasers, and there is no substantive discussion regarding a transaction; or

(6) the face-to-face meeting with the licensee or the written communication from the licensee occurs after the parties to the transaction have signed a contract to buy, sell, rent or lease the real property concerned.

(f) A licensee who represents a principal in a proposed real estate transaction shall disclose the representation at the time of the first contact with another licensee representing the other principal. The disclosure may be made orally or in writing.

(g) The licensee should retain a copy of the form signed by the prospective buyer, seller, landlord or tenant or authorized representative in order to demonstrate compliance with this section.

(h) Licensees may use a revised disclosure form adopted under this section prior to the effective date of a revision.

In addition to presenting and discussing the TREC Form Number 3 or any subsequent disclosure notice, the seller and the listing broker should discuss:

- whether the property is to be listed in the MLS;
- whether the prospective listing broker intends to operate as a dual agent with buyers produced from the broker's client buyer pool;
- who will have access to this listing information;
- whether other brokers are authorized to cooperate in the search for buyers;
- whether these brokers are subagents of the seller or buyers' agents; and
- whether the listing broker intends to share fees with these subagents and/or with buyer's agents. (*See* NAR® Code of Ethics & Standards of Practice 9-10(e) in Appendix D.)

The timing of the disclosure to a buyer or tenant is frequently a problem, and is especially difficult with respect to first-time buyers, who may have walked into the broker's office in response to a general advertisement or who may have met the listing broker at an open house. No one seriously contends that the listing broker should stop buyers after a friendly handshake and read them TREC Form Number 3. On the other hand, Texas law is quite specific in that the disclosure take place at the first face-to-face meeting regarding a real estate transaction, with, of course, the exceptions listed in the Rule. The broker must be sensitive to the problems created if the buyer is led to reveal confidential bargaining and financial information to the broker, who, it turns out, actually represents the seller. Because the broker is then obligated to pass on such information to the seller, this gives the seller and his agent an unfair advantage over the buyer.

In practice, the real estate licensee may not, at first meeting, know whether to work with the buyer on a client or on a customer basis. The first meeting might cover only general business practices, commission structures and market area specialty and be designed to convince the buyer to work with the broker. Nevertheless, TREC Agency Disclosure Form Number 3 must be given. Take the case of a real estate licensee who views a number of new listings of other brokers while out on a company caravan tour. The broker may not yet know whether the agent later will be revisiting such properties on behalf of a client or a customer; however, if meeting the seller face to face he or she must present the form to the seller. If only meeting with the seller's agent, the licensee minimally should discuss his or her status and future possibilities.

A licensee must be especially careful to address squarely such undecided status in any discussions with the buyer, seller, tenant or landlord and other brokers. Agency and other working relationships should be firmed up as soon as possible in dealing with the buyer but definitely before preparation of the buyer's offer.

What some listing brokers do at an open house, for example, is to show the buyer the property and to answer general questions of a factual nature on such topics as available financing, municipal services and estimated closing costs. Questions concerning the seller's marketing position are addressed by the listing or cooperating broker in ways designed to encourage the buyer to make his or her best offer. If the conversation begins to move into any substantive discussion regarding a transaction, the broker should immediately take the time to discuss and identify what the working relationship will be before going further.

Document

To establish that the required disclosures have been given, the broker should keep a copy of the disclosure forms signed by the buyer or the seller. In addition, the broker should obtain written confirmation on the final contract that the broker disclosed who he or she represented and that the status of that representation has not changed. It is important that the broker obtain such written proof because the declaration of the broker in a lawsuit is given little weight in proving who the broker represented. It is sometimes equally important for a broker to prove that he or she was not an agent of the buyer or the seller.

Do As You Say

If the buyer and broker decide that the broker will not represent the buyer but instead show the buyer properties as a subagent of sellers who have their properties listed in the MLS, then the broker should act as a subagent. A subagent of the seller, for example, would not suggest that the buyer start off by testing the seller with a nothing-down offer and a requirement that the seller carryback a note with interest deferred until the final balloon payment. Nor would a subagent of the seller suggest certain negotiating strategies contrary to the best interests of the seller.

DEVELOPING A COMPANY POLICY

With the variety of agency relationships available, it is essential that every brokerage firm develop their own policy, In fact, the NAR® Code of Ethics & Standards of

Practice 9-10(a) and 9-10(b) requires a company to detail its office policies on agency practices.

The most effective way to establish a company policy on agency practice is to follow a simple but organized approach. Here's a suggested method:

Phase 1: Review the various agency choices. The most popular choices are:

- exclusive seller agency;
- exclusive buyer agency;
- seller/buyer agency with consensual dual agency for in-company transactions; and
- single agency.

Phase 2: Review the advantages and disadvantages of each choice as outlined previously.

Phase 3: Consider the size and experience of the office staff, the type of specialization, local market opportunities and your financial expectations. For example, if most of your income comes from working on outside listings, then exclusive seller agency is probably not the best choice.

Phase 4: Write a company policy. Start off with a preliminary plan (*see* Figure 9.1) but make sure to also submit the plan to key members of your staff and business and legal advisers for additional input.

A comprehensive plan should include a basic statement of policy. The plan should describe the procedures for handling common situations from the perspective of the listing office and the selling office. The plan should discuss the use of TREC and company agency forms, especially the timing of making disclosures to buyer and to seller. Above all the plan should comply with all state laws. Company plans taken from textbooks or borrowed from out-of-state brokers should be carefully modified to conform to the Texas environment.

For example, a policy manual may include the following section on dealing with buyers at open house:

> ***Open House.*** *Meeting potential buyers at an open house offers arguably one of the most complex agency situations in real estate. When a prospect comes into your open house, our duty is to the seller and we must use our efforts to sell the house to the prospect. This means that you cannot suggest other competing properties or offer to represent buyers until they have communicated to you that they are not interested in the property. If the buyer shows interest in the property or indicates that he or she might like to purchase the property, you must treat them as a customer and make immediate disclosures concerning agency choices and positions as required by 22 TAC 535.164 as follows:*
>
> 1. *Determine that the prospect is interested in the property.*
> 2. *Before substantive discussions concerning the buyer's qualifications for buying or points of negotiation in any subsequent offer, provide the buyer with TREC Agency Disclosure Form Number 3 and* Our Valued Customer *disclosure letter.*

3. *Confirm in writing and orally that the buyer understands that you represent the seller and answer any questions that her or she might have.*

4. *Document in your file that you have delivered and discussed the disclosure. Request that the buyer sign TREC Form Number 3, give him or her the original and retain copies for the company file on this property and a separate file on this customer.*

5. *Do not include the agency disclosure form as an addendum to any resulting contract. The TREC Broker-Lawyer Committee maintains the position that this document is not intended to be used as such.*

Phase 5: The broker should commence in-company training sessions and monitor the effectiveness of the policy. By using role play and sample dialogue in training sessions, the sales staff can become more comfortable and competent in discussing agency in a way that showcases their professionalism. Rather than isolate discussions of agency, salespeople should be taught to integrate agency into their regular presentation. Lastly, once you are certain your sales staff understand the policy, make sure they follow it. Be prepared to make exceptions in justified cases and to make changes to existing policy if exceptions begin to be the rule.

SUMMARY

Much of the confusion that exists on the issue of agency relationships can be eliminated as brokers become more comfortable and competent in discussing their roles in a real estate transaction. Brokers should develop a company disclosure policy so that they take control over agency relationships and avoid unintended and illegal agencies. A basic policy consists of these four steps: decide, disclose, document and do. Without a doubt, timely, proper disclosure is the key ingredient to a successful and effective agency program.

SUGGESTIONS FOR BROKERS

Develop a personalized disclosure brochure that outlines the types of working relationships your firm offers to buyers and to sellers. Outline some of the customer-level services you can provide to one person while remaining the exclusive agent of the other person. Be careful not to use confusing language that might weaken the impact of meaningful agency disclosure and duties. A broker who attempts to cloud the issues may find such a brochure being used in a lawsuit. Use of the TREC form should help set the stage for meaningful discussions of your professional relationship and the needs of the prospect. Be sure to attempt to get the prospect to sign the form and discuss the chosen type of client or customer relationship. State law does not require the consumer to sign the form as must the licensee.

Figure 9.1 Company Policy Ingredients

Basic agency philosophy

- State disclosure law
- Company disclosure rules
- Summary of company policy

Procedures for handling common situations

- Listing presentation
- Open house
- In-house sale
- Buying for own account

Procedures for dealing with outside companies

- Cooperation regarding fee splitting, showing, presenting offer
- Offer subagency
- Act as buyer's agent/subagent

Guidelines for the use of company agency forms

- Why
- When
- How
- Benefits

Common agency questions

QUIZ

1. When is the best time to disclose to the buyer the agency status of the listing broker?

    a. Upon recordation of the deed
    b. When the purchase contract is signed
    c. When the buyer expresses a clear interest in buying a property listed with the broker or seeks help in locating properties
    d. When the buyer telephones the broker to arrange an introductory meeting

2. When is the best stage of the transaction to present the TREC disclosure notice to the seller regarding agency choices?

    a. Offer
    b. Listing
    c. Closing statement
    d. Deed

3. The other broker working with a buyer might represent:

    a. the buyer.
    b. the seller.
    c. neither buyer nor seller.
    d. All of the above

4. The listing broker should discuss all of the following with the seller at the time of the listing *except:*

    a. offer of subagency.
    b. sharing of the listing fee.
    c. the listing in the MLS.
    d. the buyer's motivation.

5. If a buyer customer tells the listing broker that the buyer will pay up to the listed price but wants to first submit an offer 10 percent below that price, what should the broker tell the seller?

    a. The buyer is qualified.
    b. The buyer has made a good offer.
    c. Don't risk losing the buyer by making a counteroffer.
    d. The buyer said he or she will pay up to the listed price.

DISCUSSION QUESTIONS

1. What are the four steps a broker should take to clarify agency relationships?
2. In deciding whether to act as an agent of a buyer, what are some relevant questions for a listing broker to ask?
3. In deciding whether to act as a subagent of a listing broker while working with a buyer, what are some relevant questions for an other broker to ask?
4. What are some key areas of the prospective agency relationship that the listing broker should discuss with the seller during the listing appointment?
5. When is the best time to make the disclosure of seller agency to the buyer?

CHAPTER 10 PUTTING IT ALL TOGETHER

In earlier chapters we saw Sally facing situations involving possible lawsuits in which her agency status was the main issue. If Sally had practiced "preventative brokerage," she might have lessened her risk.

This chapter discusses the following:

PREVENTIVE BROKERAGE

Regardless of whether a broker represents the seller or the buyer, her or she should do three things:

1. Use written disclosures
2. Clarify his or her role in the transaction
3. Use the help of others when needed

Brokers should recognize that the most frequent basis for complaints against real estate agents is their failure to disclose material facts. As the listing agent, brokerages must be prepared to prove in a legal dispute with a buyer customer that important information was, in fact, provided or, on the other hand, that such disclosure was prohibited by law.

Brokers also can help protect themselves by clarifying their role in the transaction to the buyer and the seller. When Sally represents the seller, she should discuss openly what she can and cannot do. For example, if she has never handled a tax-deferred exchange or the sale of a business opportunity, she should discuss her limitations and the possible use of other experts. To present one's self as an expert is not only grounds for loss of license, but could also form the basis of a DTPA lawsuit. [TRELA §15(a)(6)(W) and 22 TAC §535.157] Sally should discuss her duties and responsibilities and those of other agents, as well as the use of subagents and the MLS. If Sally is working with the buyer, she should clarify whether the buyer is her client or her customer. If she is showing property to a buyer client, she should make sure that the buyer understands that she is not warranting the condition of the property.

SUBJECTS TO DISCUSS AT LISTING PRESENTATION

Listing Broker Working with Seller

The listing broker, in working with the seller, should:

- at the beginning of the listing appointment but before an agency relationship is established or the listing agreement is discussed, explain and discuss in detail TREC Agency Disclosure Form Number 3;
- explain what subagency means and the optional use of subagents in an MLS and obtain the seller's authorization to use subagents;
- explain how commission fees may be split and obtain the seller's approval or disapproval to split fees with seller's subagents and/or buyer's brokers;
- if the listing broker is a member of the MLS, verify that the listing agreement contains a provision granting the seller's permission to use the MLS and to release marketing and sales data to the MLS. If the seller elects not to have the listing broker offer subagency or elects to offer it on a selective basis, then a decision must be made regarding the use of an MLS;
- on the subject of compensation, explain to the seller how commissions may be split with cooperating brokers. Because there is a big difference between authorizing the listing broker to split commissions with a buyer's broker and authorizing the broker to split with a subagent of the seller, the seller's attention should be clearly directed to this provision prior to signing the listing. If the listing broker decides to offer other brokers a less-than-attractive commission split, the seller should be notified because it may mean that other brokers will be less motivated to show the seller's property;
- explain that many offers presented by buyer brokers will contain a provision for the seller to pay the buyer broker's fee and that the listing brokerage may be willing to compensate the seller by lowering its commission. The seller should be informed that compensation of the buyer broker is another negotiable concession, like fixing the roof or paying the buyer's discount points, and that he or she is under no obligation to pay the buyer's broker;
- explain how the seller may permit the listing broker to offer a commission split to other brokers but not offer subagency (subagency optional);
- explain the brokerage's policy on dual agency; and
- explain to the seller that it is customary to work with other real estate brokers or their associates to increase the likelihood of finding a suitable buyer for the seller's property.

Listing Broker Working with Buyer Customer

The listing broker should present and explain the following information to a buyer customer at first contact concerning a specific property:

- the difference between a client and a customer in terms of services, duties and appropriate expectations;
- that the broker is employed by the seller to sell the seller's property;
- that the buyer is free to seek and retain his or her own technical advisers;
- that if the buyer decides not to buy the listed property, the buyer may wish to use the services of the listing broker to search for other appropriate property; if so, the agency relationship and whether the buyer is a customer or a client must be clarified;
- the in-house sales practices of the listing broker; and
- that it is customary for a broker to show prospective buyers other listed properties.

In addition, listing brokers may: provide ready access to inventory, including the MLS; collect pertinent data on property taxes, utility costs, general real estate values; provide information on municipal services and amenities; discuss financing alternatives; discuss loan qualification and processing; show properties; make appointments and conferences; suggest ways to improve suitability of the home; clarify the buyer's needs versus wants and affordability; evaluate need for property management; arrange for and review fire or liability insurance; check inventory of personal property; check applicable zoning and building permits; estimate closing costs and monthly payments; explain standard forms; explain escrow or settlement procedures; transmit offer and act as liaison between the buyer and seller (though negotiating at all times for seller's interests); monitor closing and time deadlines; and recognize the buyer's need for expert advice and suggest possible advisers.

Properties the buyer should see. The seller's agent or subagent can make appointments, show properties meeting the buyer's stated criteria, describe general features and conditions, direct the buyer to needed sources of information, complete standard forms and transmit offers to the seller.

If the buyer decides that neither the seller's property nor any other properties listed with the broker are suitable, the listing broker then can discuss what further services the broker can provide to help the buyer locate the right property. When the broker suggests that the buyer search through the MLS system for suitable properties, the broker must decide whether to act as a cooperating broker in a seller's subagent capacity or as a buyer's broker. In either case, a written agreement should be prepared.

Listing Broker and Buyer's Broker

If the listing broker receives an offer through a buyer broker, the listing broker should:

- be cooperative while respecting the agency relationships between him- or herself and the seller and those between the buyer's broker and the buyer;
- agree as to how best to handle payment of commissions consistent with the authorization of the seller and the buyer;
- communicate to the seller the buyer's intention for payment of fees relative to the buyer's broker;

- be prepared for healthy and open negotiations; and
- evaluate all terms of the buyer's offer, recognizing that they were prepared with the buyer's best interest in mind.

Listing brokers should be prepared for the likelihood that they will receive offers from other brokers submitted on behalf of buyer clients and should welcome these offers, working work with the buyer's broker in a spirit of cooperation and goodwill. At the same time, the listing broker should respect the fact that each broker owes undivided loyalty to his or her respective principal, recognizing it is in the best interest of the seller to cooperate with all brokers, one of whom may have the ultimate buyer for the seller's property. The key question regarding any offer, whether from a buyer or from a buyer's broker, is what is the net effect to the seller?

Other Broker as Subagent of Seller

In those cases in which the other broker is a subagent of the seller, the other broker:

- must discuss the appropriate TREC disclosure forms, sign and deliver a copy to the buyer or tenant, check the seller box to indicate who the broker represents and seek to obtain buyer's or tenant's signature on broker's copy to provide proof to TREC that Rule 22 TAC §535.164 has been complied with;
- should discuss with the buyer or tenant what type of services the subagent can and cannot give;
- notify all listing brokers that the cooperating broker is a subagent of the seller;
- verify each proposed commission split arrangement;
- inquire if there are any special instructions, new information or if the house is already under contract;
- inquire about the listing broker's policies regarding the handling of earnest money deposits, using a lockbox, drafting of offers, choosing the escrow company or placing the loan; and
- must at all times act as a subagent of the seller, i.e, for the best interests of the seller.

In deciding whether to represent the seller, cooperating brokers should understand that as subagents of the seller, they may not be privy to the same information as the listing broker because many sellers are reluctant to pass on confidential information to a cooperating broker for fear the cooperating broker will divulge this information to the buyer. Cooperating brokers are normally viewed by sellers as conduits for the flow of facts and figures between buyers and sellers.

Other Broker as Buyer's Broker

If the other broker decides to act as a buyer's broker, then, at initial contact when discussing the property and the seller, the cooperating broker should:

- disclose to all listing brokers of properties shown or to owners selling their own property that he or she is a buyer's broker; and
- disclaim any agency or subagency relationship with the seller or the listing agent. Immediate disclosure will enable the listing broker to take appropri-

ate action to represent the seller's best interests in any showing of the property to the prospective buyer.

As a practical matter, a broker may not have any particular customer or client in mind at the time of initial contact, for instance as on a MLS tour of homes. A broker who sometimes represents buyers should, however, inform the listing broker or seller that he or she may later return either with a client or with a customer. Therefore, the listing broker should keep this in mind when discussing any information concerning the seller's marketing position.

Buyer's Broker

The buyer's broker should:

- explain to the buyer the services to be rendered by first presenting and discussing TREC Form Number 3 and that broker is not his or her agent unless and until an agreement has been reached;
- after consultation as to the role of a buyer's broker and consent of the buyer, obtain from the buyer or tenant a written representation agreement;
- determine how fees are to be paid;
- disclose to all listing brokers and/or sellers of properties at the time of initial contact, before showing any properties, that the broker is a buyer's broker and is rejecting any offer of agency or subagency from the seller, builder or listing broker; and
- discuss with the listing broker either the possibility of a fee splitting arrangement or how the buyer's broker's fee may affect the offering price.

Dual Agent

A dual agent must:

- notify all principals and brokers that might become involved in a particular transaction, at the earliest practical point, and obtain a written dual agency agreement, using a dual agency contract that sets forth the source of any expected compensation; and
- discuss with buyer and seller the specifics of how the broker intends to act as a fiduciary to both at the same time and clarify state law, including limitations as to opinions of market value, negotiating strategies and advocacy.

OTHER CONSIDERATIONS

Retained Earnest Money in the Event of a Default

TREC-promulgated Residential Earnest Money Contract forms do not contain a standard provision that permits the listing broker to share in a portion of the earnest money deposit retained by the seller as liquidated damages in the event the buyer defaults. However, most listing agreements do contain such a protection for the listing broker. Few agreements permit the cooperating broker, as a subagent of the seller, to share in the portion allocated to the listing broker in the event of default. The Agreement Between Brokers section of the TREC form is silent as to a subagent broker's right to share in earnest money distributions in the event of default. If the listing broker has agreed to split commissions with the buyer's broker, however, the contract should clarify whether the listing broker is under any obligation to share the earnest money with the buyer's broker in the event of the default of the buyer. The buyer would have to consent to such an arrangement in the case of a buyer broker being entitled to any of the earnest money. It is probably a very poor practice to have the buyer's broker participating in any such default fee split. The buyer's broker should protect him- or herself by means of a buyer's broker agreement and/or upfront non-refundable retainer.

Commissions. One of the most important considerations is how to handle commissions. All commissions are negotiable. Who pays the commission does not determine who represents who. The listing and the selling commissions normally are paid out of the sales proceeds at closing, but do not have to be. Brokerage commissions are normally paid from the seller's proceeds, but do not have to be; the buyer or tenant may pay the broker by agreement as well.

Many offers from buyer brokers provide that the buyer broker's commission will be paid from the sales proceeds at closing. The offer may state that the broker represents the buyer and will participate in the commissions paid to the listing broker by the seller at closing. The listing broker and the seller will have to decide whether such a commission arrangement is consistent with their mutual best interests. In most cases the listing broker and the seller already have discussed this possibility, perhaps at the listing stage, and have decided to modify the listing commission distribution, just as they do when there is a subagency commission split to pay. The listing broker should counsel the seller early in the transaction about working with various types of offers, including those prepared by a buyer's broker. Such preparedness helps the listing broker deal properly with a buyer's broker and represent the seller in a professional manner.

If the listing broker refuses to adjust the listing commission, the transaction may not work because too much money may then be directed to brokerage commissions. This may be unacceptable to the seller, the buyer and any lender. Note that the decision to adjust commissions belongs to the broker and not to the licensed associate who obtained the listing and is working with the seller.

The buyer's broker was hired to help the buyer prepare the best offer (sometimes in conjunction with the buyer's attorney or accountant) on the most suitable property. Open, honest and healthy negotiations usually precede a well-drawn offer. The listing broker can expect negotiations with a buyer's broker to be more active than they would be if the cooperating broker were a subagent of the seller. The listing broker should inspect the offer carefully, ask the buyer's broker questions about it and then recommend appropriate action to the seller.

If the cooperating broker is a subagent of the seller, the issue of compensation is usually much easier. The listing broker is obligated to pay the cooperating broker the amount set forth in the offer of subagency, assuming the transaction closes.

Written Agreements. Prudent brokers should attempt to enter into a written agency agreement with clients. While it is sometimes legal, it is nonetheless unwise to proceed on oral agreements. The broker must recognize that some buyers are reluctant to sign a representation contract, even though they will be loyal customers, because:

- such an arrangement is not customary;
- they fear the closing costs will increase by an additional broker fee;
- they do not want to be tied to an exclusive contract; or

- they do not understand the benefits of representation.

USING REHEARSED DIALOGUE

The broker's newly licensed real estate associates are usually uncomfortable in making cold calls to obtain listings. Through sales and counseling training sessions that employ role-playing and sample dialogue, associates often overcome their initial uneasiness. In fact, many associates are able to use these acquired presentation and counseling skills to help distinguish themselves from their competitors.

Many top programs that deal with real estate counseling and buyer brokerage stress learning the practical skills of how to ask more effective questions of prospects or client applicants and how to listen actively. The goal is to select from a group of prospects those who may be clients and those who may be customers.

The following section on possible questions to use and dialogue to develop in discussing the agency relationship issue is an introduction to the kinds of role-playing situations designed to reduce the anxiety level of real estate agents when discussing agency. Brokers should develop their own role-play situations for use in training sessions and expand upon the brief dialogue included here. Some agents may prefer to write out these dialogues and practice them with a tape recorder. Often, it is not what is said, but how it is said, that makes the difference in explaining an important issue, such as what role you will play in the transaction and who you represent.

Dialogue for Brokerage Situations

The best way to become comfortable and competent in discussing agency alternatives is to role-play common situations. The following short scenarios indicate how some brokers handle such discussions of agency in a way that actually serves as a tool to enhance the professional image of the real estate agent. Using this as a guideline, write the dialogue in your own language and style. After completing your own version of a possible dialogue for a situation, begin developing dialogues for other common situations. Try them out, critique them and refine them based on the concepts of agency that you have learned in this text and developed on your own additional research.

Dialogue: Betty is a customer; Sally is an associate of a firm that practices exclusive seller agency. Betty walks into an open house where Sally of Bay Realty is on duty for the broker. Sally hands Betty a fact sheet and shows her around. She asks Betty general types of questions concerning Betty's wants and needs in housing, the general price range Betty was considering and square footage requirements. Sally notices that Betty is not the typical looker but is serious about purchasing a property and seems very interested in this house. Sally decides to turn the discussion to the subject of agency before the conversation gets too specific and Betty begins to reveal confidences or begins to develop unwarranted expectations of services and information.

Sally: *Has anyone explained to you, Betty, how real estate licensees work and the agency relationships licensees are allowed to develop with clients?*

Betty: *No.*

Sally: *Regarding this house you're looking at, I am the agent for the seller. The reason I'm holding this open house is to expose the seller's property to the market in the hope that a buyer such as yourself will decide to purchase the property. As the seller's agent, I can point out the many features of the property, answer many of your questions about financing, ownership and closing, assist you in preparing the offer the way you want it and promptly present your offer to the seller. By law, I am obligated to treat you, as a customer for my seller's property, honestly and fairly in the transaction. I am not able to negotiate on your behalf, contrary to the best interest of my client, or give you my professional advice or opinions. As the seller's agent, I am not allowed to prepare a competitive market analysis for you with an opinion of the market value of this or any other home in which my brokerage and I represent the owner. However, if you feel confident at this point to represent your own interests relative to this property at this time, we can continue, but first I would like to give you the Texas Real Estate Commission's Agency Disclosure form that each real estate licensee is required by law to give to you before finding out confidential information about your financial qualifications, before any serious talks about your purchasing a particular property begin and before they become your agent.*

After finishing development of this dialogue as if Sally was an exclusive seller broker, start again from the beginning as though she and her broker practiced single agency and see where the dialogue takes you. Critique your results in class. Then attempt the same process assuming Sally and her brokerage practiced disclosed or consensual dual agency. Have several classmates or family members play the part of the open house owner who has accidentally overheard the entire series of dialogues and then ask what would the owner think about the agent's conduct.

Dialogue: A buyer's broker has an advantage over other brokers in contacting an FSBO. The buyer's broker is not looking to the seller for either a listing or a attempting to bargain a commission from him or her.

Sally: *Good morning, Mr. Owner, I am Sally of Bay Realty. I am a real estate licensee but I am not here [calling] to ask for a listing on your home. The reason for my visit [call] is to see if your property might fit the needs of my client. I saw your for-sale sign [ad]. Do you have a few minutes to see if you can be of help to my buyer and me?*

Owner: *Yes, but not a whole lot more than a few minutes. And I don't want to list my property.*

Sally: *I can see you're busy. I'll be very brief. My buyer, through his buyer representation agreement with me, has agreed to include enough money in any offer he might make for your property to cover any concessions he might ask you to make, including such things as roof repairs, discount points and my fee for services to him. Therefore, I will not be personally attempting to negotiate a fee for myself from you. I am the agent for the buyer and I will not be your agent. You will not have to list your property or publicly advertise it for sale. My buyer is ready, willing and able to pay a fair price should you and he be able to come to a mutually acceptable agreement. If you are willing to sell for an acceptable price and terms, then I would appreciate the opportunity to preview your house, with or without my client, and develop a report to my client regarding your property's suitability for his needs. Then we could prepare an offer for your consideration. Could I make an appointment with you to preview your property sometime today or early tomorrow?*

Owner: *I'm telling you right now, I'm not listing with you and I'm not paying any commissions for anybody.*

Sally: *I understand Mr. Owner, and I hear your frustration. As far as the real estate fees are concerned, my agreement with my buyer client is an enforceable written contract in which my client has agreed to either pay my fee for services to him by including enough in the offer to the owner so that the owner can pay it and net out just as well or, should he not be able to negotiate that point with the owner but still desires the property, my client has agreed to compensate me in addition to whatever the final purchase price agreement is. If that is acceptable to you, I'd like to come out and give you some state-required forms on agency disclosure and seller's property condition information, discuss them with you for ten to fifteen minutes and then preview your house for my client.*

Sally, in the above scenario, is practicing exclusive buyer agency. If she were practicing single agency,would her conversation with the owner be different? Could she start talking with the owner about becoming his agent for the purchase of his next home? What conflicts of interest could develop? What if her brokerage practiced the hybrid form of single agency where the client is required to consent to dual agency, in advance, should the situation require it? Develop dialogue and disclosures in that case.

SUMMARY

When you become comfortable in handling your relationship both with customers and with clients, you will experience enhanced professional stature and esteem. You will discover a sense of freedom in being able more actively to represent the best interests of your clients, whether they are buyers or sellers, when you are negotiating against the other side, whether they are represented or unrepresented.

SUGGESTIONS FOR BROKERS

Practice real-life situations in your training classes and learn the most effective way to discuss agency relationships to prepare yourself for future discussions. Then put your practice sessions to work in the field.

QUIZ

1. Sellers may be bound by and responsible for the acts of all of the following except the:
   a. listing broker.
   b. authorized subagent.
   c. buyer's broker.
   d. listing salesperson.
2. All of the following descriptions of a typical MLS are true *except:*
   a. blanket unilateral offer of subagency
   b. permits subagency.
   c. requires subagency.
   d. allows commission sharing arrangement.
3. Who can pay the buyer's broker's fee?
   a. The seller
   b. The buyer
   c. Both buyer and seller
   d. Neither buyer nor seller
4. Which term best describes a real estate licensee who is paid a fee for working with a buyer but is not an agent of the buyer or the seller?
   a. Listing broker
   b. Cooperating broker-subagent
   c. Finder
   d. Buyer's broker
5. If a listing broker receives an offer from a buyer's broker in which the buyer's broker's fee is to be paid by the seller, the listing broker should:
   a. reject the offer.
   b. renegotiate the offering.
   c. increase the listing fee.
   d. present the offer to the seller.

DISCUSSION QUESTIONS

1. You are the listing agent. A buyer wants to submit an offer to buy through you. The buyer hands you three envelopes with instructions to present a certain one first. Only if the seller rejects the offer found in the first envelope are you to present the others. What should you advise your seller? Would you do anything differently if you were a cooperating broker acting as a subagent on a MLS listing? Suppose you were a buyer's broker?
2. A buyer asks you how much she'll have to pay each month under the loan. You explain that the monthly payment is $1,400, a portion of which will be used to pay principal, interest, taxes and insurance. The buyer neglects to obtain fire insurance because she thinks it is included in the monthly payment when, actually, the monthly payment includes only the mortgage insurance premium. The house burns down. Are you liable? Are you more likely to be liable if you are the buyer's agent than if you are the listing agent?

3. As a cooperating broker acting in a subagency capacity with the seller, you find a buyer who buys a home at $20,000 in excess of the true market value. Nine months later the buyer comes to you and asks you to list the property for sale. What listing price do you suggest? How do you explain your previous action when you helped the buyer acquire the property, which was clearly overpriced?

4. Sally of Bay Realty signs a listing with George on a penthouse apartment. George asks Sally to find him a bigger penthouse.

    a. Who does Sally represent on the current penthouse?
    b. Who does Sally represent if she shows George one of Bay Realty's listings that was obtained by another agent?
    c. Who does Sally represent if she shows George a property listed with another brokerage through the MLS?
    d. How does Sally explain to George the various working relationships open to them?

CHAPTER 11 EMPLOYMENT ISSUES

The extent of legal responsibility of a person who hires someone else to act for him or her depends upon the relationship between them. As a general rule, the more extensively the person for whom a service is being performed controls the manner in which the service is performed the greater that person's responsibility. For example, an employer has appreciable control over how an employee works. If an employee is acting within the scope of his or her employment, the employer is responsible for any harm the employee causes. In real estate brokerage, the agent's classification as an independent contractor or as an employee is important for several reasons, including establishing agency relationships through employment contracts and listing agreements. This chapter explores some general employment issues and agreements as they affect the broker and licensed associate in their roles as principals and agents.

BROKER-SALESPERSON RELATIONSHIP

Real estate licensees who operate on behalf of a licensed real estate broker are known as real estate salespersons. A *salesperson* is responsible only to the broker under whom he or she is licensed and can carry out only those responsibilities assigned by that broker. A broker is licensed to act as the principal's agent and can collect a commission for performing assigned duties. A salesperson, however, has no authority to make contracts or receive compensation directly from a principal. All compensation to the salesperson must be paid through the sponsoring broker, who is fully responsible for the actions of all salespersons licensed under him or her. All of a salesperson's activities must be performed in the name of his or her supervising broker because the salesperson is the agent of the broker and subagent of the seller. Remember that agency with the principal is at the broker level.

Employee versus Independent Contractor

Brokers engage salespersons as either employees or independent contractors. Any agreement between a broker and a salesperson should be in the form of a written contract that defines the obligations and responsibilities of the relationship. Whether a salesperson operates under the broker as an employee or as an independent contractor will affect the relationship between them (*see* Figure 11.1.)

The nature of the employer-employee relationship allows a broker to exercises certain controls over salespersons who are employees. The broker may require an employee to adhere to regulations concerning such matter as working hours, office routine and dress or language standards. As an employer, a broker is required by the federal government to withhold Social Security and income taxes from wages paid to employees. He or she is also is required to pay unemployment compensation tax as required by state and federal laws. In addition, a broker may be required to provide employees with such benefits as health insurance and profit-sharing plans.

An independent contractor operates more freely than an employee, and the broker might not control his or her activities in the same way. The broker may control what the independent contractor does, but not how it is done. A crucial element of preserving independent contractor status is that the independent contractor's services be performed under the terms of a written contract between the broker and the associate and that the terms of the contract specifically provide that the independent contractor will not be considered an employee for purposes of payment of federal taxes. An independent contractor assumes responsibility for paying for his or her own income and Social Security taxes and receives nothing from the broker that could be construed as an employee benefit. In Texas, brokers do not have to carry workmen's compensation coverage for independent contractors.

To ensure that all licensed associates are treated by the Internal Revenue Service and the Texas Employment Commission as independent contractors, brokers are urged to maintain close contact with competent tax counsel and have their policies and procedures frequently reviewed for compliance. The broker should exercise great care to ensure that independent contractors understand their personal obligations under law.

Some people believe that the difference between an independent contractor and an employee is that the former works on a commission-only basis and the employee is salaried. That may be relevant, but not conclusive. Many salespeople are paid on commission but are considered employees because of other features of their employment situation.

COMPENSATION

Broker Compensation

The broker's compensation is specified in the listing agreement, management agreement or other contract with the principal. Compensation usually is in the form of a commission or brokerage fee computed as a percentage of the total amount of money involved. Such commission typically is considered earned once the broker has accomplished the work for which he or she was hired and payment is due at the closing or upon the principal's default. Most sales commissions are payable when the sales is consummated by the delivery of the seller's deed or immediately upon default by the seller. These provisions should be included in the listing agreement or real estate contract. When no time is specified in the sales or listing agreement for payment of

Figure 11.1 Independent Contractor versus Employee

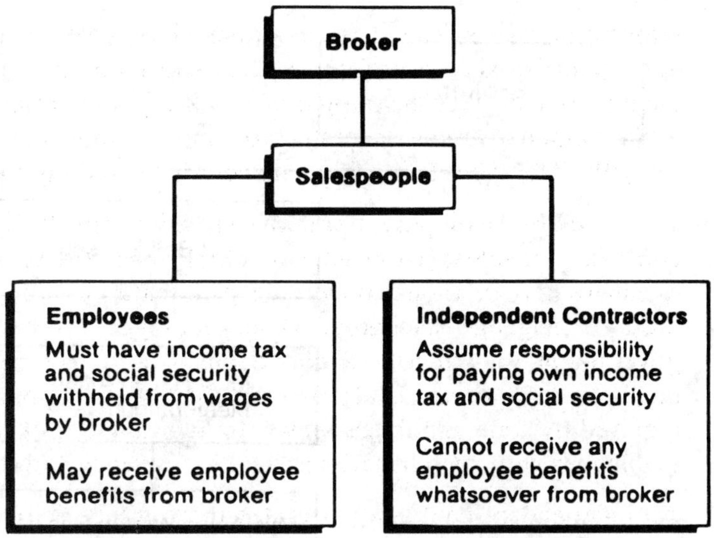

the broker's commission, it generally is earned when a completed sales contract has been signed by a ready, willing and able buyer and accepted by the seller.

Because the broker's commission is earned when the broker performs under the terms of the listing contract, if the listing contract expires prior to the closing date of the earnest money contract, the broker's commission still is vested, i.e., it is not necessary that listing contract be extended to include the closing date.

According to common law, to be entitled to a sales commission a selling broker must be able to show that he or she was the procuring cause of a sale—that the broker had taken action to start or cause a chain of events that resulted in the sale.

In addition, in Texas, to be entitled to a sales commission, a broker also must prove that he or she:

- held a valid real estate broker's license;
- had written a memorandum authorizing his or her role as an agent. This requirement signifies that the broker must show in writing that he or she was employed by the seller (*see* Figure 11.2); and
- advised the buyer in writing prior to closing that the buyer should obtain or be furnished with a title insurance policy or have the abstract covering the subject property examined by an attorney of the buyer's choice.

Upon accepting an offer from a ready, willing and able buyer, the seller is technically liable for the broker's commission, regardless of whether the seller completes the sale. The courts, however, tend to prevent a broker from seeking a commission from the seller if the broker knew, or should have known, that the buyer was not financially able to complete the purchase. A broker who has produced a buyer who is ready, willing and able to meet the listing terms usually is still entitled to a commission if the transaction is not consummated for any of the following reasons:

- The owner has a change of mind and refuses to sell.
- The owner's spouse refuses to sign the deed.
- The owner's title is defective.

Figure 11.2 Broker's Compensation

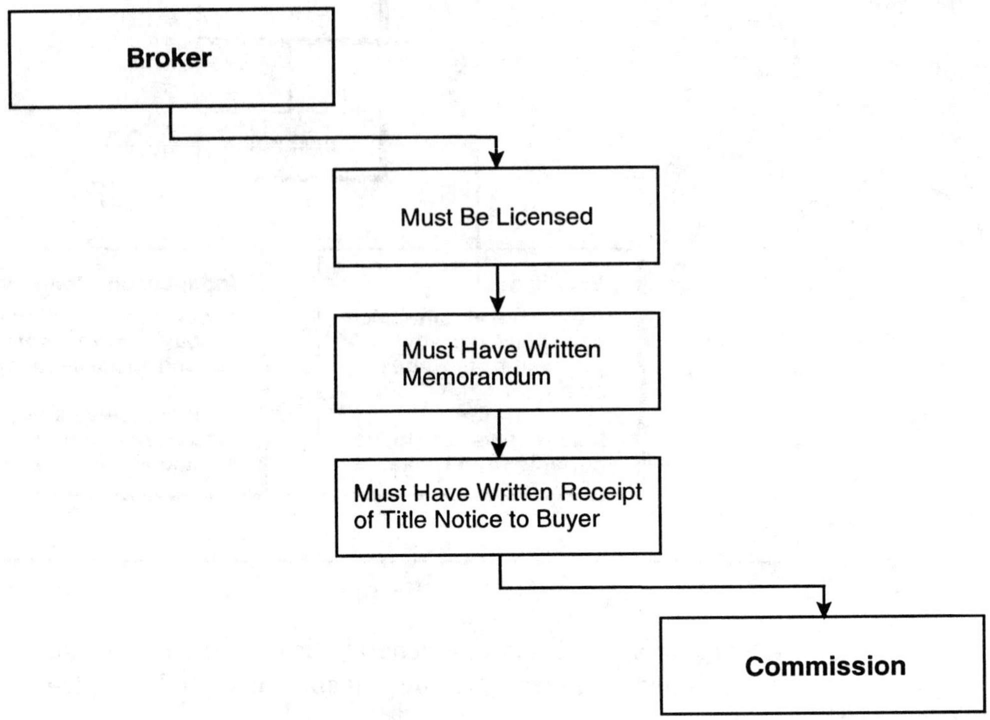

- The owner commits fraud with respect to the transaction.
- The owner is unable to deliver possession within a reasonable time.
- The owner insists on terms not in the listing (for example, the right to restrict the use of property).
- The owner and the buyer agree to cancel the transaction.

The rate of the broker's commission is negotiable in every case. Any attempt by members of the profession, no matter how subtle, to impose uniform commission rates is a clear violation of state and federal antitrust laws. If no amount or percentage rate of commission is stated in the listing contract, the broker may not be able to collect any fee at all.

In Texas, it is illegal for a broker to share a commission with someone who is not licensed as a salesperson or broker or someone exempt from licensure pursuant to Sections 3 and 14 of the Texas Real Estate License Act. This has been construed to include the giving of certain items of personal property and other premiums as well a finder's fee and portions of the commission. Additionally, a 1990 Texas law prohibits a broker from sharing a sales commission with an attorney unless the attorney perform brokerage services in the transaction.

Salesperson Compensation

A salesperson's compensation is set by mutual agreement between broker and salesperson. A broker may agree to pay a salary or share of the commissions from transactions originated by a salesperson. A salesperson may have a drawing account against his or her earned share of commissions. In such cases the salesperson should sign a note for each draw to preserve the independent contractor status.

A recent innovation in salesperson compensation is the 100 percent commission plan. In a brokerage firm where this system has been adopted, all salespeople who achieve a predetermined sales quota pay a monthly service charge to their broker (to cover the costs of office space, telephone and supervision) and receive 100 percent of the commissions from the sales they negotiate.

RELATIONSHIP BETWEEN BROKERS AND SELLERS

The first step in hiring a broker is discussion regarding the authority, responsibilities and compensation of the broker. The most common method of establishing an agency relationship between a seller and a broker is through a written agency contract called a *listing agreement.*

Listing Agreements

A listing agreement is defined in TREC Rule 22 TAC §535.148(b) as:

> *Listing contract* means an agreement whereby the owner of real property confers authority to a real estate licensee to act as an agent for said owner in the sale, rental, lease, exchange, or trade of property subject to the agreement. A management agreement is not a "listing contract" for the purposes of this section.

From the state's definition of a listing agreement, it can be inappropriate to refer to a buyer representation agreement as a *buyer listing contract,* even though the use of that term is increasing.

All listings under Texas law must have a definite termination date that is not subject to prior notice. TREC Rule 22 TAC §535.148(a) states, "Every listing contract shall have a definite termination date, upon which date the listing will automatically expire without any requirement of notice to the real estate licensee." It is grounds for loss of license for failing to specify in a listing contract a definite termination date not subject to prior notice.

There are four basic categories of listing agreements, differentiated by the different treatment of the broker relative to his or her right to compensation upon the sale of the listed property: open, exclusive agency, exclusive right-to-sell and one-time showing agreements.

Open Listing

Most common in commercial real estate, the *open* listing agreement generally entitles the broker to compensation only if the broker is in fact the procuring cause of the sale or lease of the property. The open listing does not give the broker any exclusive opportunity to be the procuring cause, but rather allows the owner of the property to give one or more brokers the same opportunity simultaneously, with the broker who produces an accepted offer being the only broker to be compensated. The open listing allows the seller to continue to procure potential buyers him- or herself and negotiate independently of the broker; if successful, the seller would not owe any broker a commission. A listing will generally be considered to be an open listing unless its terms clearly indicate that a more restrictive agreement is intended by both parties.

Depending upon the terms of a specific open listing, the broker may be entitled to sue for commission if he or she produces an offer from a buyer that meets or exceeds the exact terms of the listing and the owner refuses to sell. The buyer, however, has no rights under the broker's listing agreement to force the owner to sell the property, even if the buyer's offer meets or exceeds the terms of the listing agreement.

One disadvantage of the open listing is that brokers and their associates may expend a great deal of energy and time advertising and showing the property, only to have another broker provide the actual buyer and receive the commission for so doing. Most MLS systems refuse to take open listings because of the potential for disputes over procuring cause and commission entitlements. The only broker entitled to a commission under an open listing agreement is the one that procures the buyer. Any broker procuring a buyer for the seller and not having his or her own open listing agreement with the seller would simply be declared a volunteer.

Brokers who feel they are being denied payment of a legal commission should consult legal counsel; "self-help" remedies may be interpreted by the courts in Texas as tortious interference with a contract or breach of fiduciary duty. Any precipitous action could cause lawsuits from both parties and loss of license. Counsel might suggest that the broker let the transaction close and then sue the seller for damages and breach of contract.

Exclusive Agency Listing

The exclusive agency listing is different from the open listing in that the broker and owner agree that the contracting broker shall be the only (exclusive) broker that will be entitled to a commission and that no other brokers will have a direct contractual relationship with the seller. The seller however, retains the right to sell the property independently of the broker, as in the open listing, and to owe no compensation to the broker.

Many brokers are reluctant to take an exclusive agency listing. Under this type agreement, if the seller does accept an offer made directly through a competing broker, the seller still owes compensation to his or her exclusive agency broker and thus must pay two separate commissions on one sale. Most MLS systems will take exclusive agency listings but they must be so designated. This type listing is not unusual in commercial sales and leasing.

Exclusive Right-to-Sell Listing

For many brokers, the preferred category of listing contract is the exclusive right-to-sell or lease contract, which entitles the contracted broker to compensation regardless of who is the procuring cause, including the owner or other brokers. The exclusive right-to-sell listing is a more restrictive form of an exclusive agency listing. All MLS systems will take, and prefer, the exclusive right-to-sell listing agreement because use of this type of listing greatly reduces procuring cause disputes.

One-Time Showing Agreement

The one-time showing agreement is a very limited listing agreement. In its usual format it is, in effect, an exclusive right-to-sell listing agreement limited to coverage of only one specific buyer. The buyer is generally named in the agreement.

One-time listing agreements may be very risky to the broker because the danger of creating an undisclosed dual agency and other disclosure issues.

BUYER/TENANT REPRESENTATION AGREEMENTS

As in the case of their counterpart seller/landlord-oriented listing agreements, buyer and tenant representation agreements fall into the same basic four categories: open, exclusive agency, exclusive right-to-purchase and one-time purchase agreements. They also fall under TREC Rule 22 TAC 535.148(a) regarding a definite termination date.

Open Representation Agreement

In this type of buyer/tenant agreement, the buyer or tenant contracts with a broker or indirectly through one of the broker's licensed associates to have the broker be the agent of the buyer or tenant. The buyer or tenant in this way has true fiduciary representation in the purchase or lease transaction. The broker only receives compensation from the buyer or tenant if he or she is the procuring or producing cause of the transaction. If the buyer or tenant decides to contract with another buyer's broker or tenant rep on a different property, the buyer or tenant may do so and has no obligation to compensate the first broker. Similarly, if the buyer or tenant decides to contract for the purchase or lease of a property on his or her own, without broker participation, the broker will not be entitled to a fee.

Frequently in this type arrangement, especially when it is an oral agreement, the broker or his or her licensed associates neglect to make clear the source and/or amount of any expected commission or indicate that they will collect their fee from the seller or landlord. This is not a safe practice for the broker, who has no assurance that the owner of the suitable property will agree to such an arrangement. If there is no signed, written agreement, the broker cannot maintain a legal action to recover a commission should the buyer not pay the commission.

Exclusive Agency Purchase Agreement

The exclusive agency buyer/tenant representation agreement, if drawn properly, makes the purchaser or tenant liable to protect his or her broker's compensation, even if another broker produces the subsequently acquired property. But, like the exclusive agency listing, if the buyer or tenant deals directly with an owner without the broker's involvement, the broker is owed nothing.

Exclusive Right-to-Purchase Agreement

As in the case of exclusive-right-to-sell listing agreements, the exclusive right-to-purchase buyer representation agreement calls for compensation to be due to the contracted broker whether the buyer finds the property and negotiates the transaction with or without the broker's assistance or even through another broker. In the latter case, the buyer or tenant may be liable for compensating both brokers.

One-Time Representation Agreement

Like the one-time listing agreement, the one-time representation agreement stipulates compensation for the location and/or negotiation of a particular property purchase or lease. It does not restrict the buyer or tenant from independently looking at other properties, contracting for them and owing the broker nothing.

All four of these type agreements are subject to the problems mentioned under the open agency agreement. While it is not required they be in writing, it is preferable, both to clarify and to protect expectations. Negotiating with the non-client for commission is ripe with conflicts of interest and potential complaints of breach of fiduciary duty and/or undisclosed dual agency.

SUBAGENCY AGREEMENTS

In any of the agency contracts described above the contracted broker may attempt to include a clause that allows the broker to appoint subagents. A buyer's broker, if given such permission, may appoint subagents as readily as a seller's broker.

MLS Subagency Agreements

Under most pre-1993 MLS rules, all listings submitted to a MLS had to a contain a mandatory offer of subagency to all other members. After discovering numerous potential legal problems with such a practice, most MLS systems now offer participants optional subagency, that is, the system allows its participants to either place listings that offer subagency and compensation to other MLS members or, optionally, offer cooperation and compensation but not subagency.

Non-MLS Subagency Agreements

Any brokers, even if they are not members of an MLS system, can voluntarily contract with each other to create their own broker-to-broker subagency agreements, either on one property at a time or to cover all properties in their respective inventories for any agreed-upon period of time. Such subagency agreements generally do or should contain a pre-agreed compensation amount.

Agreements Between Brokers

Not all agreements for compensation between brokers for cooperation in a particular transaction contain an offer of subagency. The Agreement Between Brokers that appears on the last page of the TREC residential earnest money contract is such an agreement. It is merely an agreement for the listing broker to compensate the other broker in a transaction by an amount specified in this abbreviated agreement, when and if the listing broker is compensated by his or her seller-principal. If the buyer broker is not protected in his or her own agreement with the client-buyer, and at the closing the seller refuses to compensate the listing broker because of an alleged breach of fiduciary duty by the listing broker, the buyer's broker has no way to secure compensation from anyone in the transaction. Although buyer's brokers are probably not served adequately by this TREC developed compensation agreement, it can serve as a useful memorandum of the initial intent of the parties to the agreement.

Non-agent Compensation. TRELA §14(a) states, "It is unlawful for a licensed broker to employ or compensate directly or indirectly a person for performing an act enumerated in the definition of real estate broker in Section 2 of this Act if the person is not a licensed broker or licensed salesman in this state. However, a licensed broker may pay a commission to a licensed broker of another state if the foreign broker does not conduct in this state any of the negotiations for which the fee, compensation, or commission is paid." However, 22 TAC §535.131(c) states, "An unlicensed person may share in the income earned by a real estate brokerage operation, provided that such unlicensed person performs none of the activities of a real estate agent and the public is not led to believe that such unlicensed person is in the real estate brokerage business." "Commission or fees" includes any form of compensation received for services as a real estate agent; "services as a real estate agent" refers to the acts of a "real estate broker" as enumerated in Section 2(2)(A-J) and Section 2(3), when those acts are performed for another and for compensation.

A real estate licensee may no longer compensate an attorney "for performing an act enumerated in the definition of real estate broker in Section 2;" however, the principals to a transaction may compensate a lawyer for acting as a broker. A real estate licensee is not prohibited by the License Act from compensating one of the principals to the transaction so long as there is full disclosure to and consent of all parties, including any third party lenders. The reasoning is that a principal to the transaction does not perform as a broker because the action is for oneself and not for another. If a principal also happens to be an attorney, that principal is not divested of his or her right to compensation because of possessing an attorney's license.

Net Listings

Net listings do not fit into the same categorical arrangements as the previously mentioned listings. Regardless of the degree of exclusivity of the agency and freedom of the owner to sell the property independently, the net listing is any type of listing in which the broker's compensation is agreed to be any amount over an amount the seller wants to net after all expenses of the sale, including the broker's compensation.

This type listing may present some legal and ethical problems, particularly with an inexperienced seller. Net listings are not illegal in Texas. However, two specific rules of the commission are especially designed to curb potential abuse.

1. **22 TAC §535.16(c) & (d):** (c) A broker should take net listings only when the principal insists upon a net listing and when the principal appears to be familiar with current market values of real property. When a broker accepts a listing, he [or she] enters into a fiduciary relationship with his principal, whereby the broker is obligated to make diligent efforts to obtain the best price possible for the principal. The use of a net listing places an upper limit on the principal's expectancy and places the broker's interest above his [or her] principal's interest with reference to obtaining the best possible price. Net listings should be qualified so as to assure the principal of not less than his [or her] desired price and to limit the broker to a specified maximum commission.

   (d) A real estate licensee is obligated to advise a property owner as to the licensee's opinion of the market value of a property when negotiating a listing or offering to purchase the property for the licensee's own account as a result of contact made while acting as a real estate agent.

2. **TREC Rule 22 TAC §535.144:** A licensee shall not use his [or her] expertise to the disadvantage of a person with whom he [or she] deals.

For many years, TREC has included a warning to licensees stating that TREC officially discourages the taking of net listings because of their possible manipulation and harm to the public, which TREC is designed to protect.

Dual Agency Agreements

A dual agency agreement is the only agency agreement that is required to be in writing to be legal. Not only must it be in writing, but it must set forth the source of any expected compensation and include the following provisions from TRELA in conspicuous bold or underlined print:

15c. A real estate broker who acts as an agent for more than one party to a transaction shall:

(1) not disclose to the buyer or tenant that the seller or landlord will accept a price less than the asking price unless otherwise instructed in a separate writing by the seller or landlord;

(2) not disclose to the seller or landlord that the buyer or tenant will pay a price greater than the price submitted in a written offer to the seller or landlord unless otherwise instructed in a separate writing by the buyer tenant;

(3) not disclose any confidential information or any information a party specifically instructs the real estate broker in writing not to disclose unless otherwise instructed in a separate writing by the respective party or required to disclose such information by law; and

(4) treat all parties to the transaction honestly and impartially so as not to favor one party or work to the disadvantage of any party.

15d. The real estate broker shall use due diligence to assist the parties in understanding the consents, agreements, or instructions under this section in which the real estate broker is permitted to represent more than one party to a transaction.

Reinforcing the previous subsection is TRELA §15(a)(6)(D), which creates another basis for loss of license for "failing to make clear, to all parties of a transaction, which party he [or she] is acting for, or receiving compensation from more than one party except with the full knowledge and consent of all parties."

In addition to the strict requirements for a dual agency agreement as noted above, the two provisions cited in the section on net listings should be mentioned.

Property Management Agreements

Property management agreements are not listing agreements. However, they are employment agreements and involve agency duties. Experienced legal counsel should be retained to assist in the drafting of property management agreements.

SUMMARY

Although brokerage firms vary widely in size, few brokers perform their agency duties without the assistance of salespeople. Consequently, much of the business's success hinges on the broker-salesperson relationship. Agreements between a broker and a salesperson should be set in a written contract that defines the obligations and responsibilities of the each party; there are four basic types of such agreements. The salesperson may work on the broker's behalf as either an employee or as an independent contractor. The broker's compensation generally takes the form of a commission, which is a percentage of a property's selling price, and the broker is considered to have earned this commission when he or she procures a ready, willing and able buyer for a seller.

QUIZ

1. In the phrase, "ready, willing and able," the word *ready* means that the buyer

   a. intends to buy at the time the contract was made.
   b. intends to buy at the time the parties were scheduled to perform.
   c. has financial resources sufficient to complete the transaction.
   d. has examined the title and is ready to proceed.

2. A broker would have the right to dictate which of the following to an independent contractor?

   a. Numbers of hours worked
   b. Work schedule
   c. Acceptable dress code
   d. Commission rate

3. While in the employ of a real estate broker, a salesperson has the authority to:

   a. act as an agent for the seller.
   b. assume responsibilities assigned by the broker.
   c. accept a commission from another broker.
   d. advertise the property on his or her own behalf.

4. As an independent contractor for a real estate broker, a salesperson has the authority to:

   a. act as an agent for another person.
   b. assume only responsibilities assigned by the broker.
   c. arrange a real estate advertising contract with a local newspaper.
   d. make contracts and receive compensation directly from the principal.

5. The statement "a broker must be employed to recover a commission for his or her services" means that:

   a. the broker must work in a real estate office.
   b. the seller must have signed an agreement to pay a commission broker for selling the property.
   c. the broker must have asked the seller the price of the property and then found a ready, wiling and able buyer.
   d. the broker must have signed the listing agreement.

DISCUSSION QUESTIONS

1. Explain why classifying a real estate salesperson as an independent contractor does not relieve the broker of responsibility for the salesperson's actions.
2. Define *procuring clause.*
3. Discuss the differences between how a broker and a salesperson are compensated.
4. Discuss the two TAC rules concerning net listings in Texas.

CHAPTER

12 CONSUMER PROTECTION ACT

No evidence exists that misrepresentation and fraud are more prevalent in the real estate industry than they are in other sectors of the economy. If, however, deceptive acts occur in a real estate transaction, they may a greater impact than they do in other areas, for several reasons. First, most real estate transactions involve large sums of money; as a result, people who feel deceived are more apt to take action to assert their rights. A second reason is that licensing laws have placed substantial supervisory responsibility upon brokers for the conduct of salespeople. Unauthorized and even unintentional deception by salespeople can subject brokers to liability, including the loss of license. Finally, in many transactions, little direct contract takes place between buyer and seller. Because information is often transmitted through a third party, misunderstanding and error can result in the buyer, seller or both feeling that they have been deceived.

In Texas, a consumer's rights are protected by the Texas Deceptive Trade Practices-Consumer Protection ACT (DTPA). This act declares, among other things, that "false, misleading or deceptive acts or practices" in the advertising, offering for sale, selling or leading of any real or personal property are unlawful. This chapter explores how the DTPA affects real estate brokers and salespeople.

DECEPTIVE TRADE PRACTICES-CONSUMER PROTECTION ACT

The Deceptive Trade Practices-Consumer Protection Act was passed by the Texas Legislature in 1973. As the act was originally drafted, real estate transactions were excluded from coverage. In 1975, the act was amended to include transactions involving real property purchased or leased for use. The purpose of the law is to protect consumers against false, misleading and deceptive business practices, unconscionable actions and breaches of warranty.

This law creates a powerful weapon for consumers. There are two reasons for its effectiveness. First, proving that a deceptive act has occurred is easier under this law than under previous real estate statutes and even common law (*See* Figure 12.1). Second, the law provides that consumers may recover more than their actual losses. Although an injured party can recover punitive damages for fraud, the Deceptive Trade Practices Act does not require proof that the defendant intended to deceive or mislead. The mere occurrence of a deceptive act can result in damages in excess of the actual economic losses.

The first use of the Deceptive Trade Practices Act in the real estate area involved cases concerning breach of warranty in the sale of new homes. The initial draft of the law allowed a consumer to recover three times the amount of actual damages suffered as a result of defective or unworkmanlike construction in a new home purchase. This generous remedy prompted consumers to bring all breach of warranty cases under the Deceptive Trade Practices Act. In recent years, the law has been used by consumers against sellers of used homes, brokers and lenders. The law no longer provides for the automatic trebling of damages; however, it still allows for a recovery of damages in excess of the actual economic loss.

Consumer Defined

The act protects only consumers. *Consumer* means an "individual, partnership, corporation, this state or a subdivision or agency of the state who seeks or acquires by purchase or lease, any goods or services." [T.B.C.A. 17.45] Specifically excluded are business consumers with assets of $25 million or more. Goods include both real and personal property; services include any type of labor or work performed for another and for which compensation is received.

Deceptive Acts

The act prohibits all false, misleading or deceptive acts in the conduct of business. The law specifically enumerates 23 activities that are violations of the act. Although an awareness of the enumerated prohibited acts is important, a violation of the act is not limited to those listed. The enumerated acts include, among others:

- misrepresenting or causing confusion and misunderstanding regarding the source, approval, certification or affiliation of goods or services;
- misrepresenting the characteristics, benefits, qualities or uses of goods or services;
- misrepresenting that goods are new;
- disparaging the goods, services or business of another by misleading or false representations;
- misleading advertising, such as advertising goods or services for sale with intent not to sell them as advertised or a fraudulent representation that one is going out of business;
- making false or misleading statements concerning the reasons for a price reduction;
- misrepresenting the authority of an agent to negotiate the final terms of a consumer transaction;

Figure 12.1 Comparison of Actions for Fraud and Misrepresentation

Common Law Fraud

1. Was a false statement made?
2. Was it made intentionally or negligently?
3. Was the misstatement a material fact?
4. Was the misstatement relied upon?
5. Was anyone "injured?"

Statutory Fraud

1. Was a false promise made with intent not to perform?
2. Did the person who benefited from the misrepresentation know that it had been made and fail to disclose truth?

Deceptive Trade Practices-Consumer Protection Act

1. Were any acts specifically listed committed?
2. Were any deceptive acts committed?
3. Were any misleading statements made?
4. Were any false statements made, including innocent misstatements?
5. Was an unconscionable act or course of action practiced against the victim?
6. Were acts the producing cause of harm to the victim?

- representing that a contract, agreement, warranty or guaranty confers rights or benefits that it does not;
- representing that work or services have been performed when in fact they were not; and
- failing to disclose information concerning goods or services that were known at the time of the transaction if the purpose of the lack of disclosure was to induce the consumer into a transaction into which the consumer would not have entered had the information been disclosed.

There are two aspects of the enumerated acts that are important to remember. First, there is no requirement that the consumer prove that the offending party intended to deceive or misrepresent the facts. In most cases an innocent misrepresentation is as much a violation of the act as a fraudulent misrepresentation; it is not a defense to a lawsuit brought under this act that the defendant did not know that his or her action was illegal. Second, the act prohibits not only misrepresentations but also misleading statements. A misleading statement is one that leads the consumer in the wrong direction or creates a misconception of the facts.

Case Brief

***Orkin Exterminating Co., Inc. v. LeSassier*, 688 S.W.2d 651 (Tex. Civ. App. 9 Dist. 1985).** Ms. LeSassier contracted with Orkin Extermination Co., Inc., for termite extermination services. On the date the serviceman came to Ms. LeSassier's home, she let him in and then returned to her employment. Almost a year later she noticed evidence of termite activity. An Orkin employee returned and treated her home. When she continued to have problems, she hired another firm to exterminate her home. She had the damage repaired and sued Orkin, alleging violation of the Deceptive Trade

Practices Act in that Orkin had "represented that work or services had been performed when such work or services had not been performed." Orkin defended that the Deceptive Trade Practices Act did not apply because there was no verbal assertion made by it that the termite treatment had been performed. The court held that the serviceman coming to Ms. LeSassier's home, beginning treatments and then leaving, never to return, was a representation that all the treatments called for in the contract had been performed.

Unconscionable Conduct

The Deceptive Trade Practices Act also provides that a consumer can sue if he or she has suffered actual damages produced by unconscionable action by another. Unconscionable action is a form of deception and therefore should be explored. The act defines it as "an act or practice which, to a person's detriment: (a) takes advantage of the lack of knowledge, ability, experience, or capacity of a person to a grossly unfair degree; or (b) results in a gross disparity between the value received and consideration paid, in a transaction involving transfer of consideration."

Unconscionable action is a type of equitable relief afforded to a person who has been tricked or swindled to such an extent that it would be unfair to allow the transaction to stand. Unconscionability is a difficult legal concept to grasp because it is intentionally vague. In the case that follows, the Texas Supreme Court provides some guidance in understanding the type of conduct prohibited.

Case Brief

***Chastain v. Koonce,* 700 S.W.2d 579 (Supreme Court of Texas, 1985).** This deceptive trade practices case required the court to first determine if petitioners were consumers under the DTPA and, if so, whether the evidence supported a finding of unconscionable action or course of action.

In 1979, Charles Koonce and J.P. Stroud began to sell five acre-tracts on the northern boundary of the 320-acre farm. At trial, there was ample testimony that Koonce and Stroud told the purchasers that Lot 1 at the northeastern corner would be commercial but that Lots 2 through 15 would be restricted for residential-use only. Claiming that they relied on these representations, the Chastains and three other couples independently purchased Lots 4, 5, 6 and 9 by warranty deed. In January 1981, Koonce and Stroud sold Lot 2 to David Metts who, about seven months after the Chastains and other residential purchases had constructed houses on their lots, built an oilfield pipe storage yard on his property.

The Supreme Court of Texas found that the DTPA defines a consumer to be an "individual who seeks or acquires by purchase or lease any goods or services" and that the goods or services sought or acquired by lease or purchase must form the basis of the complaint. The defendants contended that the purchasers did not meet this second part of the test because they based their complaint on Lot 2, a piece of property that none of the couples owned. However, the court decided that the purchasers were covered by the DTPA, because their complaint centered on representations made during the transaction that resulted in their purchase of the lots, statements made to induce the purchasers to buy the lots and that enhanced the desirability of the property.

Having decided that the purchasers were covered by the DTPA, the court then considered the second point, the presence of evidence to support a finding of unconscionability. Under the facts of the case, the court found that the purchasers failed to show any disparity between the value received and the consideration paid in the transaction. In order for the purchasers to recover, they must have proven that Koonce and Stroud took advantage of the purchasers' lack of knowledge, ability or capacity to a grossly unfair degree. Justice Kilgarlin wrote, "A slight disparity between the consideration paid and the value received is not unconscionable; a glaring and flagrant disparity is. Unfairness is perhaps a more nebulous term than disparity, but this is not a reason to create a new definition for *gross*." Based on the record as a whole, the court found no evidence that the Chastains and the other three couples were taken advantage of to a grossly unfair degree, although they did have standing to sue under the DTPA.

Producing Cause

Under DTPA, the consumer must prove that a misleading, deceptive or fraudulent act was a producing cause of loss. A *producing cause* is a contributing factor that in the ordinary sequence produces injury or damage. In common law and statutory fraud causes of action, the injured party is required to prove that the misrepresentation was of a relevant (*material*) fact and that this misrepresentation directly caused economic loss. Under the DTPA, the consumer is not required to prove that the deceptive act related to material fact or that the consumer relied upon that misrepresentation. Furthermore, the consumer is not required to prove that the misleading or deceptive act directly caused his or her injury.

Case Briefs

***Cameron v. Terrell and Garrett, Inc.*, 618 S.W.2d 535 (Tex. 1981):** Jerry and JoAnn Cameron purchased a house. The house had been listed for sale by the sellers with their real estate agent, Terrell and Garrett, Inc. Terrell and Garrett had listed the house in the multiple-listing service and in doing so included a statement that the house contained 2,400 square feet. The Camerons were shown this information about this house by their real estate agent. Subsequently, the Camerons closed the sale and moved in. The Camerons then had the house measured and discovered that it contained 2,245 square feet of heated and air-conditioned space. However, if the garage, porch and wall space were included, there was a total of 2,400 square feet. The Camerons sued Terrell and Garrett, Inc., under the Texas Deceptive Trade Practices Act, alleging misrepresentation. They claimed that Terrell and Garrett, Inc., had falsely represented the number of square feet in the house. They sought actual damages of $3,419.30.

After a trial and two appeals, judgment was rendered for the Camerons. The court stated that Terrell and Garrett had misrepresented the number of square feet through the MLS and that the Camerons were consumers under the law, even though there was no contact with Terrell and Garrett. The Camerons were required to prove that they had been adversely affected by the misrepresentation.

***Weitzel v. Barnes,* 691 S.W.2d 598 (Tex. 1985):** On February 8, 1983, Barnes/Segraves Development Company, seller, and the Weitzels, buyers, signed a contract to purchase a remodeled home. The written contract gave the Weitzels the right to inspect, among other things, the plumbing and air-conditioning systems in the house. The contract provided that if the Weitzels were dissatisfied with the systems, they could reject the contract. A contract addendum further provided that failure of the buyer to inspect and give written notice of repairs to the seller constituted a waiver of buyer's inspection rights and amounted to buyer's consent to purchase the property as-is. The Weitzels did not inspect the house. Prior to and after signing the contract, the seller told the Weitzels that the plumbing and air-conditioning systems complied with the Fort Worth building code specifications. After moving into the house the Weitzels found that the equipment did not function properly and was not in compliance with the city code. The Weitzels claimed that the oral representations were deceptive acts under the Deceptive Trade Practices Act. Barnes/Segraves asserted as their defense the written contract provision regarding inspections, repairs and waiver. The seller also argued that the buyer did not rely upon the representations and in fact had notice prior to consummation of the sale that the city had posted a condemned notice on the house.

The court held for the Weitzels, reasoning that the buyers were not seeking to contradict the terms of the written agreement, nor were they claiming a breach of contract. Therefore, the verbal misrepresentations were admissible to prove a violation of the Deceptive Trade Practices Act. Next the court stated that the act does not require proof that the Weitzels relied upon the oral misrepresentation. Reliance is not an element of producing cause. The court did point out that, had the seller remained silent and not spoken to the quality or characteristics of the plumbing and air-conditioning system, the seller would not have been liable. The contract provision regarding inspection, repairs and waiver would have been controlling.

DAMAGES

The Deceptive Trade Practices Act provides that a prevailing consumer can recover his or her actual damages, attorney fees and court costs. In addition, the judge or jury can award the consumer a sum of money in excess of his or her actual losses. The consumer may receive two times that portion of the actual damages not exceeding $1,000. For example, if a purchaser was actually damaged in the sum of $2,300, he could receive $2,300 plus an additional $2,000 ($1,000). Further, if the court finds that the defendant committed the prohibited act knowingly, the plaintiff could receive three times the amount of damages in excess of $1,000.

DEFENSES

How can a person limit his or her liability for a deceptive or misleading act or practice? The act specifically makes unenforceable any waiver (written or oral) by the consumer to sue under the Deceptive Trade Practices Act. However, the act does establish a procedure for limiting liability and for recovery of damages from a consumer if the suit is filed in bad faith by notice and settlement provisions amended in 1989. The consumer must give 60 days' written notice to the defendant of his or her specific complaint and the amount of actual damages and expenses, including attorney fees. The defendant then has 60 days to respond to the complaint and tender to the consumer a written offer of settlement. If the consumer ignores or rejects this offer and the court later determines that the offer is the same or substantially the same as the actual damages found by the court, then the defendant's liability can be limited to the amount of the offer, if it is less than that awarded by the court. The law also states that the tender of an offer of settlement is not an admission of guilt.

A second defense is the giving of timely written notice to the consumer of the broker's reliance on some other written information. This can greatly assist brokers and salespeople because they frequently rely upon information provided by others, such as the seller, an appraiser, an engineer or perhaps even a governmental agent. The key to the success of this defense is that:

1. the broker or agent must have received the information in writing;
2. the broker must give written notice to the consumer prior to consummation of the sale that the broker is relying upon this written information; and

3. the broker must establish that he or she did not know and could not have known that the information was false or inaccurate.

It is important for a broker or an agent to remember that reliance upon the written information must be reasonable considering his or her expertise in the area. However, a broker or an agent who can prove that he or she has met this defense will not be liable for the consumer's damages.

Case Briefs

***Kennemore v. Bennett,* 755 S.W.2d 89 (Tex. 1988):** Thomas and Charles Kennemore contracted with builder Bill Bennett for the construction of a home. When the Kennemores refused to pay Bennett the balance due on the contract and $4,542.55 for extras, he placed mechanic's and materialman's liens against the property. Bennett then sued to foreclose his lien. The Kennemores defended against Bennett's suit and counterclaimed that Bennett had failed to construct the house in a good and workmanlike manner. The Kennemores asserted this breach of warranty action under the Texas Deceptive Trade Practices Act. Prior to trial, the Kennemores paid Bennett in full but proceeded to trial on their DTPA claim against Bennett. Bennett argued that the Kennemores had waived their DTPA action by moving into the house and paying Bennett the money demanded in Bennett's lawsuit. The Texas Supreme Court held that the DTPA claims are not waived by consumers simply by accepting the allegedly defective home.

***Ojeda de Toca v. Wise,* 748 S.W.2d 449, (Tex. 1988).** On November 15, 1979, Rocio Ojeda de Toca purchased a house from Wise Developments, Inc. Approximately 11 months prior to the purchase, the City of Houston had recorded a document ordering that the house be demolished and placed a lien against the property for the demolition costs. Although Wise was aware of the demolition order, it did not notify Toca. While Toca was out of the country, the City demolished the house pursuant to the demolition order. Toca sued Wise for misrepresentation, fraud and violation of the Texas Deceptive Trade Practices Act. Wise asserted in its defense that Toca had constructive notice of the demolition order under the recording statute. The court held that the legislature, in passing the Deceptive Trade Practices Act, did not intend to bar a consumer's DTPA or fraud claim because an examination of the county records could have disclosed the seller's deception and that the recording statute is not to protect perpetrators of fraud. Therefore, Toca was allowed to receive from Wise for its failure to disclose the existence of the Demolition Order.

***Alvarado v. Bolton,* 749 S.W.2d 47, (Tex. 1988).** The Alvarados purchased 50 acres of land in Fort Bend County, Texas, from Bolton. The earnest money contract did not reserve any mineral rights for the seller (Bolton), but at the closing the deed specifically reserved to Bolton one-half of the mineral rights. After oil was discovered on the land, the Alvarados learned of Bolton's mineral reservations and sued to reform the deed and for damages under DTPA. Bolton asserted that under the doctrine of merger, once a deed is delivered and accepted, the earnest money contract becomes merged into the deed and only those terms in the deed can be used for resolving disputes. Therefore, because the deed specifically reserved the mineral rights and the Alvarados accepted the deed, the Alvarados were not entitled to the mineral rights. The court held that the doctrine of merger cannot be used to defeat a DTPA claim for breach of an express warranty made in an earnest money contract. Therefore, the Alvarados can prevail against Bolton if they can prove that the earnest money contract had been breached by Bolton.

SUMMARY

Fraud is a deceptive act practiced deliberately by one person in an attempt to gain an unfair advantage over another. *Misrepresentation* is a false statement made negligently or innocently that is a material factor in another's decision to contract. In Texas, one of the methods for holding a person liable for fraud or misrepresentation is the Deceptive Trade Practices Act, which prohibits not only false statements but also misleading statements or acts. A consumer who can prove that a misleading act was the producing cause of the injury can recover his or her actual damages, attorney fees, court costs and additional compensation up to twice the amount of the actual losses. One defense that can be particularly useful to brokers is giving written notice to a buyer or seller that they are relying upon written information supplied by someone else. If this notice is given in a timely and proper manner, the broker is relieved from liability for false or misleading statements contained in such written reports.

QUIZ

1. Which of the following is not true with respect to the Texas Deceptive Trade Practices Act?
   a. A broker can safely rely upon a signed written waiver.
   b. There is no requirement that the offending party intended to deceive.
   c. In order to prevail, the injured party must be a consumer as defined in the act.
   d. A written offer of settlement is a defense.
2. Which of the following is not an example of damages available under the Texas Deceptive Trade Practices Act?
   a. Actual damages
   b. Mandatory four times the actual damages
   c. Court costs and attorney fees
   d. Two times the actual damages, not exceeding $1,000
3. In defending against a DTPA case, a broker or salesperson using the timely written notice defense must include all of the following *except:*
   a. the broker must give written notice to the consumer prior to consummation of the sale that the broker is relying on this written notice.
   b. the broker or agent must have received the information in writing.
   c. the broker must establish that he or she did not and could not know that the information was false or inaccurate.
   d. the broker must produce evidence that three independent sources were consulted before the written notice was submitted to the consumer.
4. Which of the following is provided by the Texas Deceptive Trade Practices-Consumer Protection Act?
   a. A reasonable offer of settlement made within specified time limits is a defense.
   b. Transmittal of written information prepared by others along with a written statement of reliance on such information is a defense.
   c. Recovery of court costs and attorney fees is possible if the lawsuit was frivolous or harassing.
   d. All of the above
5. All the following are included in the DTPA definition of consumer *except:*
   a. individuals.
   b. partnerships or corporations.
   c. business consumers with assets of $25 million of more.
   d. the state of Texas.

DISCUSSION QUESTION

1. What types of statement might a broker make that would lead to possible innocent misrepresentation under the DTPA?

CHAPTER

13

LOOKING AHEAD

The issue of who real estate agents represent will continue to be a major issue for the remainder of the 1990s, just as real property securities registration was major national issues in the 1970s and the impact of the due-on-sale clause was the hot issue for the 1980s. This chapter discusses the following:

Gradual change
Differing Degrees
Disclosure
  Consumer Awareness
  Choices
  Adapting to Change

GRADUAL CHANGE

In the years to come, we can expect that brokerage practice will not change drastically, but there will be more disclosure of agency. Companies will spend more time on developing policy on agency and on training sales staff on correct procedure.

The trend in brokerage will be toward single agency in all transactions, except for consensual dual agency with in-house sales, because more buyers will be seeking buyer representation. Thus, large firms will have a greater number of buyer clients, many of whom may become interested in company listings. When dual agency is used, the disclosure and consent will be more extensive. Even though they may be representing adversaries, brokers will continue to cooperate in an honest manner to complete a transaction to the satisfaction of the buyer and seller.

The study of agency relationships has revealed a number of real estate customs and practices that are no longer suited to the modern real estate market, such as:

- the concept that all brokers represent the seller;
- the failure to inform and educate clients and customers in advance regarding real estate principles and practices;
- failure to refer to other professionals;
- automatic use of subagency;

- lack of formal contracts with buyers; and
- lack of understanding of agency.

DIFFERING DEGREES

The agency/subagency disclosure issue is not a problem of equal degree in all states. It may be less of a problem where the real estate broker's main role is to match a buyer with a seller and where, thereafter, lawyers for both parties take over to prepare contracts and closing documents. In states in which a neutral escrow agent closes the sale, however, the role of the broker extends beyond introducing the parties, with buyers and sellers each expecting reasonable representation by "their agent," who often turns out to be the same agent.

Also, the problem may be more extensive in some fields of real estate than in others. There may, for example, be a greater problem in residential sales than in large commercial or industrial property acquisitions, where the parties tend to be more sophisticated, represented by specialists and in which decisions tend to be based on objective facts and figures. California limits its disclosure law to residential real property; Washington's disclosure law does not apply to lease transactions.

DISCLOSURE

Disclosure should be required in all real estate transactions. In residential real estate, brokers are commonly agents of the sellers, whereas in commercial real estate it is common for brokers to represent the buyer. Nevertheless, there is no reason for the legislature to disturb or limit these practices or to prefer one over the other. As long as agency relationships are identified, discussed and documented at the appropriate time, then real estate practices and preferences should be left to the marketplace.

All participants in a real estate transaction should recognize the need for clarification to buyers and sellers of what level of service will be provided and to whom. Further discussion, clear and timely disclosure and education will produce several benefits, such as less ambiguity and potential for dispute and a more prestigious professional image for real estate brokers, salespeople and the industry as a whole.

Consumer Awareness

The main goal of increased disclosure of agency relationships is consumer awareness and protection. By highlighting alternatives, consumers can make knowledgeable choices about:

- who, if anyone, they want to represent them;
- what services they want to receive;
- what compensation they are willing to pay; and
- what liabilities they are prepared to accept.

The present media attention on agency affords the industry an opportunity to step forward and demonstrate its professionalism and concern for protecting the best interests of the client. It also affords brokers a chance to use the agency issue in a positive, constructive way to increase their level of competence, professionalism and, in the process, their volume of business.

CHOICES

Several choices are open to brokers. There will be some brokers who choose to ignore the liabilities; these brokers are gambling that upon closing, buyers and sellers will be satisfied with the transaction and with the broker's performance. Based on high past levels of consumer satisfaction, this could be a good gamble; however, based on the high dollar amount involved in some transactions, the amount of commissions and the potential damages recoverable, it can also be an expensive gamble if something goes wrong.

Most brokers take a cautious yet realistic approach to disclosure. For those so willing, discussion of agency can become a routine step in the development of every working relationship with buyers and sellers. This discussion can be supplemented with a simple written statement that identifies all possible agency relationships. As the relationship develops, a more specific understanding can be reached through practice. Developing a comprehensive yet comfortable disclosure policy will lead to well informed, conscious choices of the most effective and successful types of agency.

Adapting to Change

The real estate industry has the ability to adapt to change. Disclosure of agency is no more difficult to adapt to than rules concerning disclosure of property condition or financing. It was not too long ago that brokers switched from open listings to exclusive listings.

We are now experiencing another evolution toward a system of listing the buyer and providing the same level of client services previously reserved for sellers. Single-client agency representation is now being used by small real estate firms to compete with larger firms, which may have a harder time making the switch because of the potential conflicts of interest arising from in-house sales. However, large firms have the advantage of expert management and in-house training that can develop programs to help salespeople promote the benefits of buyer agency. These firms can also develop the forms and procedures needed for dual agency.

SUMMARY

There is no magical solution to the representation issues discussed in this book. The various alternatives to the traditional seller representation approach have imperfections as well. But by openly discussing the problems, exploring alternatives and maintaining flexibility, the marketplace should be able to develop its own solutions.

Real estate agents should evaluate their role in each transaction. Although their primary purpose is to protect the client and conclude a successful transaction, they need not assume the adversarial role of a trial attorney. Brokers should continue to cooperate with other brokers while respecting the agency relationships of others.

The goal of real estate agents should be to simplify legal relationships, avoid ambiguities and encourage their coworkers to act in a manner that complies with both the law and the reasonable expectations of buyers and sellers.

Only by improved communication among buyers, sellers, brokers and salespeople will we truly know the answer to the most often asked question in the real estate industry, "who do you represent?"

APPENDIX

A SELECTED STATUTES AND TREC RULES

It is important to know what the law says before trying to decide what the law means. Therefore, the following legal excerpts should be researched and studied by real estate agents. It is the licensee's responsibility to be familiar with laws that affect his or her daily business.

Note: *Section 2(7) states, "If the sense requires it, words in the present tense include the future tense; in the masculine gender include the feminine or neutral gender; in the singular number include the plural number; the word* and *may be* or; *and the word* or *may be read* and. *This Act is substantive in character and is intended to be applied prospectively only."*

22 TAC Section 531.1

A real estate broker or salesman, while acting as an agent for another, is a fiduciary. Special obligations are imposed when such fiduciary relationships are created. They demand

(a) that the primary duty of the real estate agent is to represent the interests of his client and his position, in this respect, should be clear to all parties concerned in a real estate transaction; that, however, the agent in performing his duties to his client shall treat other parties to a transaction fairly;

(b) that the real estate agent be faithful and observant to trust placed in him and be scrupulous and meticulous in performing his functions;

(c) that the real estate agent place no personal interest about that of his client.

22 TAC Section 531.2

A real estate broker or salesman has a special obligation to exercise integrity in the discharge of his responsibilities, including employment of prudence and caution as so to avoid misrepresentation, in any wise, by acts of commission or omission.

22 TAC Section 531.3

It is the obligation of a real estate agent to be knowledgeable as a real estate brokerage practitioner. He should

(a) be informed on market conditions affecting the real estate business and pledged to continuing education in the intricacies involved in marketing real estate for others;

(b) be informed on national, state and local issues and developments in the real estate industry;

(c) exercise judgment and skill in the performance of his work.

TRELA Section 1

(a) This Act shall be known and may be cited as "The Real Estate License Act."

(b) It is unlawful for a person to act in the capacity of, engage in the business of, or advertise or hold himself out as engaging in or conducting the business of a real estate broker or a real estate salesman within this state without first obtaining a real estate license from the Texas Real Estate Commission. It is unlawful for a person licensed as a real estate salesman to act or attempt to act as a real estate broker or salesman unless he is, at such time, associated with a licensed Texas real estate broker and acting for the licensed real estate broker.

(c) Each real estate broker licensed pursuant to this Act is responsible to the commission, members of the public, and his clients for all acts and conduct performed under this Act by himself or by a real estate salesman associated with or acting for the broker.

(d) No real estate salesman shall accept compensation for real estate sales and transactions from any person other than the broker under whom he is at the time licensed or under whom he was licensed when he earned the right to compensation.

(e) No real estate salesman shall pay a commission to any person except through the broker under whom he is at the time licensed.

22 TAC Section 535.1(g)
(g) Real estate licensure is required of a real estate broker's employees, agent or associates who direct or supervise other employees, agents or associates while the other employees, agents or associates are performing acts for which licensure is required. Provided, however, that licensure if not required for the performance of administrative tasks. Administrative tasks include but are not limited to the following: (1) training or motivating personnel; (2) performing duties generally associated with office administration and personnel matters.

22 TAC Section 535.2(a), (b), (c), (d), (f) and (g)
(a) Other than is contemplated by this section, the Real Estate License Act does not regulate the working agreements between or among licensees.
(c) A broker is responsible for his salesman's authorized acts, but the broker may absent himself as he chooses.
(d) A salesman may work in or out of a real estate office without direct supervision of his sponsoring broker. This in no way lessen the degree of responsibility of the sponsoring broker for his salesman's actions.
(f) A real estate agent owes the very highest fiduciary obligation to his principal and is obligated to convey to his principal all information of which the agent has knowledge and which may affect the principal's decision. It is the broker's obligation under a listing contract to negotiate the best possible transaction for his principal, the person he has agreed to represent.
(g) a broker is responsible for the authorized acts of his associates whether they are licensed as salesmen or brokers.

TRELA Section 2. As used in this Act:

(1) "Real estate" means a leasehold, as well as any other interest in land, whether corporeal, incorporeal, freehold or nonfreehold and whether the real estate is situated in this state or elsewhere.

(2) "Real estate broker" means a person who, for another person and for a fee, commission, or other valuable consideration, or with the intention or in the expectation or on the promise of receiving or collecting a fee, commission, or other valuable consideration from another person:

- (A) sells, exchanges, purchases, rents, or leases real estate;
- (B) offers to sell, exchange, purchase, rent, or lease real estate;
- (C) negotiates or attempts to negotiate the listing, sale, exchange, purchase, rental, or leasing of real estate;
- (D) lists or offers or attempts or agrees to list real estate for sales, rental, lease, exchange, or trade;
- (E) appraises or offers or attempts or agrees to appraise real estate;
- (F) auctions, or offers or attempts or agrees to auction, real estate;
- (G) buys or sells or offers to buy or sell, or otherwise deals in options on real estate;
- (H) aids, attempts, or offers to aid in locating or obtaining for purchase, rent, or lease any real estate;
- (I) procures or assists in the procuring of prospects for the purpose of effecting the sale, exchange, lease, or rental of real estate; or

(J) procures or assists in the procuring of properties for the purpose of effecting the sale, exchange, lease, or rental of real estate.

TRELA Section 14

(a) It is unlawful for a licensed broker to employ or compensate directly or indirectly a person for performing an act enumerated in the definition of real estate broker in Section 2 of this Act if the person is not a licensed broker or licensed salesman in this state. However, a licensed broker may pay a commission to a licensed broker of another state if the foreign broker does not conduct in this state any of the negotiations for which the fee, compensation, or commission is paid.

22 TAC Section 535.131 (c)
An unlicensed person may share in the income earned by a real estate brokerage operation, provided that such unlicensed person performs none of the activities of a real estate agent and the public is not led to believe that such unlicensed person is in the real estate brokerage business.

TRELA Section 15

(a) The commission may, on its own motion, and shall, on the signed complaint in writing of a consumer or service recipient, provided the complaint, or the complaint together with evidence, documentary or otherwise, presented in connection with the complaint, provides reasonable cause, investigate the actions and records of a real estate broker or real estate salesman. The commission may suspend or revoke a license issued under the provisions of this Act at any time when it has been determined that:

(2) the licensee has procured, or attempted to procure, a real estate license, for himself or a salesman, by fraud, misrepresentation or deceit, or by making a material misstatement of fact in an application for a real estate license;

(3) the licensee, when selling, buying, trading, or renting real property in his own name, engaged in misrepresentation or dishonest or fraudulent action;

(4) the licensee, while performing an act constituting an act of a broker or salesman, as defined by this Act, has been guilty of:

(A) making a material misrepresentation, or failing to disclose to a potential purchaser any latent structural defect or any other defect known to the broker or salesman. Latent structural defects and other defects do not refer to trivial or insignificant defects but refer to those defects that would be a significant factor to a reasonable and prudent purchaser in making a decision to purchase;

(B) making a false promise of a character likely to influence, persuade, or induce any person to enter into a contract or agreement when the licensee could not or did not intend to keep such promise;

(C) pursuing a continued and flagrant course of misrepresentation or making of false promises through agents, salesmen, advertising, or otherwise;

(D) failing to make clear, to all parties to a transaction, which party he is acting for, or receiving compensation from more than one party except with the full knowledge and consent of all parties;

(E) paying a commission or fees to or dividing a commission or fees with anyone not licensed as a real estate broker or salesman in this state or in any other state for compensation for services as a real estate agent;

(F) failing to specify in a listing contract a definite termination date which is not subject to prior notice;

(G) acting in the dual capacity of broker and undisclosed principal in a transaction;

(H) placing a sign on real property offering it for sale, lease, or rent without the written consent of the owner or his authorized agent;

(I) inducing or attempting to induce a party to a contract of sale or lease to break the contract for the purpose of substituting in lieu thereof a new contract;

(J) negotiating or attempting to negotiate the sale, exchange, lease, or rental of real property with an owner or lessor, knowing that the owner or lessor had a written outstanding contract, granting exclusive agency in connection with the property to another real estate broker;

(K) offering real property for sale or for lease without the knowledge and consent of the owner or his authorized agent, or on terms other than those authorized by the owner or his authorized agent;

(L) establishing an association, by employment or otherwise, with an unlicensed person who is expected or required to act as a real estate licensee, or aiding or abetting or conspiring with a person to circumvent the requirements of this Act;

(M) conduct which constitutes dishonest dealings, bad faith, or untrustworthiness;

(N) acting negligently or incompetently in performing an act for which a person is required to hold a real estate license.

22 TAC Section 535.141(c)

A real estate broker is responsible for all acts and conduct performed by a real estate salesman associated with or acting for the broker. A verified complaint which names a licensed real estate salesman as the subject of a complaint but does not specifically name the salesman's sponsoring broker is a complaint against the broker sponsoring the salesman at the time of any alleged violation for the limited purposes of determining the broker's involvement in any alleged violation and whether the broker fulfilled his or her professional responsibilities to the commission, members of the public and his or her clients, provided the complaint concerns the conduct of the salesman as an agent for the broker.

22 TAC Section 535.144

A licensee, when engaging in a real estate transaction on his own behalf, is obligated to inform any person with whom he deals that he is a licensed real estate broker or salesman acting on his own behalf either by disclosure in any contract of sale or rental agreement or by disclosure in any other writing given prior to entering into any contract of sale or rental agreement. A licensee shall not use his expertise to the disadvantage of a person with whom he deals.

22 TAC Section 535.147(b)

Commission or fees includes any form of compensation received for services as a real estate agent.

22 TAC Section 535.148

(a) Every listing contract shall have a definite termination date, upon which date the listing will automatically expire without any requirement of notice to the real estate licensee.

22 TAC Section 535.152

"Written consent" as required by this section of the Act may be obtained in a listing agreement or any other appropriate agreement that has been reduced to writing.

22 TAC Section 535.156

(a) A licensee's relationship with his principal is that of a fiduciary. A licensee shall convey to his principal all known information which would affect the principal's decision on whether or not to accept or reject offers; however, the licensee shall have no duty to submit offers to the principal after the principal has accepted an offer.

(b) The licensee must put the interest of his principal above his own interest. A licensee must deal honestly and fairly with all parties; however, he represents only his principal and owes a duty of fidelity to such principal.

22 TAC Section 535.157

A licensee should not undertake to perform a service or handle a transaction for which he lacks the requisite knowledge or expertise.

TRELA Section 15C

(a) A real estate broker may not act as an agent for more than one party to a transaction unless:

(1) the real estate broker, prior to entering into any written agreements to represent more than one party to the transaction, in accordance with the rules of the commission, provides the parties with the applicable agency disclosure form promulgated by the commission which defines common agency relationships, duties of the broker, and potential conflicts that may develop.

(2) the real estate broker enters into written agreements in which all parties to the transaction consent to and authorize the real estate broker to represent more than one party to the transaction; and

(3) the written agreements set forth the source of any expected compensation to the real estate broker.

(b) A written listing agreement to represent a seller or landlord or a written agreement to represent a buyer or tenant which authorizes a real estate broker to act as agent for more than one party to a transaction is sufficient to establish written consent of the party to the agreement for the real estate broker to represent more than one party to the transaction under this section if the written agreement sets forth, in conspicuous bold or underlined print, the broker's obligations under Subsection (c) of this section.

(c) A real estate broker who acts as an agent for more than one party to a transaction shall:

(1) not disclose to the buyer or tenant that the seller or landlord will accept a price less than the asking price unless otherwise instructed in a separate writing by the seller or landlord;

(2) not disclose to the seller or landlord that the buyer or tenant will pay a price greater than the price submitted in a written offer to the seller or landlord unless otherwise instructed in a separate writing by the buyer or tenant;

(3) not disclose any confidential information or any information a party specifically instructs the real estate broker in writing not to disclose unless otherwise instructed in a separate writing by the respective party or required to disclose such information by law; and

(4) treat all parties to the transaction honestly and impartially so as not to favor one party or work to the disadvantage of any party.

(d) The real estate broker shall use due diligence to assist the parties in understanding the consents, agreements, or instructions under this section in which the real estate broker is permitted to represent more than one party to a transaction.

22 TAC Section 535.164(a)

The Texas Real Estate Commission adopts by reference Agency Disclosure Form 3, approved by the Texas Real Estate Commission in 1993.

TRELA Section 15D. No licensed real estate broker, licensed real estate salesman, or not for profit real estate board or association which provides information about real property sales prices or terms of sale for the purpose of facilitating the listing, selling, leasing, financing, or appraisal of real property shall be liable to any other person as a result of so providing such information unless the disclosure of same is otherwise specifically prohibited by statute.

TRELA Section 16

(a) A license granted under the provisions of this Act shall be suspended or revoked by the commission on proof that the licensee, not being licensed and authorized to practice law in this state, for a consideration, reward, pecuniary benefit, present or anticipated, direct or indirect, or in connection with or as a part of his employment, agency, or fiduciary relationship as a licensee, drew a deed, note, deed of trust, will, or other written instrument that may transfer or anywise affect the title to or an interest in land, except as provided in the subsections below, or advised or counseled a person as to the validity or legal sufficiency of an instrument or as to the validity of title to real estate.

(b) Notwithstanding the provisions of this Act or any other law, the completion of contract forms which bind the sale, exchange, option, lease, or rental of any interest in real property by a real estate broker or salesman incident to the performance of the acts of a broker as defined by this article does not constitute the unauthorized or illegal practice of law in this state, provided the forms have been promulgated for use by the commission for the particular kind of transaction involved, or the forms have been prepared by an attorney at law licensed by this state and approved by said attorney for the particular kind of transaction involved, or the forms have been prepared by the property owner or prepared by an attorney and required by the property owner.

(c) A Texas Real Estate Broker-Lawyer Committee is hereby created which, in addition to other powers and duties delegated to it, shall draft and revise contract forms capable of standardization for use by real estate licensees and which will expedite real estate transactions and reduce controversies to a minimum while containing safeguards adequate to protect the interests of the principals to the transaction.

(e) In the best interest of the public the commission may adopt rules and regulations requiring real estate brokers and salesmen to use contract forms which have been prepared by the Texas Real Estate Broker-Lawyer Committee and promulgated by the commission; provided, however, that the commission shall not prohibit a real estate broker or salesman from using a contract form or forms binding the sale, exchange, option, lease, or rental of any interest in real property which have been prepared by the property owner or prepared by an attorney and required by the property owner. For the purpose of this section, contract forms prepared by the Texas Real Estate Broker-Lawyer Committee appointed by the commission and the State Bar of Texas and promulgated by the commission prior to the effective date of this Act shall be deemed to have been prepared by the Texas Real Estate Broker-Lawyer Committee. The commission may suspend or revoke a license issued under the provisions of this article when it has determined that the licensee failed to use a contract form as required by the commission pursuant to this section.

22 TAC Section 537.11 (c-e, g)

(c) A licensee shall not practice law, offer, give nor attempt to give advice, directly or indirectly; he shall not act as a public conveyance nor give advice or opinions as to the legal effect of any contracts or other such instruments which may affect the title to real estate; he shall not give opinions concerning the status or validity of title to real estate and he shall not attempt to prevent nor in any manner whatsoever discourage any principal to a real estate transaction from employing a lawyer. However, nothing herein shall be deemed to limit the licensee's fiduciary obligation to disclose to his principals all pertinent facts which are within the knowledge of the licensee, including such facts which might effect the status of or title to real estate.

(d) A licensee shall not undertake to draw or prepare documents fixing and defining the legal rights of principals to a transaction. In negotiating real estate transactions, the licensee may fill in forms for such transactions, using exclusively forms which have been approved and promulgated by the Texas Real Estate Commission or such forms as are otherwise permitted by these rules . . . it is not the practice of law as defined in this Act for a real estate licensee to complete a contract form which is approved and promulgated by the Texas Real Estate Commission or prepared by the Texas Real Estate Broker-Lawyer Committee and made available for trial use by licensees with the consent of the Texas Real Estate commission.

(e) Where it appear that, prior to the execution of any such instrument, there are unusual matters involved in the transaction and which should be resolved by legal counsel before the instrument is executed or that the instrument is to be acknowledged and filed for record, the licensee shall advise the principals that each should consult a lawyer of his choice before executing same.

(g) A broker shall advise the principals that the instruments they are about to execute is [intended to be] binding on them.

APPENDIX

B

AGENCY CASES FROM 50 STATES

This appendix contains an annotation of 600 cases from all 50 states illustrating a number of the agency issues raised in the text.

CHAPTER 1. THE REAL ESTATE LICENSEE

Definition of Agency

An agency relationship is defined by the Restatement (Second) of Agency, Section 1, to be:

> . . . a consensual, fiduciary relation between two persons, created by law by which one, the principal, has a right to control the conduct of the agent, and the agent has a power to affect the legal relations of the principal.

CHAPTER 2. AGENCY RELATIONSHIPS

Payment of Fee

A review of the legal cases reveals that the mere fact that the buyer undertakes to pay the commission does not itself create an agency relationship between the buyer and broker. The courts have held that the establishment of an agency relationship does not stand or fall on the determination of whether a commission was to be paid. *Business Properties, Inc. v. Thomas,* 46 S.E.2d 337 (VA 1948); *Richardson v. DuPree,* 122 S.E. 707 (GA 1924); *Velten v. Robertson,* 671 P.2d 1011 (CO 1983). Broker is entitled to commission if licensed at time brokerage services rendered, even if not licensed at closing. *Bersani v. Basset,* 585 NYS 2d 245 (NY 1992).

Even though the seller pays the fee, the broker may still be deemed to be the agent of the buyer. In *Brean v. North Campbell Professional Building,* 548 P.2d 1193 (AZ 1976), the broker first contacted the potential buyer with the idea of finding a desirable property and then searched for land and obtained a listing. *Mead v. Hummel,* 121 P.2d 423 (AZ 1942); *Wright v. Dutch,* 296 P.2d 34 (CA 1956); *Stephens v. Ahrens,* 178 P. 863 (CA 1919), holding that an agency is a consensual relationship and the broker is the agent of the person who first employs the broker. *Sands v. Eagle Oil & Refining Co.,* 188 P.2d 782 (CA 1948); *Norville v. Palant,* 545 P.2d 454 (AZ 1976); *Duffy v. Setchell,* 347 N.E.2d 218 (IL 1976); *Tanner Associates v. Ciralddo,* 161 A.2d 725 (NJ 1960); *Downing v. Buck,* 98 N.W.388 (MI 1904); *Walters v. Marler,* 147 Cal.Rptr.655 (CA 1978), *Pepper v. Underwood,* 122 Cal.Rptr. 343 (CA 1975).

As stated in *Wise v. Dawson,* 353 A.2d 267 (DE 1975), the splitting of fees between two brokers is not an indication of agency but only a recognition of the mutual effort and cooperation used to effect the sale of the property. The splitting of fees frequently occurs in independent contractor situations. As held in *Banner v. Elm,* 248 A.2d 452 (MD 1968), it is not uncommon to provide in the purchase contract that the seller will pay the buyer's broker.

Dunatoo v. Home of the Good Shepherd of Omaha, 228 N.W.2d 287 (NE 1975); *Antle v. Haas,* 251 S.W.2d 290 (KY 1952); *Price v. Martin,* 147 S.E.2d 716 (VA 1966).

Other cases hold that no compensation is necessary to create an agency relationship. A gratuitous agent may become an agent without compensation. *Kurtz v. Farrington,* 132 A. 540 (CT 1926). In *Walter v. Moore,* 700 P.2d 1219 (WY 1985), the court found that no agency was created with the buyer when the broker was doing a favor and not receiving any compensation. In *Canada v. Kearns,* 624 S.W.2d 755 (TX 1981), the broker unsuccessfully argued that the broker should not be responsible for the misrepresentation of one of the broker's salespeople selling the salesperson's own home through the broker for no fee.

Because agency is a consensual relationship, there is no legal barrier to having the seller authorize the listing broker to share fees with a buyer's broker. But consent is essential. Any secret agreement by a broker to split fees with the broker of the other principal is void as against public policy. *Sweeney & Moore Inc. v. Chapman,* 294 N.W. 711 (MI 1940); *Devine v. Hudgins,* 163 A. 83 (ME 1932); *Quinn v. Burton,* 81 N.E. 257 (MA 1907); *Corder v. O'Neill,* 106 S.W. 10 (MO 1907); *Ornamental and Structural Steel, Inc. v. BBG Inc.,* 509 P.2d 1053 (AZ 1973); *Greater Bloomfield Real Estate Co. v. Braun,* 235 N.W.2d 168 (MI 1975). Broker may compensate unlicensed finder who simply finds and introduces parties, but not someone who acts as a broker and is unlicensed. *Preach v. Monter Rainbow,* 12 Cal.App.4th 1441 (CA 1993).

Despite the fact that payment of the commission does not necessarily determine agency, the prudent broker will nevertheless document whom the broker represents. If no agency documentation exists, then courts will likely use the commission payment as strong evidence of an agency relationship. *Price v. Eisan,* 15 Cal.Rptr. 202 (CA 1961); *St. James American Church of Los Angeles v. Kurkjian,* 121 Cal.Rptr. 214 (CA 1975); *Hickam v. Colorado Real Estate Commission,* 534 P.2d 1220 (CO 1975); *Standard Realty & Development Co. v. Ferrara,* 151 Cal.App.2d 514 (CA 1957); *Wilkie v. Abbott's Executrix,* 178 S.W.2d 210 (KY 1944); *Prichard v. Reitz,* 223 Cal.Rptr. 734 (CA 1986).

A "finder" is subject to licensing law and cannot qualify for a commission. *Cooney v. Ritter,* 939 F.2d 81 (3rd Cir. 1991). For special rules related to lawyers acting as brokers, see *Matter of Roth,* 577 A.2d 490 (NY 1990), *Lovett v. Estate of Lovett,* 593 A.2d 382 (NJ 1991).

The buyer's broker entitled to commission from buyer if the procuring cause of sale. *Douros Realty v. Kelley Properties,* 799 S.W.2D 179 (MO 1990). Buyer claimed that sales agent concealed facts about roof condition and about agent representing seller. Court held for agent because agency disclosure was made in sales contract prior to alleged concealment. *Magliaro v. Lewis,* Case No. A91A1912 (GA 1992). Broker entitled to commission from buyer based on oral agreement. *Weichert Co. Realtors v. Ryan,* 128 N.J. 427 (NJ 1992). Buyer broker held not to have an enforceable agency agreement in commercial lease situation. *White & Associates v. Decker & Hallman,* Case No. A91A1595 (GA Ct. of Appeals Feb. 1992). Brokers successfully sued for commission on a contract not consummated. *Callaway v. Overholt,* 796 S.W.2d 828 (TX 1990).

The Fiduciary Relationship

Fiduciary Duties—Persons dealing with a real estate licensee may naturally assume that the broker possesses the requisites of an honest and ethical person. *Ellis v. Flink* 301 So.2d 493 (FL 1974); *Department of Employment v. Bake Young Realty,* 560 P.2d 504 (ID 1977); *Easton v. Strassburger,* 199 Cal.Rptr. 383 (CA App. 1984); *Zichlin v. Dill,* 25 So.2d 4 (FL 1946). Brokers hold themselves out to the public as having particular skills and knowledge in the real estate field. In essence, the law creates a public duty.

In any lawsuit alleging that the broker breached a fiduciary duty, the broker must prove there was no breach of duty. *Vogt v. Town & Country Realty of Lincoln,* 231 N.W.2d 496 (NE 1975).

In a suit for negligence against a real estate broker, the Nebraska Supreme Court held a special two-year statute of limitations for "professional negligence" was inapplicable because "real estate brokers are not professionals." *Tylle v. Zouche,* 412 N.W.2d 438 (NE 1987).

Duty of Loyalty—Of all the obligations imposed by the fiduciary duty, loyalty is the essential virtue required of a broker. *Rose v. Showalter,* 701 P.2d 251 (ID 1985); *Wegg v. Henry Broderick, Inc.,* 557 P.2d 861 (WA 1976); *Cogan v. Kidder, Mathews & Segner, Inc.,* 648 P.2d 875 (WA 1982).

Disclosure

1. ***Relationship****—Mersky v. Multiple Listing Bureau of Olympia, Inc.,* 437 P.2d 897 (WA 1968); *Kimmell v. Clark,* 520 P.2d 851 (AZ 1974); *Ross v. Perelli,* 538 P.2d 834 (WA 1975) (relationship between subagent and buyer); *Wilkinson v. Smith,* 639 P.2d 768 (WA 1982); *John J. Reynolds v. Snow,* 174 N.E.2d 753 (NY 1961); *Velten v. Robertson,* 671 P.2d 1011 (CO 1983); *Smith v. Zak,* 98 Cal.Rptr. 242 (CA 1971); *Jenkins v. Wise,* 574 P.2d 1337 (HI 1978); *Silva v. Bisbie,* 628 P.2d 214 (HI 1981); *Ramsey v. Sedlar,* 454 P.2d 416 (WA 1969); *Abell v. Watson,* 317 P.2d 159 (CA 1957) (buyer was broker's wife). See also *Handy v. Garmarker,* 324 N.W.2d 168 (MN 1982); *Christman v. Seymour,* 700 P.2d 898 (AZ 1985); *Drake v. Hasley,* 713 P.2d 1203 (AK 1986).

The broker must disclose any interest in a corporation offering to buy a listed property, even if the broker is a minority stockholder or is only a director or officer and has no stock ownership. *Bell v. Routh Robbins Real Estate Corp.,* 147 S.E.2d 277 (VA 1966); *McKinney v. Christmas,* 353 P.2d 373 (CO 1960); *Treat v. Schmidt,* 193 P.666 (CO 1920); *Newell-Murdoch Realty Co. v. Wickham,* 190 P. 359 (CA 1920); *Batson v. Strehlow,* 441 P.2d 101 (CA 1968); *Wendt v. Fischer,* 154 N.E. 303 (NY 1926); *Travagliante v. J. W. Wood Realty Company,* 425 S.W.2d 208 (MO 1968). Brokerage breached fiduciary duty owed seller by not disclosing that one of its general partners was part purchaser of listed property. *Designer Showrooms v. Kelley,* 405 S.E.2d 417 (SC 1991).

The fact the broker is licensed or has an interest in the buyer does not preclude the broker from participating in the transaction and earning a commission, provided the seller receives full disclosure of the conflicting interests. In *re Estate of Baldwin,* 110 Cal.Rptr. 189 (CA App 1973); *Rosenfeld v. Glick Real Estate Co.,* 291 S.W.2d 863 (MO 1956); *Stevens v. Hutton,* 163 P.2d 479 (CA 1946). Failure to disclose broker's romance with client's ex-spouse's divorce attorney might influence complete loyalty to client. *Silverman v. Pitterman,* 574 So.2d 275 (FL 1991).

Note that a licensee acting as a principal in the sale or purchase of real estate should disclose to the other party the fact of licensure. An inactive licensee may have no duty of disclosure, although it would be preferable to disclose. *Gregory v. Selle,* 206 N.W.2d 147 (WI 1973). Upheld ruling that use of phrase by broker "for sale by owner" was misleading. *HelpSell v. Maine REC,* 611 A.2d 981 (ME 1992). Broker not liable for making repairs as personal guarantor when he signed agreement on line marked "witness." *McGinney v. Jackson,* 575 So.2d 1070 (ALA 1991).

2. ***Other Offers***—The broker must present all offers as a matter of top priority. It is also advisable to inform the seller of facts that indicate another offer may be presented shortly and to present offers even after the seller has accepted an offer, in the event the seller wishes to have a back-up offer. Brokers should tell buyers that making a full-price offer does not mean the seller must accept such offer. Brokers should avoid giving to buyers "rights of first refusal" or assuring them that the seller will accept a certain amount.

The broker must submit an offer even if the broker believes it is too low to warrant consideration. *E. A. Strout Realty Agency, Inc. v. Wooster,* 99 A.2d 689 (VT 1955).

The listing broker is under an affirmative duty to disclose a second offer to purchase and, by failing to disclose such offer, has made a representation that no other offer exists. Failure to disclose could result in loss of commission, loss of license or even punitive damages. The buyer may sue the broker for money damages resulting from the broker's failure to present the buyer's offer. Such cases usually involve situations in which the broker purchases the property. *Simone v. McKee,* 298 P.2d 667 (CA 1956); *Cisco v. Van Lew,* 141 P.2d 433 (CA 1943); *Southern Cross Industries, Inc. v. Martin,* 604 S.W.2d 290 (TX 1980); *Hickman v. Colorado Real Estate Commission,* 534 P.2d 1220 (CO 1975); *Virginia Real Estate Commission v. Bias,* 308 S.E.2d 123 (VA 1983); *Githens v. Johnson,* 192 N.W. 270 (IA 1923); *Brown v. Carpenter,* 134 S.W. 1150 (KY 1911); *Barbat v. M.E. Arden Co.,* 254 N.W.2d 779 (MI 1977); *Harper v. Adametz,* 113 A.2d 136 (CT 1955); *Arnato v. Latter & Blum, Inc.,* 79 So.2d 873 (LA 1955); *Phillips v. Lynch,* 704 P.2d 1083 (NEV 1985).

Brokers must respect the confidentiality of offers. The listing broker should not disclose to other salespeople in the broker's office the amount of a cooperating broker's offer. Nor should the listing broker reveal the amount of a previous counteroffer made by the seller. Likewise, the listing broker should not disclose the amounts of previously rejected offers unless the seller agrees to this strategy. Buyers should be encouraged to submit their best offers.

Knowledge of other offers may result in the buyer's submitting a lower offer than originally planned.

Brokers must also disclose any information that a prospective buyer may be willing to offer better terms or a higher price than the offer presented. *Carter v. Owens,* 50 So. 641 (FL 1909); *Gillespie v. Rosenbaum,* 173 N.Y.S.429 (NY 1918); *Raleigh Real Estate & Trust Co. v. Adarns,* 58 S.E. 1008 (NC 1907); *Mason v. Bulleri,* 543 P.2d 478 (AZ 1975). Broker not liable to buyer for failure to convey purchase offer accurately to seller. *Andrie v. Crystal-Anderson,* 466 N.W.2d 393 (MI 1991).

3. Status of Deposit Money—*De St.Germain v. Watson,* 214 P.2d 99 (CA 1950) (failed to disclose payment in form of promissory note); *Nugent v. Scharff,* 476 S.W.2d 414 (TX 1971); *Roy H. Long Realty Company v. Vanderkolk,* 547 P.2d 497 (AZ 1976); *Merkeley v. MacPherson's Inc.,* 420 P.2d 205 (WA 1966); *Hughey v. Rainwater Partners,* 661 S.W.2d 690 (TN 1983) (seller awarded 100 percent of deposit); *Reich v. Christopulos,* 256 P.2d 238 (UT 1953); holding no violation of licensing law to fail to disclose postdated check is *Lowe v. State Dept. of Commerce, Real Estate Division,* 515 P.2d 388 (NV 1973); *Huizenga v. Withey Sheppard Associates,* 167 N.W.2d 120 (MI 1969); see *Wilson v. Lewis,* 165 Cal.Rptr. 396 (CA 1980).

A broker is liable for failure to disclose to the property owner that the broker did not collect the security deposits as indicated in the rental agreements. In *Murphy & Fritz's Place, Inc. v. Loretta,* 447 N.Y.S.2d 205 (NY 1982), the broker was held liable for failure to disclose that he had not received the initial or additional deposit the contract required the buyer to make. Broker liable for advising buyer to make a $50,000 down payment to person claiming falsely to be the owner of the property (rather than place money in escrow). *Keystone Realty v. Osterhus,* 807 P.2d 1385 (NEV 1991).

4. Buyer's Financial Condition—*Miller v. Berkoski,* 297 N.W.2d 334 (IA 1980) (broker loaned buyer money for down payment); *McGarry v. McCrone,* 118 N.E.2d 195 (OH 1954); *Farrell v. Score,* 411 P.2d 146 (WA 1966); *Mason v. Bulleri,* 543 P.2d 178 (AZ 1975); *Alhino v. Starr,* 169 Cal.Rptr. 136 (CA 1980); *Banville v. Schmidt,* 112 Cal.Rptr. 126 (CA 1974); *R.A. Poff & Co. v. Ottaway,* 62 S.E.2d 865 (VA 1951). In *Fulsom v. Egner,* 79 N.W.2d 25 (MN 1956), the broker failed to disclose that the buyer's ability to pay was contingent on the outcome of a pending lawsuit.

When the broker makes a credit check of the buyer and discovers many negative features, the broker must disclose this information to the seller. Even though a failure to disclose may not amount to misrepresentation, it is still a breach of fiduciary duty sufficient to justify nonpayment of commission, as held in *White v. Boucher,* 322 N.W.2d 560 (MN 1982).

The seller is justified in relying upon the broker's representation that the buyer is financially sound, without having to make an independent investigation of the buyer's finances. *Phillips v. JCM Development Corporation,* 666 P.2d 876 (UT 1983). But if the broker makes reasonable inquiry into the buyer's financial condition and discloses this to the seller, the broker is not liable just because the buyer later defaults. *Zwick v. United Farm Agency, Inc.,* 556 P.2d. 508 (WY 1976).

Disclosure of financial condition is especially important when the buyer is a salesperson of the cooperating broker. *L.A. Grant Realty v. Cuomo,* 396 N.Y.S.2d 524 (NY 1977); *Hercules v. Robedeaux Inc.,* 329 N.W.2d 240 (WI App. 1982).

In *Prall v. Corum,* 403 So.2d 991 (FL 1981), the broker was held liable for failure to disclose the buyer's financial inability to purchase the property and the fact that the broker loaned the buyer money to close.

5. Property Value—The broker is liable for rendering a false opinion of value. *Eastburn v. Joseph Esphalla Jr. & Co.,* 112 So. 232 (AK 1927); *Moore v. Turner,* 71 S.E.2d 342 (WV 1952); *Iriart v. Johnson,* 411 P.2d 226 (NM 1966). In *Duhl v. Nash Realty, Inc.,* 429 N.E.2d 1267 (IL 1982), the seller bought another property relying on the broker's assurance that the property would sell quickly. A mere mistake in judgment of value is not a breach. *Smith v. Fidelity & Columbia Trust Co.,* 12 S.W.2d 276 (KY 1928). No commission is owed a broker who withholds information that a property being taken by the broker's client in an exchange is overvalued due to faulty construction. The client may be justified in relying on the professional opinion of the broker without making an independent investigation. *Smith v. Carroll Realty Co.,* 335 P.2d 67 (UT 1959); *Frederick v. Sguillante,* 144 So.2d 848 (FL 1962). In some cases, the broker is liable for deliberately undervaluing the property and then attempting to buy it and resell at a quick profit. *Barnard v. Gardner Inv. Corporation,* 106

S.E. 346 (VA 1921). Broker not liable for negligent misrepresentation of value of land. *1488, Inc. v. Philsec Inc.*, 939 F.2d 1281 (5th Cir. 1991).

When the broker learns of factors affecting the value of the property after the listing is signed, the broker must disclose such factors so the price can be adjusted in accordance with actual conditions. It is sometimes difficult, however, to pinpoint when a market is surging upwards. *Holmes v. Cathcart,* 92 N.W. 956 (MN 1903). In *Ramsey v. Gordon,* 567 S.W.2d 868 (TX 1978), the broker/buyer was to be paid a commission by the seller. The seller was allowed to void the contract because the broker breached a fiduciary duty by not disclosing the increasing value of the property during the listing period. In *Ridgeway v. McGuire,* 158 P.2d 893 (OR 1945), the broker/buyer was held liable for failure to advise the seller that the property would be valued higher if it were subdivided. In *Schoenberg v. Benner,* 59 Cal.Rptr. 359 (CA 1967), the listing broker was held negligent for failing to verify the appraised value of property that secured the buyer's purchase money note carried back by the seller.

6. Commission Split—Failure to disclose a secret fee splitting arrangement with the buyer's broker (as opposed to a subagent) can result in loss of commission by the listing broker. *Tracey v. Blake,* 118 N.E. 271 (MA 1918); *Devine v. Hudgins,* 163 A.83 (ME 1932); *Peaden v. Marler,* 189 P.741 (OK 1920). There is generally no prohibition against the listing broker dividing the commission with the buyer, as such a reduction in commission is a personal sacrifice on the broker's part to further the interest of the seller. *Banner v. Elm,* 248 A.2d 452 (MD 1968); *McCall v. Johns,* 294 S.W.2d 869 (TX 1956); *Douell v. Rosenstein,* 208 N.W. 651 (MN 1926); but see *Greenberg v. Meyer,* 363 N.E.2d 779 (OH 1977), in which broker was held to have breached duty of loyalty.

7. Contract Provisions—The broker must disclose important provisions of contracts that the client is expected to sign. Brokers have been held liable for not discussing with the seller the effect of accepting an unsecured promissory note or the fact that the seller would receive minimal cash. *Morley v. J. Pagel Realty & Ins.,* 550 P.2d 1104 (AZ 1976); *Buffington v. Haas,* 601 P.2d 1320 (AZ 1979); *Wesco Realty, Inc. v. Drewry,* 515 P.2d 513 (WA 1973); *Reese v. Harper,* 329 P.2d 410 (UT 1958). While a listing broker clearly has a duty to advise the seller concerning tying up the seller's VA eligibility on an assumption by a nonveteran buyer, it has been held that a buyer's broker has no such duty. *Hurney v. Locke,* 308 N.W.2d 764 (SD 1981). The broker may be liable for failure to disclose that a listing agreement is an exclusive-right-to-sell, *Lyle v. Moore,* 599 P.2d 336 (MT 1979), or the effect of an extender or carryover clause, *Baird v. Madsen,* 134 P.2d 885 (CA 1943).

Some courts extend the duty of the broker to discuss with the buyer certain contract provisions, such as the seller's remedies upon default of the buyer. *Wegg v. Henry Broderick, Inc.,* 557 P.2d 861 (WA 1976); *Swift v. White,* 129 N.W.2d 748 (IA 1964); for a contrary result, see *Crawford v. Powers,* 419 F.Supp. 723 (D.S.C.), applying South Carolina law, *Kidd v. Maldonado,* 688 P.2d 461 (UT 1984). In an exchange, the broker was liable for failing to disclose that a second mortgage contained a due-on-sale clause and plaintiff lost the property through foreclosure, *Pepitone v. Russo,* 134 Cal.Rptr. 709 (CA 1976). In *Alhino v. Starr,* 169 Cal.Rptr.136 (CA 1980), the salesperson failed to disclose to the seller that the purchase money note was unsecured and did not contain the customary attorney's fees and acceleration provisions. Broker acting as buyer owes duty of fair disclosure to seller (explain consequence of taking subject to as compared to assumption of loan). *Sigmen v. Arizona Dept. Real Estate,* 819 P.2d 969 (AZ 1991).

Sellers not required to pay commission when broker failed to comply with state disclosure law. *Huijers v. DeMarrais,* 12 Cal.App.4th 676 (CA December 1992).

Faithfulness

A broker who induces a buyer to believe that a property can be bought for less than the asking price may fail to discharge the duty of loyalty and therefore forfeit the commission. See *Beckwith v. Clevenger Realty Co.,* 360 P.2d 596 (AZ 1961), in which the broker told the buyer the seller was anxious to sell due to poor health; *Haymes v. Rogers,* 222 P.2d 789 (AZ 1950), in which the court held the broker liable only if done in bad faith. Likewise, the broker should not make an unauthorized statement that the property is listed at $195,000 but the seller yesterday countered another buyer's offer at $187,000.

Preparing two ascending offers for the buyer and presenting only the lower one without informing the seller that the buyer will go higher violates the broker's duty of loyalty. It is unfaithful for the broker to attempt to sell property well above the listing price to pocket the difference. *Mason v. Bulleri,* 543 P.2d 478 (AZ 1975); *Gillespie v. Rosenbaum,* 173 N.Y.S.429 (NY 1918); *Rattray v. Scudder,* 169 P.2d 371 (CA 1946); *Sankey v. Cramer,* 131 P. 288 (CO 1913). A broker who persuaded the buyer to buy elsewhere breached the fiduciary duty of good faith in *Lyon v. Giannoni,* 335 P.2d 690 (CA 1959). Broker breached duty of honesty to buyer of second home (former seller-client of broker). *Youngblood v. Wall,* 815 S.W.2d 512 (TN 1991).

Any collusion by the broker with the buyer will forfeit the broker's right to a commission, even though the seller obtains the full asking price. *Carter v. Owens,* 50 So. 641 (FL 1909); *Sternberger v. Young,* 75 A. 807 (NJ 1908). In *Greenfield v. Bausch,* 263 N.Y.S. 19 (NY 1933), the buyer agreed to pay the broker half of any amount by which the seller's listing price was reduced through the broker's efforts. The broker cannot suggest that the buyer offer terms less advantageous to the seller than the buyer had indicated the buyer would make. *Investment Exchange Realty, Inc. v. Hillcrest Bowl, Inc.,* 513 P.2d 282 (WA 1973); *Mitchell v. Gould,* 266 P. 565 (CA 1928).

Brokers cannot make false promises to induce their principals to enter into contracts, as in *Brown v. Coates,* 253 F.2d 36 (DC 1958). In *Jory v. Bennight,* 542 P.2d 1400 (NV 1975), the broker was held liable for the misconduct of its two salespeople who falsely promised that the seller would receive additional monies outside of escrow.

Denial of commission due to conflict of interest when listing broker failed to disclose that salesperson in office was selling similar property to same buyer. *Reinhold v. Mallery,* 599 A.2d 126 (NH 1991).

Broker not liable to seller for damages caused as a result of buyer receiving inaccurate income financial information supplied by seller. *Burton v. Mackey,* 102 Or.App. 361 (OR 1990).

In *Moser v. Bertram,* No. 20692 (August 10, 1993), the New Mexico Supreme Court faced the issue of whether the listing salesperson was liable to a buyer-client of the firm for breach of fiduciary duty. The buyer failed to close on an earlier contract with the listing salesperson's seller. The buyer subsequently arranged financing expecting to consummate the sale but was told the seller had accepted another offer. Buyer sued for loss of investment opportunity. The listing salesperson was the only one left with money. The court held that "although agency fiduciary obligations and liabilities may extend from a salesperson to the qualifying broker, the fiduciary duties of one real estate salesperson are not attributable to another salesperson operating under the same qualifying broker unless one salesperson is at fault in appointing, supervising, or cooperating with the other." See *Restatement (Second) of Agency "358(1)* (1957).

Brokers should not return deposit money to the buyer without first checking with the seller, as in *Kruger v. Soreide,* 246 N.W.2d 764 (ND 1976).

Many of the reported cases involve buyers' brokers who find the ideal properties for their clients but first buy the properties themselves and then sell them to the buyers at a secret profit. *Des Fosses v. Notis,* 333 A.2d 822 (ME 1975); *Green v. Jones-Murphy Properties, Inc.,* 335 S.W. 2d 822 (AR 1960); *Hyman v. Burmeister,* 216 Ill.App. 98 (IL 1919); *Kurtz v. Farrington,* 132 A. 540 (CT 1926).

If the broker is not the agent of the buyer, however, then the broker may owe no duty to disclose to the buyer the broker's interest in purchasing the property. *Fish v. Teninga,* 161 N.E. 515 (IL 1928); *Warren v. Mangels Realty,* 533 P.2d 78 (AZ 1975). Buyers' brokers cannot profit by their own unfaithfulness. *Hilbolt v. Wisconsin Real Estate Brokers' Board,* 137 N.W.2d 482 (WI 1965); *Neff v. Bud Lewis Company,* 548 P.2d 107 (NM 1976); *Pouppirt v. Greenwood,* 110 P. 195 (CO 1910); *Roquemore v. Ford Motor Company,* 290 F.Supp. 130 (TX 1967); *United Homes, Inc. v. Moss,* 154 So.2d 351 (FL 1963); *Kroeker v. Hurlbert,* 101 P.2d 101 (CA 1940); *Degner v. Moncel,* 93 N.W.2d 857 (WI 1959); *Smith v. Howard,* 322 P.2d 1034 (CA 1958).

In *Sawyer Realty Group, Inc. v. Jarvis Corp.,* 432 N.E.2d 849 (IL 1982), the seller's brokers breached a duty of good faith to the buyer by not disclosing the fact that after the buyer submitted an offer, the seller sold the property to the brokers. In *Funk v. Tiff,* 515 F.2d 23 (9th Cir. FL 1975), the buyer made an offer through the listing broker, who, in turn, submitted a similar offer for himself and partner. The court held that the listing broker had a duty to deal fairly and honestly with the buyer and that outbidding the prospective buyer without adequate disclosure to the buyer was a breach. The listing broker held the property as a constructive trustee for the benefit of the buyer.

Self-Dealing

> The real estate broker is brought by his calling into a relation of trust and confidence. Constant are the opportunities by concealment and collusion to extract illicit gains. We know from our judicial records that the opportunities have been not lost. *Roman v. Lobe,* 152 N.E. 461 (NY 1926) (Cardoza, J.).

Unfortunately, the casebooks are filled with lawsuits in which the real estate broker purchased property and was sued because either (1) the broker did not disclose to the seller that the broker or a relative was the real buyer or (2) the buyer's broker secretly purchased a property and then resold it to the buyer-client at a profit in a double escrow or "flip" transaction. Some of the self-deal cases in which the broker is an undisclosed buyer are *Batson v. Strehlow,* 441 P.2d 101 (CA 1968); *Riley v. Powell,* 665 S.W. 2d 578 (TX 1984); *Rodes v. Shannon,* 35 Cal.Rptr. 339 (CA 1963); *Rosenfeld v. Glick Real Estate Co.,* 291 S.W.2d 863 (MO 1956); *Buckley v. Savage,* 7 Cal.Rptr. 328 (CA 1960). When the broker fully discloses the facts and takes no unfair advantage, there is no breach of fiduciary duty, as in *Fisher v. Losey,* 177 P.2d 334 (CA 1947).

In some cases the broker uses a dummy purchaser to buy and then sell at a secret profit. *Loughlin v. Idora Realty Company,* 66 Cal.Rptr. 747 (CA 1968); *Schepers v. Lautenschlager,* 112 N.W.2d 767 (NE 1962); *Alley v. Nevada Real Estate Division,* 575 P.2d 1334 (NV 1978) ("double escrow"); *Carluccio v. 607 Hudson Street Holding Co.,* 57 A.2d 452 (NJ 1948); *M.S.R., Inc. v. Lish,* 527 P.2d 912 (CO 1974); *Wendt v. Fischer,* 154 N.E. 303 (NY 1926); *Simone v. McKee,* 298 P.2d 667 (CA 1956).

Listing agent found out about their seller's bid on a replacement home. The agent used the information to outbid the sellers. Court found no breach of fiduciary duty. *Walter v. Murphy,* 573 N.E.2d 677 (OH 1988).

Punitive damages awarded to buyer whose offer was never presented by listing agent who bought the property at lower price from desperate seller. *Forbus v. City Realty,* Case No. 90-131 (AL 1992).

In *Thompson v. Searl,* 301 P.2d 804 (WY 1956), the seller broker breached its fiduciary obligation by accepting a commission from the buyer for selling the buyer's home that was used as part payment of the sales price, without first obtaining the seller's consent.

In some cases, the self-dealing broker is sued by the buyer who hired the broker to locate a property. *Henderson v. Hassur,* 594 P.2d 650 (KS 1979); *Quinn v. Phipps,* 113 So. 419 (FL 1927); *Rogers v. Genung,* 74 A.473 (NJ 1909); *Kurtz v. Farrington,* 132 A.540 (CT 1926); *Zichlin v. Dill,* 25 So.2d 4 (FL 1946); *Volz v. Burkeheimer, Inc.,* 21 P.2d 285 (WA 1933); *Barber's Super Markets, Inc. v. Stryker,* 500 P.2d 1304 (NM 1972); *Baskin v. Dam,* 239 A.2d 549 (CT 1967); *Spindler v. Krieger,* 147 N.E.2d 457 (IL 1958); *Jarvis v. O'Brien,* 305 P.2d 961 (CA 1957); often the buyer sues to impose a constructive trust in favor of the buyer, *Mitchell v. Allison,* 213 P.2d 231 (NM 1949); *Ward v. Taggart,* 336 P.2d 534 (CA 1959); *Antle v. Haas,* 251 S.W.2d 290 (KY 1952), *Green v. Jones-Murphy Properties, Inc.,* 335 S.W.2d 822 (AR 1960); *Burton v. Pet, Inc.,* 509 S.W.2d 95 (MO 1974); *Sierra Pacific Industries v. Carter,* 163 Cal.Rptr. 764 (CA 1980); *Hughes v. Miracle Ford, Inc.,* 676 S.W.2d 642 (TX 1984).

Duty of Obedience

When the seller instructed the broker not to return the buyer's deposit money without first obtaining a written appraisal (confirming the buyer's contingency that the sales price be at or below fair market value) and the broker failed to obtain such appraisal, the broker could not recover its commission. The seller's instructions were reasonable, material and if carried out could have prevented litigation. *Jackson v. Williams,* 510 S.W.2d 645 (TX 1974). When the listing agreement stated that the broker was to lease a warehouse subject to the owner's approval of the tenant, and the broker allowed the tenant to move in without prior owner approval, the broker was not entitled to receive a commission. *Latter & Blum v. Richmond,* 388 So.2d 368 (LA 1980); *Owen v. Shelton,* 277 S.E.2d 189 (VA 1981).

The broker was held to have breached its fiduciary duty of obedience by failing to obey the seller's instruction to revoke a counteroffer prior to the buyer's acceptance. *Abboud v. State Real Estate Commission,* 316 N.W.2d 608 (NE 1982).

Duty to Use Reasonable Skill and Care

The broker's duty of care and disclosure is greater when the client is unsophisticated and unknowledgeable in real estate transactions. *Prall v. Gooden,* 360 P.2d 759 (OR 1961); *Bjornstad v. Perry,* 443 P.2d 999 (ID 1968); and *Fairfield S&L v. Kroll,* 246 N.E.2d 327 (IL 1969).

The duty to exercise reasonable skill and care is imposed not only by the common law of agency, but frequently is also required by the terms of the listing contract and thus supports a breach of contract action or defense. In most professional liability lawsuits, it is necessary to produce expert testimony regarding the standard of care required of the professional. This is not required in malpractice actions against a real estate broker. *Jorgensen v. Beach 'N' Bay Realty, Inc.,* 177 Cal.Rptr.882 (CA 1981); *Easton v. Strassburger,* 199 Cal.Rptr.383 (CA 1984). The complaining party's testimony may be sufficient to prove broker malpractice. Buyer's broker held to have fiduciary duty to discover and disclose material facts such as existence of declaration of restriction against property prohibiting business use. *Lewis v. Long & Foster Real Estate,* 584 A.2d 1325 (MD 1991).

The broker should make a reasonable inquiry into the creditworthiness of a proposed buyer seeking to have the seller's carryback financing. The broker must exercise care in evaluating or preparing contract provisions and must use correct information, facts and figures. Important facts must be carefully researched and verified, such as sewer connections and zoning. The real estate broker is held to a standard of care that requires that the broker possess ordinary professional knowledge concerning the title and natural characteristics of the property being sold. *Brady v. Carmanl,* 3 Cal.Rptr. 612 (CA 1960). Broker not liable when buyer defaulted on a seller carryback mortgage. *Garcia v. Unique Realty,* 92 FCDR 2162 (GA 1993).

The case of *Perkins v. Thorpe,* 676 P.2d 52 (ID 1984) involved the question of whether the broker breached a fiduciary duty owed to the seller by negligently misadvising the seller on the value of the listed property and failing to disclose that the broker represented the buyer in a separate but related transaction. The court stated that:

> The law imposes upon a real estate broker a fiduciary obligation of utmost good faith, integrity, honesty, and loyalty as well as a duty of due care and diligence. Breach of the fiduciary duty may result in the broker's loss of commission and in liability in damages. A broker ultimately is responsible to the public for the actions of real estate sales persons whom he employs.
>
> A broker is obligated to employ that degree of skill in his calling usually possessed by others in the same business. The broker's conduct is required to meet a standard of competence because he is issued a license and permitted to hold himself out to the public as qualified by training and experience to render a specialized service in the field of real estate transactions. The law requires that the broker perform [at] a certain level of skill; for if he failed to do so, instead of being the badge of competence and integrity it is supposed to be, the broker's license would serve only as a foil to lure the unsuspecting public in.

The broker is liable to the seller whenever the broker's carelessness results in a buyer being successful in suing the seller for money damages or rescission. This is true even when the broker is acting gratuitously, as in *Green v. Jones-Murphy Properties, Inc.,* 335 S.W.2d 822 (AR 1960). A gratuitous buyer's broker was held liable for failure to transfer the seller's insurance policy to the buyer as agreed in *Estes v. Lloyd Hammerstad, Inc.,* 503 P.2d 1149 (WA 1972). Consider the following:

1. Broker innocently misstated the net operating income to indicate a positive cash flow.
2. Broker failed to reveal that seller only had oral permission for a driveway access.
3. Broker failed to ascertain that the property being sold was owned jointly, only one owner signed the acceptance and the transaction failed; likewise, when the unsophisticated seller only owned a life estate.
4. Broker failed to verify the issuance of a valid septic tank permit, a critical contingency to the sales contract. The broker is required to employ a reasonable degree of effort and professional expertise to confirm or refute important information obtained from the seller. *Tennant v. Lawton,* 615 P.2d 1305 (WA 1980).

5. Broker assisted the seller in preparing a financial statement based on a check register. Buyer canceled due to erroneous financial information supplied to the buyer. Although brokers are not usually held to the standard of care of accountants, a broker must exercise extreme care when acting like an accountant in voluntarily assisting in the preparation of financial information for the broker's principal. *Lunden v. Smith,* 632 P.2d 1344 (OR 1981).

In some cases, the broker is liable to the seller for failing to properly advise and protect the seller's best interest. *Nolan v. Wisconsin Real Estate Brokers' Board,* 89 N.W.2d 317 (WI 1958). Suppose the broker allows the seller to carry back a $50,000 note not secured by a mortgage or deed of trust without first making sure that the seller understands the consequences of taking an unsecured note. See *Morley v. J. Pagel Realty & Insurance,* 550 P.2d 1104 (AZ 1976), in which the court said the broker must employ all his professional ability and knowledge to make sure the client understands the facts. Or suppose in a contemplated transaction that (1) the broker promises the seller that a sale will occur by a date sufficient to have funds to purchase another property, (2) the broker fails to recommend protective contingency language in both contracts and (3) the broker represents both ends of the transaction. Or suppose the broker advises the seller that the seller is entitled to keep the earnest money deposit on default, yet fails to mention that escrow usually requires mutual releases and first deducts cancellation charges prior to paying out the deposit.

What if the broker fails to tell the seller about restrictions on VA and FHA financing, such as substitution of VA eligibility and the need to make repairs under "minimum property requirements"? See *Monty v. Peterson,* 540 P.2d 1377 (WA 1975); *Reese v. Harper,* 329 P.2d 410 (UT 1958). In *Jones v. Maestas,* 696 P.2d 920 (ID 1985), the court held that the broker was not required to communicate the meaning of an exclusive listing agreement that was unequivocally expressed by the instrument itself.

The broker was held liable when the broker wrote the purchase contract wrong and not according to specifications in *Mattieligh v. Poe,* 356 P.2d.328 (WA 1960). The broker is required to act with due diligence to inquire about an apparent discrepancy in property size. The broker must point out the desirable features of the seller's property. *Schackai v. Lagreco,* 350 So.2d 1244 (LA 1977); *Mallallieu-Golder, Inc. v. O'Neal,* 16 Pa. D & C 2d 594 (PA 1959).

The real estate broker is expected to do more than find a buyer for a seller's property. The broker must diligently exercise skill and care on behalf of the client. To illustrate the extent of the broker's obligation beyond matchmaking, refer to the checklist of listing broker responsibilities in the typical residential transaction (Appendix B).

Duty to Account

The broker must not commingle client funds with the broker's own funds. Brokers usually maintain a separate client trust fund account. The broker should use one account for sales transactions and another one for rental property management transactions.

State licensing law usually contains strict rules on trust fund accounting. The Real Estate Commission can suspend or revoke a broker's license for not properly accounting for client funds. *Kilgore v. Texas Real Estate Commission,* 565 S.W.2d 114 (TX 1978). Brokers must deposit checks by the next business day after receipt unless special permission is obtained to hold the check in uncashed form. Rather than use a client trust fund account, some brokers suggest the buyer's deposit check be payable directly to the escrow company or settlement agent.

Misrepresentation

Regarding the element of reliance, courts have held that the buyer is entitled to relief if the representations were a material inducement to the contract, even though the buyer may have made efforts to discover the truth thereof and did not rely wholly on the veracity of the representations. *Foxley Cattle Co. v. Bank of Mead,* 241 N.W.2d 495 (NE 1976); *Erickson v. Midgarden,* 31 N.W.2d 918 (MN 1948); *Schechter v. Brewer,* 344 S.W.2d 784 (MO 1961).

It is sometimes difficult to distinguish between fact and opinion. "Real property taxes are low" is different from "real property taxes are $1,000 per year." In *Foreman & Clark Corporation v. Fallon,* 479 P.2d 362 (CA 1961), the court found no breach because the statements as to the tenant's future sales in a percentage lease case were mere expressions of opinion, were not material and were not relied on by the landlord. *Coleman v. Goran,* 168 N.E.2d 56 (IL 1960); *Lone Star Machinery Corporation v. Frankel,* 564 S.W.2d 135 (TX 1978). In *Peterson v. Auvel,*

552 P.2d 538 (OR 1976), the buyer relied on the broker's opinion that the earnest money contract was not enforceable. *Eyers v. Burbank Co.*, 166 P.656 (WA 1917). See *Gross v. Sussex, Inc.*, 630 A2d 1156 (MD 1993).

Examples of Misrepresentation

Even though brokers act in good faith, they may still be liable for failure to exercise reasonable care or competence in obtaining or communicating information that the broker knew or should have known. Brokers may be liable for (1) negligently failing to discover and disclose building defects that were discoverable upon exercising reasonable care, *Easton v. Strassburger,* 199 Cal.Rptr. 383 (CA 1984); *Gouveia v. Citicorp.*, 686 P.2d 262 (NM 1984); *Amato v. Rathbun Realty, Inc.*, 647 P.2d 433 (NM 1982); (2) making representations regarding title that the agent does not know to be true, *Hall v. Wright,* 156 N.W.2d 661 (IA 1968); or (3) representing the property as a "buildable site," *Tennant v. Lawton,* 615 P.2d 1305 (WA 1980).

It normally is no defense that the broker was simply passing on information received from the seller. *Dugan v. Jones,* 615 P.2d 1239 (UT 1980) (total acreage conveyed was 7 acres, not 23 acres as represented); *Nordstrom v. Miller,* 605 P.2d 545 (KS 1980); *Gaurrky v. Rozga,* 332 N.W.2d 804 (WI 1983); *Hoffman v. Connall,* 718 P.2d 814 (WA 1986). For a broker to recover from the seller based on indemnity, the broker must show that the broker used due care and was justified in relying on the seller's representations. *Barnes v. Lopez,* 544 P.2d 694 (AZ 1976). Seller told broker the water well was "good" in *Bevins v. Ballard,* 655 P.2d 757 (AK 1982). See *Rach v. Kleiber,* 367 N.W.2d 824 (WI 1985).

The broker has been held liable for misrepresentation in the following types of cases:

1. *Water leakage.* Broker should have known basement had a seepage problem. Broker knew of serious problems with leaking sewage from neighbor's yard and with drainage of water from property. *Sawyer v. Tildahl,* 148 N.W.2d 131 (MN 1967); *McGerr v. Beals,* 145 N.W.2d 579 (NE 1966); *McRae v. Bolstad,* 646 P.2d 771 (WA 1982); *Berryman v. Reigert,* 175 N.W.2d 438 (MN 1970); *Richmond v. Blair,* 488 N.E.2d 563 (IL 1985). Broker liable for misrepresentation regarding leaks and dampness. *Silva v. Stevens,* 589 A.2d 852 (VT 1991). Broker not liable when broker pointed out water stains and recommended buyer hire home inspector. *Connor v. Merrill Lynch Realty,* 581 N.E.2d 196 (IL 1991).

2. *Operating expenses and income.* Broker showed the buyer falsified operating statements and promised to help run the restaurant. *Jennings v. Lee,* 461 P.2d 161 (AZ 1969). Broker incorrectly assured the buyer that the property would generate monthly income of $900 without having checked available income records. *Ford v. Cournale,* 111 Cal.Rptr. 334 (CA 1974). Broker carelessly assured the buyer that the property could be rented. *Emily v. Bayne,* 371 S.W.2d 663 (MO 1963).

3. *Free of termites.* Seller's broker who assured buyer that the property was free of termites, dry rot and fungi was held liable in *Johnson v. Sergeants,* 313 P.2d 41 (CA 1957), and *Saporta v. Barbagelata,* 33 Cal.Rptr. 661 (CA 1963). *Maples v. Porath,* 638 S.W.2d 337 (MO 1982); *Neveroski v. Blair,* 358 A.2d 473 (NJ 1976); *Miles v. McSwegin,* 388 N.E.2d 1367 (OH 1979); *Obde v. Schlemeyer,* 353 P.2d 672 (WA 1960). Broker with two termite reports intentionally concealed termite condition and was liable for punitive damages for intentionally inflicting emotional distress on buyer by concealing negative termite report and showing only the positive report in *Godfrey v. Steinpress,* 180 Cal.Rptr. 95 (CA 1982); *Lynn v. Taylor,* 642 P.2d 131 (KS 1982); and *Dicker v. Smith,* 523 P.2d 371 (KS 1974). Failure to disclose termites. *Wire v. Jackson,* 576 So.2d 1198 (LA 1991). Real estate broker acting as seller had plastered over the termite damage. In a subsequent sale the buyer not able to recover against original broker/seller. *Katz v. Schacter,* 251 N.J.Super. 467 (NJ 1991).

   The mere use of an "as is" clause without a more specific explanation of the defect may not eliminate a customary requirement of the seller to provide a termite clearance report nor protect against claims for concealed termite damage. Seller liable for not disclosing known latent termite damage despite "as is" clause. *Stemple v. Dobson,* 400 S.E.2d 561 (WV 1990). Buyer denied recovery in *Van Gessel v. Fold,* 569 N.E.2d 141 (IL 1991). Fraudulent concealment of termite report despite "as is" clause. *Rayner v. Wise Realty,* 504 So.2d 1361 (FL 1987).

4. *Free of liens and encumbrances.* Broker erroneously represented that the seller owned the property free and clear of all encumbrances. *Floyd v. Myers,* 333 P.2d 654 (WA 1959);

Carl Needham, Inc. v. Camilleri, 533 P.2d 765 (NV 1975); *Wilson v. Hisey,* 305 P.2d 686 (CA 1957); *Mayflower Mortgage Company v. Brown,* 530 P.2d 1298 (CO 1975); *Grandchamp v. Patzer,* 197 N.W.2d 537 (MI 1972). Minor encroachments sometimes do not render title unmarketable (free and clear of encumbrances) if the encroachment would not cause a prudent person to hesitate before buying.

5. *Filled land.* Broker told buyer that the property listed was not a "filled lot." Buyer's house sank and buyer successfully recovered against seller, who then sued broker for the loss caused by broker's unauthorized false representation. *Kruse v. Miller,* 300 P.2d 855 (CA 1956); *Sorrell v. Young,* 491 P.2d 1312 (WA 1971) (constructive fraud); *Thacker v. Tyree,* 297 S.E.2d 885 (WV 1982); *Ashburn v. Miller,* 326 P.2d 229 (CA 1958).

6. *Property condition.* Salesperson stated the heater was in good working condition. Actually, the seller had concealed the fact that the heater was broken. "Fraud includes the pretense of knowledge when there is none." *Spargnapani v. Wright,* 1 10 A.2d 82 (DC 1954). In *Fowler v. Benton,* 185 A.2d 344 (MD 1962), the broker failed to disclose that the house was built in a slide area. Silence is not golden when there is a duty to speak. Silence breaches an implied duty to warn of defects. *Henderson v. Johnson,* 403 P.2d 669 (WA 1965); *Easton v. Strassburger,* 199 Cal.Rptr. 383 (CA 1984); leaking roof, *Hunter v. Wilson,* 355 So.2d 39 (CA App. 1978); *Berman v. Watergate West, Inc.,* 391 A.2d 1351 (DC 1978) (defective air-conditioning system); *Brown v. Pritchett,* 633 S.W.2d 294 (MO 1982); *Milliken v. Green,* 583 P.2d 548 (OR 1978); *Robert v. Estate of Barbagallo,* 531 A.2d 1125 (PA 1987). Faulty heating system was known to broker who had managed the property for a former owner. *Ne Bud v. Lewis Company,* 548 P.2d 107 (NM 1976); *Byrn v. Walker,* 267 S.E.2d 601 (SC 1980); *Sorensen v. Gardner,* 334 P.2d 471 (OR 1959) (misrepresented that plumbing complied with building code). Building in state of disrepair and had been placed for condemnation by city officials. *Lingsch v. Savage,* 29 Cal.Rptr. 201 (CA 1963); *Cooper v. Jevne,* 128 Cal.Rptr. 724 (CA 1976); *Merrill v. Buck,* 375 P.2d 304 (CA 1962). Cracked foundation. *Pinger v. Guaranty Investment Co.,* 307 S.W.2d 53 (MO 1957); *Josephs v. Austin,* 420 So.2d 1181 (LA 1982). Sewer not connected or backs up. *Kraft v. Lowe,* 77 A.2d 554 (DC 1950); *Shane v. Hoffman,* 324 A.2d 532 (PA 1974); *Crum v. McCoy,* 322 N.E.2d 161 (OH 1974). Broker misrepresented condition of foundation and past repairs. *Schechter v. Brewer,* 344 S.W.2d 784 (MO 1961). Relied on broker's advice to purchase new house with substantial defects. *Menzel v. Morse,* 362 N.W.2d 465 (IA 1985).

   No duty to warn buyer of readily observable condition (stepped on insulation and fell through attic). *Zaffiris v. O'Loughlin,* 585 NYS 2d 94 (NY 1992). Seller's agreement to repair faulty septic system not terminated by doctrine of merger. *Andreychak v. Lint,* 607 A.2d 1346 (NJ 1992). Seller liable for innocent misrepresentation regarding repairs to septic system. *Zimmerman v. Kent,* 575 N.E.2d 70 (MASS 1991). Broker not liable for failure to disclose latent defect; seller normally has no duty to disclose defect in used property unless asked by buyer. *Commercial Credit Corp. v. Lisenby,* 579 So.2d 1291 (ALA 1991). Broker held to have no duty to buyer to inspect property for defects beyond asking sellers if such defects existed. *Kubinsky v. Van Zandt Realtors,* 811 S.W.2d 711 (TX 1991). Former seller not liable to buyer for concealment of defects even though seller now mortgagee and buyer defaulted under mortgage. *Kovach v. McLellan,* 564 So.2d 274 (FL 1990). Agent failed to disclose that an "independent" property inspector had previously inspected home; house later found to be not structurally sound. *Johnson v. Beverly-Hanks,* 400 S.E.2d 38 (NC 1991). Seller/broker represented house needed no repair. Both seller and appraiser held liable because house needed $23,000 of repairs to make it eligible for FHA financing. *Rene Lenoir v. Judy Hill Realty,* Case No. 5200 (2d District, MS 1990). Lead paint, see *Richwind v. Brunson,* 625 A2d 326 (MD 1993).

7. *Easements.* When the buyer questioned the broker about an easement, the broker said not to worry. Three months after closing, the city used the easement to lay water pipes. The broker was held liable. *Brady v. Carman,* 3 Cal.Rptr. 612 (CA 1960); *Gilby v. Cooper,* 310 N.E.2d 268 (OH 1973); *Norgren v. Harwell,* 172 So.2d 723 (LA 1965); *Stone v. Lawyers Title Insurance Corp.,* 554 S.W.2d 183 (TX 1977).

8. *Zoning.* Broker disclosed zoning restrictions but negligently failed to disclose private recorded restrictions that diminished the value of the lot, in *Monty v. Peterson,* 540 P.2d 1377 (WA 1975). Broker negligently misrepresented actual zoning. *Barnes v. Lopez,* 544 P.2d 694 (AZ 1976), in which broker merely affirmed the erroneous information given by the seller. *Brandt v. Koepnick,* 469 P.2d 189 (WA 1970); *Asleson v. West Branch Land*

Co., 311 N.W.2d 533 (ND 1981); *Burien Motors, Inc. v. Balch*, 513 P.2d 582 (WA 1973); *Granberg v. Turnham*, 333 P.2d 423 (CA 1958). Broker represented that it would be easy to change the zoning. *Nantell v. Lim-Wick Construction Company*, 228 So.2d 634 (FL 1969). See *Blaine v. Jones Construction*, 841 SW2d 703 (MO 1992).

Holding seller had no duty to disclose zoning problem in *City of Aurora v. Green*, 467 N.E.2d 1069 (IL 1984); *Denton v. Hood*, 461 N.E.2d 1069 (IL 1984); *O'Brien v. Noble*, 435 N.E.2d 554 (IL 1982); *Goldfarb v. Dietz*, 506 P.2d 1322 (WA 1973) (nonconforming use). Some courts distinguish statements of law from statements of fact and hold the seller liable only for misstatements of fact. Whether a statement was one of law or fact is not relevant in an equitable action for rescission based on mutual mistake. *Gartner v. Eikell*, 319 N.W.2d 397 (MN 1982); *Gardner Homes, Inc. v. Gaither*, 228 S.E.2d 525 (NC 1976). But see *Steinberg v. Bay Terrace Apt. Hotel Inc.*, 375 So.2d 1089 (FL 1979).

9. *Size of property.* Brokers frequently get into trouble because they say "Here is the boundary line" when they're not sure, rather than "I don't know; let's order a survey and find out." This is especially true with unintentional misrepresentations of square footage or acreage. *Alexander Myers & Company v. Hopke*, 565 P.2d 80 (WA 1977); *Nathanson v. Murphy*, 282 P.2d 174 (CA 1955); *Mikkelson v. Quail Valley Realty*, 641 P.2d 124 (UT 1982); *Carrel v. Lux*, 420 P.2d 564 (AZ 1966); *Dixon v. MacGillivray*, 185 P.2d 109 (WA 1947); *Cameron v. Terrell & Garrett, Inc.*, 618 S.W.2d 535 (TX 1981); *Shaffer v. Earl Thacker Co., Ltd.*, 716 P.2d 163 (HI 1986). Broker liable for misrepresentation of home's square footage even though buyer toured home. *John v. Robbins*, 764 F.Supp. 379 (NC 1991).

   Broker not liable for statement that boundary line "probably went to that stake." *Bischoff Realty v. Ledford*, 562 N.E.2d 1321 (IN 1990).

10. *"As Is" Clause.* Use of a general "disclaimer" clause does not protect against fraud. *Smith v. Rickards*, 308 P.2d 758 (CA 1957); *Wittenberg v. Robinov*, 173 N.E.2d 868 (NY 1961). An "as is" clause is generally sufficient to indicate that the seller is not going to make any repairs. *Lenawee County Bd. of Health v. Messerly*, 331 N.W.2d 203 (MI 1982). Selling a property "as is" does not relieve the broker from revealing known defects that are not readily observable to the buyer. *Lingsch v. Savage*, 29 Cal.Rptr. 201 (CA 1963); *Crawford v. Nastos*, 6 Cal.Rptr. 425 (CA 1960); *Katz v. Dept. of Real Estate*, 158 Cal.Rptr. 766 (CA 1979); *Weitzel v. Barnes*, 691 S.W.2d 598 (TX 1985); *Prichard v. Reitz*, 223 Cal. Rptr. 734 (CA 1986); *Davies v. Bradley*, 676 P.2d 1242 (CO 1983); *Prudential v. Jefferson Associates*, 839 S.W.2d 866 (TX 1992); *George v. Lumbrazo*, 584 NYS 2d 704 (1992); *Grube v. Thieol*, Wisconsin Ct.App. 91-2322 (WI 1992).

    Buyer could not recover for injuries to child from falling tree because bought property in "as is" condition. *Stonecipher v. Kornhaus & Moorman*, Miss. S.Ct. (MI June 17, 1993).

11. *Lawful use.* The doctrine of caveat emptor continues to govern the disclosure of unlawful land usages. In many jurisdictions, the buyer is responsible for determining whether existing land uses are unlawful by checking zoning ordinances, building codes, occupancy rules and restrictive covenants. These courts see the risk of illegal use as foreseeable and place that risk on the buyer. *Cousinea v. Walker*, 613 P.2d 608 (AK 1980) (caveat emptor in general); *Oates v. Jag, Inc.*, 311 S.E.2d 369 (NC 1984). Holding that the seller has no duty to disclose to the buyer a large increase in the assessed value of the property is *Lenzi v. Morkin*, 469 N.E.2d 178 (IL 1984). Once buyer asked broker why other homes were built on stilts, broker obligated to disclose material facts about building code violation and flood insurance. *Revitz v. Terrell*, 572 So.2d 996. See *Randels v. Best Real Estate*, 243 ILL App. 3d 801 (IL 1993).

    The recent trend is to interpret certain seller conduct as an implied representation of lawful use, which would support a buyer's claim for misrepresentation. *Iverson v. Solsbery*, 641 P.2d 314 (CO 1982); *Strickland v. Vescovi*, 484 A.2d 460 (CT 1984); *Kannavos v. Annino*, 247 N.E.2d 708 (MA 1969); *Dettler v. Santa Cruz*, 403 S.W.2d 651 (MO 1966).

12. *Miscellaneous.* Concealed fact of prior grisly murder on the property, *Reed v. King*, 193 Cal.Rptr.130 (CA 1983); misrepresented location of lots, *Blanke v. Miller*, 268 S.W.2d 809 (MO 1954); misrepresented that property bounded on a river, *Carrington v. Graves*, 89 A. 237 (MD 1913). Broker intentionally inflated price of comparable sales in the area,

Miller v. Boeger, 405 P.2d 573 (AZ 1965). Broker misrepresented the value of a property to be exchanged, *Quistgard v. Derby,* 250 P.2d 2 (CA 1952). Broker sent to jail for misrepresenting to lender existence of second mortgage on property purchased by broker in violation of 18 U.S.C.A. 1015. *U.S. v. Gregoria,* 956 F.2d 341 (1st CIR 1992).

Broker misrepresented the duration of the lease because the broker failed to read the lease completely; the court also held that the buyer had no independent duty to investigate because the buyer had no reason to believe that the representations were false. *Hagar v. Mobley,* 638 P.2d 127 (WY 1981). Broker liable for failing to disclose to buyer that property undergoing foreclosure procedure. *Gray v. Boyle,* 803 S.W.2d 678 (TN 1990).

Positive misrepresentations as to the asking price were held to go beyond the scope of "clever salesmanship." *Collins v. Philadelphia Oil Co.,* 125 S.E. 223 (WV 1924); *Booker v. Pelkey,* 180 N.W. 132 (WI 1920); *Huttig v. Nessy,* 130 So. 605 (FL 1930); *Stevens v. Reilly,* 156 P. 157 (OK 1916).

In *Jerger v. Rubin,* 471 P.2d 726 (AZ 1970), the salesperson misrepresented that he was negotiating with a potential resale client, which would enable the plaintiff-buyer to sell off a portion of the property being purchased and thus afford the payoff of the additional financing. In *Foster v. Cross,* 650 P.2d 406 (AK 1982), the buyer's broker misrepresented the buyer's development experience and financial condition.

Question of fact whether broker breached duty to homeowner to disclose recent "lock box burglaries" in area. *Moore v. Harry Norman Realtors,* 404 S.E.2d 793 (GA 1991). Suspicion of the presence of ghosts in residential property deemed a latent defect that must be disclosed to buyer. *Stambovsky v. Ackley,* 572 NYS 2d 672 (NY 1991). Broker held not liable for alleged negligent misrepresentation concerning railroad service to site. *Chicago Export Packing v. Teledyne,* 566 N.E.2d 326 (IL 1990). Adequate circumstantial evidence to prove fraud and justify million dollar punitive damage award. *Kuhnert v. Allison,* No. 14956 (HI Supreme Court 1993). Duty to disclose known pollution problem limited to residential properties; the rule is caveat emptor with commercial properties. *Futura Realty v. Lone Star,* 578 So.2d 363 (FL 1991). Tenant in shopping center sued broker for misrepresentation allegedly based on written material supplied by seller. *Henry S. Miller v. Bynum,* 797 S.W.2d 51 (TX 1990).

Termination of Agency Relationship

Like marriage, an agency relationship is easy to create but can be hard to terminate. The two main ways to terminate an agency are by acts of the parties or by operation of law.

An agency may end at the time stated in the listing agreement or, if no time is specified, then within a reasonable period of time. A principal is justified in revoking the agency if the agent has breached any fiduciary duty. Also, the principal has the unilateral power to revoke the agency at any time, except in the rare case in which an agency is coupled with some interest of the broker in the property. Thus, the principal could revoke the agency and forbid the agent to show the property. Or a rental agent may be fired and asked to turn over keys and security deposits. The principal may have the power to terminate an agency but not the legal right. If the principal wrongfully terminates the agency, the principal may be liable for the damages caused the agent in revoking the agency prior to the termination date. *Roth v. Moeller,* 197 P.62 (CA 1921); *Sunshine v. Manos,* 496 S.W.2d 195 (TX 1973); *Chain v. Pye,* 429 S.W.2d 630 (TX 1968). Likewise, the agent can renounce the agency relationship but only after adequate notice is given the principal. Fiduciary duty did not end when seller rejected a full price offer. *Quechee Lakes v. Boggers,* No. 89-87 (Vermont S.C. 1992).

Courts are sometimes asked to determine when the agency relationship is ended, especially when the broker decides to become a principal in the transaction or decides to represent an adverse party. In cases in which the commission is earned only if the transaction closes, the broker's fiduciary duty continues throughout the entire closing and does not cease when the buyer is found and the purchase contract is signed. The broker's duties of disclosure as well as the other fiduciary duties continue until the transaction closes and the purpose of the agency comes to an end. *Cooke v. Iverson,* 500 P.2d 830 (ID 1972); *Zikratch v. Stillwell,* 16 Cal.Rptr. 660 (CA 1961); *Bate v. Marsteller,* 346 P.2d 903 (CA 1959); *Menzel v. Salka,* 4 Cal.Rptr. 78 (CA 1960); *Rarnsey v. Sedlar,* 454 P.2d 416 (WA 1969); *Wesco Realty Inc. v. Drewry,* 515 P.2d 513 (WA 1973); *One Twenty Realty Co. v. Baer,* 272 A.2d 377 (MD 1971); *Pilling v. Eastern & Pacific Enterprises,* 702 P.2d 1232 (WA 1985), which held that a subagent has no duty to attend closing or perform services to the seller during closing.

In *Hardy v. Davis,* 164 A.2d 281 (MD 1960), the broker secretly loaned the buyer money to complete the purchase. The court held the agency terminated when the sale was made. Thus, the agent could properly deal with the other party if such dealing is not inconsistent with the broker's duty to the principal. *Sears v. Polans,* 243 A.2d 602 (MD 1968); *Olson v. Brickles,* 124 S.E.2d 895 (VA 1962).

The fiduciary relationship between a real estate broker and principal may, under certain circumstances, exist even in the absence or after the expiration of a listing agreement. *Swallows v. Laney,* 691 P.2d 874 (NM 1984); *Wheeler v. Carl Rabe Inc.,* 599 P.2d 902 (CO 1979); *West v. Touchstone,* 620 S.W.2d 687 (TX 1981); *Cogan v. Kidder, Mathews & Segner, Inc.,* 600 P.2d 655 (WA 1979); *Harvey v. Tucker,* 12 P.2d 847 (ECS 1932). The burden of proving a termination of agency is upon the party asserting it. In canceling an agency for an indefinite term, notice to the other party is generally required. *George v. Bolen,* 580 P.2d 1357 (KS 1978).

If state law requires that the agent's authority be express and in writing, then the sales contract is unenforceable when one seller signs both sellers' names to a contract and that seller was not authorized in writing to act as the other's agent and when the nonsigning seller did not ratify the contract in writing. *Fejta v. GAF Companies, Inc.,* 800 F.2d 1395 (LA 1986).

The agency relationship may also be terminated through operation of law. Death of the agent or principal prior to the broker finding a ready, willing or able buyer will terminate the listing, as will insanity, destruction of the listed premises (or a taking by eminent domain) and bankruptcy of the principal, who loses all control of the property to the court. If the broker is adjudicated a bankrupt, the broker may be required to surrender the license to the Real Estate Commission.

CHAPTER 5. SUBAGENCY

The rules of the multiple listing service (MLS) usually create a system whereby members offer subagency to other members on behalf of the seller. People ex rel. *Woodard v. Colorado Springs Board of REALTORS*® 692 P.2d 1055 (CO 1984); *United States v. Realty Multi-Lists,* 629 F.2d 1351 (5th Cir. 1980); *Iowa v. Cedar Rapids Board of REALTORS*®, 300 N.W.2d 127 (IA 1981); *Derish v. San Mateo-Burlingame Board of REALTORS*®, et al., 186 Cal.Rptr. 390 (CA 1982). See also 1983-2 Trade Cas (CCH) Section 65,718; 1978-2 Trade Cas (CCH) Section 62,388; and 1977-1 Trade Cas (CCH) Section 61,435. In *State v. Black,* 676 P.2d 963 (WA 1984), the court found no antitrust violation against certain brokers after they lowered their commission splits with alternative brokers who provided limited service to sellers at a reduced fee. MLS may be guilty of unlawful tie-in when it requires participants belong to the Board of REALTORS®. *Fletcher Thomson v. Metropolitan Multi-List, Inc.,* 934 F.2d 1566 (11th Cir. 1991).

In *Wolfson v. Berls,* 295 N.W.2d 562 (MN 1980), the court held that the cooperating broker was the subagent of the seller. It was immaterial that the seller did not know the cooperating broker or authorize his actions. The cooperating broker did not become an agent of the buyer by merely preparing a purchase agreement with terms provided by the buyer. *First Church v. Dunton Realty, Inc.,* 574 P.2d 1211 (WA 1978); *Hale v. Wolfson,* 81 Cal.Rptr. 23 (CA 1969); *White v. Lobdell,* 638 P.2d 1057 (MT 1982); *Fred Tuke and Son v. Burkhardt,* 160 N.E.2d 283 (OH 1959); *Elliot v. Barnes,* 645 P.2d 1136 (WA 1982); *Granberg v. Turnham,* 333 P.2d 423 (CA 1958); *White v. Boucher,* 322 N.W.2d 560 (MN 1982); *Coons v. Gunn,* 69 Cal.Rptr. 876 (CA 1968); *Price v. Eisan,* 15 Cal.Rptr. 202 (CA 1961); *Timmerman v. Ankrom,* 487 S.W.2d 567 (MO 1972); *Hicks v. Wilson,* 240 P.289 (CA 1925); *Van Denberg v. Northside Realty Associates, Inc.,* 323 S.E.2d 839 (GA 1984); *Award Realty, Inc. v. Copeland,* 698 S.W.2d 337 (TN 1985); *Buzzard v. Bolger,* 453 N.E.2d 1129 (IL 1983).

In *Reich v. Christopulous,* 256 P.2d 238 (UT 1953), the agency relationship was created with the subagent by the MLS agreement and express language in the listing. In *Pilling v. Eastern & Pacific Enterprises,* 702 P.2d 1232 (WA 1985), the court held that the selling broker, in a multiple listing situation, is an authorized subagent of the listing broker and therefore owes the seller the same duties owed by the listing broker. In *Fennell v. Ross,* 711 S.W.2d 793 (AR 1986), the court was concerned with the issue of reliance on a misrepresentation when the cooperating broker knew the falsity of the statements about commercial use and a floodplain zone. The court concluded that the selling broker in an MLS listing is the subagent of the seller, even though the broker had worked with these buyers for a year before locating the property in question. Therefore, the knowledge of the cooperating broker was not imputed to the buyer.

Subagencies may be created even though the property is not listed in an MLS, as is frequently the case in commercial real estate transactions. *Marra v. Katz,* 347 N.Y.S.2d 143 (NY 1973).

Not all courts agree that the cooperating broker is the subagent of the seller. *Cashion v. Ahmadi,* 345 So.2d 268 (AL 1977); *Lester v. Marshall,* 352 P.2d 786 (CO 1960); *Lageschulte v. Steinbrecher,* 344 N.E.2d 750 (IL App. 1976). A participating member of an MLS was found to be the buyer's broker in *Gillen v. Stevens,* 330 S.W.2d 253 (TX 1959). Finding neither seller nor listing broker liable for the misrepresentation of the cooperating broker, the court in *Wise v. Dawson,* 353 A.2d 207 (DE 1975) found that no agency relationship existed between listing brokers and cooperating brokers in an MLS-type system. See *Pumphrey v. Quillen,* 141 N.E.2d 675 (OH 1955). The Supreme Court of Arizona ruled that the selling broker was not the agent of the seller in *Buffington v. Haas,* 601 P.2d 1320 (AZ 1979); *Brean v. North Campbell Professional Building,* 548 P.2d 1193 (AZ 1976); *Norville v. Palant,* 545 P.2d 454 (AZ 1976). The fact that the selling broker may share in the listing broker's fee does not necessarily create a subagency, *Hiller v. Real Estate Commission,* 627 P.2d 769 (CO 1981). In *Sullivan v. Jefferson,* 400 A.2d 836 (NJ 1979), the listing broker was held not liable for the wrongful act of an MLS cooperating broker who stole the buyer's earnest money deposit in a situation in which it was customary for the cooperating broker to hold the deposit check.

Imputed Notice

Notifying an agent is the same thing as notifying a principal. *Haislmaier v. Zache,* 130 N.W.2d 801 (WI 1964); *3 Am.Jur.2d Agency* Section 152, page 543: "Notice to a subagent appointed by authority is imputable to, and is the equivalent of, notice to the principal." This imputed notice rule may make it critical in a lawsuit whether the cooperating broker is held to be a subagent of the seller or an agent of the buyer. Consider these situations:

1. The purchase contract required buyer to give seller written notice of loan approval by May 8. Buyer notified the cooperating broker on May 8 but the broker did not tell the seller, who then attempted to cancel on May 10. The court in *Grant v. Purdy* 73 D & C 2d 42 (PA 1974) held that the cooperating broker is, in reality, a subagent of the seller and thus notice was imputed to the seller by the May 8 deadline. Thus, the seller could not cancel.

2. Buyer notified the cooperating broker with whom they were working that they accepted seller's counteroffer on a property listed in the MLS. Meanwhile, seller had received a higher offer, so seller attempted to revoke the counteroffer. If the cooperating broker is held to be a subagent of the seller, then the revocation, coming after notice of acceptance to the seller's subagent, is too late and the contract is binding. If the cooperating broker is held to be the buyer's broker, there is no binding contract because seller's revocation was effective before the seller was notified of the acceptance. *Stortroen v. Beneficial Finance Co.,* No.85CA0548 (CO 1985); *Shriver v. Carter,* 6S I P.2d 436 (CO 1982), *Darling v. Nineteen-Eighty Corporation,* 176 N.W.2d 765 (IA 1970).

3. Betty Buyer was working with salesperson Alice of South Side Realty, a large brokerage firm. Alice helped Betty Buyer prepare an offer on a property listed by South Side Realty salesperson Tom. The offer was contingent on Betty Buyer receiving a title report by July 10. Tom received the title report by July 10, but failed to tell Betty Buyer, who later attempted to cancel the contract. The trial court held that timely receipt of the report by South Side Realty as agent of Betty Buyer was imputed to Betty Buyer and thus the contract was binding. *Little v. Rohauer,* 707 P.2d 1015 (CO 1985).

4. Note, to avoid the effect of the imputed notice rules, the seller could require that notice is not effective until delivered directly to the seller.

Good Faith

The subagent is under the same duty as the listing broker to exercise utmost good faith toward the principal and the listing broker. It is bad faith for the subagent to lead the buyer to believe the property could be bought for less than the listed price, because this could "either force from the seller a lower price than that fixed or delay the sale, even if he finally buys at the price fixed, both detrimental to the interest of the seller." There is a similar duty to disclose all material facts. In *re Sivert's Estate,* 135 N.W.2d 205 (MN 1965); *Kruse v. Miller,* 300 P.2d

855 (CA 1956); *Alford v. Creagh,* 62 So.254 (AL 1913); *Hughey v. Rainwater Partners,* 661 S.W.2d 690 (TN 1983); *Skopp v. Weaver,* 546 P.2d 307 (CA 1976).

The subagent may also be liable for the misrepresentations of the listing broker. In *First Church, etc. v. Cline J. Dunton Realty, Inc.,* 574 P.2d 1211 (WA 1978), the subagent was liable for not confirming the boundary description, even though the subagent relied on the information provided by the listing broker. Also, *Gauerke v. Rozga,* 332 N.W.2d 804 (WI 1983).

The listing broker must disclose any relationship between the proposed buyer and the subagent. This is true even if the MLS regulations do not create a seller subagency. *Frisell v. Newman,* 429 P.2d 864 (WA 1967). Even if the listing broker was unaware of the kinship ties between one of its subagents and the buyer, the seller may still have the right to rescind the sale and recover any profit gained by the broker or recoup the commission paid. *Mersky v. Multiple Listing Bureau of Olympia, Inc.,* 437 P.2d 897 (WA 1968). Also, *Kline v. Pyms Suchman Real Estate Company,* 303 So.2d 401 (FL 1974); *Ross v. Perelli,* 538 P.2d 834 (WA 1975).

Does a buyer who is a broker and also a member of the MLS have a fiduciary duty to the seller as a subagent? The cases holding no fiduciary duty of disclosure are *Case v. Business Centers, Inc.,* 357 N.E.2d 47 (OH 1976); *Cook v. Westersund,* 179 Cal.Rptr. 396 (CA App. 1981); *Blocklinger v. Schlegel,* 374 N.E.2d 491 (IL 1978); *Stout v. Edmonds,* 225 Cal.Rptr. 345 (CA 1986). When the prospective buyer was an MLS member, the listing broker owed a duty as agent to the seller only, and not to the broker-buyer in *Carroll v. Action Enterprises, Inc.,* 292 N.W.2d 34 (NE 1980). Nor does the broker-buyer have a duty to discover listing mistakes made by the listing broker, even if the broker-buyer receives a commission split. *Asleson v. West Branch Land Co.,* 311 N.W.2d 533 (ND 1981); *Lageschute v. Steinbrecher,* 344 N.E.2d 750 (IL 1976).

Compensation

Many of the subagency cases are concerned with the cooperating broker seeking a commission. The majority of the cases hold that the cooperating broker and the listing broker are joint venturers who owe certain fiduciary duties between themselves, including the payment of fees even under oral arrangements. *Nutter v. Bechtel,* 433 P.2d 993 (AZ 1967); *Moore v. Sussdorf,* 421 S.W.2d 460 (TX 1967) (even if the listing between seller and broker is not in writing, as required by law); *J.A. Cantor & Associates, Inc. v. Devore,* 281 So.2d 245 (FL 1973); *Sorenson v. Brice Realty Company,* 282 P.2d 1057 (OR 1955); *Hapsas Realty, Inc. v. McCoun,* 579 P.2d 785 (NM 1978); *Dean Vincent, Inc. v. Russell's Realty, Inc.,* 521 P.2d 334 (OR 1974). But in *Gray v. Fox,* 198 Cal.Rpts 720 (CA 1984), the buyer identified himself as a licensed real estate broker and received a share of the listing broker's commission. Unknown to anyone, the buyer immediately resold the property at a profit in a double escrow. The court found that the buyer was an agent for the seller and breached fiduciary duties owed to the seller by failing to disclose the resale and the secret profit.

While there is a fiduciary relationship between the cooperating broker and the seller, there is no contractual relationship; therefore, the cooperating broker usually has no cause of action against the seller for payment of commission. *Gibson v. W.D. Parker Trust,* 527 P.2d 301 (AZ 1974); *Panorama of Homes v. Catholic Foreign Mission,* 404 N.E.2d 1104 (IL 1980); *Goodwin v. Glick,* 294 P.2d 192 (CA 1956); *Smith v. Wright,* 10 Cal.Rptr. 675 (CA 1961); *Philbrick v. Chase,* 58 A.2d 317 (NH 1948). In *Ju v. Jacoby,* 177 Cal.App.3rd 239 (CA 1986), the court held that the mere designation of a cooperating broker in a contract between buyer and seller did not give such a broker a right to enforce the contract in the absence of an intention on the part of the seller to personally secure for the cooperating broker the benefit of the contract. For a contrary result, see *Vanderschuct v. Christiana,* 198 N.Y.S.2d 768 (NY 1960); *Steve Schmidt & Co. v. Berry,* 228 Cal.Rptr. 689 (CA 1986) permitting recovery by the cooperating broker subagent on a third-party beneficiary theory.

A salesperson could sue the client for a commission but could sue a creditor of the broker who had put a hold on all commission monies owed the broker. *Best-Morrison Properties v. Dennison,* 468 So.2d 483 (FL 1985).

In *Walters v. Marler,* 147 Cal.Rptr. 655 (CA 1978), the court held that a broker retained by the buyer is the agent of the buyer and owes the buyer a fiduciary duty, even though as cooperating broker his fee is paid by the seller.

In *Richard H. Huff Realty, Inc. v. Andrews,* 564 P.2d 93 (AZ 1977), the listing salesperson unsuccessfully sought to collect the selling agent's portion of the listing fee when the buyer was another salesperson in the listing broker's office. The court upheld the salesperson-buyer's claim to the selling commission. See *Fitzgerald v. Shannon & Luchs Co.,* 600 F. Supp.106 (DC 1984).

CHAPTER 7. DUAL AGENCY

A real estate broker cannot act as the agent for buyer and seller in the same transaction without the informed consent of both. When the broker assumes to act in a dual capacity without the intelligent consent of both parties, the transaction is voidable as a matter of law. *Taborsky v. Mathews,* 121 So.2d 61 (FL 1960); *Brockman v. Delta Mfg. Co.,* 87 P.2d 968 (OK 1939); *Darling v. Nineteen Eighty Corporation,* 176 N.W.2d 765 (IA 1970); *Shepley v. Green,* 243 S.W.2d 772 (MO 1951) (consent implied by failure to object); *Gordon v. Beck,* 239 P.309 (CA 1925); *Quest v. Barge,* 41 So.2d 158 (FL 1949); *Price v. Martin,* 147 S.E.2d 716 (VA 1966). Undisclosed dual agency has been held "a species of fraud." *Peyton v. Cly,* 7 Cal.Rptr. 504 (CA 1960); *Moore v. Mead,* 182 N.W. 29 (MI 1921); *Greater Bloomfield Realty Co. v. Brown,* 235 N.W.2d 168 (MI 1975). Listing broker breached duty to seller by actively participating in assisting the buyer without informing seller of the dual capacity. *Gillmore v. Morelli,* 472 N.W.2d 738 (ND 1991).

In addition, the undisclosed dual agent cannot recover any commission. *Leno v. Stewart,* 95 A. 539 (VT 1915); *Spratlin et al. v. Hawn,* 156 S.E.2d 402 (GA 1967); *Investment Exchange Realty, Inc. v. Hillcrest Bowl, Inc.,* 513 P.2d 282 (WA 1973); *Panorama of Homes, Inc. v. Catholic Foreign Mission Society, Inc.,* 404 N.E. 2d 1104 (IL 1980); *Phillips v. Campbell,* 480 S.W.2d 250 (TX 1972); *Meerdink v. Kreiger,* 550 P.2d 42 (WA 1976); *Miller v. Berkoski,* 297 N.W.2d 334 (IA 1980). Even if the seller is not injured by the failure to disclose, the broker forfeits any right to a commission. A broker may act for both parties only if there is a full disclosure to both principals, so that the principals may deal at arm's length. *Silverman v. Bresnahan,* 114 A.2d 307 (NJ 1955); *Lawton v. McHale Realty Co.,* 131 A.2d 679 (RI 1957). For want of proof that the parties consented to a dual commission arrangement, payments by one precluded recovery from the other. *Porter v. Striegler,* 533 S.W.2d 478(TX 1976). No rule of law is better settled than the one that an agent cannot serve two masters. *McMichael v. Burnett,* 17 P.2d 932 (KS 1933); *Mortgage Bankers Assn. of New Jersey v. New Jersey Real Estate Commission,* 491 A.2d 1317 (NJ 1985).

Dual agency situations can also arise in real estate exchanges in which one broker represents both sides of the transaction. *Hays v. Ryker,* 118 So. 199 (MS 1928); *Rodenkirch v. Layton,* 176 N.W. 897 (IA 1920); *Hageman v. Colombet,* 198 P. 842 (CA 1921); *Hughes v. Robbins,* 164 N.E.2d 469 (OH 1959); *Homefinders v. Lawrence,* 335 P.2d 893 (ID 1959); *Galyen v. Voyager Inn, Inc.,* 328 F.Supp. 1299 (MO 1971).

Sometimes the dual agency arises because of a prior long-standing relationship between the listing broker and the buyer. *Koller v. Belote,* 528 P.2d J 000 (WA 1974); *Adarns v. Kerr,* 655 S.W.2d 49 (MO 1983) (listing broker also managed properties for buyer). Other times the broker "adopts" the buyer prior to or during the closing process. The broker might reach an agreement with the buyer prior to presenting the offer that the broker will manage the property or sell it at a profit for the buyer, as in *Dickinson v. Tysen,* 103 N.E. 703 (NY 1913); or receive a percentage commission upon resale of the property at a profit, as in *Wilson v. Southern Pacific Land Company,* 215 P. 396 (CA 1923).

It may not be a breach of duty to reach an agency agreement with the buyer after the contract is signed, although the broker still should disclose this fact to the seller. *Currier v. Letourneau,* 373 A.2d 521 (VT 1977). It may not be a dual agency for the listing broker also to become the listing broker of the buyer's existing home, although the professional broker will disclose this fact to all parties. *Hall v. Williams,* 50 S.W.2d 138 (MO 1932); *Fred Tuke & Son v. Burkhardt,* 156 N.E.2d 490 (OH 1958). In *Harvey v. Tucker,* 12 P.2d 847 (KS 1932), the court held that fraud would not be presumed and dual agency would not apply when an agent immediately resells a property for the buyer, although the transaction was near the "danger zone." In *Urban Investments, Inc. v. Branham,* 464 A.2d 93 (DC App. 1983), the court recognized that a broker can act as a dual agent when the buyer first engages the broker to sell the buyer's home and the broker subsequently represents the buyer in the purchase of a new home.

A broker may be the agent of two contracting parties in certain instances, but only on the fullest disclosure by the broker of the fact that the broker is representing both parties, and the fullest comprehension of that fact by those contracting. *Quest v. Barge,* 41 Sa.2d 158 (FL 1949); *Barbat v. M.E. Arden Co.,* 254 N.W.2d 779 (MI 1977); *Napier v. Adams,* 158 S.E.18 (GA 1931); *Holley v. Jackson,* 158 A.2d 803 (DE 1954). The duty of care owed to each party by a dual agent is to exercise the same full and truthful disclosure of all known facts, or facts reasonably discoverable, in the exercise of due diligence, that are likely to affect either principal's interest and action. *Brandt v. Koepnick,* 469 P.2d 189 (WA 1970); *Martin v. Hieken,* 340 S.W.2d 161 (MO 1960). For example, when a dual agent broker discovers an encumbrance and fails to further inquire whether the seller has marketable title, the broker has breached a fiduciary duty to the buyer and is liable for the loss of the buyer's down payment. *Garl v. Mihuta,* 361 N.E.2d 1065 (OH 1975). In *Wilson v. Lewis,* 165 Cal.Rptr. 396 (CA 1980), a cooperating broker retained by the buyer was held to also be the agent of the seller because the broker was receiving a 3-percent commission from the seller. The broker breached a duty by failing to disclose to the seller that the buyer's deposit check was postdated and could not be negotiated until after inspection of the property.

Dual agency was disclosed in an in-house sale but the disclosure was inadequate when the broker intentionally misled the seller into thinking the buyer was an owner-occupant, whereas the buyer was an investor, and the broker had a substantial personal stake in retaining the buyer's continued business. *Jorgensen v. Beach 'N' Bay Realty,* 177 Cal.Rptr. 882 (CA 1981).

When several principals employ the same broker, misconduct of the broker cannot be imputed to any one of the principals who is not actually at fault, each of the principals being under an equal duty to supervise the broker and protect the principal's interest. *Whittlesey v. Spence,* 439 S.W.2d 195 (MO 1969).

In *Smith v. Sullivan,* 419 So.2d 184 (MS 1982), the broker breached its fiduciary duty to the seller by representing the buyer in a purchase from the seller after the listing had expired. The broker failed to disclose the identity and financial responsibility of the buyer. Buyer's agent obtained a "one-time showing" listing from seller. Held to be a dual agent. *Culver & Associates v. Jaoudi Industries,* 1 Cal.Rptr.2d 680 (CA 1991).

The dual agent has a duty to act with fairness to each party and to disclose to each all facts that the agent knows or should know would reasonably affect the judgment of each in permitting such dual agency. According to the *Restatement (Second) of Agency,* Section 392,

> The agent's disclosure must include not only the fact that he is acting on behalf of the other party, but also all facts which are relevant in enabling the principal to make an intelligent determination . . . The agent, however, is under no duty to disclose, and has a duty not to disclose to one principal, confidential information given to him by the other, such as the price he is willing to pay. If the information is of such a nature that he cannot fairly give advice to one without disclosing it, he cannot properly continue to act as advisor . . . .

In *Foster v. Blake Heights Corporation,* 530 P.2d 815 (UT 1974), the court held that a broker negotiating a transaction does not have to be exclusively the agent for either the buyer or seller but may be a go-between acting for both.

Consent must be knowing, intelligent and obtained in such a way as to ensure that the client has had adequate time to reflect upon the choice. Consent must not be forced upon the client by the pressures of closing. *Matter of Dolan,* 384 A.2d 1076 (NJ 1978). In a complex commercial real estate transaction, an attorney may not represent both buyer and seller, even if both gave their informed consent. *Baldasarre v. Butler,* A 49-50 N.J. S.C. 1993. *Bokusky v. Edina Realty,* Civ. 3-92-223 (D. Minn. 1993). Issue is the adequacy of informed consent to a dual agency. The only disclosure was a statement in the sales contract that the individual sales agent represented the buyer and the listing brokerage represented the seller. Certified as a class action suit with remedy sought being the disgorgement of all commissions earned on in-house sales.

Even though the broker acts as a dual agent, there will be no rescission and no forfeiture of commission if both parties intelligently consent to the common representation. *Nahn-Heberer Realty Co. v. Schrader,* 89 S.W.2d 142 (MO 1936), although the court still inquired whether the broker was disloyal to either party; *Panebianco v. Berger,* 199 N.W. 545 (NE 1924); *Lamb v. Milliken,* 243 P. 624 (CO 1926); *Cole v. Brundage,* 344 N.E.2d 583 (IL 1976); *Bonaccorso v. Kaplan,* 32 Cal.Rptr. 69 (CA 1963); *Lemons v. Barton,* 186 N.E.2d 426 (IN 1962);

Zimmerman v. Garvey, 71 A. 780 (CT 1909); *Phillips v. Campbell,* 480 S.W.2d 250 (TX 1972); *Hladik v. Allen,* 147 P.474 (CA 1915); *Olson v. Brickles,* 124 S.E.2d 895 (VA 1962). As a general rule, dual agency does not apply to insurance agents, a rule some real estate agents sometimes refer to. *Wright v. Providence Washington Ins. Co.,* 286 P.237 (KS 1930).

Broker breached fiduciary duty resulting in forfeiture of commission. *Wallace v. Odham,* 579 So.2d 171 (FL 1991). A buyer broker who shows property listed in the MLS which offers subagency takes the risk of being a dual agent. *Stefani v. Baird & Warner,* 510 N.E.2D 65 (IL).

Middleman Exception

One limited exception to the rule that a broker cannot collect a fee from both parties without their prior approval is the so-called middleman exception. The middleman exception, in which the broker merely brings the parties together to negotiate their own contract, does not apply if the broker exercises any discretion or authority to negotiate for the principal. *Faiar v. Smith,* 79 N.W. 633 (MI 1899); *McConnell v. Cowan,* 28 S P.2d 261 (CA 1955); *Devine v. Hudgins,* 163 A. 83 (ME 1932); *Whiston v. David Mayer Blvd. Corporation,* 84 N.E.2d 858 (IL 1949); *Anderson v. Anderson,* 197 N.W.2d 720 (MN 1972); *Barber's Super Markets, Inc. v. Stryker,* 500 P.2d 1305 (NM 1972); *Knudson v. Weeks,* 394 F.Supp. 963 (OK 1975); *Tyrone v. Kelley,* 507 P.2d 65 (CA 1973); *Property House, Inc. v. Kelley,* 715 P.2d 805 (HI 1986). If the broker is involved in promises of service, representations, preparation of escrow documents, advice and assistance, the broker is an agent and not a middleman. In actual practice, true middleman status occurs only in rare situations. One example of a middleman is a "broker's broker," that is, a broker who puts the seller's broker and the buyer's broker in touch with each other.

APPENDIX

C

ETHICAL AND LEGAL RESPONSIBILITIES

This appendix contains:

- a comprehensive list of common state licensing law violations;
- examples of what constitutes unlawful conduct and unethical practices;
- interpretations of the Code of Ethics involving subagency cases;
- a checklist of listing broker's obligations;
- nine practical steps to lessen the risk of misrepresentation claims; and
- procuring cause guideline

COMMON STATE LICENSING LAW VIOLATIONS

In addition to the common law agency responsibilities of a fiduciary, the real estate broker and salesperson also must abide by contract obligations and by ethical responsibilities found in the licensing law of the state in which they do business and in industry rules of conduct. Some of the more common rules of ethical conduct follow, many of which are grounds for the suspension or revocation of the real estate agent's license. In this section, the word "licensee" refers to the broker or the salesperson.

1. Making any substantial misrepresentation or false promise of a character likely to influence, persuade or induce.
2. Acting for more than one party in a transaction without the knowledge or consent of all parties thereto.

Comment: Many states require written consent to a dual agency. Note that this section means only that the dual agent with written consent will not lose its license. If the dual agency consent is successfully challenged in a civil lawsuit as being obtained without full disclosure of all facts, the broker may still forfeit the right to a commission. For example, assume the dual agent did not tell the seller that the property was undervalued and that the broker already had another buyer lined up to pay a 20 percent higher purchase price. Any consent of the seller would not be "informed consent" because the seller was not given all the facts. The seller could lawfully cancel the pending sale.

3. Commingling the money or other property of others that is received and held by the licensee with the licensee's own money or property.

Comment: It is commingling to keep commission monies in a client trust account after closing.

4. Demanding a fee under an exclusive listing that fails to contain a definite, specified date of final and complete termination. This rule also applies to buyer's listings.
5. Claiming or taking any secret or undisclosed amount of compensation, commission or profit by a licensee.
6. The use by a licensee of an option to purchase in a listing agreement except when the licensee, prior to exercising such option, obtains the owner's consent approving the amount of the disclosed profit.
7. Willfully using the term REALTOR® or any tradename or insignia of membership in any real estate organization of which the licensee is not a member.
8. Demonstrating negligence or incompetence.
9. As a broker, failing to exercise reasonable supervision over the salespersons' activities.
10. Soliciting or inducing the sale, lease or listing for sale or lease, of residential property on the ground, wholly or in part, of loss of value, increase in crime. or decline of the quality of the schools, due to the present or prospective entry into the neighborhood of a person or persons of another race, sex, color, religion, ancestry or national origin.
11. Acceptance by a salesperson of any compensation from anyone other than the employing broker.

Comment: Even if the owner wants to give the salesperson a bonus for doing a great job, this money must first go through the salesperson's broker.

12. A salesperson's acting as a broker.

Comment: Sometimes a salesperson handles the rental of a property purchased by a client. The salesperson cannot independently set up a rental management account. This is a licensed activity and must go through the broker.

13. The licensee shall not be a party to the naming of a false consideration in any document, unless it be the naming of an obviously nominal consideration.

Comment: Brokers should avoid preparing dual contracts, especially if their purpose is to circumvent government financing regulations covering VA and FHA transactions.

14. For the protection of all parties with whom the licensee deals, the licensee shall see that financial obligations and commitments regarding real estate transactions are in writing, expressing the exact agreements of the parties, and that copies of those agreements, at the time they are executed, are placed in the hands of all parties involved.

Comment: Although brokers cannot engage in the unauthorized practice of law, they nevertheless are obligated to make sure that their clients understand the key points of the purchase contract and that the contract contains the necessary protective provisions. It is often advisable to assist the client in retaining an attorney to advise on the legal aspects of the contract and the transaction.

15. When acting as agent in the management of property, the broker shall not accept any commission, rebate or profit on expenditures for an owner without the owner's knowledge and consent.
16. The broker shall not submit or advertise property without written authorization or franchise and, in any offering, the price quoted shall not be other than that agreed on with the owner as the offering price.

Comment: The most common violation here is the practice of stating without the seller's permission that the property is listed at $100,000 but the seller will take $95,000. Rather than suggesting a low price, the professional agent should encourage buyers to make their best offer, which the broker will then submit to the seller.

17. Each written offer, on receipt by the listing broker, shall be transmitted to the seller as a matter of top priority. In the event that more than one formal written offer on a specific property is made before the owner has accepted an offer, any other formal written offer presented to the broker, whether by a prospective purchaser or another broker, shall be immediately transmitted to the owner for decision. If an offer or counteroffer is rejected, the rejection shall be noted on the offer or counteroffer or, in the event of the seller's or buyer's neglect or refusal to do so, the broker for the rejecting party shall note the

rejection on the offer or counteroffer and return a copy immediately to the originator of the offer or counteroffer.

18. The broker shall not compensate a licensee of another broker in connection with a real estate transaction without the knowledge of the other broker. This requirement shall not apply in cases where the licensee is receiving compensation from a former broker for a commission earned while affiliated with that former broker.
19. A licensee shall not place any sign indicating that a property is for sale, rent, lease or exchange without the written authorization of the owner or seller.
20. A broker shall maintain a fixed office located in the state in which he or she is licensed at a business address registered with the Commission, and it shall be an office from which the broker does, in fact, conduct business and where the broker's books and records are maintained.
21. The licensee shall ascertain and disclose all pertinent facts concerning every property for which the licensee accepts the agency, so that the licensee may fulfill the obligation to avoid error, misrepresentation or concealment of pertinent facts.

Comment: The licensee should take care to discover and disclose such relevant information as sewer connections, known building code violations, terms of lease, private restrictions and easements, zoning, boundary problems, condominium parking stalls and pending assessments, the owners of record, and property condition, such disclosure to include any known roof or water infiltration problems.

22. The licensee shall not claim to be an expert in an area of specialization in real estate brokerage, e.g., appraisal, property management, commercial leasing or business opportunities, if, in fact, the licensee has had no special training, preparation or experience in such area.
23. The licensee shall recommend that title be examined, survey be conducted and appraisal or legal counsel be obtained when the interest of either party requires it. When accepting an exclusive listing, the licensee shall provide written comparable market data and/or shall advise that a professional appraisal be secured. The licensee shall adequately explain the meaning and probable significance of a contingency clause or unique provisions, such as an "as is" clause, or shall recommend that the parties seek legal counsel.
24. An exclusive listing must state a definite termination date. No later than five calendar days after the termination of any exclusive listing, the licensee must register any prospective buyers with the owner and disclose the exercise of the extension period in the listing contract, if any.
25. The licensee shall not knowingly underestimate the probable closing costs, including loan fees, in a transaction to the prospective buyer or seller of real property to induce that person to make or to accept an offer to purchase the property.
26. Any listing agreement shall contain a statement that "the amount or rate of a real estate commission is not fixed by law. They are set by each broker individually and may be negotiable between the seller and the broker."
27. The principal broker or designated representative of the listing broker shall review each purchase contract prior to acceptance.
28. While the broker may discuss the different methods of holding title for the buyer, the broker may not determine the best form of ownership for the buyer. This should be determined by the buyer and/or buyer's attorney or accountant.

EXAMPLES OF UNLAWFUL CONDUCT

1. Knowingly making a substantial misrepresentation of the likely market value of real property to its owner, either for the purpose of securing a listing or for the purpose of acquiring an interest in the property for the licensee's own account.
2. The statement or implication by a licensee to an owner of real property during the listing negotiations that the licensee is precluded by law, regulation or by the rules of an

organization, other than the brokerage firm seeking the listing, from charging less than the commission or fee quoted to the owner by the licensee.

3. The failure by a licensee acting in the capacity of an agent in a transaction for the sale, lease or exchange of real property to disclose to a prospective purchaser or lessee facts known to the licensee that materially affect the value or desirability of the property when the licensee has reason to believe that such facts are not known to or are not readily observable by a prospective purchaser or lessee.
4. When seeking a listing, representation to an owner of the real property that the soliciting licensee has obtained a bona fide written offer to purchase the property, unless at the time of the representation the licensee has possession of a bona fide written offer to purchase.
5. The willful failure by a listing broker to present or cause to be presented to the owner of the property any offer to purchase received prior to the closing of a sale, unless expressly instructed by the owner not to present such an offer or unless the offer is patently frivolous.

Comment: In many states, offers have to be presented only up to the time the seller first accepts an offer. The better practice is one of full disclosure of all offers throughout the closing process. The seller may want to accept a "back-up offer" in the event the buyer defaults under the first contract.

6. Presenting competing offers to purchase real property to the owner by the listing broker in such a manner as to induce the owner to accept the offer that will provide the greatest compensation to the listing broker, without regard to the benefits, advantages and/or disadvantages to the owner.
7. Knowingly underestimating the probable closing costs in a transaction in a communication to the prospective buyer or seller of real property to induce that person to make or accept an offer to purchase the property.
8. Failing to explain to the parties or prospective parties to a real estate transaction the meaning and probable significance of a contingency in an offer or contract that the licensee knows or reasonably believes may affect the closing date of the transaction or the time the property is vacated by the seller or occupied by the buyer.
9. Knowingly making a false or misleading representation to the seller of real property as to the form, amount and/or treatment of a deposit toward purchase of the property made by an offeror.

Comment: Sometimes the broker tells the seller that the seller will receive the entire earnest money deposit if the buyer defaults. Sellers should know that escrow agents are reluctant to transfer the deposit to the seller unless both buyer and seller sign a cancellation letter authorizing such transfer. Also, costs and expenses may be deducted before transferring the deposit money.

10. The refunding by a licensee, when acting as an agent or subagent for seller, of all or part of a buyer's purchase money deposit in a real estate sales transaction after the seller has accepted the offer to purchase, unless the licensee has the express permission of the seller to make the refund.
11. Failing to disclose to the seller of real property in a transaction in which the licensee is acting in the capacity of an agent the nature and extent of any direct or indirect interest that the licensee expects to acquire as a result of the sale. The prospective purchase of the property by a person related to the licensee by blood or marriage, purchase by an entity in which the licensee has an ownership interest, or purchase by any other person with whom the licensee has a special relationship where there is a reasonable probability that the licensee could be indirectly acquiring an interest in the property, shall be disclosed.
12. A representation made as principal or agent to a prospective purchaser of a promissory note secured by real property with respect to the fair market value of the securing property without a reasonable basis for believing the truth and accuracy of the estimate of fair market value.
13. Making an addition to or modification of the terms of an instrument previously signed or initialed by a party to a transaction without the knowledge and consent of the party.

EXAMPLES OF UNETHICAL PRACTICES

1. Representing, without a reasonable basis, the nature and/or condition of the interior or exterior features of a property when soliciting an offer.
2. Failing to respond to reasonable inquiries of a principal as to the status or extent of efforts to market property listed exclusively with the licensee.
3. Representing as an agent that any specific service is free when, in fact, it is covered by a fee to be charged as part of the transaction.
4. Failing to disclose to a person, when first discussing the purchase of real property, the existence of any direct or indirect ownership interest of the licensee in the property.
5. Recommending that a particular lender or escrow service be used when the salesperson believes his or her broker has a significant beneficial interest in such entity without disclosing this information at the time the recommendation is made.
6. Using the term "appraisal" in any advertising or offering for promoting real estate brokerage business to describe a real property evaluation service to be provided by the licensee unless the evaluation process will involve a written estimate of value based upon the assembly, analysis and reconciliation of facts and value indicators for the real property in question.
7. Representing to a customer or prospective customer that because the licensee or broker is a member of, or is affiliated with, a franchised real estate brokerage entity, that such entity shares substantial responsibility with the licensee, or broker, for the proper handling of transactions if such is not the case.
8. Demand for a commission or discount by a licensee purchasing real property for his or her own account after an agreement in principle has been reached with the owner as to the terms and conditions of purchase without any reference to price reduction because of the agent's licensed status.

HOW TO AVOID MISREPRESENTATION CLAIMS

1. Question the seller thoroughly regarding the property. Use a "Property Condition Disclosure" form and cover the following questions
   - Owners and interests?
   - Condition of improvements, utility systems?
   - History of repairs? Warranties?
   - Easements? Where? Purpose? Restrictions on use?
   - Boundaries and encroachments? Stakes visible?
   - Nonconforming or illegal uses?
   - Lease restrictions, permitted uses?
   - Current and future zoning?
   - Special ordinances concerning height limits, design standards?
   - State and municipal improvements, assessments?
   - Outstanding building permits and violations? Citations?
   - Financing restrictions?
   - Is land filled?
   - Any Declaration of Covenants, Conditions and Restrictions ("CC&R's")?
   - On income properties, are expense and income projections accurate?
   - Any significant neighborhood trends? School busing?
   - Termite or rodent problems?

- Any other matters that might affect the value of the property?

2. Make an independent investigation of the property.

   Remember that the real estate agents' job is not simply to pass on information from sellers but to keep themselves and the sellers out of trouble by verifying the completeness and accuracy of information. As the agent, you owe a duty of due care to the seller and the buyer. Satisfying yourself, because you may be the one left holding the bag after the seller leaves the state. A disgruntled buyer may prefer to sue a stationary broker, rather than a moving seller.

   - Check out the items under Section 1, above, especially those you find to be sensitive or suspicious.
   - Pay attention to decorative improvements that might conceal defects, such as new plaster over a cracked wall.
   - If a matter is technical and important, suggest to the seller that it might be wise to bring in expert assistance, such as a soil engineer or a swimming pool contractor.

3. On condominium sales, check into the following common problem areas:

   - House rules regarding children, pets, waterbeds and barbecuing;
   - Location of lockers, parking stalls;
   - Any special assessments? For what and how much?; and
   - Maintenance fee, what is included, any proposed increases.

4. Check into factors external to the property that might influence its value and affect a person's decision to buy. For example:

   - Abutting and nearby uses (present and proposed), a rock band next door; or
   - Highway expansion, rerouting of a bus line.

5. Do not make statements concerning matters about which you do not have first-hand knowledge or that are not based on expert opinion or advice.

   - Avoid statements such as "A neighbor told me that . . . ." It would be better to say "According to Mr. Jones at the Building Department, who handles these matters . . . ."
   - If you do not know the answer to a buyer's question, it is better to say: "I don't know but I'll find out for you or find someone who will."

6. Have a list of government agencies you can or should call to get further information.

   - Use the list to investigate the seller's information and find out things for the buyer. Urge the buyer to check things out, too, by giving the buyer the proper departments and numbers to call.
   - Offer to assist the buyer but don't volunteer highly technical information. That should come directly to the buyer from the government agency.

7. Do not participate with the seller in nondisclosure of information. If the seller refuses to disclose such things as citations for building code violations, decline the listing. No listing is worth damages, loss of reputation and loss of license.

8. Avoid exaggeration and be circumspect with opinions.

   - Exaggeration is unethical and could even be considered misrepresentation, depending on the statement's context and the listener's background.
   - If you wish to venture a "quick" opinion, make sure the buyer understands that it is only a guess, that it is not necessarily an educated one, and that the buyer should not rely on it in making his or her decision. While it is permissible to give factual sales data, try to avoid giving an opinion of value increases. If you feel compelled to give such an opinion, it is best to do so in writing and with proper caveats and disclaimers.

9. Obtain and disclose certain pertinent information in writing.
    - Obtain a "Property Condition Form" disclosure from the seller.
    - Give a fact sheet, memo or "tactful" letter to the buyer whenever disclosures are appropriate. For example, such a letter would confirm earlier discussions in which you pointed out, perhaps, a leaky roof or the need to consult with a soil engineer, and affirm that neither you nor the seller makes any warranty as to the condition of the roof or the foundation.
    - Keep copies of these in the client's file; maintain a "paper trail" in the event you later have to testify about the transaction.

PROCURING CAUSE

The following guidelines are excerpts from the NAR Code of Ethics and Arbitration Manual:

Communication and Contact—Abandonment and Estrangement

Many arbitrable disputes will turn on the relationship (or lack thereof) between a broker (often a cooperating broker) and a prospective purchaser. Panels will consider whether, under the circumstances and in accord with local custom and practice, the broker made reasonable efforts to develop and maintain an ongoing relationship with the purchaser.

Panels will want to determine, in cases in which two cooperating brokers have competing claims against the listing broker, whether the first cooperating broker actively maintained ongoing contact with the purchaser or whether the broker's inactivity, or perceived inactivity, may have caused the purchaser to reasonably conclude that the broker had lost interest or disengaged from the transaction (abandonment).

In other instances, a purchaser, despite reasonable efforts by the broker to maintain ongoing contact, may seek assistance from another broker. The panel will want to consider why the purchaser abandoned the first broker.

In still other instances, there may be no question that there was an ongoing relationship between the broker and purchaser; the issue then becomes whether the broker engaged in conduct which caused the purchaser to terminate the relationship (estrangement). This can be caused, among other factors, by words or actions. Panels will want to consider whether such conduct caused a break in the series of events leading to the transaction and whether the successful transaction was actually brought about through the initiation of a separate, subsequent series of events by the second cooperating broker.

CONSIDERATION OF THE ENTIRE COURSE OF EVENTS

The standard of proof in Board-conducted arbitration is a preponderance of the evidence and the initial burden of proof rests with the party requesting arbitration (see Professional Standards Policy Statement 26). This does not, however, preclude panel members from asking questions of the parties or witnesses to ensure their understanding of testimony concerning the events that led to the transaction and to the request for arbitration. Because each transaction is unique, it is impossible to develop a comprehensive list of all issues or questions that panel members may want to consider in a particular hearing. Panel members are advised to consider the following which are representative of the issues and questions frequently involved in arbitration hearings.

- What was the nature of the transaction giving rise to the arbitration request?
- Was the property listed or subject to a management agreement?
- Who was the listing agent?
- What was the nature of the listing or other agreement: exclusive-right-to-sell, exclusive agency, open, or some other form of agreement?
- Was the agreement in writing?

- Was it in effect at the time the dispute arose?
- Who was the cooperating broker or brokers?
- Are all appropriate parties to the matter joined?
- Is or was the matter the subject of litigation?
- Were any of the parties acting as subagents? As buyer brokers? In some other capacity?
- Did any of the cooperating brokers have an agreement, written or otherwise, to act as agent or in some other capacity on behalf of any of the parties?
- Were any of the brokers (including the listing broker) acting as a principal in the transaction?
- Did all brokers comply with all disclosures mandated by law or the Code of Ethics?
- Who introduced the ultimate purchaser or tenant to the property?
- When and how was the introduction made?
- Did the introduction of the purchaser or tenant to the property start an uninterrupted series of events leading to the sale (or to any other intended objective of the transaction), or was the series of events hindered or interrupted in any way?
- If there was an interruption or break in the original series of events, how was it caused, and by whom?
- Did the broker making the introduction to the property maintain contact with the purchaser or tenant or could the broker's inaction have reasonably been viewed by the buyer or tenant as the broker's withdrawal from the transaction?
- Did the broker making the introduction to the property engage in conduct (or fail to take some action) that caused the purchaser or tenant to choose to utilize the services of another broker?
- Was there interference in the series of events from any outside or intervening cause or party?
- What were the brokers' relationships with respect to the seller, the purchaser, the listing broker, and any other cooperating brokers involved in the transaction?
- What offers (if any) of cooperation and compensation were extended to cooperating brokers acting as subagents, buyers' brokers, or to brokers acting in any other capacity?
- If an offer of cooperation and compensation was made, how was it communicated?
- If the cooperating brokers were subagents, was there a faithful exercise of agency on their part or was there any breach or failure to meet the duties owed to a principal?
- If the cooperating brokers were buyer-agents or were acting in a nonagency capacity, were their actions in accordance with the terms and conditions of the listing broker's offer of cooperation and compensation (if any)?
- If more than one cooperating broker was involved, was either (or both) aware of the other's role in the transaction?
- If more than one cooperating broker was involved, how and when did the second cooperating broker enter the transaction?
- If more than one cooperating broker was involved, was the second cooperating broker aware of any prior introduction of the purchaser to the property by the listing broker or by any other cooperating broker?
- Was the entry of any cooperating broker into the transaction an intrusion into an existing relationship between the purchaser and another, or was it the result of abandonment or estrangement of the purchaser, or at the request of the purchaser?

- Did the cooperating broker (or second cooperating broker) initiate a separate series of events, unrelated to and not dependent on any other broker's efforts, which led to the successful transaction?
- Is there any other information that would assist the hearing panel in having a full, clear understanding of the transaction giving rise to the arbitration request or in reaching a fair and equitable resolution to the matter?

These questions are typical but not all-inclusive of the questions that may assist hearing panels in understanding the issues before them. The objective of a panel is to carefully and impartially weigh and analyze the whole course of conduct of the parties and render a reasonable peer judgment with respect to the issues and questions presented and to the request for an award.

THE DUTY OF REASONABLE SKILL AND CARE—CHECKLIST OF LISTING BROKER'S OBLIGATIONS

Research of the Property

To adequately complete a listing contract, research of the property to ascertain pertinent facts should combine the following:

- ☐ *Comparable Market Data.* Provide written comparable market data on the properties previously sold and recommend appraisal when needed.
- ☐ *Estimate of Value.* Provide substantiation for market value.
- ☐ *Tax Office.* Research the public field books and tax records, including maps, to determine seller's property interests and pertinent facts.
- ☐ *Other Offices and/or Departments.* Research property data as needed:
  - ☐ *Governmental Agencies.* Recording Office; Planning Department, Sewer Division; Department of Education; and Department of Health
  - ☐ *Private Groups and Parties.* Lender of Record; Lessor of Record; and Condominium Association of Owners.

Property Inspection

Be observant.

- ☐ *Condition of Improvements.* Note condition of the following for possible problem areas: visible wood damage (e.g., woodrot, termites and other pests); roof and ceilings; foundations, wiring and security systems; plumbing, including sprinklers; carpets; appliances and warranties, pool and pool equipment; fences and walls; sewer connection; solar energy devices; and removal of trash and debris. If possible problem area is found, advise seller to consult professional.
- ☐ *Land Area.* Inspect all land area: (a) Compare with available documentation. (b) Check property boundaries for easements, possible encroachments, location of stakes and setback compliance. (c) Check if property is located in or on a flood zone, beach front, slide activity area or is on fill land.
- ☐ *Compliance of Improvements.* (a) Compare improvements with tax office drawings. If improvements differ from drawings, check for building permits. If none, improvement must be brought into compliance or lack of building permit revealed to buyer. (b) Compare with zoning usage. (c) Review lease or deed restrictions.
- ☐ *Horizontal Property Regime.* For property under condominium Horizontal Property Regime: (a) Ascertain maintenance fee amount and what it includes. (b) Check common elements noting general repairs and maintenance. (c) Check for assessments: (current; immediate or near future); possible maintenance fee increase; and pending litigation. (d) Verify parking stall. Check for: location: size (compact, regular); type (covered, uncovered); and actual number of stalls involved (e.g., two stalls or one stall which would accommodate two compact cars).
  - ☐ *Seller's Papers and Documents.* Examine seller's papers and documents as applicable (1) Plot plans; (2) tax statements; (3) lease documents—note if consents are required; (4) financial documents; (5) liens, foreclosures, defaults, (6) Deeds—note legal description; (7) Condominium documents: (a) House rules—note restrictions re children, pet, number of occupants; (b) Bylaws; and (c) Current financial statement and status of reserve account; (8) Tenant rental leases; (a) Verify: monthly rent; amount of security deposit; term of lease; and options to extend or purchase; (b) Decide proper time to give notice to vacate; (9) Property management agreements; (10) Assessments: road and sewer; (11) Declaration of restrictions; and (12) Uniform Commercial Code Financing Statement on personal property.
  - ☐ *Defects and Repair Record.* (1) Ask seller about known defects and repair record and (2) Ask property manager (condominium and/or rental) about known problems.
  - ☐ *Legal Consultation.* Suggest legal consultation when necessary.
  - ☐ *Title Search.* Suggest a title search where clouds on title are a possibility.

☐ *Personal Property.* Have seller confirm whether potential "fixtures" are to be included in the sale: chandelier, ceiling fan, basketball set, garage door opener, blinds, satellite dish, microwave, portable air conditioner, showerhead massager, built-in bar, sprinklers, stereo system, security system and mirrors.

Listing Agreement

☐ *Agency Relationship.* Explain the responsibilities and relationships of the following: seller; listing agent; listing company; other real estate agent working for the listing company; real estate agents working for other real estate companies and members of the Multiple Listing Service; and sharing of commissions.

☐ *Prior Listings.* Ask if seller is under obligation to another broker through: prior client listing agreements or client protection agreements.

☐ *Written Agreement.* Put in writing the specific termination date and specify all agreements, including: right to advertise; permission to place a "For Sale" sign on the property; lock-box permission; commission agreement; extension provisions; and withdrawal and cancellation provisions.

☐ *Marketing.* Explain and discuss fully the market data, including: comparables and/or appraisal; terms and conditions of sale, including market conditions; seller's degree of urgency to sell; pricing strategy; and the Multiple Listing Service.

☐ *Financial Options.* Discuss buyer's basic financing alternatives, their liability and cost, and how they relate to the seller. (1) Cash; (2) Mortgage assumptions; (3) New financing: (a) Conventional; (b) FHA—discuss points, repairs; and (c) VA—discuss points, repairs, substitution of eligibility and release of liability; (4) Second mortgages—note usury law; preparation of release; (5) Purchase money mortgages; (6) Installment contracts of sale (land contracts); (7) Review underlying mortgage provisions regarding: prepayment penalties; due on sale; assumption; and (8) Check status of reserve or impound account.

☐ *Listing Company's Services and Policies.* Advise fully of services and policies, including: merchandising methods; advertising policies; lock-box policy; key policy; and updating of market data.

☐ *Recheck Listing Information and Terms.* Recheck with seller all information and terms in listing agreement to verify accuracy and completeness.

☐ *Closing Costs.* Review with seller the estimated closing costs for each type of financing.

☐ *Seller's signature.* Have all owners sign: (1) Listing Agreement; (2) Release of Information form: mortgage; condominium association; and (3) Property Disclosure Statement.

☐ *Broker's Review of Listing.* Have principal broker or other authorized company representative review and sign acceptance of listing agreement.

☐ *Copies.* Give copies of listing agreement to seller and broker.

Marketing Responsibilities

☐ *Communications with Seller.* Inform seller continually of marketing efforts. Respond to seller's inquiries as to status or extent of efforts to market exclusively listed property.

☐ *Market Conditions.* Counsel seller on changing conditions in the market.

☐ *Price Quote.* Quote only the price agreed on with the seller as the offering price.

☐ *Pertinent Facts.* Ascertain and disclose all pertinent facts.

Presenting Offers

☐ *Submit Offers.* Submit all offers as a matter of top priority.

☐ *Prepare for Presentation.* (1) Review terms of offer thoroughly, especially items of personal property to be included; (2) Analyze any contingencies; (3) Review qualifications of all offerors; (4) Protect and promote seller's interests; and (5) Move with a sense of immediacy.

☐ *Present All Offers in a Fair and Unbiased Manner*

- ☐ *Disclose Participation.* Disclose in writing your participation in the purchase if buying for: self; any member of immediate family or firm; or any entity in which you have ownership interest.
- ☐ *Contingencies.* (a) Review any contingencies including their effect on occupancy and closing dates; and (b) If seller has any problem with a contingency, advise seller to consult an attorney.
- ☐ *Deposits.* Explain how deposits will be treated in the event of default or cancellation.
    - ☐ *Misrepresentation of Deposits.* Avoid making false or misleading representations to seller as to the form, amount, and/or treatment of offeror's deposit.
    - ☐ *Client Trust Account.* In accordance with state law, all monies received in trust for other persons must be kept in a special bank account or deposited with a neutral depository. *Records.* Records of monies held in a client trust account should be kept in accordance with sound accounting principles.
- ☐ *Changes Constitute Counteroffer.* Explain that any change to the buyer's offer constitutes a counteroffer.
- ☐ *Unqualified Acceptance Results in Contract.* Explain that an unqualified acceptance communicated to the buyer results in a binding, enforceable contract; there is no right of rescission, absent a special state law provision.
- ☐ *Professional Consultation.* Encourage consultation with an attorney and/or certified public accountant if in seller's best interest.
- ☐ *Recommendation of Escrow Company or Lender.* Disclose any significant beneficial interest you or your brokerage company have with escrow/title company or lending institution recommended by you or your company.
- ☐ *Discrimination.* Avoid discrimination against any party based on race, sex, color, religion, marital status, parental status, ancestry, physical handicap or other grounds covered by state or federal law.

Acceptance of Offer

- ☐ *Communicate Immediately.* Communicate acceptance to buyer's agent or buyer immediately. *Binding Contract.* A binding contract does not materialize until acceptance is communicated.
- ☐ *Notice of Acceptance.* Have buyer acknowledge notice of acceptance.
- ☐ *Closing Costs and Check.* Explain and give seller estimated closing costs. Point out when seller can expect to receive his or her check.
- ☐ *Copies.* Ensure that all parties have a copy of the final accepted contract.

Counteroffer by the Seller

- ☐ *Counteroffer Form.* Use counteroffer form. (1) *Seller's Signature.* Have seller sign and attach original signed purchase contract. Note that attached counteroffer applies. (2) *Delivery.* Deliver counteroffer to selling agent or buyer.
- ☐ *Counteroffer on Purchase Contract.* (1) *Changes.* Ensure that all changes are dated and initialed by all parties. (2) *Expiration.* Specify date and time counteroffer expires. (3) *Delivery.* Deliver counteroffer to selling agent or buyer.
- ☐ *If Counteroffer Unacceptable to Buyer,* prepare new offer.

Rejection of Offer by Seller

- ☐ *Seller's Signature.* Have seller sign and date rejection on offer if offer is rejected.
- ☐ *Inform Selling Agent or Buyer.* Advise selling agent or buyer immediately of rejection of offer.
- ☐ *Return Offer.* Return copy of rejected offer to buyer's agent or buyer.

Closing Responsibilities: Pre-closing

- ☐ *Submit Contract and Instructions to Closing Agent.* Upon acceptance of offer, submit:

- ☐ *Contract.* Submit one of the following: original *OR* copy with telegram stating acceptance followed by original signed purchase contract.
- ☐ *Closing Instructions.* Instruct closing agent to: incur no costs until contingencies are removed; and have documents available for seller's review prior to closing date.
- ☐ *Keep Seller Informed.* Keep seller informed of proceedings.
- ☐ *Cooperate with Selling Broker.* Cooperate with selling broker in arranging for appraisal, survey and appliance inspection where needed.
- ☐ *After Contingencies Removed.* When all contingencies are removed. (1) *Moving Arrangements.* Instruct seller to begin moving arrangements. (2) *Repairs.* Advise seller that any repairs should be done during this period. (3) *Termite Inspection.* With seller's concurrence, order termite inspection if required by contract.

Final Closing

- ☐ *Accompany Seller to Closing.* Answer questions; double check charges; explain payment and recording procedure; and review closing statement.

☐ *Conveyance of Title.* (1) *Time and Date.* Inform seller of time and date of recordation. (2) *Keys.* Give keys to selling agent or buyer. (3) *Final Documents.* Explain that final documents will be mailed.

APPENDIX

D NAR® CODE OF ETHICS AND STANDARDS OF PRACTICE

CODE OF ETHICS

The National Association of REALTORS® has designed its own Code of Ethics to establish a public and professional consensus against which the practice and conduct of REALTORS® and REALTOR® Associates may be judged. All members must subscribe to this Code of Ethics. Each Board is specifically responsible for enforcing the Code of Ethics within its own jurisdiction. The Code is admissible in evidence to establish the standard of care of members of the real estate industry (*Pepper v. Underwood,* 122 Cal. Rptr. 343 [CA 1975]; *Menzel v. Morse,* 362 N.W.2d 465 [Iowa 1985]).

STANDARDS OF PRACTICE

The Standards of Practice relating to the Code of Ethics are interpretations of various articles of the Code and are not part of the Code itself. A Standard of Practice is a statement of general principle to guide REALTORS® as to the professional conduct required in the specific situations described.

CASES FROM THE INTERPRETATIONS OF THE CODE OF ETHICS

Many of the provisions of the NAR® Code of Ethics are based on the subagency relationship between listing brokers and cooperating brokers. The *Interpretations of the Code of Ethics,* Eighth Edition (1983), published by the National Association of REALTORS®, contains the following subagency cases:

1. Case #7-14. The cooperating broker conditioned the submission of the offer on the buyer signing a prelisting agreement. The hearing committee found this action inconsistent with the terms of the subagency, which included no such condition.
2. Case #9-25. The listing broker was held obligated to disclose to subagents a special agreement in which the listing broker would credit the seller with a discount if the property were sold in-house.
3. Case #9-26. The listing broker must give timely notification to subagents of any modification in compensation for subagency services.
4. Case #19-10. The subagent has no authority to *advertise* participation as a subagent in a real estate transaction unless authorized by the listing broker.
5. Case #21-12. The cooperating broker improperly presented an offer that required the listing broker to pay a higher subagency commission than that specified in the MLS.

6. Case #22-5. It is no violation for a REALTOR® to refuse to offer subagency in the sale of new homes in which he is the builder-owner.
7. Case #22-6. It is a violation for a REALTOR® to make a blanket decision not to cooperate or extend subagency to other MLS participants.

Code of Ethics and Standards of Practice

of the

NATIONAL ASSOCIATION OF REALTORS®

Effective January 1, 1994

Where the word REALTORS® is used in this Code and Preamble, it shall be deemed to include REALTOR-ASSOCIATE®s.

While the Code of Ethics establishes obligations that may be higher than those mandated by law, in any instance where the Code of Ethics and the law conflict, the obligations of the law must take precedence.

Preamble...

Under all is the land. Upon its wise utilization and widely allocated ownership depend the survival and growth of free institutions and of our civilization. REALTORS® should recognize that the interests of the nation and its citizens require the highest and best use of the land and the widest distribution of land ownership. They require the creation of adequate housing, the building of functioning cities, the development of productive industries and farms, and the preservation of a healthful environment.

Such interests impose obligations beyond those of ordinary commerce. They impose grave social responsibility and a patriotic duty to which REALTORS® should dedicate themselves, and for which they should be diligent in preparing themselves. REALTORS®, therefore, are zealous to maintain and improve the standards of their calling and share with their fellow REALTORS® a common responsibility for its integrity and honor. The term REALTOR® has come to connote competency, fairness, and high integrity resulting from adherence to a lofty ideal of moral conduct in business relations. No inducement of profit and no instruction from clients ever can justify departure from this ideal.

In the interpretation of this obligation, REALTORS® can take no safer guide than that which has been handed down through the centuries, embodied in the Golden Rule, "Whatsoever ye would that others should do to you, do ye even so to them."

Accepting this standard as their own, REALTORS® pledge to observe its spirit in all of their activities and to conduct their business in accordance with the tenets set forth below.

Articles 1 through 5 are aspirational and establish ideals REALTORS® should strive to attain.

ARTICLE 1

In justice to those who place their interests in a real estate professional's care, REALTORS® should endeavor to become and remain informed on matters affecting real estate in their community, the state, and nation. (Amended 11/92)

ARTICLE 2

In the interest of promoting cooperation and enhancing their professional image, REALTORS® are encouraged to refrain from unsolicited criticism of other real estate practitioners and, if an opinion is sought about another real estate practitioner, their business or their business practices, any opinion should be offered in an objective, professional manner. (Amended 11/92)

ARTICLE 3

REALTORS® should endeavor to eliminate in their communities any practices which could be damaging to the public or bring discredit to the real estate profession. REALTORS® should assist the governmental agency charged with regulating the practices of brokers and sales licensees in their states. (Amended 11/87)

ARTICLE 4

To prevent dissension and misunderstanding and to assure better service to the owner, REALTORS® should urge the exclusive listing of property unless contrary to the best interest of the owner. (Amended 11/87)

ARTICLE 5

In the best interests of society, of their associates, and their own businesses, REALTORS® should willingly share with other REALTORS® the lessons of their experience and study for the benefit of the public, and should be loyal to the Board of REALTORS® of their community and active in its work.

Articles 6 through 23 establish specific obligations. Failure to observe these requirements subjects REALTORS® to disciplinary action.

ARTICLE 6

REALTORS® shall seek no unfair advantage over other REALTORS® and shall conduct their business so as to avoid controversies with other REALTORS®. (Amended 11/87)

- **Standard of Practice 6-1**

  REALTORS® shall not misrepresent the availability of access to show or inspect a listed property. (Cross-reference Article 22.) (Amended 11/87)

- **Standard of Practice 6-2**

  Article 6 is not intended to prohibit otherwise ethical, aggressive or innovative business practices. "Controversies," as used in Article 6, does not relate to disputes over commissions or divisions of commissions. (Adopted 4/92)

ARTICLE 7

When representing a buyer, seller, landlord, tenant, or other client as an agent, REALTORS® pledge themselves to protect and promote the interests of their client. This obligation of absolute fidelity to the client's interests is primary, but it does not relieve REALTORS® of their obligation to treat all parties honestly. When serving a buyer, seller, landlord, tenant or other party in a non-agency capacity, REALTORS® remain obligated to treat all parties honestly. (Amended 11/92)

- **Standard of Practice 7-1(a)**

  REALTORS® shall submit offers and counter-offers as quickly as possible. (Adopted 11/92)

REALTOR®
NATIONAL ASSOCIATION OF REALTORS®
430 North Michigan Avenue
Chicago, Illinois 60611-4087

- **Standard of Practice 7-1(b)**

When acting as listing brokers, REALTORS® shall continue to submit to the seller/landlord all offers and counter-offers until closing or execution of a lease unless the seller/landlord has waived this obligation in writing. REALTORS® shall not be obligated to continue to market the property after an offer has been accepted by the seller/landlord. REALTORS® shall recommend that sellers/landlords obtain the advice of legal counsel prior to acceptance of a subsequent offer except where the acceptance is contingent on the termination of the pre-existing purchase contract or lease. (Cross-reference Article 17.) (Amended 11/92)

- **Standard of Practice 7-1(c)**

REALTORS® acting as agents of buyers/tenants shall submit to buyers/tenants all offers and counter-offers until acceptance but have no obligation to continue to show properties to their clients after an offer has been accepted unless otherwise agreed in writing. REALTORS® acting as agents of buyers/tenants shall recommend that buyers/tenants obtain the advice of legal counsel if there is a question as to whether a pre-existing contract has been terminated. (Adopted 11/92)

- **Standard of Practice 7-2**

REALTORS®, when seeking to become a buyer/tenant representative, shall not mislead buyers or tenants as to savings or other benefits that might be realized through use of the REALTOR®'s services. (Amended 11/92)

- **Standard of Practice 7-3**

REALTORS®, in attempting to secure a listing, shall not deliberately mislead the owner as to market value.

- **Standard of Practice 7-4**

(Refer to Standard of Practice 22-1, which also relates to Article 7, Code of Ethics.)

- **Standard of Practice 7-5**

(Refer to Standard of Practice 22-2, which also relates to Article 7, Code of Ethics.)

- **Standard of Practice 7-6**

REALTORS®, when acting as principals in a real estate transaction, remain obligated by the duties imposed by the Code of Ethics. (Amended 11/92)

- **Standard of Practice 7-7**

REALTORS® may represent the seller/landlord and buyer/tenant in the same transaction only after full disclosure to and with informed consent of both parties. (Cross-reference Article 9.) (Adopted 11/92)

- **Standard of Practice 7-8**

The obligation of REALTORS® to preserve confidential information provided by their clients continues after the termination of the agency relationship. REALTORS® shall not knowingly, during or following the termination of a professional relationship with their client:

1) reveal confidential information of the client; or
2) use confidential information of the client to the disadvantage of the client; or
3) use confidential information of the client for the REALTOR®'s advantage or the advantage of a third party unless the client consents after full disclosure unless:
   a) required by court order; or
   b) it is the intention of the client to commit a crime and the information is necessary to prevent the crime; or
   c) necessary to defend the REALTOR® or the REALTOR®'s employees or associates against an accusation of wrongful conduct. (Cross-reference Article 9.) (Adopted 11/92)

ARTICLE 8

In a transaction, REALTORS® shall not accept compensation from more than one party, even if permitted by law, without disclosure to all parties and the informed consent of the REALTOR®'s client or clients. (Amended 11/92)

ARTICLE 9

REALTORS® shall avoid exaggeration, misrepresentation, or concealment of pertinent facts relating to the property or the transaction. REALTORS® shall not, however, be obligated to discover latent defects in the property, to advise on matters outside the scope of their real estate license, or to disclose facts which are confidential under the scope of agency duties owed to their clients. (Amended 11/92)

- **Standard of Practice 9-1**

REALTORS® shall not be parties to the naming of a false consideration in any document, unless it be the naming of an obviously nominal consideration.

- **Standard of Practice 9-2**

(Refer to Standard of Practice 21-3, which also relates to Article 9, Code of Ethics.)

- **Standard of Practice 9-3**

(Refer to Standard of Practice 7-3, which also relates to Article 9, Code of Ethics.)

- **Standard of Practice 9-4**

REALTORS® shall not offer a service described as "free of charge" when the rendering of a service is contingent on the obtaining of a benefit such as a listing or commission.

- **Standard of Practice 9-5(a)**

REALTORS® shall, with respect to offers of compensation to another REALTOR®, timely communicate any change of compensation for cooperative services to the other REALTOR® prior to the time such REALTOR® produces an offer to purchase/lease the property. (Amended 11/93)

- **Standard of Practice 9-5(b)**

Standard of Practice 9-5(a) does not preclude the listing broker and cooperating broker from entering into an agreement to change cooperative compensation. (Adopted 4/93)

- **Standard of Practice 9-6**

REALTORS® shall disclose their REALTOR® status and contemplated personal interest, if any, when seeking information from another REALTOR® concerning real property. (Cross-reference to Article 12.) (Amended 11/92)

- **Standard of Practice 9-7**

The offering of premiums, prizes, merchandise discounts or other inducements to list, sell, purchase, or lease is not, in itself, unethical even if receipt of the benefit is contingent on listing, purchasing, or leasing through the REALTOR® making the offer. However, REALTORS® must exercise care and candor in any such advertising or other public or private representations so that any party interested in receiving or otherwise benefiting from the REALTOR®'s offer will have clear, thorough, advance understanding of all the terms and conditions of the offer. The offering of any inducements to do business is subject to the limitations and restrictions of state law and the ethical obligations established by

Article 9, as interpreted by any applicable Standard of Practice. (Amended 11/92)

- **Standard of Practice 9-8**

REALTORS® shall be obligated to discover and disclose adverse factors reasonably apparent to someone with expertise in only those areas required by their real estate licensing authority. Article 9 does not impose upon the REALTOR® the obligation of expertise in other professional or technical disciplines.
(Cross-reference Article 11.) (Amended 11/86)

- **Standard of Practice 9-9**

REALTORS®, acting as listing brokers, have an affirmative obligation to disclose the existence of dual or variable rate commission arrangements (i.e., listings where one amount of commission is payable if the listing broker's firm is the procuring cause of sale/lease and a different amount of commission is payable if the sale/lease results through the efforts of the seller/landlord or a cooperating broker). The listing broker shall, as soon as practical, disclose the existence of such arrangements to potential cooperating brokers and shall, in response to inquiries from cooperating brokers, disclose the differential that would result in a cooperative transaction or in a sale/lease that results through the efforts of the seller/landlord. If the cooperating broker is a buyer/tenant representative, the buyer/tenant representative must disclose such information to their client. (Amended 4/93)

- **Standard of Practice 9-10(a)**

When entering into listing contracts, REALTORS® must advise sellers/landlords of:

1) the REALTOR®'s general company policies regarding cooperation with subagents, buyer/tenant agents, or both;
2) the fact that buyer/tenant agents, even if compensated by the listing broker, or by the seller/landlord will represent the interests of buyers/tenants; and
3) any potential for the listing broker to act as a disclosed dual agent, e.g. buyer/tenant agent. (Adopted 11/92)

- **Standard of Practice 9-10 (b)**

When entering into contracts to represent buyers/tenants, REALTORS® must advise potential clients of:

1) the REALTOR®'s general company policies regarding cooperation with other firms; and
2) any potential for the buyer/tenant representative to act as a disclosed dual agent, e.g. listing broker, subagent, landlord's agent, etc. (Adopted 11/92)

- **Standard of Practice 9-11**

Factors defined as "non-material" by law or regulation or which are expressly referenced in law or regulation as not being subject to disclosure are considered not "pertinent" for purposes of Article 9. (Adopted 11/92)

ARTICLE 10

REALTORS® shall not deny equal professional services to any person for reasons of race, color, religion, sex, handicap, familial status, or national origin. REALTORS® shall not be parties to any plan or agreement to discriminate against a person or persons on the basis of race, color, religion, sex, handicap, familial status, or national origin. (Amended 11/89)

- **Standard of Practice 10-1**

REALTORS® shall not volunteer information regarding the racial, religious or ethnic composition of any neighborhood and shall not engage in any activity which may result in panic selling. REALTORS® shall not print, display or circulate any statement or advertisement with respect to the selling or renting of a property that indicates any preference, limitations or discrimination based on race, color, religion, sex, handicap, familial status or national origin. (Adopted 11/93)

ARTICLE 11

REALTORS® are expected to provide a level of competent service in keeping with the standards of practice in those fields in which the REALTOR® customarily engages.

REALTORS® shall not undertake to provide specialized professional services concerning a type of property or service that is outside their field of competence unless they engage the assistance of one who is competent on such types of property or service, or unless the facts are fully disclosed to the client. Any persons engaged to provide such assistance shall be so identified to the client and their contribution to the assignment should be set forth.

REALTORS® shall refer to the Standards of Practice of the National Association as to the degree of competence that a client has a right to expect the REALTOR® to possess, taking into consideration the complexity of the problem, the availability of expert assistance, and the opportunities for experience available to the REALTOR®.

- **Standard of Practice 11-1**

Whenever REALTORS® submit an oral or written opinion of the value of real property for a fee, their opinion shall be supported by a memorandum in the file or an appraisal report, either of which shall include as a minimum the following:

1. Limiting conditions
2. Any existing or contemplated interest
3. Defined value
4. Date applicable
5. The estate appraised
6. A description of the property
7. The basis of the reasoning including applicable market data and/or capitalization computation

This report or memorandum shall be available to the Professional Standards Committee for a period of at least two years (beginning subsequent to final determination of the court if the appraisal is involved in litigation) to ensure compliance with Article 11 of the Code of Ethics of the NATIONAL ASSOCIATION OF REALTORS®.

- **Standard of Practice 11-2**

REALTORS® shall not undertake to make an appraisal when their employment or fee is contingent upon the amount of appraisal.

- **Standard of Practice 11-3**

REALTORS® engaged in real estate securities and syndications transactions are engaged in an activity subject to regulations beyond those governing real estate transactions generally, and therefore have the affirmative obligation to be informed of applicable federal and state laws, and rules and regulations regarding these types of transactions.

ARTICLE 12

REALTORS® shall not undertake to provide professional services concerning a property or its value where they have a present or contemplated interest unless such interest is specifically disclosed to all affected parties.

- **Standard of Practice 12-1**

(Refer to Standards of Practice 9-4 and 16-1, which also relate to Article 12, Code of Ethics.) (Amended 5/84)

ARTICLE 13

REALTORS® shall not acquire an interest in or buy or present offers from themselves, any member of their immediate families, their firms or any member thereof, or any entities in which they have any ownership interest, any real property without making their true position known to the owner or the owner's agent. In selling property they own, or in which they have any interest, REALTORS® shall reveal their ownership or interest in writing to the purchaser or the purchaser's representative. (Amended 11/90)

• Standard of Practice 13-1

For the protection of all parties, the disclosures required by Article 13 shall be in writing and provided by REALTORS® prior to the signing of any contract. (Adopted 2/86)

ARTICLE 14

In the event of a contractual dispute between REALTORS® associated with different firms, arising out of their relationship as REALTORS®, the REALTORS® shall submit the dispute to arbitration in accordance with the regulations of their Board or Boards rather than litigate the matter.

In the event clients of REALTORS® wish to arbitrate contractual disputes arising out of real estate transactions, REALTORS® shall arbitrate those disputes in accordance with the regulations of their Board, provided the clients agree to be bound by the decision. (Amended 11/93)

• Standard of Practice 14-1

The filing of litigation and refusal to withdraw from it by REALTORS® in an arbitrable matter constitutes a refusal to arbitrate. (Adopted 2/86)

• Standard of Practice 14-2

Article 14 does not require REALTORS® to arbitrate in those circumstances when all parties to the dispute advise the Board in writing that they choose not to arbitrate before the Board. (Amended 11/92)

ARTICLE 15

If charged with unethical practice or asked to present evidence or to cooperate in any other way, in any disciplinary proceeding or investigation, REALTORS® shall place all pertinent facts before the proper tribunals of the Member Board or affiliated institute, society, or council in which membership is held and shall take no action to disrupt or obstruct such processes. (Amended 11/89)

• Standard of Practice 15-1

REALTORS® shall not be subject to disciplinary proceedings in more than one Board of REALTORS® with respect to alleged violations of the Code of Ethics relating to the same transaction.

• Standard of Practice 15-2

REALTORS® shall not make any unauthorized disclosure or dissemination of the allegations, findings, or decision developed in connection with an ethics hearing or appeal or in connection with an arbitration hearing or procedural review. (Amended 11/91)

• Standard of Practice 15-3

REALTORS® shall not obstruct the Board's investigative or disciplinary proceedings by instituting or threatening to institute actions for libel, slander or defamation against any party to a professional standards proceeding or their witnesses. (Adopted 11/87)

• Standard of Practice 15-4

REALTORS® shall not intentionally impede the Board's investigative or disciplinary proceedings by filing multiple ethics complaints based on the same event or transaction. (Adopted 11/88)

ARTICLE 16

When acting as agents, REALTORS® shall not accept any commission, rebate, or profit on expenditures made for their principal, without the principal's knowledge and consent. (Amended 11/91)

• Standard of Practice 16-1

REALTORS® shall not recommend or suggest to a client or a customer the use of services of another organization or business entity in which they have a direct interest without disclosing such interest at the time of the recommendation or suggestion. (Amended 5/88)

• Standard of Practice 16-2

When acting as agents or subagents, REALTORS® shall disclose to a client or customer if there is any financial benefit or fee the REALTOR® or the REALTOR®'s firm may receive as a direct result of having recommended real estate products or services (e.g., homeowner's insurance, warranty programs, mortgage financing, title insurance, etc.) other than real estate referral fees. (Adopted 5/88)

ARTICLE 17

REALTORS® shall not engage in activities that constitute the unauthorized practice of law and shall recommend that legal counsel be obtained when the interest of any party to the transaction requires it.

ARTICLE 18

REALTORS® shall keep in a special account in an appropriate financial institution, separated from their own funds, monies coming into their possession in trust for other persons, such as escrows, trust funds, clients' monies, and other like items.

ARTICLE 19

REALTORS® shall be careful at all times to present a true picture in their advertising and representations to the public. REALTORS® shall also ensure that their professional status (e.g., broker, appraiser, property manager, etc.) or status as REALTORS® is clearly identifiable in any such advertising. (Amended 11/92)

• Standard of Practice 19-1

REALTORS® shall not offer for sale/lease or advertise property without authority. When acting as listing brokers or as subagents, REALTORS® shall not quote a price different from that agreed upon with the seller/landlord. (Amended 11/92)

• Standard of Practice 19-2

(Refer to Standard of Practice 9-4, which also relates to Article 19, Code of Ethics.)

• Standard of Practice 19-3

REALTORS®, when advertising unlisted real property for sale/lease in which they have an ownership interest, shall disclose their status as both owners/landlords and as REALTORS® or real estate licensees. (Amended 11/92)

• Standard of Practice 19-4

REALTORS® shall not advertise nor permit any person employed by or affiliated with them to advertise listed property without disclosing the name of the firm. (Adopted 11/86)

- **Standard of Practice 19-5**

Only REALTORS® as listing brokers, may claim to have "sold" the property, even when the sale resulted through the cooperative efforts of another broker. However, after transactions have closed, listing brokers may not prohibit successful cooperating brokers from advertising their "cooperation," "participation," or "assistance" in the transaction, or from making similar representations.

Only listing brokers are entitled to use the term "sold" on signs, in advertisements, and in other public representations. (Amended 11/89)

ARTICLE 20

REALTORS®, for the protection of all parties, shall see that financial obligations and commitments regarding real estate transactions are in writing, expressing the exact agreement of the parties. A copy of each agreement shall be furnished to each party upon their signing such agreement.

- **Standard of Practice 20-1**

At the time of signing or initialing, REALTORS® shall furnish to each party a copy of any document signed or initialed. (Adopted 5/86)

- **Standard of Practice 20-2**

For the protection of all parties, REALTORS® shall use reasonable care to ensure that documents pertaining to the purchase, sale, or lease of real estate are kept current through the use of written extensions or amendments. (Amended 11/92)

ARTICLE 21

REALTORS® shall not engage in any practice or take any action inconsistent with the agency of other REALTORS®.

- **Standard of Practice 21-1**

Signs giving notice of property for sale, rent, lease, or exchange shall not be placed on property without consent of the seller/landlord. (Amended 11/92)

- **Standard of Practice 21-2**

REALTORS® acting as subagents or as buyer/tenant agents, shall not attempt to extend a listing broker's offer of cooperation and/or compensation to other brokers without the consent of the listing broker. (Amended 11/92)

- **Standard of Practice 21-3(a)**

REALTORS® shall not solicit a listing which is currently listed exclusively with another broker. However, if the listing broker, when asked by the REALTOR®, refuses to disclose the expiration date and nature of such listing; i.e., an exclusive right to sell, an exclusive agency, open listing, or other form of contractual agreement between the listing broker and the client, the REALTOR® may contact the owner to secure such information and may discuss the terms upon which the REALTOR® might take a future listing or, alternatively, may take a listing to become effective upon expiration of any existing exclusive listing. (Amended 4/93)

- **Standard of Practice 21-3(b)**

REALTORS® shall not solicit buyer/tenant agency agreements from buyers/tenants who are subject to exclusive buyer/tenant agency agreements. However, if a buyer/tenant agent, when asked by a REALTOR®, refuses to disclose the expiration date of the exclusive buyer/tenant agency agreement, the REALTOR® may contact the buyer/tenant to secure such information and may discuss the terms upon which the REALTOR® might enter into a future buyer/tenant agency agreement or, alternatively, may enter into a buyer/tenant agency agreement to become effective upon the expiration of any existing exclusive buyer/tenant agency agreement. (Adopted 4/93)

- **Standard of Practice 21-4**

REALTORS® shall not use information obtained by them from the listing broker, through offers to cooperate received through Multiple Listing Services or other sources authorized by the listing broker, for the purpose of creating a referral prospect to a third broker, or for creating a buyer/tenant prospect unless such use is authorized by the listing broker. (Amended 11/92)

- **Standard of Practice 21-5**

The fact that an agency agreement has been entered into with a REALTOR® shall not preclude or inhibit any other REALTOR® from entering into a similar agreement after the expiration of the prior agreement. (Amended 11/92)

- **Standard of Practice 21-6**

The fact that a client has retained a REALTOR® as an agent in one or more past transactions does not preclude other REALTORS® from seeking such former client's future business. (Amended 11/92)

- **Standard of Practice 21-7**

REALTORS® are free to enter into contractual relationships or to negotiate with sellers/landlords, buyers/tenants or others who are not represented by an exclusive agent but shall not knowingly obligate them to pay more than one commission except with their informed consent. (Cross- reference Article 7.) (Amended 4/93)

- **Standard of Practice 21-8**

When REALTORS® are contacted by the client of another REALTOR® regarding the creation of an agency relationship to provide the same type of service, and REALTORS® have not directly or indirectly initiated such discussions, they may discuss the terms upon which they might enter into a future agency agreement or, alternatively, may enter into an agency agreement which becomes effective upon expiration of any existing exclusive agreement. (Amended 11/92)

- **Standard of Practice 21-9**

In cooperative transactions REALTORS® shall compensate cooperating REALTORS® (principal brokers) and shall not compensate nor offer to compensate, directly or indirectly, any of the sales licensees employed by or affiliated with other REALTORS® without the prior express knowledge and consent of the cooperating broker.

- **Standard of Practice 21-10**

Article 21 does not preclude REALTORS® from making general announcements to prospective clients describing their services and the terms of their availability even though some recipients may have entered into agency agreements with another REALTOR®. A general telephone canvass, general mailing or distribution addressed to all prospective clients in a given geographical area or in a given profession, business, club, or organization, or other classification or group is deemed "general" for purposes of this standard.

Article 21 is intended to recognize as unethical two basic types of solicitations:

First, telephone or personal solicitations of property owners who have been identified by a real estate sign, multiple listing compilation, or other information service as having exclusively listed their property with another REALTOR®; and

Second, mail or other forms of written solicitations of prospective clients whose properties are exclusively listed with another REALTOR® when such solicitations are not part of a general mailing but are directed specifically to property owners identified through compilations of current listings, "for sale" or "for rent" signs, or other sources of information required by Article 22 and Multiple Listing Service rules to be made available to other REALTORS® under offers of subagency or cooperation. (Amended 11/92)

- **Standard of Practice 21-11**

REALTORS®, prior to entering into an agency agreement, have an affirmative obligation to make reasonable efforts to determine whether the client is subject to a current, valid exclusive agreement to provide the same type of real estate service. (Amended 11/92)

- **Standard of Practice 21-12**

REALTORS®, acting as agents of buyers or tenants, shall disclose that relationship to the seller/landlord's agent at first contact and shall provide written confirmation of that disclosure to the seller/landlord's agent not later than execution of a purchase agreement or lease. (Cross-reference Article 7.) (Amended 11/92)

- **Standard of Practice 21-13**

On unlisted property, REALTORS® acting as buyer/tenant agents shall disclose that relationship to the seller/landlord at first contact for that client and shall provide written confirmation of such disclosure to the seller/landlord not later than execution of any purchase or lease agreement.

REALTORS® shall make any request for anticipated compensation from the seller/landlord at first contact. (Cross- reference Article 7.) (Amended 11/92)

- **Standard of Practice 21-14**

REALTORS®, acting as agents of sellers/landlords or as subagents of listing brokers, shall disclose that relationship to buyers/tenants as soon as practicable and shall provide written confirmation of such disclosure to buyers/tenants not later than execution of any purchase or lease agreement. (Amended 11/92)

- **Standard of Practice 21-15**

Article 21 does not preclude REALTORS® from contacting the client of another broker for the purpose of offering to provide, or entering into a contract to provide, a different type of real estate service unrelated to the type of service currently being provided (e.g., property management as opposed to brokerage). However, information received through a Multiple Listing Service or any other offer of cooperation may not be used to target clients of other REALTORS® to whom such offers to provide services may be made. (Amended 11/92)

- **Standard of Practice 21-16**

REALTORS®, acting as subagents or buyer/tenant agents, shall not use the terms of an offer to purchase/lease to attempt to modify the listing broker's offer of compensation to subagents or buyer's agents nor make the submission of an executed offer to purchase/lease contingent on the listing broker's agreement to modify the offer of compensation. (Amended 11/92)

- **Standard of Practice 21-17**

(Abolished effective 1/94)

- **Standard of Practice 21-18**

All dealings concerning property exclusively listed, or with buyers/tenants who are exclusively represented shall be carried on with the client's agent, and not with the client, except with the consent of the client's agent. (Adopted 11/92)

ARTICLE 22

REALTORS® shall cooperate with other brokers except when cooperation is not in the client's best interest. (Amended 11/92)

- **Standard of Practice 22-1**

It is the obligation of subagents to promptly disclose all pertinent facts to the principal's agent prior to as well as after a purchase or lease agreement is executed. (Cross-reference to Article 9.) (Amended 11/92)

- **Standard of Practice 22-2**

REALTORS® shall submit offers and counter-offers, in an objective manner. (Amended 11/92)

- **Standard of Practice 22-3**

REALTORS® shall disclose the existence of an accepted offer to any broker seeking cooperation. (Adopted 5/86)

- **Standard of Practice 22-4**

REALTORS®, acting as exclusive agents of sellers/landlords, establish the terms and conditions of offers to cooperate. Unless expressly indicated in offers to cooperate, cooperating brokers may not assume that the offer of cooperation includes an offer of compensation. Terms of compensation, if any, shall be ascertained by cooperating brokers before beginning efforts to accept the offer of cooperation. (Amended 4/93)

ARTICLE 23

REALTORS® shall not knowingly or recklessly make false or misleading statements about competitors, their businesses, or their business practices. (Amended 11/91)

The Code of Ethics was adopted in 1913. Amended at the Annual Convention in 1924, 1928, 1950, 1951, 1952, 1955, 1956, 1961, 1962, 1974, 1982, 1986, 1987, 1989, 1990, 1991, 1992 and 1993.

EXPLANATORY NOTES (Amended 11/88)

The reader should be aware of the following policies which have been approved by the Board of Directors of the National Association:

In filing a charge of an alleged violation of the Code of Ethics by a REALTOR®, the charge shall read as an alleged violation of one or more Articles of the Code. A Standard of Practice may only be cited in support of the charge.

The Standards of Practice are not an integral part of the Code but rather serve to clarify the ethical obligations imposed by the various Articles. The Standards of Practice supplement, and do not substitute for, the Case Interpretations in ***Interpretations of the Code of Ethics.***

Modifications to existing Standards of Practice and additional new Standards of Practice are approved from time to time. The reader is cautioned to ensure that the most recent publications are utilized.

Articles 1 through 5 are aspirational and establish ideals that a REALTOR® should strive to attain. Recognizing their subjective nature, these Articles shall not be used as the bases for charges of alleged unethical conduct or as the bases for disciplinary action.

NATIONAL ASSOCIATION OF REALTORS®
430 North Michigan Avenue
Chicago, Illinois 60611-4087

Form No. 166-288-2 (12/93)

APPENDIX

E

BROKERAGE CLAUSES AND FORMS

This appendix contains

- sample clauses that could be used in buyer brokerage agreements;
- sample disclosure statements that may be used in sales contracts to clarify whom the agent represents in the real estate transaction;
- a sample real estate services contract;
- a buyer's listing agreement;
- a sample customer letter for the seller-oriented firm;
- Disclosure form regarding real estate agency relationships.
- TAR® Residential Real Estate Listing Agreement (MLS)/Exclusive Right to Sell
- Buyer Representation Agreement/Exclusive Right to Buy

CANCELLATION AND REPRESENTATION CLAUSES FOR BUYER-BROKER CONTRACTS

Important

The sample clauses that follow are for illustration purposes only. They are not intended to apply to all situations and should be used only after consultation with a real estate attorney who can adapt them to the facts of the particular case.

Clause 1—Buyer acknowledges and agrees that Broker may act for other Buyers as agents in connection with the location of properties for purchase by said Buyers and may negotiate on behalf of such Buyers with the Sellers. In the event Broker undertakes to represent and act for other Buyers, Broker shall not disclose to such other Buyers any offer or other information received from Buyer in connection with any property shown to, and considered by, Buyer for purchase.

Comment: Because a Broker may represent more than one Buyer. the Broker should protect against "lost opportunity claims" from clients disappointed that they did not get a chance to bid first on an available property.

Clause 2—Buyer and Seller acknowledge that Bay Realty (herein called "Broker") and all agents associated with Broker, have previously been retained by Buyer to acquire real property. As regards Seller's property only, the agency relationship between Buyer and Broker is terminated. A copy of the Buyer's Agency Agreement with Broker has been received by Seller and is attached to this contract.

The Seller is aware and fully understands both the prior relationship between Broker and Buyer and the current relationship as it relates to Seller's property.

Comment: When a Buyer's Broker discovers that the Buyer wants to purchase a property that has already been listed with the Broker, the Broker may be faced with a dual agency conflict. One method of eliminating this conflict is to withdraw from the Buyer agency as it relates to this one property.

Clause 3—If, as to any interest in real property within the stated purposes of this agency, Broker has any ownership interest, or has any listing contract with the owner for sale or lease of the property under which he may be collecting a commission, and Buyer acquires such property, this agency contract shall be void with respect to such acquisition by Buyer, except that Broker shall immediately notify Buyer of the facts regarding Broker's interest in such real property, or Broker's contractual relationship with its owner, and Broker shall return to Buyer anything of value received by Broker attributable to such property pursuant to this agency contract.

Comment: In cases of conflict of interest, such as when the Buyer desires to buy one of the Broker's own properties or one of the Broker's listings, the Buyer agency contract can be terminated as regards this particular acquisition.

COMPENSATION ALTERNATIVES FOR BUYER-BROKER CONTRACTS

Clause 1—If Broker is to receive a portion of any commission from a Seller or Listing Broker in connection with the sale of property covered under this agreement, Broker shall immediately disclose to Buyer this fact and the amount of any commission. Buyer may, at the option of Buyer, require that any such commission paid by Seller be divided between Broker and Buyer so that the Buyer receives the difference between the amount due under this Buyer-Broker agency agreement and the amount paid over by Seller.

The foregoing adjustments to the methods of compensation of Broker shall in no way affect the obligations of Broker to act as agent and fiduciary of the Buyer in connection with the locating and purchase of real estate as set forth in this agreement.

Clause 2—Broker agrees to act for Buyer and will not accept any fee from Seller or Seller's agent unless disclosure is made to Buyer prior to the execution of an offer to purchase.

In the event Seller has agreed to pay a fee and, with the consent of the Buyer, Broker is entitled to receive any portion thereof, then the amount so payable shall be credited against the obligations of Buyer hereunder.

Clause 3—Buyer understands Broker is a member of the Multiple Listing Service, and Buyer agrees that Broker may work with other Brokers who represent the Seller in marketing a property. They will be the Seller's agents and Broker will be the Buyer's Agent. Broker may share in the commission that the Seller pays to his agent, if such is fully disclosed to Buyer. The amount of any commission paid Broker by the Seller of a property will be applied against the commission that Buyer owes Broker under this agreement.

Clause 4—Al the earliest practical point, and again in the offer to purchase, Broker shall fully inform all prospective Sellers and Seller's Agents with whom Broker negotiates pursuant to this agency contract, that Broker is acting on behalf of a Buyer-principal, and shall be paid exclusively by such Buyer-principal.

Comment: It is important to give notice to the Seller and Seller's Agents that the Broker represents the Buyer. Sellers are thus alerted to the fact that the Broker has disclaimed any subagency (especially important in MLS transactions) and that no commission splits are expected.

When submitting a net offer, some Buyer Brokers disclose the amount of their fee so that everyone can see how the offer was structured. Other Buyer Brokers feel strongly that the amount of the Buyer Broker fee is none of the Seller's or Listing Broker's business.

SAMPLE DISCLOSURES

Below are sample disclosure clauses that the broker might insert into the sales contract to clarify the broker's relationships with the buyer and seller.

SITUATION 1 Broker represents Buyer in purchase of an unlisted property and Seller has agreed to pay the fee. Seller is unrepresented.

The Seller agrees that Broker is acting as agent of Buyer, but Broker will be compensated by Seller and not by Buyer. Seller affirms that Broker is being paid solely for introducing Seller to Buyer and that Seller is not relying on Broker for any advice or counsel regarding the sale. Broker has advised Seller that Seller is free to obtain his/her own independent counsel.

SITUATION 2 Bay Realty represents Buyer. Main Realty represents the Seller. Each party pays its own Broker and Buyer takes this into account when setting the offering price.

All parties confirm that Bay Realty is acting as agent of the Buyer and Main Realty is acting as agent of the Seller in this transaction. Bay Realty will be paid by Buyer only through escrow pursuant to a separate agreement. Main Realty will be paid by Seller pursuant to the listing agreement, minus the amount specified in the MLS listing to have been paid to the Selling Broker.

SITUATION 3 Listing Broker wants to clarify that Buyer's agent is not a subagent.

Buyer and Seller each recognize and agree that Buyer's agent is an independent representative of the Buyer owing a direct fiduciary obligation to the Buyer, and that no subagency relationship exists between Buyer's Agent and either the Seller or the Listing Broker. Any exception must be expressly set forth in writing signed by all parties and their agents. It is further recognized and agreed that the Seller shall not be responsible or liable for any breach of a fiduciary duty owed by Buyer's Agent to Buyer.

Seller hereby instructs the Listing Broker to pay to Buyer's Agent from the total commission received from the Seller, a fee of ______% of the sales price. Seller acknowledges that Seller has been informed that the above fee shall be credited against obligations the Buyer has to Buyer's Agent, with any excess being credited to Buyer's closing costs.

SITUATION 4 Buyer and Seller each have individual agents and the parties want to protect against a dual agency claim.

The parties agree that Main Realty is the exclusive agent of Alice Seller and has no fiduciary duties to anyone else; that Bay Realty is the exclusive agent of Bob Brown and has no fiduciary duties to anyone else.

The agents are authorized to share commissions between themselves without thereby creating any agency relationship to any person other than their respective designated principal stated above.

It is the express intention of the undersigned that this dual agency disclaimer shall result in no dual agency relationship being created in this transaction.

SITUATION 5 Seller wants to clarify that Broker represents Seller alone.

Buyer is hereby informed that Bay Realty, and all agents associated with Bay Realty, is the agent of the Seller only, to whom it owes fiduciary duties and from whom it will be compensated. Buyer hereby acknowledges that neither Bay Realty nor any of its sales agents are the agent of the Buyer in this transaction.

SITUATION 6 Broker is acting as agent of Buyer only.

By placing their initials here ________________________________
Buyer and ________________________________ Seller acknowledge that:

(1) In negotiating the purchase by Buyer of Seller's property, Bay Realty is acting as the agent of Buyer;

(2) As independent agent of Buyer, Bay Realty owes an exclusive fiduciary duty to Buyer, not Seller;

(3) The payment by Seller of a commission to Bay Realty in this transaction does not thereby create an agency relationship between Seller and Bay Realty; and

(4) A subagency relationship will not be deemed created between Bay Realty and Seller's Listing Broker or Seller by reason of Listing Broker listing the property with the Multiple Listing Service.

SITUATION 7 Broker is buying a FSBO.

The Seller agrees that Broker is acting for his own account and may later resell the property at a profit. Broker is not an agent of the Seller. Seller is not relying on Broker for any advice or counsel regarding the sale. Broker has advised Seller that Seller is free to obtain his/her own independent counsel.

Comment: It is not advisable to accept a commission in a purchase of a FSBO. The risk is too great. You may thereby be held to have fiduciary duties of disclosure and loyalty to the Seller. The disadvantage is that the loan amount may be less, although a knowledgeable lender may understand the economics of the situation and increase the loan amount accordingly.

SITUATION 8 Selling broker is submitting an offer to a seller who has authorized the listing broker to split commissions but with no offer of subagency. The addendum might read:

(1) Listing Broker's disclosure of commission split agreement with no offer of subagency.

____, owner(s) of property located at __________________________________, has employed Bay Realty as exclusive agents for the sale of real property and has agreed to allow payment of one-half of the agreed-upon commission to a licensed Broker other than Bay Realty for finding a ready, willing and able Buyer for the property. This authorization to split commission with the agent for the Buyer is not to be deemed an employment agreement as a subagent of the Seller or agent of Bay Realty.

The selling agent, ____, hereby waives any agency or fiduciary relationship with the owner or Bay Realty. Throughout negotiations the selling agent shall be presumed to be representing the Buyers and not the Sellers.

(2) Buyer's Broker's request for commission split.

The undersigned Buyer has employed Main Realty as exclusive agent for the purchase of real property. The undersigned Seller has listed a property under an exclusive-right-to-sell agreement with __________________________________ and has offered a subagency commission of _________% to cooperating Brokers finding a Buyer for the property. In the event Buyer makes an offer that seller accepts, Buyer requests that Seller authorize the listing broker to release to and Main Realty accepts the commission split offered as full compensation for professional services performed on behalf of the Buyer.

Seller acknowledges that Main Realty is acting solely on the Buyer's behalf and has not, by acceptance of the commission split offered, formed any agency or fiduciary relationship to the Seller or the listing Broker.

REAL ESTATE SERVICES CONTRACT

Note

Some agents spend countless hours helping buyers find a property, only to "lose" the buyer to another agent or the seller. This form is designed to evidence a moral commitment on the buyer's part in return for receiving the professional services of the broker. The form recognizes that the broker is the agent of the seller and not the buyer. If the buyer is not willing to work exclusively through the broker, the broker may decide not to spend much time working with this buyer on properties other than in-house listings.

CONTRACT

Based on the mutual promises set forth below, ________________________________ (Customer) engages Bay Realty (Broker) to locate real property suitable for purchase by Customer.

This agreement begins at signing and ends on ________________________________

Customer deposits the sum of $____________________ to ensure Broker is paid for services. This amount will be returned to Customer at the closing of a property purchased through Broker.

Broker will:

1. Use professional skill and judgment to locate real property that is available for purchase and suitable for Customer
2. Assist Customer throughout the entire transaction, including (a) property selection; (b) gathering valuable information on neighborhood characteristics, utility costs, financing alternatives, closing costs, and loan qualification; (c) preparation of offer, and (d) monitoring the closing.

Customer will:

1. Work exclusively through Broker during this agreement.
2. Purchase property only if Broker is paid a fee by the seller.
3. Cooperate with Broker in providing personal and financial information and being available to inspect properties.

Customer understands and acknowledges that Broker's fee will be paid by the seller and that the Broker's loyalty and responsibility will be to the seller, the client who has employed the Broker. The Broker is not the agent of the buyer.

Date____________________________ Customer ____________________________

Broker___________________________ Customer ____________________________

BUYER'S LISTING AGREEMENT

BUYER'S LISTING AGREEMENT
Exclusive Right-to-Represent

RETAINER AGREEMENT:

The "Buyer" named below, also called the "Client," retains and authorizes the "Buyer's Broker" named below on an exclusive basis to locate and/or negotiate for the purchase of real property of a general nature described below.

RETAINER PERIOD:

This Agreement begins upon signing and ends on __________, or upon the earlier closing of a property under this Agreement.

BROKER'S OBLIGATIONS:

The Buyer's Broker will:

(1) use diligence in locating a property acceptable to Client,
(2) use professional knowledge and skills to negotiate for the purchase of the property,
(3) assist Client throughout the transaction and act in the Client's best interest at all times.

CLIENT'S OBLIGATIONS:

The Client will:

(1) work exclusively with Buyer's Broker for the purchase of this property,
(2) furnish Buyer's Broker with relevant personal and financial information to insure Client's ability to purchase property.

NOTICE: The amount or rate of real estate commissions is not fixed by law. They are set by each broker individually and are negotiable between the Buyer and the Broker.

COMPENSATION:

Client agrees to compensate Buyer's Broker if the Client, or any other person acting in the Client's behalf, buys, exchanges for, or obtains an option on any real property of the general nature described below.

The amount of the compensation is $________ or ________% of the purchase price of the property, payable at closing.

The Buyer's Broker is authorized to negotiate for a commission paid by the Seller, the payment of which will satisfy the Client's obligation to pay a commission under this Agreement. The payment of any commission by the Seller from the sales proceeds will not make the Buyer's Broker either the agent or subagent of the Seller.

GENERAL NATURE OF PROPERTY:

TYPE: ____________________

____________________ APPROXIMATE PRICE: ____________________

LOCATION: ____________________

TERMS: ____________________

ADDITIONAL TERMS AND CONDITIONS: ____________________

BUYER'S BROKER:

I agree to render services to Buyer on the terms and conditions stated above.

Date: ____________________, 19____

Buyer's Broker: ____________________

Address: ____________________

____________ Phone ____________

By ____________________

Supervising Broker's Approval: ____________________

Date: ____________________

BUYER:

I agree to employ Buyer's Broker on the terms and conditions stated above.

Date: ____________________, 19____

Buyer's Name: ____________________

Address: ____________________

____________ Phone ____________

____
Buyer's Signature

____
Buyer's Signature

CUSTOMER LETTER

Note

This is a draft of a letter to buyer prospects of a large seller-oriented brokerage firm. It is designed to soften the chilling effect of a disclosure to the buyer that the broker is the agent of the seller.

Dear Buyer:

We at Big City Realty Company are pleased to assist you in your efforts to locate a property to satisfy your needs. We have many excellent properties listed with our firm. We have many sellers who are looking for qualified buyers. In addition, we are members of the Multiple Listing Service and have ready access to literally hundreds of other listings.

We offer many services to help you decide on the right property and the right terms of purchase. Our sellers recognize that not all buyers prefer the same property. Sellers know that it is in their best interests that we work closely with prospective buyers like yourself to provide you with the type of service and information you need to select the right property. Although we are employed and paid by the seller, here's what we can do for you:

Explain Real Estate. We will spend a lot of time explaining some of the complex terms, principles and practices of real estate. For example, you may want clarification of such things as easements, condominium bylaws, title insurance and closing procedures.

Review Affordability. We review your financial situation so you don't waste time looking at properties you can't afford. This helps you set the right price range. To do this, we need the same type of information about yourself as you would tell a lender or the seller to show your financial qualifications.

Compare Properties. We can screen the various listed properties. We will collect detailed information on each property that meets your needs. such as property taxes, zoning, building permits, utility costs, square footage and comparative values.

Provide Neighborhood Information. We will help acquaint you with your new community by providing information on municipal services, schools, churches and shopping centers.

Compare Financing Alternatives. Our salespeople are in close contact with local lenders and we can help you choose from the long menu of financing plans available to you. We can make appointments for you with the lender, help explain the loan application forms and monitor the loan processing.

Present Offers. We can help you understand the standard offer to purchase contract form. We will present your offer immediately to the seller and report back any acceptance or request for changes.

Estimate Costs. We can help estimate the closing costs to complete the purchase, as well as the monthly costs of ownership.

Please let us know if there are any other services you would like. In certain cases, you may want to hire us to be your exclusive agent. If so, we will want to discuss this further with you so both of us agree in writing on the specific terms of this employment and how we will be paid.

EQUAL HOUSING OPPORTUNITY

TEXAS ASSOCIATION OF REALTORS®
RESIDENTIAL REAL ESTATE LISTING AGREEMENT MULTIPLE LISTING SERVICE (MLS) EXCLUSIVE RIGHT TO SELL

REALTOR®

1. **PARTIES:** The parties to this agreement (this Listing) are ______________________________ (Owner) and ______________________________ (Broker). In consideration of services to be performed by Broker, Owner appoints Broker as Owner's sole and exclusive agent and grants to Broker the irrevocable and exclusive right to sell the Property for the price and on terms described below.

2. **PROPERTY:** The Property is described as Lot______________, Block ______________, Unit __________, of ______________________ Addition in the City of______________________, ______________________ County, Texas, known as ______________________________ (address and zip code), or as described on an attached exhibit, together with the following items, if any: curtains and rods, draperies and rods, valances, blinds, window shades, screens, shutters, awnings, wall-to-wall carpeting, mirrors fixed in place, ceiling fans, attic fans, mail boxes, television antennae and satellite dish with controls, permanently installed heating and air-conditioning units and equipment, built-in security and fire detection equipment, lighting and plumbing fixtures, water softener, built-in kitchen equipment, garage door openers with controls, built-in cleaning equipment, all swimming pool equipment, shrubbery, permanently installed outdoor cooking equipment, built-in fireplace screens, and all other property owned by Owner and attached to the above described real property except the following property which is not included: ______________________________.

The Property ☐ is ☐ is not subject to a mandatory membership in an owners' association and its assessments and requirements.

3. **LISTING PRICE:** Owner lists the Property for the gross amount of $______________ (Listing Price) and agrees to sell the Property for the Listing Price or for any other price as Owner may accept. A sale of the Property may be financed through any one or a combination of the following terms: ☐ a conventional loan; ☐ an F.H.A. insured loan; ☐ a V.A. guaranteed loan; ☐ a loan under the Texas Veteran's Housing Assistance Program; ☐ an assumption of an existing note; ☐ cash; ☐ a loan financed by Owner; or through such other terms as Owner may accept. Owner shall pay all usual or typical closing costs charged to sellers of residential real property in Texas, including loan discount points and prepayment penalties (sellers' usual closing costs are those set forth in the residential earnest money contracts promulgated by the Texas Real Estate Commission). **NOTICE TO OWNER: Broker does not guarantee that the Property will be appraised or sold for the Listing Price stated above nor does Broker guarantee any net amount Owner might realize from the sale of the Property.**

4. **TERM:** This Listing shall commence on the ______ day of ______________________, 19_____ (commencement date) and shall terminate at 11:59 p.m. on the ______ day of ______________________, 19 _____ (termination date). However, if on the termination date there is a pending contract for the sale of the Property in effect between Owner and a prospective buyer and the transaction described in such a contract has not closed and funded, this Listing shall continue in effect until the earlier of either: (a) the transaction has closed and funded; (b) the transaction has otherwise terminated; or (c) within ________ days after the termination date of this Listing.

5. **M.L.S. FILING:**

(a) Broker is a member of the Multiple Listing Service (MLS) of the ______________________________ Association or Board of REALTORS® (the Association), and is bound by its rules. Broker shall file this Listing with MLS within four (4) days after the commencement date of this Listing.

(b) As a condition of filing this Listing with MLS, Owner authorizes Broker, upon a final and closed sale of the Property to submit information about the sale, including price and terms, to MLS for publication to members of the Association for market evaluation or appraisal purposes and for disclosure of the sales price to bonafide customers and clients. Owner shall not enter into a contract for the sale of the Property that prohibits disclosure of the sale and its terms to MLS. **NOTICE TO OWNER: MLS rules require Broker to submit such information to MLS for the purpose of insuring that all persons who use and benefit from MLS also contribute information to MLS.**

Residential Listing Agreement concerning ______________________________
(Property Address)

(c) **NOTICE TO OWNER: MLS rules require your Broker, as a condition of filing this Listing with MLS, to unilaterally offer to cooperate with and compensate other MLS participants or other brokers who procure or assist in procuring a purchaser for the sale of your Property. Cooperating with and compensating other brokers means that your Broker will allow other brokers to show the Property to prospective buyers and that if another broker procures an acceptable offer, your Broker will agree to pay the other broker part of the fee or commission that you agree to pay your Broker under paragraph 7(a) of this Listing. Your Broker may offer to cooperate with and compensate other brokers who act as: (1) subagents of your Broker; (2) agents who represent buyers; or (3) both subagents and buyer agents. Your Broker should advise you of your Broker's general policies regarding cooperation with and compensation of subagents, buyer agents, or both.**

(d) Broker shall cooperate with and compensate, on terms and conditions as Broker determines, any other broker who procures or assists in procuring a buyer for the sale of the Property as follows (check only one):

❑ (1) only if the other broker is a subagent of Broker.

❑ (2) only if the other broker is a buyer's agent (NOTE: A buyer's agent represents the interest of the buyer even though the buyer's agent may be compensated by Broker).

❑ (3) whether the other broker is a subagent or a buyer's agent (NOTE: This choice includes choices 1 and 2 above).

NOTICE TO OWNER: Excluding or limiting cooperation with other brokers may impact the exposure the Property receives from potential buyers or other brokers.

6. **CONFLICTS OF INTEREST AND MULTIPLE REPRESENTATION:** During the term of this Listing, Broker is Owner's agent and shall represent the interests of Owner in any negotiations for the sale of the Property unless Owner authorizes Broker, as set forth below, to represent both Owner and a prospective buyer of the Property, in which event certain restrictions and limitations apply to Broker's representation of Owner's interests.

<u>**Discussion of Agency Relationships:**</u> Owner is advised that real estate brokers who hold themselves out as buyer brokers or buyer agents represent buyers. Real estate brokers who hold themselves out as listing brokers or listing agents represent sellers. Real estate brokers who hold themselves out as subagents represent sellers through cooperation with the listing broker. Owner should know that Broker, as part of Broker's business, may work with both buyers and sellers and Broker may enter into buyer representation agreements to represent buyers and listing agreements to represent sellers. In the event Broker does work with both buyers and sellers, it is possible that one or more of the buyers Broker has agreed to represent may be interested in looking at the Property and making an offer to purchase the Property. In such an event, Broker may be faced with a potential conflict of interest. <u>The law in the State of Texas states that a broker may not act as an agent for more than one party to a transaction unless both parties consent to and authorize the broker to represent more than one party.</u>

To resolve potential conflicts of interests, Owner and Broker agree to the following (choose either (a) or (b)).

❑ (a) <u>No Dual Agency</u>. Broker and Broker's associates shall represent Owner exclusively and shall not represent a buyer of the Property or act as an agent for anyone other than Owner in any negotiations for the purchase of the Property. Owner understands that (choose either (1) or (2)):

❑ (1) Broker exclusively represents sellers of real property and does not represent buyers.

❑ (2) Broker represents both buyers and sellers of real property, however, Broker shall not show the Property to any buyer whom Broker represents. If a buyer, whom Broker represents, desires to purchase the Property, Broker shall refer the buyer to another broker.

❑ (b) <u>Dual Agency</u>. Owner authorizes Broker to show the Property to prospective buyers whom Broker has agreed to represent. If a buyer whom Broker has agreed to represent wishes to make an offer to purchase the Property, Owner authorizes Broker to present any offer such buyer may wish to make, to assist both Owner and the buyer in negotiations for the sale of the Property, and to act as an agent for both Owner and the buyer of the Property. Broker's compensation shall be paid by Owner as provided in paragraph 7 of this Listing. **In the event Broker acts as an agent for Owner and a buyer in the sale of the Property, Broker (or any associates of Broker) shall:**

(1) not disclose to the buyer that the Owner will accept a price less than the asking price (Listing Price) unless otherwise instructed in a separate writing by the Owner;

Residential Listing Agreement concerning ______________________________________
(Property Address)

(2) not disclose to the Owner that the buyer will pay a price greater than the price submitted in a written offer to the Owner unless otherwise instructed in a separate writing by the buyer;

(3) not disclose any confidential information or any information Owner or a buyer specifically instructs Broker in writing not to disclose unless otherwise instructed in a separate writing by the respective party or required to disclose such information by law; and

(4) treat all parties to the transaction honestly and impartially so as not to favor one party or work to the disadvantage of any party.

Broker shall not knowingly, during the term of this Listing or after its termination, disclose information obtained in confidence from Owner except as authorized by Owner or as required by law. Broker shall not disclose to Owner any information obtained in confidence regarding any other person Broker represents or may have represented except as required by law.

7. BROKER'S FEE:

(a) Owner shall pay Broker a fee of $ ____________________or________% (select only one) of the sales price, in cash in ____________________ County, Texas when Broker's fee is earned and payable as set forth in paragraph 7. In the event of exchange, the Listing Price shall be the sales price for purposes of computing Broker's Fee.

(b) Broker's Fee shall be earned when any one of the following events occurs: (1) Broker, during the term of this Listing, individually or in cooperation with another broker procures a buyer who enters into a contract with Owner to buy the Property; (2) Broker, during the term of this Listing, individually or in cooperation with another broker procures a buyer ready, willing, and able to buy the Property at the Listing Price and on terms stated in paragraph 3 or at any other price and on terms acceptable to Owner; or (3) Owner sells, exchanges, agrees to sell, or agrees to exchange the Property during the term of this Listing to anyone at any price on any terms.

(c) Broker's Fee, once earned as stated in paragraph 7(b), shall be payable, either during term of this Listing or after its termination, at the time of any one of the following events: (1) the closing and funding of any sale or exchange of the Property; (2) Owner's refusal to sell the Property; or (3) at such time as otherwise set forth in this Listing.

(d) If Owner breaches this Listing or leases, rents or otherwise transfers the Property without Broker's written approval, Broker's Fee shall be earned and payable and the Listing Price shall be the sales price for purposes of computing Broker's Fee.

(e) In the event a buyer, with whom Owner has entered into a contract for the sale of the Property during the term of this Listing, breaches such a contract and Owner receives earnest money or a portion thereof as liquidated damages, Owner shall pay Broker one-half of such amount, but not exceeding Broker's Fee as stated in paragraph 7(a) of this Listing.

(f) In the event Owner initiates a cause of action, mediation, or arbitration against or with a buyer, with whom Owner has entered into a contract for the sale of the Property during the term of this Listing and who breached such a contract, and if Owner collects the purchase price and/or damages either by suit, compromise, settlement or otherwise, Owner shall pay Broker, after deducting attorneys' fees and other expenses of collection, an amount equal to one-half of the amount collected after deductions or the full amount of the Broker's Fee described in Paragraph 7(a), whichever is less.

(g) Broker's Fee shall not be payable if a sale of the Property does not close or fund as a result of: (1) Owner's failure, without fault of Owner, to deliver a title policy to a buyer; (2) loss of ownership due to foreclosure or other legal proceeding; or (3) Owner's failure to restore the Property, as a result of casualty loss, to its previous condition by the closing date set forth in a contract for the sale of the Property.

(h) If within 90 days after the termination of this Listing (the Protection Period) Owner enters into a contract to sell the Property or sells, exchanges or otherwise transfers a legal or equitable interest (excluding a lease with no right to purchase) of the Property to any person whose attention has been called to the Property by Broker, any other broker, or Owner during the term of this Listing, or to any person with whom Broker, any other broker, or Owner negotiated the sale, exchange, or transfer of the Property during the term of this Listing, Owner shall pay Broker the Broker's Fee as provided in paragraph 7(a), provided Broker, prior to or within five (5) days after the termination of this Listing, has delivered or sent by regular or certified mail to Owner written notice specifying the names of the persons to whose attention Broker, any other broker, or Owner has called to the Property or negotiated with during the term of this Listing. If during the term of the Protection Period such sale, exchange or transfer occurs while the Property is listed exclusively with another Texas licensed real estate broker this paragraph shall not apply and Owner shall not be obligated to pay Broker's Fee.

8. BROKER'S AUTHORITY: Broker shall make reasonable efforts and act diligently to sell the Property. Owner authorizes Broker or Broker's associates to: (a) advertise the Property by means and methods as Broker determines; (b) place a "For Sale" sign on the Property in compliance with any State and local laws, rules, ordinances, restrictions, or covenants; (c) remove from the Property all other signs offering the Property for sale or lease; (d) furnish comparative marketing and sales information about other properties to

Residential Listing Agreement concerning ______________________________
(Property Address)

prospective buyers; (e) disseminate information about the Property to other brokers or their associates through MLS or other means as Broker determines; (f) enter the Property at reasonable times to show the Property to prospective buyers; (g) authorize other brokers or their associates, home inspectors, appraisers, and/or repair personnel to enter the Property at reasonable times to show the Property to prospective buyers or for other pertinent purposes; (h) obtain information from any holder of any note secured by a lien on the Property concerning information about the note or lien; (i) upon a final and closed sale of the Property, disclose the sales price to the local county appraisal district; and (j) accept earnest money and deposit the earnest money in trust in accordance with the terms of the earnest money contract. Broker is not authorized to execute any document in the name of or on behalf of Owner with respect to the Property.

9. OWNER'S REPRESENTATIONS AND ADDITIONAL PROMISES:

(a) Owner represents that: (1) Owner has fee simple title to the Property, peaceable possession of the Property, all improvements and fixtures thereon, unless rented, and the legal capacity to convey the Property; (2) Owner is not now a party to a listing agreement with another broker for the sale, exchange or lease of the Property; and (3) all written information relating to the Property provided to Broker by Owner is true and correct.

(b) Owner shall: (1) not rent or lease the Property during the term of this Listing without the prior written approval of Broker; (2) not negotiate with any prospective buyer who may contact Owner directly, but refer all prospective buyers to Broker; (3) not enter into a listing agreement with another broker for the sale, exchange or lease of the Property during the term of this Listing; and (4) provide Broker with copies of all leases or rental agreements, if any, pertaining to the Property and advise Broker of any tenants in the Property.

10. TITLE INSURANCE AND DEED: Owner shall furnish, at Owner's expense, to any buyer of the Property: (a) an Owner's Policy of Title Insurance, in the amount of the sales price and dated at or after the closing of a sale of the Property; (b) a General or Special Warranty Deed conveying title to the Property subject only to liens securing payment of a debt created or assumed as part of the sales price, taxes for the current year, usual restrictive covenants and utility easements common to any regularly platted subdivision where the Property is located, and any other reservations or exceptions acceptable to a buyer; (c) property tax statements showing no delinquent taxes; and (d) copies of restrictive covenants and documents evidencing exceptions to any title commitment other than the standard printed title exceptions.

11. SELLER'S DISCLOSURE NOTICE: Effective January 1, 1994, Section 5.008 of the Texas Property Code requires a seller of residential real property of not more than one dwelling unit to deliver, on or before the effective date of a contract for the sale of the property, a Seller's Disclosure Notice which provides, to the best of the seller's belief and knowledge, information regarding the condition of the property including any material defects and other material facts affecting the property. Owner authorizes Broker and Broker's associates to furnish prospective buyers and other brokers with a copy of the attached required Seller's Disclosure Notice relating to the condition of the Property. Owner represents that the attached Seller's Disclosure Notice is a true and correct representation as to the condition of the Property to the best of Owner's knowledge and belief and that Owner has disclosed all known material defects and material facts affecting the Property in the attached Seller's Disclosure Notice. **NOTICE TO OWNER: If a contract is entered without the seller providing the required Seller's Disclosure Notice, the buyer may terminate the contract for any reason within seven (7) days after receiving the notice. Prospective buyers, brokers, other brokers, and their associates may rely upon any statement or representation you make, whether in writing or otherwise, including but not limited to the Seller's Disclosure Notice, as true and correct. If the information you provide or statements you make are false or inaccurate you may be held liable for damages.**

12. BACK-UP OFFERS: Broker shall not be obligated to continue to market the Property after Owner has entered into a binding contract to sell the Property. If a subsequent or back-up offer for the sale of the Property is submitted to Broker after Owner has entered into a binding contract to sell the Property, Broker ☐ shall ☐ shall not submit the subsequent or back-up offer to Owner. If Broker is to submit subsequent or back-up offers, Owner shall specifically provide in any contract for the sale of the Property with a buyer that Owner may continue to market the Property for the purpose of receiving and negotiating subsequent or back-up offers.

13. KEYBOX:

(a) NOTICE TO OWNER: A keybox is a locked container placed on the Property in which a key to the Property is placed. The keybox may be opened with a special combination, key, programmer key, or electronic or other special card. Keyboxes make it more convenient for cooperating brokers and their associates, home inspectors, appraisers, and/or repair personnel to facilitate the showing, inspecting, or repairing of the Property. All persons who have special combinations, keys, programmer keys, or electronic or other special cards will have access to the Property at any time a keybox containing a key to the Property is placed on the Property. The use of the keybox will probably increase the number of showings, but involves risks (such as unauthorized entry, theft, property damage, or personal injury). Neither the Association nor MLS requires the use of a keybox. Please discuss the advantages and disadvantages of keyboxes with your Broker, insurance agent, and/or attorney.

Residential Listing Agreement concerning ______________________________
(Property Address)

(b) If a keybox is authorized, Owner shall protect, defend, indemnify and hold harmless Broker, Broker's associates, and other brokers and their associates, the Association, MLS, and any keybox provider of and from any damages or claims arising from the use of a keybox including, but not limited to, damages to or loss of real or personal property or personal injury. Owner shall assume all risk of any loss, damage, or injury. Broker advises Owner to obtain personal property insurance.

(c) If authorized, the keybox will remain on the Property for the term of this Listing. Broker shall remove the keybox by 6:00 p.m. of the following business day after Broker receives written notice from Owner instructing Broker to remove the keybox or by 6:00 p.m. of the following business day after termination of this Listing.

(d) In the event the Property is occupied by a tenant at any time during this Listing, Owner shall furnish Broker a written statement, signed by all tenants, authorizing the use of a keybox on the Property or Broker may refuse to place or may remove any keybox from the Property.

(e) Broker ☐ is ☐ is not authorized to place a keybox containing a key to the Property on the Property.

14. LIMITATION OF LIABILITY: Broker and any other broker shall not be responsible in any manner for personal injury to Owner resulting from acts of third-parties or loss or damage of personal or real property due to vandalism, theft, freezing water pipes, or any other damage or loss whatsoever. In the event the Property is or becomes vacant during the term of this Listing, Owner shall notify Owner's casualty insurance company and request a "Vacancy Clause" to cover the Property. Broker shall not be responsible for the security of the Property nor for inspecting the Property on any periodic basis. Owner shall protect, defend, indemnify, and hold harmless Broker, Broker's associates, any other brokers and their associates, and the Association of and from any damages, costs, attorneys' fees, or expenses whatsoever, arising from: (a) acts of third parties or loss or damage of personal or real property due to vandalism, theft, freezing water pipes or any other damage; and (b) Owner's failure to disclose any material or relevant information or the giving of any incorrect information to Broker, Broker's associates, any other brokers or their associates, or prospective buyers.

15. ESCROW AUTHORIZATION: Owner authorizes any escrow or closing agent authorized to close a transaction for the purchase or acquisition of the Property to collect and disburse to Broker the Broker's Fee due under this Listing. Owner authorizes Broker to instruct any closing or escrow agent to collect and disburse all brokers fees due under this Listing.

16. IRS: The Internal Revenue Service (IRS) requires a closing agent to report the gross sales price, seller's tax identification number and other required information to the IRS. Owner shall provide to the closing agent such information at time of closing. IRS requires a buyer of real property to withhold a percentage of the sales price from the seller if the seller is a foreign person. A foreign person includes nonresident aliens, foreign corporations, foreign partnerships, foreign trusts, or foreign estates. In most closings of sales of residential properties the Owner will be required to deliver an affidavit that Owner is not a foreign person. Owner certifies that Owner: ☐ is ☐ is not a foreign person.

17. SPECIAL PROVISIONS:

18. ATTORNEYS' FEES: If Owner or Broker is a prevailing party in any legal proceeding brought as a result of a dispute under this Listing, such party shall be entitled to recover from the non-prevailing party all costs of such proceeding and reasonable attorneys' fees. **NOTICE TO OWNER: It is the policy of the State of Texas to encourage the peaceable resolution of disputes through alternative dispute resolution procedures. The parties are encouraged to submit to mediation or arbitration (services which are provided by most associations or boards of REALTORS® and others) disputes which cannot be resolved in good faith through informal discussion.**

19. ACKNOWLEDGMENT, ENTIRE AGREEMENT, ASSIGNABILITY, BINDING EFFECT, AND SAVING CLAUSE: Owner acknowledges that Owner has read this Listing and understands its contents. This Listing contains the entire agreement between Owner and Broker and cannot be changed except by written agreement. Owner and Broker acknowledge there are no other agreements or conditions other than as set forth in this Listing. This Listing may not be assigned by either party without the written approval of the other party. This Listing is binding upon the parties, their heirs, administrators, executors, successors, and assigns. Should any clause in this Listing be found invalid or unenforceable by a court of law, the remainder of this Listing shall not be affected and all other provisions of this Listing shall remain valid and enforceable to the fullest extent permitted by law.

Residential Listing Agreement concerning ______________________________
(Property Address)

20. ADDITIONAL NOTICES TO OWNER:

(a) Commission rates, broker's fees, or the division of commissions between brokers are not fixed, controlled, recommended, suggested, or maintained by the Association of REALTORS® or MLS. The amount an owner agrees to pay a broker is not prescribed by law and is negotiable between the owner and the broker.

(b) Fair housing laws require the Property to be shown and made available for sale to all persons without regard to race, color, religion, national origin, sex, handicap or familial status.

(c) Whether a keybox is authorized or not, Owner is advised to safeguard and/or remove jewelry and other valuables located in the Property.

(d) HOME WARRANTIES: Broker advises Owner that residential service contracts (home warranties) are available from Residential Service Companies licensed under Article 6573b, Texas Civil Statutes. A residential service contract is an agreement whereby the residential service company may, under the terms of the agreement, repair or replace all or any part of the appliances, or electrical, plumbing, heating, cooling, or other systems of the Property.

(e) Broker cannot give legal advice. This is intended to be a legally binding agreement. READ IT CAREFULLY. If you do not understand the effect of this Listing, consult your attorney BEFORE signing.

AGREED BETWEEN:

BROKER'S PRINTED NAME — LICENSE NO.	OWNER'S SIGNATURE — DATE
By: AGENT 'S OR BROKER'S SIGNATURE — DATE	OWNER'S SIGNATURE — DATE
	OWNER'S SOCIAL SECURITY NUMBER OR TAX I.D. NUMBER
ADDRESS	ADDRESS
CITY/STATE/ZIP	CITY/STATE/ZIP
TELEPHONE	TELEPHONE

BUYER'S RESOURCE - PARK CITIES
Buyer Representation Agreement
(Exclusive Right To Buy)

THIS AGREEMENT ("Agreement") is made and shall commence on the date ("Effective Date") set forth herein, by and between the **BUYER'S RESOURCE - PARK CITIES** ("Broker"), a real estate broker duly authorized and licensed by the Texas Real Estate Commission, license number 0407283, located at 5944 Luther Lane, Suite 130, Dallas, Texas, 75225, telephone (214) 363-7400, and ____

____("Buyer"),

currently residing at ____.

WITNESSETH:

In consideration of the real estate brokerage services and duties to be performed by Broker in assisting Buyer in locating suitable property, in exclusively representing Buyer's interests, and in negotiations for the purchase or other acquisition of ownership or any equity interest (absolute or contingent) in real property, or as may otherwise be provided for herein, whether one or more tracts (the "Property"), within the perimeter boundaries of the following defined territory ("Market Area"), described as follows:____

____,

and in consideration of the mutual promises and covenants contained herein, the parties agree as follows:

1. **APPOINTMENT OF BROKER.** Buyer hereby appoints Broker as Buyer's exclusive agent and grants to Broker the exclusive right to represent and assist Buyer in locating suitable Property within the Market Area, or as may otherwise be provided for herein, and to assist in negotiating the terms and conditions for the purchase or other acquisition of Property within the Market Area, or as may otherwise be provided for herein, in accordance with the lawful directions of Buyer and the terms and provisions contained herein.

2. **DUTIES OF BROKER.** Broker shall (a) use diligence to locate Property which satisfies the requirements and criteria of Buyer within the Market Area; (b) use Broker's best efforts, skills and talents to procure the purchase of Property within the Market Area on terms and conditions acceptable to Buyer; and (c) represent Buyer only as Buyer's agent in negotiating the terms and conditions for the purchase of Property. As Buyer's agent, Broker's additional duties include: undivided loyalty, full disclosure of known information concerning the Property or the sellers thereof, confidentiality of information concerning Buyer not otherwise authorized to disclose, accounting of funds and property delivered by Buyer to Broker, obedience to Buyer's lawful instructions, and due diligence and reasonable care in the performance of all duties. Broker will not knowingly create conflicts with sellers which would disadvantage Buyer, or as otherwise provided for in §4.

3. **DUTIES OF BUYER.** Unless otherwise agreed in writing between Buyer and Broker, Buyer shall conduct through Broker all efforts to locate suitable Property within the Market Area and shall conduct through Broker all negotiations for the purchase or other acquisition of any Property during the term herein and any and all extensions granted herein. Buyer shall cooperate and communicate fully with Broker in said purchase negotiations and in locating Property acceptable to Buyer. Regarding any property inquiries made or received by Buyer, Buyer shall timely notify other brokers, if any, and property owners that Buyer is a client of Broker. Buyer shall provide pertinent information to Broker about Buyer's specific purchase requirements and criteria and/or the anticipated Property Buyer intends to buy.

4. **CONFLICTS OF INTEREST.** Broker advises Buyer that potential conflicts may occur (a) between Broker and other competing buyers, (b) as a result of Broker's prior relationships with property owners, or (c) other unknown conflicts. In the event of competing buyers represented by Broker, for the same Property Buyer is considering purchasing, Broker, with the written consent of Buyer, may refer Buyer to another broker, acceptable to Buyer, for representation or other services concerning that Property only. Broker's decision to refer any competing Buyer shall be based on referring out the particular competing Buyer whose Buyer Representation Agreement is executed with the latest Effective Date. In the event Broker, or Buyer, determines that a prior and conflicting relationship exists with a property owner, Broker, with the written consent of Buyer, may refer Buyer to another broker for representation or other services concerning that Property only. In the event Buyer is referred to another broker, as provided for herein, Buyer's obligations to pay Broker a Professional Service Fee ("Fee"), pursuant to §8, shall be waived for that Property only.

5. **TERM OF AGREEMENT.** This Agreement shall commence on ______________________, 199___ ("Effective Date"), and shall terminate at 11:59 p.m. (CST) on ______________________, 199___ ("Termination Date"); or at any time prior to the Termination Date, upon the written consent of Buyer and Broker.

6. **DISCLOSURE OF BUYER'S FINANCIAL PRE QUALIFICATION.** Buyer ☐ does, ☐ does not, consent for Broker to disclose to third parties that Buyer has been pre qualified, or qualified otherwise, for a home mortgage loan only. Unless otherwise authorized by Buyer in writing, Broker shall neither disclose specific loan amounts which Buyer has been approved for by a lender, nor other personal financial information about Buyer. Broker recommends that Buyer obtain loan pre qualification from a lender of Buyer's choice and to request lender to furnish Buyer with written notice from the lender so indicating that Buyer has been pre qualified for a certain loan amount.

Initialed By Buyer ______________ / ______________.

7. **DISCLOSURE OF BUYER'S IDENTITY.** Buyer ☐ does, ☐ does not, authorize Broker to disclose Buyer's identity to third parties.

8. **PROFESSIONAL SERVICE FEE.** If Buyer acquires any Property within the Market Area, or as otherwise provided for herein, with or without the assistance of Broker, during the term hereof or any extension or renewal hereof, or in the event Buyer defaults in Buyer's contractual obligations with a Property owner in accordance with the terms of this Agreement, and pursuant to the provisions of §4, then, in such event, Buyer shall pay to Broker, in cash, at the closing (or as may otherwise be provided for herein), in Dallas County, Texas, of each Property purchased, a Fee as follows:

(a) As a contingency Fee of ____________________, due and payable ____________________, or
(b) As a flat Fee in the amount of ____________________, due and payable ____________________, or
(c) As an hourly Fee of ____________________ per hour, due and payable ____________________, or
(d) Other: ____, due and payable ____.

The Fee shall be paid to Broker (a) directly by Buyer as provided for above, (b) as provided by the purchase contract, or (c) as provided for in any separate agreement consented to by Buyer and Broker in writing. Notwithstanding the source of Fee payment to Broker, Buyer shall at all times be obligated for the Fee payment to Broker until the Fee obligation is satisfied.

As an alternative, Buyer may negotiate for the payment of the Fee from the seller, or any third party, from the purchase contract and/or from the proceeds of such purchase transaction, and in the event any part or all of such Fee is paid, the amount so paid shall be credited against Buyer's Fee obligation herein. Broker's receipt of the Fee from any party other than Buyer, and Broker's waiving of Buyer's obligation to pay all or part of the required Fee, shall not be deemed a conflict of interest for Broker. ***Except as provided for in §17, and unless otherwise authorized by Buyer in writing, Broker shall not disclose the specific provisions of this section to third parties.***

NOTICE: In accordance with 15(a)(6)(D) of the Texas Real Estate License Act, Broker is prohibited from receiving compensation from more than one party except with the full knowledge and consent of all parties.

The Professional Service Fee specified herein is the result of negotiations concerning the value of the services to be provided by Broker. The amount of compensation and the contract terms herein are not prescribed by law and are subject to negotiation between Broker and Buyer.

9. **FEE PAYMENT FOR LEASE.** If a lease agreement is executed during the term of this Agreement, and unless otherwise agreed in writing between Buyer and Broker, Buyer, as Tenant, shall pay to Broker a Fee for negotiating any Lease Agreement equal to one half of one month's lease payment for each year of the Lease Agreement, prorated to the actual term of the Lease Agreement, including renewals and extensions, and payable at the time the Lease Agreement is executed and thereafter at the time of any extension or renewal.

10. **RETAINER FEE.** Not later than the Effective Date of this Agreement, Buyer shall pay to Broker a non-refundable retainer fee in the amount of $ ____________________, as advanced partial payment for Broker's services. However, this retainer fee shall be refundable to Buyer within ten (10) days following any Property closing, provided the Fee described in §8 has been received by Broker, or unless otherwise applied as a credit against the Fee obligation described in §8.

11. **PROTECTION PERIOD.** If within ______ days (the "Protection Period") after the Termination Date, Buyer enters into a contract to purchase a Property within the Market Area which was called to the attention of Buyer by Broker, any other broker, Buyer, or any other party, during the term of this Agreement, Buyer shall pay to Broker the Fee specified in §8 provided Broker has delivered to Buyer, prior to or within ten (10) days after the Termination Date, written notice specifying the address or location of each Property called to the attention of Buyer. If during the Protection Period, Buyer enters into another Buyer Representation Agreement with another Texas real estate licensee before (a) executing a purchase contract, or (b) purchasing or acquiring a Property, Buyer shall not be obligated to pay the Fee to Broker.

12. **DIVISION OF FEE.** Broker may divide the Fee payable herein on any terms acceptable to Broker with any other licensed broker(s), including, but not limited to, a broker acting as an agent or subagent of a seller.

13. **LEGAL FEES.** In the event that it becomes necessary for Broker to retain an attorney to initiate legal proceedings of any nature in order to secure payment of the Fee provided for in §8, in addition to all other amounts to which Broker may be entitled, Broker shall be entitled to recover all costs of suit and reasonable attorneys fees.

14. **NONDISCRIMINATION.** Broker and Broker's agents shall perform their obligations herein without regard to the race, color, religion, national origin, marital status, sex, handicap, ancestry, or familial status of any party.

15. **ASSIGNMENT.** Any assignment of Buyer's rights to an agreement to purchase or acquire any interest in Property shall not release Buyer from Buyer's obligations herein. Neither party shall assign this Agreement without the prior written consent of the other party.

16. **DISBURSEMENT.** Buyer hereby authorizes any escrow agent or title company which closes any transaction covered by this Agreement to collect and disburse to Broker the Fee due under this Agreement.

17. **DISCLOSURE OF BROKER'S ROLE.** At the time of initial contact, Broker shall clearly inform all prospective sellers, lessors, and their agents that Broker is acting on behalf of a Buyer client only and is not representing the interests of the seller, lessor, listing broker or landlord. At all times Broker shall comply with the applicable real estate agency disclosure requirements of the Texas Real Estate Commission and other real estate agency disclosure requirements.

Initialed By Buyer ____________________ / ____________________.

18. BINDING EFFECT. This Agreement shall be binding upon the parties hereto and their respective heirs, administrators, executors, successors, and permitted assigns. If this Agreement is executed by more than one Buyer, each Buyer shall be jointly and severally obligated for the payments and performance required of Buyer herein.

10. DISCLOSURE OF PRICE AND TERMS. Buyer ☐ does, ☐ does not, authorize Broker to disclose the purchase price and terms of any Property acquired by Buyer through any reporting services and/or appraisal service providers. In the event Buyer authorizes Broker not to disclose price and terms, Buyer shall include such request as a requirement in a purchase contract and shall further furnish Broker, if requested by Broker, with a separate written notice indicating that the terms and conditions of the purchase are confidential, which notice Buyer consents for Broker to furnish, if requested, to any reporting services.

20. YARD SIGN. Buyer ☐ does, ☐ does not, consent for Broker to place a yard sign ("BOUGHT") on the purchased Property following the closing of the purchase transaction for a period of _______ days after such closing, or as otherwise permitted by applicable zoning ordinances. Buyer ☐ does, ☐ does not, authorize Broker to remove any other real estate yard signs present on the purchased Property following closing.

21. CONTROLLING LAW, MERGER, AND SAVING CLAUSE. This Agreement shall be governed by and construed in accordance with the laws of the State of Texas. Buyer acknowledges that Buyer has read this Agreement and that this instrument contains the entire agreement and understanding of the parties hereto with respect to the subject matter contained herein. All prior negotiations, understandings and agreements, both oral and written are hereby superseded and merged into this Agreement. Should any clause in this Agreement be found invalid or unenforceable by a court of law, the remainder of this Agreement shall not be affected and all other provisions of this Agreement shall remain valid and enforceable to the fullest extent permitted by law. This Agreement shall not be modified except by written amendment duly executed by Buyer and Broker.

22. SELLER'S DISCLOSURE OF PROPERTY CONDITION (Section 5.008 Property Code). Texas law currently requires the seller of a residential property, subject to certain limitations, to provide the Buyer with a completed copy of a **SELLER'S DISCLOSURE OF PROPERTY CONDITION** (the "Notice") disclosing the condition of the Property, including any known property defects. If seller fails to deliver the Notice within the time allowed, Buyer may terminate the purchase contract within three days after the time for delivery of the Notice. If seller timely delivers the Notice, Buyer may terminate the purchase contract for any reason within seven days after Buyer receives the Notice.

23. TIME. Time is of the essence in the performance of this Agreement.

24. LEGAL OR TAX ADVICE. Broker cannot give legal or tax advice. This Agreement is intended to be a binding legal document. Read it carefully. If you do not understand the effect of any part of this Agreement or any subsequent agreements, seek competent legal advice and/or advice from a competent tax specialist before entering into any agreements.

25. SPECIAL PROVISIONS.

(a) The attached Addendum One, **IMPORTANT BUYER INFORMATION**, is incorporated herein for all purposes. Broker recommends that Buyer read and become aware of its provisions before executing this Agreement and before entering into any purchase contracts.

(b) As required by the Texas Real Estate Commission, Broker has furnished Buyer a copy of the **INFORMATION AND DISCLOSURE REGARDING REAL ESTATE AGENCY TRANSACTIONS (TREC 3)** prior to the execution of this Agreement by Buyer.

BROKER	**BUYER**
BUYER'S RESOURCE - PARK CITIES	
5944 Luther Lane, Suite 130	_______________
Dallas, Texas 75225	
(214) 363-7400 Fax: (214) 363-5731	_______________
_______________	_______________
By:	**City, State, Zip**
_______________	_______________
Date	**Telephone**
	_______________
	Date

ADDENDUM ONE

IMPORTANT BUYER INFORMATION:

A. ALTERNATIVE BUYER SERVICE CHOICES. ***Broker provides Exclusive Buyer Agency services only and does not represent sellers in real estate transactions.*** Broker recognizes, however, that Buyer has the right and may choose, prior to entering into this Agreement, to employ the services of any other real estate broker to provide other property purchase services which may include: (a) Non Exclusive Single Agency, wherein a broker may represent either seller or buyer, but not both seller and buyer in the same transaction; (b) Dual Agency, wherein a broker may represent both buyer and seller in the same transaction; or (c) Non Agency or Facilitation, wherein a broker may work with, but not for, either or both buyer and seller in the same transaction. Broker encourages Buyer to interview other brokers and/or obtain additional information regarding alternative real estate services before entering into this Agreement with Broker or any agreement with any other real estate company.

B. **SURVEY**. Buyer is advised to timely obtain, or to request seller to furnish, a current survey plat made by a Registered Professional Land Surveyor, of the Property Buyer purchases, in a form Buyer requires, or may be required by a third party lender, and to timely request seller to cure any objections Buyer may have with such survey plat, and as otherwise provided for, by example, in the TREC Earnest Money Contract (TREC No. 20-2).

C. **NOTICE TO BUYER IN ACCORDANCE WITH THE TEXAS REAL ESTATE COMMISSION (TREC).**

(1) Broker advises Buyer to have an Abstract covering the property examined by an attorney of Buyer's selection, or Buyer should be furnished with or obtain a Title Policy. If a Title Policy is furnished, the Commitment should be promptly reviewed by an attorney of Buyer's choice due to the time limitations on Buyer's right to object.

(2) If the Property is situated in a utility or other statutorily created district providing water, sewer, drainage, or flood control facilities and services, Chapter 50 of the Texas Water Code requires seller to deliver and Buyer to sign the statutory notice relating to the tax rate, bonded indebtedness, or standby fee of the district prior to final execution of the purchase contract.

(3) Buyer is advised that the presence of wetlands, toxic substances including lead-base paint or asbestos and wastes or other environmental hazards or the presence of a threatened or endangered species or its habitat may effect Buyer's intended use of the Property. If Buyer is concerned about these matters, an addendum either promulgated by TREC or required by the parties should be used.

(4) If the Property adjoins and shares a common boundary with the tidally influenced submerged lands of the state, Section 33.135, Texas Natural Resources Code, requires a notice regarding coastal area property to be included in the purchase contract. An addendum either promulgated by TREC or required by the parties should be used.

D. **FOREIGN PERSON.** The Tax Reform Act of 1984 requires the Buyer of real property from a foreign person to withhold ten percent (10%) of the sales price from the seller. No tax amount need be withheld if Buyer is acquiring the Property for use as a principal residence and the amount of the purchase price is not in excess of $300,000.00. A foreign person, for purposes of U.S. income taxation, includes nonresident aliens, foreign corporations, foreign partnerships, foreign trusts, or foreign estates. If the seller is not a foreign person, Broker hereby advises Buyer to obtain from seller a certification of non-foreign status at closing.

E. **HOME WARRANTY.** Broker recommends that Buyer consider the purchase of, or to require seller to furnish to Buyer, a Home Owner's Warranty, to the extent possible without pre existing conditions, effective as of or prior to the closing date of the Property acquired by Buyer.

F. **PROPERTY INSPECTIONS.** Broker recommends that Buyer engage the services of a licensed Home Inspection Service Company to inspect the physical condition of the Property and that other specialists be engaged, including but not limited to, structural engineers, heating and air conditioning contractors, roofing contractors, pest control operators (termite inspectors) and others. Buyer should personally attend all physical inspections of Property Buyer intends to acquire. Broker shall have no obligation to perform or to cause to be performed any of such services for or on behalf of Buyer.

G. **ENVIRONMENTAL.** Broker recommends that Buyer obtain independent and/or certified reports with regard to any possible adverse environmental conditions affecting any Property to be purchased by Buyer, including but not limited to: asbestos, radon, chemical, lead, electro-magnetic wave, and other adverse conditions. Broker further recommends that Buyer require any property owner to remove any such adverse environmental conditions found prior to closing. Broker shall have no obligation to perform or to cause to be performed any of such services for or on behalf of Buyer.

H. **REAL ESTATE RECOVERY FUND.** As a consumer of real estate services, and in accordance with §531.18 of the Texas Real Estate License Act, you are hereby advised of the availability of the Real Estate Recovery Fund for claims to satisfy judgments against real estate licensees involving a violation of the law. For further information, contact the Texas Real Estate Commission, P.O.B. 12188, Austin, Texas, 78711-2188, (512) 459-6544.

I. **NOTICE REGARDING NEW CONSTRUCTION.** In the event Buyer intends to purchase Property with newly constructed improvements, Buyer is advised that some home builders may require the use of certain builder purchase contract forms which may contain some contract provisions which Buyer may be unable to negotiate, depending upon Buyer's specific requirements, or may lack other provisions which Buyer might otherwise require be included in a purchase contract. Due to construction requirements and possible completion delays, information, including but not limited to survey plats, title commitments, closing and possession dates may be uncertain and/or delayed. Buyer is also advised to obtain, or to require the builder to furnish, an appropriate new home warranty, effective as of the closing date.

Initialed By Buyer ____________________ / ____________________.

Glossary of Key Terms

agency relationship. The fiduciary relationship that exists when one person (agent) represents the interests of another (principal) in dealings with others, with their consent and under their control.

agent. One who represents a principal in dealings with others. While the term more precisely refers to the broker, the term sales agent is used to refer to the salesperson.

blanket offer of subagency. The offer made by the listing broker on behalf of the seller to all other participants in the multiple listing service to act as a subagent for the seller. The seller has the option of making a blanket unilateral offer of subagency or making no offer of subagency; in either case, under MLS rules, an offer to cooperate must include an offer to compensate.

buyer's broker. A real estate broker who is employed by and represents only the buyer in the transaction, regardless of whether the commission is paid by the buyer directly or by the seller through a commission split with the listing broker. To be distinguished from brokers who represent the seller but nevertheless "work with" the buyer; these brokers are not referred to as "buyers' brokers." They are subagents of the seller. Also, brokers acting as dual agents for buyers and sellers are not referred to as buyers' brokers. Buyer brokerage is one part of a single-agency real estate practice.

client. One who engages the professional advice and services of another, and whose interests are protected by the specific duties and loyalties imposed by the fiduciary relationship.

commission split. The sharing of the seller-paid commission between the listing broker and the selling broker. An MLS listing generally indicates the compensation being offered by the listing broker to the other MLS participants, either as a percentage of the gross selling price or as a definite dollar amount. Thus, MLS members know what they will earn on finding a suitable buyer.

company policies. A set of rules and principles that establishes how a brokerage company is to operate. Every firm should have a clear company policy on agency and take steps to ensure that the sales staff follows it.

consensual dual agency. The practice of representing both the buyer and the seller provided both have given their informed consent in writing.

cooperating broker. The real estate broker working with the prospective buyer on a property listed with another broker. The cooperating broker traditionally is compensated through a commission split with the listing broker. The cooperating broker, also called the selling broker, participating broker, outside broker, or other broker, may be either a subagent acting on behalf of the seller or a buyer's broker, both of whom "cooperate" to make a sale. In some states the cooperating broker may act as a transaction broker or transaction coordinator.

customer. One who purchases property with the assistance of a broker who is not acting as an agent for the customer. The customer is, therefore, without the protection of a fiduciary relationship but does have the protection of the state licensing law and the NAR Code of Ethics if the broker is a REALTOR®. Also refers to a seller who is working with a real estate agent who represents the buyer only.

dual agency. The practice by which the same broker works as an agent for both the buyer and the seller in the same real estate transaction. The dual agency may be either intended or unintended. As a rule of agency law, dual agency is not legally prohibited, provided both parties give their informed consent to this limited representation. In actual practice, it may be difficult to achieve this "knowing consent" of the buyer and the seller. It is also difficult to balance the needs of the buyer and the seller without inadvertently favoring one over the other.

exclusive listing. A written listing of real property in which the seller agrees to appoint only one broker to handle the transaction. There are two types that apply to the seller

1. The "exclusive-right-to-sell listing" obligates the seller to pay a commission if anyone, including the seller, procures a ready, willing and able buyer.
2. The "exclusive agency listing" reserves to the owner the right to sell the property directly without owing a commission. The exclusive agent is entitled to a commission if the buyer is procured by anyone other than the seller.

A third type applies to the buyer

3. The "exclusive-right-to-represent" obligates the buyer to pay a commission if the buyer agrees to buy a described type of property located by the broker, the buyer or anyone else during the listing period.

facilitator. A person who assists the parties to a potential real estate transaction in communication and negotiation without being an advocate for any interest except the mutual interest of all parties to reach agreement. Also called an intermediary, middleman, mediator, nonagent or transaction broker.

fiduciary. 1. A relationship of trust and confidence between principal and agent. The law imposes on the agent duties of loyalty, confidentiality, accounting, obedience and full disclosure, as well as the duty to use skill, care and diligence. A real estate agent owes complete fiduciary duties to the principal and must act in the best interests of the principal (the client) while also being competent and honest to the other side (the customer, whether the seller or the buyer). 2. The agent is referred to as the fiduciary; one who holds the faith, confidence and trust of the client.

finder. One who produces a buyer or locates a property—nothing more. The finder is not an agent and owes no fiduciary duties.

implied agency. An agency relationship that is created by the words or conduct of the agent or principal rather than by written agreement. A listing agent who acts like a buyer's agent in negotiating for the buyer can become involved in an accidental dual agency (express agent of seller and implied agent of buyer).

informed consent. A person's approval that is based on a full disclosure of all the facts needed to make the decision intelligently. To consent to a dual agency, the buyer and seller need to understand the liability involved, the alternatives, and the role that they and the real estate licensees will play.

in-house sale. A sale involving only one brokerage firm acting as both the listing and the selling agent; the listing agent is also the selling agent. Frequently, one real estate agent in the firm secures the listing and works with the seller, and a different member of the same firm finds and works with the buyer. Unless the broker clearly discloses to the buyer that the broker, and all the salespeople, represent the seller, there is a potential dual agency conflict. Even though different salespeople from the firm work with the buyer and seller respectively, the firm itself may become the agent of both the buyer and the seller (a dual agent). Assuming careful disclosure and conduct by the listing broker, however, there is nothing improper about selling a listing "in-house"; in fact, the seller lists the property so that the broker will find qualified buyers.

limited agency. A form of agency relationship permitted under some state statutes in which the buyer and seller, with the agreement of the broker, designate one salesperson from the brokerage firm to act as agent and knowingly waive the right to individual loyalty from the firm and any of its other agents and employees. In some cases the buyer designates one salesperson and the seller designates a different salesperson; none of the other salespeople represent buyer or seller.

listing. An agreement that establishes the rights and obligations between the seller and the broker, or between the buyer and the broker. A salesperson usually obtains the listing of a seller's property in the name of the broker. The broker is called the listing broker, the salesperson is sometimes called the listing agent.

listing broker. In this textbook, refers to the seller's agent. A buyer's agent can also list the buyer.

middleman. A person who facilitates a real estate transaction by introducing a buyer to a seller, who then negotiate their own transaction; a "finder." Provided the middleman exercises no discretion in facilitating the transaction, the middleman in some states may be exempted from the traditional fiduciary duties owed by an agent to a principal. Very seldom does a real estate broker conform to this "middleman" concept. Middleman status could occur when a buyer works with a broker but specifically refuses to authorize the broker to act as the buyer's agent; likewise, the seller does not authorize the broker to act as a subagent. See *Facilitator.*

MLS (multiple listing service). An information service, generally owned and operated by a local association of brokers, in which members pool their listings (primarily residential) and agree to share commissions with other member brokers who find purchasers. Most MLSs are affiliated with the National Association of REALTORS® which considers the MLS to be a formal system of presenting listings in which blanket offers of cooperation and compensation are made to other MLS members.

open listing. A listing in which the broker has the nonexclusive right to sell the property and receive a commission. If the sale results through the efforts of the seller or another broker, then the open listing broker receives no commission. Controversies may arise over which broker actually was the "procuring cause" of the sale.

optional offer of subagency. The MLS policy that affords sellers represented by a participating member the choice whether to offer subagency. A seller can choose to make a blanket offer of subagency or to offer cooperation and compensation to buyer agents, subagents and other licensed participants in the MLS. There is no mandatory offer of subagency.

principal. 1. A person who employs an agent to represent him or her as a client, especially if referred to with the use of the pronoun "his" or "her" principal. 2. One of the primary parties to a transaction, whether or not an agency relationship is involved (i.e., the buyer or seller, especially if referred to as "the" principal).

representation. To act on another's behalf (the principal), as an agent owing fiduciary duties to such principal. There is a definite distinction between "working with" a buyer (who is then a customer or prospect) and "representing" a buyer (who is then a client). Buyers often believe they are being represented when, in fact, they either are not represented or are being "represented" by the seller's agent in an undisclosed dual agency.

While a listing broker frequently works with buyers to encourage them to buy a listed property, the listing broker should be careful that the broker's words and actions do not lead the buyer to expect that the broker is representing such buyer. It is the conduct of the broker that usually forms the basis for the reasonable expectations of the buyer and the seller. If, in fact, the broker is representing both the buyer and the seller, then appropriate dual agency disclosures must be given and the informed consents of the buyer and the seller must be obtained to this form of limited representation.

salesperson. A person who meets the state's requirements for a salesperson's or broker's license and who works for and is licensed under a broker or a brokerage firm. Salespeople are commonly referred to as real estate agents, even though they are not the primary agents of the seller or the buyer; in essence, they are agents of the agent (broker). This is an important concept to keep in mind when discussing the "in-house sale" dual agency situation in which salesperson Alice from Bay Realty is thought to be "representing" the seller and salesperson Sally, also from Bay Realty, is "representing" the buyer. In this situation, both the buyer and the seller have the same agent (i.e., Bay Realty). Separate "agents" are not representing the buyer and the seller. Salesperson Alice is not the seller's agent and salesperson Sally is not the buyer's agent—rather, Bay Realty is the only agent, in this case a dual agent. Bay Realty is the primary fiduciary that owns the listing. Bay Realty is obligated by the licensing law to supervise its salespeople and is responsible for and bound by their actions.

seller's agent. A real estate agent, also called the listing agent, who is employed by and represents only the seller in a real estate transaction. Not to be confused with the selling agent.

selling broker. The broker working with or representing the buyer in the purchase of a listed property. Also called the "cooperating broker," "participating broker" or "other broker" when the selling agent is a member of a firm other than the listing firm. The selling agent may be the listing broker, a cooperating broker (subagent) or a buyer's broker, depending on the facts of each case.

single agency. The practice of representing either the buyer or the seller but never both in the same transaction. The single-agency broker may be compensated indirectly through an authorized commission split or directly by the principal who employed the agent to represent him or her.

subagency. A theory of agency law applicable to the agent of a person who is already acting as an agent for a principal. In real estate the client (usually the seller) lists with an agent who, in turn, retains the services of subagents to find a buyer. A seller may limit the authority of the broker to appoint subagents. Cooperating broker members of the MLS may reject any blanket offer of subagency. Nevertheless, listing brokers customarily use subagents to market real estate, especially if the property is listed in the MLS.

subagent. A person empowered by an agent to act on behalf of the principal or on behalf of the agent, if not properly authorized by the principal. By custom, most sellers authorize the listing broker to appoint its sales staff to act on behalf of the seller as subagents. Listing contracts may authorize the listing broker to appoint outside brokers as subagents, including other members of the MLS. The principal who authorizes the use of subagents may be bound by the acts and representations of such agents of the seller's agent. The subagent's misrepresentations to the buyer can be asserted by the buyer against the seller. The subagent owes fiduciary duties to the agent and to the principal.

unintended dual agency. Accidental representation of both the buyer and the seller by the same broker. This is especially prevalent when the broker does not declare, and the principal does not affirm, the agency status of the broker.

BIBLIOGRAPHY

BIBLIOGRAPHY OF BOOKS AND GENERAL ARTICLES

Adler, Moshe. "Disclosure and the Buyer-Broker Relationship." *Real Estate Review* 11 (Winter 1982): 94–96, 99.

Agency Advocate, a quarterly newsletter published by Who's Who in Creative Real Estate, Inc., P.O. Box 23275, Ventura, CA 93002-3275.

Agency Compliance Manual, Ohio Association of REALTORS®, 1988.

"Agency Disclosure: Don't Sell Homes Without It." *Real Estate Today,* (August 1989): 64–70.

Agency Disclosure Law Compliance Manual, California Association of REALTORS®, 1990.

"A New Chapter in Agency Policy." *Real Estate Today* (August 1992): 25.

"Another Day, Another Agency Dilemma." *Real Estate Today* (September 1991): 42–45.

Arnold, Michael A., "The Principal-Agent Relationship in Real Estate Brokerage Services," *American Real Estate and Urban Economics Association Journal,* Vol. 20, No. 1 (Spring 1992), 89–106.

Ball, Jay N. "Issues and Interpretations." *Real Estate Review,* 20, No. 4 (Winter 1991): 15–16.

Bell, Carrie Sears. "A Real Dilemma for Real Estate." *Real Estate Salespeople,* (May/June 1986): 9.

Black, Roy T., and Hugh O. Nourse. "Real Estate Broker Liability for Agency Violations: Will the Edina Cases Create a National Trend?" *REEA Journal* (Spring 1993): 68.

Broadbent, William R. "How to Represent a Buyer." San Luis Obispo, Calif. (self-published), 1985.

———"Who Pays the Buyer's Broker?" *Creative Real Estate Magazine* (September 1985): 13.

Federal Trade Commission. *Real Estate Brokers. Facts for Consumers.* Washington, D.C.: December 1985.

"Broker/Buyer Relationship vs. The Law of Agency." *NARELLO News,* 1985.

Bryant, James A., and Donald R. Epley. The Conditions and Perils of Agency, Dual Agency, and Undisclosed Agency. *Real Estate Law Journal* 21 Fall 1992: 117.

Buchholz, Barbara. "Agent Turned Buyer." *First Tuesday,* (October 1986): 9.

Burke, D. Barlow. *Law of Real Estate Brokers.* Boston: Little, Brown & Co., 1982.

Burton, Robert C., and Ellen M. Hamilton. "Deceptive Trade Practices Act and the Real Estate Broker." *Texas Real Estate Law Reporter* (April 1986).

Butcher, Roger. "Working Free or for a Fee" (Brochure for one-day seminar on buyer brokering, 1808 Tribute Road, Suite B, Sacramento, CA 95814).

Butters, Robert D. "Who is My Client?" *Perspective* (Society of Industrial REALTORS®) (Fall 1986).

"Buyer Representation." *RB Management Issues & Trends,* NAR 5, no. 4 (1990).

"Buyers Take Their Pick." *Real Estate Today,* (Jan./Feb. 1993): 10–14.

Cheng, Jim. "Buyer Offered Extra Help When Agent is Retained." *The Burlington Free Press,* 3 March 1985, 10D.

Cole, William L. Wade. "The New Role of the Real Estate Broker." Seattle, 1986 (self-published).

Continuing Legal Education in Colorado, Inc.: "Real Estate Brokers, Life Under the New Statute." September 1993.

Earnest, G. Lane. "Agency of Surprise: The Disclosure Dilemma in real estate." *The Colorado Lawyer* (July 1986): 1185.

Ferguson, Jerry T. and Robert H. Plattner. "The Growing Importance of Buyers' Brokers." *Real Estate Review,* Vol. 21, No. 4 (Winter 1992), 83–86.

Frank, Stephen L. *Kentucky Real Estate Professionals and the Law.* Kentucky Real Estate Commission, 1986.

Frascona, Oliver E. *Paper Trail,* Denver: Denver Carrington Publishing, 1987.

Friedman, Ronald, and Benjamin N. Henszey. *Protecting Your Sales Commission: Professional Liability in Real Estate.* Chicago: Real Estate Education Co., 1982.

Hagglund, Clarance E., and Britton D. Weimer. "Caveat Realtor: The Broker's Liability for Negligent and Innocent Misrepresentations." *Real Estate Law Journal* 20, no. 2 (Fall 1991): 149–56.

———"The Practitioner's Corner, Caveat Emptor: Realty Purchaser's Duty to Investigate." *Real Estate Law Journal,* 20 (Spring 1992): 373.

Hanna, Mark J., and James. M. Richardson. "Whom do you Represent?" *South Carolina Realtor,* (July 1986): 6.

Harlan, Don, and Gail Lyons. "Beware When Rookies Work with Friends and Relatives." *Real Estate Today* (August 1992): 15.

Harney, Kenneth R. "Consumer Advocate Turns Attention to Real Estate." *The Washington Post,* July 1986.

Harwood, Bruce. "The Owner-broker Relationship." *Real Estate Principles* (Chapter 17). Englewood Cliffs, N.J.: Prentice-Hall, 1986.

Hess, Lee R. "Procuring Cause: Who Really Sold the Property?" *Real Estate Today* (October 1988): 18–21.

Houlihan, John. "Dual Agency: A Dilemma for the Real Estate Broker." Paper presented in 1985. University of Southern Maine Center for Real Estate Education.

Jacobus, Charles J. "Real Estate Brokerage and Management." *Real Estate Law* (Chapter 5, pp. 93–127). Englewood Cliffs, NJ: Prentice-Hall, 1986.

Joachim, Harry. "Buyer Broker—A New Phase in Real Estate." *Communique,* October 1986.

Johnson, Jim. "Real Estate Agent's Dual Role Debated." *San Francisco Examiner,* 3 March 1985.

Johnson, Melvin. "How to Work for a Fee in Investment Real Estate." *Real Estate Today,* (September/October 1986): 48.

Kaplan, Douglas. "The Independent Real Estate Broker." 62 FLA. B.J. 24 (1989).

Kiell, Matthew. "The Agency Relationship." *Real Estate Today* January/February 1987): 38–43.

Kottler, Norman H. "Selling Broker and Arizona Law." *Arizona Realtor Digest* (May/June 1985): 12.

Larsen, Morella. "Agency legislation." *Oregon Association of Realtors Newsletter,* May 1986.

Levi, Donald R. "The Age of Consumerism Arrives in Real Estate Brokerage: Expanded Liability to Buyers and Prospective Buyers." *Proceedings of REEA Convention,* May 22, 1985.

———"When Agency Goes to Court." *Texas Realtor* (April 1986): 29.

———"The Dual Agency Trap." *Real Estate Review,* (Spring 1985): 109.

Lyons, Gail G. "Colorado Broker Option Lets Agents Represent Real Estate Buyer—in Full." *The Denver Post,* 6 April 1986, 8-E.

Lyons, Gail, and Don Harlan. *Buyer Agency,* Chicago: Dearborn Financial Publishing, Inc., 1993.

"The Many Shades of Buyer Brokerage." *Real Estate Today* (August 1992): 18–19.

McGee, "Potential Liability For Misrepresentations In Residential Real Estate Transactions: Let The Broker Beware." 16 Fordham Urban Law Journal 127 (1988). Spring 1989. 17 Real Est. L.J. 377.

Messina, Mike. "Dual Agency: Much Ado About Nothing." *Sacramento Realtor,* February 1985, 18.

Miceli, Thomas J., "The Multiple Listing Service, Commission Splits and Broker Effort," *American Real Estate and Urban Economics Association Journal,* Vol. 19, No. 4 (Winter 1991), 548–66.

Miller, Barry M. "Serving Your Seller with a Buyer's Broker Offer." Denver Realtor News, August 1986.

Miller, Norman G. "The Changing Structure of Residential Brokerage." *Real Estate Review* 8 (Fall 1978): 46–50.

———"Buyer Brokerage: The Other Side of the Coin." *Real Estate Business* (Fall 1986): 17.

Moore, Gary S., Gerald E. Smolen and Lawrence V. Conway. "The Effects of an Informational Disclosure Form on the Real Estate Agency Representational Model," *Journal of Real Estate Research,* Vol. 7, No. 2 (Spring 1992), 217–26.

Munhall, Dale L. "Dual vs. Single Agency: The Big Controversy with a Simple Solution." *Nebraska Realtor News,* 43, no. 1 (January/February 1985): 4.

National Association of REALTORS®. *Interpretations of the Code of Ethics.* 110b Policy Reference File, 1983.

Ponto. "Listing Buyers for a Fee." *Real Estate Today* (September) 1976: 50.

Powell, Frona M. "Relief for Innocent Misrepresentation: A Retreat from the Traditional Doctrine of Caveat Emptor." 19, no. 130 (Fall 1990).

Reilly, John. *Agency Relationships in Real Estate,* 2nc Edition. Chicago: Real Estate Education Company, 1994.

Reilly, John. *The Dual Agency Dilemma* (self-published, 1984).

———*The Ultimate Language of Real Estate.* Chicago: Real Estate Education Company, 1993.

———*The Real Estate Agent: Who's On First?* (self-published, 1985).

Reinstein, Alan, Robert T. Keliman and Edward J. Farragher. "New Disclosure Requirements for Real Estate," *Real Estate Review,* 21, no. 3 (Fall 1991): 92–97.

Rohan, Patrick J., Bernard H. Goldstein and Charles S. Babis. *Real Estate Brokerage Law & Practice.* New York: Matthew Bender, Volume 1, 1985.

Sadberry, Pat A. "Ethics at work." *Tierra Grande,* No. 30 (1986): 2.

Smith, Holly. "Tips on Using an Agent to Sell or Buy." *The Record* (NJ), 2 June 1985 R–1.

Somers, Michael. "The Winds of Change. *Homes & Land of Sonoma County,* No. 3 (1986): 6.

———*A Primer On California Real Estate Agency Law & Practice.* Novato, Calif.: (self-published) 1987.

Spinelli, Ray. "Agency Dilemma: Legislation Recommended." *California Real Estate* (May 1985): 1.

Sykes, Simon. "Dual Agency Double-take." *First Tuesday's Best of 1985* (P.O. 20068, Riverside, CA 92516): 283.

Texas Real Estate Research Center. "Legal & Ethical Responsibilities in Real Estate." Publication No. 485.

Tune, Jerry. "Dealing with the Complex Agency Issue." *Honolulu Sunday Star-Bulletin & Advertiser,* 11 November 1984, G-1.

———"Buyer brokering." *Florida REALTOR®* Magazine, March 1986, p. 6; October 1986, p. 20.

Williams, Kay. "What a Real Estate Agent Does for You." Money (May 1985): 29.

Williams, Martha, and John Reilly. Agency Relationships in California Real Estate. Chicago: Longman Financial Services Institute, 1987.

Wolf, Guy P., and Marianne M. Jennings. "Seller/Broker Liability in Multiple Listing Service Real Estate Sales: A Case for Uniform Disclosure." *Real Estate Law Journal* Summer 1991. 20, no. 22 (Summer 1991).

LAW REVIEW ARTICLES AND LEGAL REFERENCES

California Continuing Education of the Bar, G. Graham and C. Scott, ed.: *California Real Property Sales Transactions,* Sec. 2.24–2.27.

Collette, Matthew M. 61 S. California Law Review 399. Note: "Sub-Agency in Residential Real Estate Brokerage: A Proposal to End the Struggle with Reality," January 1988.

Comment. "A Real Estate Broker's Duty to His Purchaser: Washington State's Position and Some Projections for the Future," 17 *Gonzaga Law Review* 79 (1981).

Comment. "Conflicts of Interest in Real Estate Transactions: Dual Representation—Lawyers Stretching the Rules," 6 *Western New England Law Review* 73 (1983).

Comment. "Conveyancing—The Rules of the Real Estate Broker and the Lawyer in Ordinary Real Estate Transactions—Wherein Lies the Public Interest?," 19 *DePaul Law Review* 319 (1969).

Comment. "Dual Agency in Residential Real Estate Brokerage: Conflict of Interest and Interests in Conflict," 12 *Golden Gate University Law Review* 379 (1982).

Comment. "Mandatory Disclosure: The Key to Residential Real Estate Brokers' Conflicting Obligations," 19 *John Marshall Law Review* 201 (1985).

Comment. "Practice of Law: Real Estate Brokers Authorized to Complete Transaction Forms," 60 *Washington Law Review* 781 (1985).

Comment. "Real Estate Broker's Fiduciary Duties," 12 *Pepperdine Law Review* 145 (1984).

Comment. "Reexamination of the Real Estate Broker-Buyer-Seller Relationship," 18 *Wayne Law Review* 1343 (1972).

Comment. "Unprofessional Conduct by Real Estate Brokers: Conflicts of Interest and Conflict in the Law I," 1 *Pacific Law Journal* 821 (1979).

Culum, Kevin C. 50 *Montana Law Review* 331 Comment. "Hidden-but-Discoverable-defects: Resolving the Conflicts Between Real Estate Buyers and Brokers," Summer 1989.

Currier, Barry A. "Finding the Broker's Place in the Typical Real Estate Transaction," 5 *University of Florida Law Review* 655 (1981).

Erxleben, William C. "In Search of Price and Service Competition in Residential Real Estate Brokerage: Breaking the Cartel," 56 *Washington Law Review* 1979 (1981).

Freyfogle, Eric T. "Real Estate Sales and the New Implied Warranty of Lawful Use," 71 *Cornell Law Review* I (1985).

Gresham, Zane O. "The Real Estate Transfer Process: A Functional Critique," 23 *Emory Law Journal* 421 (1974).

Groham, Joseph M. 61 *St. John's L. Rev.* 560. "A Reassessment of the Selling Real Estate Broker's Agency Relationship with the Purchaser," Summer 1987.

Guilfoy, Joanna L. 21 *Rutgers L.J.* 111. Note: "Home Not-So-Sweet Home: Real Estate Broker Liability in the Sale of Previously Contaminated Residential Property: Has Broker Liability Gone too Far?" Fall 1989.

Hicks, Jack B. *Easton v. Strassburger,* 18 *Loyola of Los Angeles Law Review* 809 (1985).

Hopper, Brett L. 1992 *B.Y.U.L. Rev.* 1135 Comment. "The Selling Real Estate Broker and the Purchaser: Assessing the Relationship," 1992.

Isacco, Jr., Michael D. 27 *New Eng. L. Rev.* 1211 Note: A Massachusetts Real Estate Broker's Duty to Disclose: The Quandary Presented by AIDS-Stigmatized Property," Summer 1993.

Jacobson, L. H. "Broker's Liability for Sale of Defective Homes: The Decline of Caveat Emptor," 52 *Los Angeles Bar Journal* 346 (1977).

Levin, Murray S. "Overstating the Value of Property to Induce a Listing," 34 *Kansas Law Review* 757 (1986).

———39 *U. Miami L. Rev.* 429. "Real Estate Agent Liability for Creative Financing Failures," May 1985.

Levinson, Gary A. "California Real Estate—A Practitioner's Guide Through the Broker's Legal Duties," 7 *Whittier Law Review* 613 (1985).

McGee, Dawn K. 16 *Fordham Urb. L.J.* 127. Note: "Potential Liability for Misrepresentations in Residential Real Estate Transactions: Let the Broker Beware," 1987/1988.

Meyer, Paul. 23 *Loy. U. Chi. L.J.* 241. "Illinois Real Estate Brokers: The Duties of Disclosure and Accuracy," Winter 1992.

Miceli, Thomas J. "The Multiple Listing Service, Commission Splits and Broker Effort," *Journal of the American Real Estate and Urban Economics Association,* 19, no. 4 (Winter 1991): 548–566.

Miller, Harry, and Starr Marvin. *Current Law of California Real Estate,* Sec. 4:18 (1975 and Supp. 1983).

Mortland, Jean A. 25 *Real Prop. Prob. & Tr.J.* 755. "Attorneys as Real Estate Brokers: Ethical Considerations," Winter 1991.

Murray, Paula C. 27 *Wake Forest L. Rev.* 689 "AIDS, Ghosts, Murder: Must Real Estate Brokers and Sellers Disclose?" Fall 1992.

———32 *Vill. L. Rev.* 939. "The Real Estate Broker and The Buyer: Negligence and the Duty to Investigate," September 1987.

Note. "Brokers—Dual Agency—Separable Transactions," *University of Kansas Law Review* 462 (1960).

Note. "Duties, Rights & Remedies of Real Estate Brokers," *University of Florida Law Review* 513 (1955).

Note. "*Ellsworth Dobbs, Inc. v. Johnson:* A Re-examination of the Broker-Buyer-Seller Relationship in New Jersey," 23 *Rutgers Law Review* 83 (1968).

Note. "Imposing Tort Liability on Real Estate Brokers Selling Defective Housing," 99 *Harvard Law Review* 1861 (1986).

Note. "Real Estate Brokers' Duties to Prospective Purchasers," 1976 *Brigham Young University Law Review* 513.

Note. *Reed v. King* (nondisclosure of prior murder), 45 *University of Pittsburgh Law Review* 877 (1984).

Note. "When Is a Broker Not a Broker?," 21 *Land and Water Law Review* 241 (1986).

Note. "When the Walls Come Tumbling Down: Theories of Recovery for Defective Housing," 56 *St. John 's Law Review* 670 (1982).

Raushenbush, W.B. "Who Helps the Home Buyer?," *Arizona State Law Journal* 203 (1979).

Report. "Residential Real Estate Transactions: The Lawyer's Proper Role—Services—Compensation," 14 *Real Property Probate & Trust Journal* 581 (1979).

Romero, Molly Moore. "Theories of Real Estate Broker Liability: Arizona's Emerging Malpractice Doctrine," 20 *Arizona Law Review* 767 (1968).

Sanford, Jeb C. "Conflicts of Interest in Real Estate," 17 *St. Mary's Law Journal* 79 (1985).

Sinclair, James S. "The Duty of the Broker to Purchasers and Prospective Purchasers of Real Property in Illinois," *Illinois Bar Journal* (January 1981): 260.

Stambler, A., and J.A. Stein. "The Real Estate Broker—Schizophrenia or Conflict of Interests?," 28 *Journal of Bar Association of District of Columbia 16* (1961).

Zeit, Robert M. 63 *Temp. L. Rev.* 165 "Recent Decision, Real Estate—Broker Liability to Purchasers—*Herbert v. Saffell,*" 877 F.2D 267 (4th Cir. 1989), Spring 1990.

MAJOR STUDIES ON AGENCY

1. Brown, Barry, and Eric D. Green. *The Role of the Broker in Residential Real Estate Transactions.* Report Appended to FTC Study, August 1979.
2. California Department of Real Estate. *Dual Agency Problem in California Real Estate Transactions.* February 1981.
3. California Department of Real Estate. *The Extent and Nature of Single Agency Real Estate Practices in California.* December 1981.
4. Federal Trade Commission. *The Residential Real Estate Brokerage Industry* (U.S. Superintendent of Documents, Stock #018-000-00305-8). December 1981.
5. Hawaii Real Estate Commission. *Dual Agency Study.* November 1984.
6. Association of Real Estate License Law Officials, ARELLO, three reports:

   (a) *Agency/Sub-Agency Report.* A comprehensive review of the issues and possible solutions. October 1984.

   (b) *Appendices* (261 pages). Summaries of major studies and articles; especially useful to attorneys and researchers, with more than 100 agency cases briefed.

   (c) *Update Agency Report.* A review and commentary on legislative approaches in 17 states. October 1985. All reports available directly from: ARELLO, P.O. Box 129, Centerville, UT 84014; (801) 531-8202.
7. National Association of REALTORS®, *Final Report of Agency Task Force (with Exhibits),* May 1986.
8. National Association of REALTORS®, *Report of Presidential Advisory Group on Agency,* April 1992.
9. National Association of REALTORS®, *Report of Presidential Agency Group on Facilitator,* October 1993.
10. National Association of REALTORS®, *Report of Presidential Advisory Group on Agency Coordination,* October 1993.

VIDEO PROGRAMS

1. "Agency: Choices, Challenges & Opportunities," National Association of REALTORS®, 1993.
2. "Agency: Options and Oppositions," National Association of REALTORS®, #151-950, 1993.
3. "Agency Relationships in Real Estate" and "Developing an In-House Agency Disclosure Policy," by John Reilly, REVEI. Video course, 1987. (800) 582-7979.
4. "Who Do You Represent?" Coronet Films, Deerfield, Illinois, Winter 1986.
5. "Agency Answers," by Julie Garton-Good, 1993, 1-800-445-8543.
6. "Making Agency Representation Work for You" and "Managing The Changes In Agency Representation," by Roger Turcotte, 1993, 1-603-746-5705.

INDEX